Nietzsche, Henry James, and the Artistic Will

Nietzsche, Henry James, and the Artistic Will

STEPHEN DONADIO

New York
OXFORD UNIVERSITY PRESS
1978

Library of Congress Cataloging in Publication Data
Donadio, Stephen.
Nietzsche, Henry James, and the artistic will.
Bibliography: p. Includes index.
1. James, Henry, 1843-1916—Aesthetics.
2. Nietzsche, Friedrich Wilhelm, 1844-1900—
Aesthetics. I. Title.
PS2127.A35D6   111.8′5   77-15657   ISBN 0-19-502358-7

Grateful acknowledgment is made to Macmillan Publishing Co., Inc.,
and Macmillan and Co., Ltd., for permission to reprint excerpts from two
works by William Butler Yeats included in the *Collected Poems:* "Meru"
(copyright 1934 by Macmillan Publishing Co., Inc., renewed 1962 by
Bertha Georgie Yeats), and "Crazy Jane Talks with the Bishop" (copyright 1933 by Macmillan Publishing Co., Inc., renewed 1961 by Bertha
Georgie Yeats).

Printed in the United States of America

In Memory of My Father
Anthony S. Donadio
1911-1958

Civilisation is hooped together, brought
Under a rule, under the semblance of peace
By manifold illusion; but man's life is thought,
And he, despite his terror, cannot cease
Ravening through century after century,
Ravening, raging, and uprooting that he may come
Into the desolation of reality. . . .

W. B. YEATS

Preface

Let us begin, at what might seem a distance from our subject, with a passage from William Butler Yeats's *Reveries over Childhood and Youth* (1914). The passage, which constitutes an entire, independent section of the work, presents us with two images; each of them is fully realized, but their relationship is not explained:

> Two pictures come into my memory. I have climbed to the top of a tree by the edge of the playing field, and am looking at my school-fellows and am as proud of myself as a March cock when it crows to its first sunrise. I am saying to myself, "If when I grow up I am as clever among grown-up men as I am among these boys, I shall be a famous man." I remind myself how they think all the same things and cover the school walls at election times with the opinions their fathers find in the newspapers. I remind myself that I am an artist's son and must take some work as the whole end of life and not think as the others do of becoming well off and living pleasantly. The other picture is of a hotel sitting-room in the Strand, where a man is hunched up over the fire. He is a cousin who has speculated with another cousin's money and has fled from Ireland in danger of arrest. My father has brought us to spend the evening with him, to distract him from the remorse he must be suffering.

As we contemplate these perfectly concrete but somehow elusive images, various relationships between them begin to suggest themselves: temporal, spatial, metaphorical, emotional. The first image is associated with childhood, the second with adulthood—perhaps the first recognition of the gravity of adulthood. The first scene occurs outdoors, in broad daylight, in a familiar place; the second at night, in another country, in a rented room. Children are playing in the first scene; in the second all the games have come to an end. The perspective in the first scene is from a height; all the participants in the second scene are on the same level. The confident, expansive gesture of the March cock evoked by the first scene is contradicted by the image of a man "hunched up over the fire," presumably to keep warm, in the second. The mood of the first scene is joyful, that of the second grim. In the first scene the boy identifies himself proudly as the son of an artist; in the second we are presented with a grown man who has been ruined by speculating with someone else's capital.

It would, of course, be possible to go on enumerating the various possibilities implied by this juxtaposition of images, the shifting succession of overlapping and continuous and clashing perspectives in which they might be comprehended. But by now the point should be sufficiently clear: the juxtaposition creates a resonance which makes these images, each of which we might have thought could be unpacked rather efficiently and briskly, evocative of unexpected harmonies and disharmonies in the range of experience depicted. Each of these images must be understood in light of the other; each calls the other into being, and they continue to speak to one another endlessly. Taken on its own, each represents a fragment of the artist's experience; taken together, they provide a complete account of the significance of the artistic enterprise—an account which expresses, as it were simultaneously and in a single plane, the stunning triumphs, risks, and possibilities for self-deception and bad conscience which that enterprise affords.

Something along these lines, at least in its general ambition, has been attempted in the present study, which proposes a conjunction between two figures ordinarily considered worlds apart. For some readers, the very idea of drawing parallels between a philosopher and a writer of fiction seems problematic— as if these two activities had not always sustained and offered criticisms of one another (much in the way William and Henry James themselves did). But the contrast between this particular philosopher and this particular novelist, if only from the point of view of tone, has seemed to present further obstacles, for it has not been readily apparent that any significant relationship could be established between a philosopher whose works are often characterized by a feverishness and a "desperate buffoonery" (in Karl Löwith's compelling phrase) and a novelist commonly celebrated for his magisterial detachment and restraint. And yet that wildly uncertain tone, careering from profound exaltation to self-mockery, cannot be wholly unfamiliar to readers of American literature generally—and readers of Melville in particular may find themselves almost at ease with it. Moreover, even at its most extreme, Nietzsche's thinking does not place him beyond comparison with the familiar American authors of the nineteenth century. As D. H. Lawrence pointed out over half a century ago, "the furthest frenzies of French modernism or futurism have not yet reached the pitch of extreme consciousness that Poe, Melville, Hawthorne, Whitman reached. The European moderns are all *trying* to be extreme. The great Americans I mention just were it." If one feels the force of this assertion, and regards James as a writer in the great Transcendental line (as it is surely possible to do), then the association with Nietzsche begins to appear less startling.

The association proposed here is hardly arbitrary, and it is concerned primarily with the extraordinary emotional investment made by both James and Nietzsche in the power of art as the only activity capable of creating values and raising experience from insignificance. But if we need to find a more specific common ground on which to place these figures, it is the ground of Emersonian belief. Indeed, the connections here are so extensive that the present study can only hope to suggest some of the more striking. Both William and Henry James acknowledged their indebtedness to Emerson in tributes to his genius, but (as we shall see) those explicit acknowledgments tell only a small part of the story. Nietzsche's estimation of Emerson, and profound sense of kinship with him, are not so generally well known, but it is important to remember that Nietzsche was referring to Emerson when he observed that "the author who has been richest in ideas in this century so far has been an American," and that his own feeling of closeness with Emerson's thinking was so great that he could hardly bring himself to praise the Concord philosopher lest he be obliged to convict himself of self-flattery: "Never have I felt so much at home in a book, and in *my* home, as—I may not praise it, it is too close to me." How this sense of connection reveals itself in Nietzsche's work, and how it serves to bring him into relationship with James, will become apparent in the pages that follow.

In attempting to account for such correspondences, this study inevitably becomes involved in an effort to trace what Nietzsche once described as "those most difficult and most captious of all deductions, in which the largest number of mistakes have been made,—the deduction which makes one infer something concerning the author from his work, something concerning the doer from his deed, something concerning the idealist from the need which produced this ideal, and something concerning the imperious *craving* which stands at the back of all thinking and valuing." In the course of this enterprise, I have taken heart from an observation made by Walter Pater in his *Studies in the History of the Renaissance:*

Theories which bring into connection with each other modes of thought and feeling, periods of taste, forms of art and poetry, which the narrowness of men's minds constantly tends to oppose to each other, have a great stimulus for the intellect, and are almost always worth understanding.

Middlebury, Vermont   S.D.
April 1978

Acknowledgments

A number of people read this book at various stages and offered valuable criticism and encouragement. In particular, I should like to thank Quentin Anderson, Jacques Barzun, Sacvan Bercovitch, Steven Marcus, and Roger Wertheimer for their careful reading. I am especially grateful to my friend Neal Kozodoy for his many editorial suggestions and innumerable acts of kindness. I also wish to express my thanks to Barbara Hohol, who typed every stratum of this book with efficiency and speed, and to Elaine Koss, who helped to see the typescript through publication. I have been exceedingly fortunate in working with James Raimes at the Oxford University Press; no author could wish for a more patient, discerning, and indefatigably intelligent editor. It would be futile for me to attempt an accounting of my debt to my wife, Emmie; on numerous occasions, she put aside her own work to help me with mine, and the notes for the present volume owe a great deal to her assistance. Beyond that, as she knows, she has lived with all the moods of this book for nearly a decade, and in that time has never failed to mediate between them and the continuing business of our lives.

My indebtedness to the people I have mentioned is great; but I am sure that they will understand me when I say that my greatest and most incalculable debt is to the late Lionel Trilling, without whose generosity of mind and spirit this work never would have reached completion.

A Note on Sources, Editions, and Translations

With the exception of a few discursive footnotes, in the interest of legibility footnotes have been omitted from the text that follows. Readers seeking to locate the source of a specific quotation, or interested in further bibliographical particulars, are directed to the Notes at the end of the book. Fuller accounts of certain of the issues treated in the text are also provided there.

Except where otherwise indicated, the translations of Nietzsche's works cited here are those by Walter Kaufmann, which are generally reliable and easily available, and which in many instances contain useful indexes and explanatory apparatus.

The German edition of Nietzsche's works referred to throughout is the *Werke in drei Bänden*, edited by Karl Schlecta, 3rd ed., which includes a fourth volume containing a valuable *Nietzsche-Index* and bibliography (Munich, Carl Hansers Verlag, 1965). There have, however, been a number of serious objections to Schlecta's selection and arrangement of the *Nachlass* materials in the third volume of this edition (see, for instance, Kaufmann, pp. 450-452); accordingly, all German references to the notes translated by Kaufmann and R. J. Hollingdale in *The Will to Power* are to vols. 18 and 19 of the Musarion edition (*Gesammelte Werke, Musarionausgabe*, 23 vols., Munich, 1920-1929).

When it is completed, the comprehensive *Werke: Kritische Gesamtausgabe* currently in progress, edited by Giorgio Colli and Mazzino Montinari and projected in thirty volumes (Berlin,

Walter de Gruyter, 1967ff.), will presumably be the definitive scholarly edition. As Montinari has pointed out, "it is, above all else, by virtue of its inclusiveness that the critical edition differs from previous Nietzsche editions: it assembles fragments, drafts, plans and excerpts (made by Nietzsche from books he was reading), all of which were omitted by earlier editors of the *Nachlass*." One of the hazards of this procedure is worth noting, however: in its incorporation of all the surviving *Nachlass* materials the new edition tends, at least implicitly, to blur the distinction between rejected or fragmentary drafts and finished works. This general problem has plagued Nietzsche scholarship at least since the misleading publication of the collection entitled *The Will to Power* at the turn of the century, and the danger that it continues to present to interpreters of Nietzsche is cogently articulated by R. J. Hollingdale when he observes that "the key to a balanced understanding of the *Nachlass* is the knowledge that most of Nietzsche's finished works originated in similar notebook entries, and are consequently a selection from that body of material from which the *Nachlass* is the portion not selected. That the *Nachlass* is reject material is the first datum for its assessment. How much weight and authority to give it in an exposition of 'Nietzsche's opinions' must remain an interpretive question, but any interpretation which relies heavily on it to the exclusion of the finished works seems to me unsound in principle. Such a method has to assume that, since he published what he should have rejected and rejected what he should have published, Nietzsche was unaware of what his opinions really were or deliberately sought to conceal them, and there is no evidence for either contention."

Contents

Nietzsche, Henry James, and the Artistic Will

I
The Immediate Context

. . . I have found strength where one does not look for it: in simple, mild, and pleasant people, without the least desire to rule—and, conversely, the desire to rule has often appeared to me a sign of inward weakness: they fear their own slave soul and shroud it in a royal cloak (in the end, they still become the slaves of their followers, their fame, etc.). The powerful natures dominate, it is a necessity, they need not lift one finger. Even if, during their life time, they bury themselves in a garden house.

FRIEDRICH NIETZSCHE

1. *The Appearance of the Master*

In early November of 1907, Sydney Waterlow, a well-educated young man who had recently settled in the municipality of Rye in east Sussex, recorded in his diary a number of remarks made in conversation by that town's most distinguished resident, the American novelist Henry James. In the course of the conversation, James recalled an incident in which the prolonged wailing of a cat on his lawn had at last driven him beyond the limits of endurance, and "under the extreme provocation of its obscene caterwauling" he had killed the animal. The act, Waterlow went on to note, "was followed by nausea and collapse."

The anecdote is startling, in part because it suggests a whole range of extreme emotions and responses which are not usually associated with James, who is generally taken to be an essentially high-spirited, humane, and witty novelist of manners

3

whose occasional ventures into the darker regions of the soul (as in the famous ghost stories, for instance, or even "The Beast in the Jungle") may be regarded as a function of technique, a product of the author's self-conscious search for interesting new subjects which appealed to his taste for melodrama and which he could use to display his virtuosity and consummate craftsmanship. There seems to be nothing—or almost nothing—in James's work that would suggest the loss of control recorded by Waterlow: indeed, the very possibility of such responses seems to be excluded from his temperament, and our sense of his enterprise as a whole does not incorporate these disturbing potentialities.

And yet, as will become apparent in the course of this book, what is perhaps most remarkable about the anecdote is how completely and precisely it reflects that abrupt alternation from unequivocal assertion of will to revulsion, panic, and nervous exhaustion—a reversal inextricably linked with a corresponding impulse to overwhelming self-affirmation in the face of apparent failure—which very often characterized James's own emotional life, even as that life is reflected in the life of his works. For all the apparently obsessive refinement and civility, no one who has ever looked into the unyielding eyes of the late portraits of The Master, or seen, in the photographs, just the faintest suggestion of the curled lip, or taken note of the unexpectedly massive hand gripping the end of a chair-arm, as if the novelist were established in the very seat of power, at home in some official residence considerably more worldly than the Palace of Art—no one whose consciousness has registered such details will doubt the reputedly withering power of James's personality.

Testimony to that force is hardly lacking in the accounts of his contemporaries, whether they are noting, as Edmund Gosse does, his "radically powerful and unique outer appearance," or remarking, as in the case of one young woman, "the strange power" of his eyes, which "made me feel . . . as if he had read me to the soul—and I rather think he had." ("My servants," Ford Madox Ford once recalled, "used to say: 'It always gives me a turn to open the door for Mr. James. His eyes seem to look you through to the very backbone.'") "I found him overwhelming," his extraordinary secretary wrote, recalling her first meeting with him:

> He was much more massive than I had expected, much broader and stouter and stronger. I remembered that someone had told me he used to be taken for a sea-captain when he wore a beard, but it was clear that now, with the beard shaved away, he could hardly have passed for, say, an admiral, in spite of the keen grey eyes set in a face burned to a colourable sea-faring brown by the Italian sun. No successful naval officer could have afforded to keep that sensitive mobile mouth. . . . He might perhaps have been some species of disguised cardinal, or even a Roman nobleman amusing himself by playing the part of a Sussex squire. The observer could at least have guessed that any part he chose to assume would be finely conceived and generously played, for his features were all cast in the classical mould of greatness. He might very well have been a merciful Caesar or a benevolent Napoleon, and a painter who worked at his portrait a year or two later was excusably reminded of so many illustrious makers of history that he declared it to be a hard task to isolate the individual character of the model.

The full significance of the description of James as "a merciful Caesar or a benevolent Napoleon" will become apparent several chapters from now, as this book draws to its conclusion. For the moment, however, we should be aware that Theodora Bosanquet goes on to observe of her "overwhelming" (she repeats the word) first interview with her prospective employer, that "once I was seated opposite to him, the strong, slow stream of his deliberate speech played over me without ceasing."

But at this point it is important to remember that James's

very manner of speaking (which, except for the elimination of the notorious, endless pauses, became virtually indistinguishable from his written style once the dictation of his books became habitual in the late 'nineties)—solemn, slow, elaborate, involved, exacting, marvelously controlled but sometimes maddening in its deliberateness—was, as Edith Wharton has pointed out, "really the partial victory over a stammer which in his boyhood had been thought incurable." Moreover, the same man characterized by one of his contemporaries as "magisterial," indeed "upon the whole . . . the most masterful man I have ever met," was also, especially in his later life, increasingly plagued by periods of severe anxiety and melancholy, and once described to the young Desmond McCarthy "the spiral of depression which a recent nervous illness had compelled him step after step, night after night, day after day, to descend." Yet McCarthy was equally struck by James's additional remarks on this occasion, since they seemed to reveal the novelist's essential "confidence in himself in relation to [his] art": ". . . What stages of arid rejection of life and meaningless yet frantic agitation he had been compelled to traverse! 'But,' and he suddenly stood still, 'but it has been good'—and here he took off his hat, baring his great head in the moonlight—'for my genius.' Then, putting on his hat again, he added, 'Never cease to watch whatever happens to you.' " In view of this general pattern of "conversion" (one of the clearest guiding principles of the whole James household, as F. W. Dupee has observed), it is not altogether surprising that this author for whom artistic creation represented the highest and most compelling form of activity should have described the process of composition to his secretary as if it required an insistent passivity: "It all seems," he said, "to be so much more effectively and unceasingly *pulled* out of me in speech than in writing."

These alternating aspects of James's personality find their

imaginative expression in his work, and their interrelation forms one of the underlying concerns of this book, which attempts to trace that process of transformation (or "conversion") by which one state of feeling reverses itself and becomes its opposite.* Such considerations are most obviously applicable to the novels of the so-called "major phase" (*The Ambassadors, The Wings of the Dove,* and *The Golden Bowl*), which give evidence of a general progression on the part of their protagonists from self-denial and renunciation to an undivided affirmation of the will. But this consideration of the phases of the individual will (which in the course of James's development eventually became synonymous with the very will to live) also came to provide a useful way of defining the concerns central to James's work as a whole, which Ezra Pound saw as emerging into greatness "first by reason of [James's] hatred of personal intimate tyrannies working at close range."

The pages that follow, however, attempt to do more than consider this question of individual will in relation to the dynamics of James's personal psychology, or even in relation to the intricate and endlessly fascinating psychology of the James family as a whole. They attempt rather to connect recurring patterns in this American novelist's emotional and intellectual life with similar patterns associated with a controversial European philosopher with whom he would not ordinarily be expected to have anything in common, and to suggest that, taken together, the lives and works of these two ostensibly alien figures provide us with a way of grasping the far-reaching and pervasive implications of the momentous shift in the ground of

---

* The significance of this notion for an adequate understanding of Nietzsche cannot be overestimated, as Peter Heller makes clear in his enormously persuasive discussion of "Reversal as Doctrine, Method, and Symptom" in *Dialectics and Nihilism: Essays on Lessing, Nietzsche, Mann, and Kafka,* Amherst, Mass., Univ. of Massachusetts Press, 1966, 138-143.

religious and aesthetic belief which occurred in Europe and America in the course of the nineteenth century, and which is ultimately responsible for producing the complex and often contradictory cultural phenomenon we have come to identify as modernism.

2. *Transcendental Relations*

Ever since T. S. Eliot's overpowering dictum that James "had a mind so fine that no idea could violate it," any enterprise proceeding from what appear to be contrary assumptions has been considered at least slightly suspect. Eliot's remark was presumably intended to be understood as praise, as a tribute to the novelist's ability to remain free of any intellectual prejudice; but the remark has (not surprisingly, perhaps) been taken as a *caveat* regarding the discussion of James's work in relation to the world of general ideas. In any case, the categories considered proper to a discussion of this author's fiction have usually been derived either from the domain of novelistic theory or from that of the nineteenth-century novel of manners: his work is almost invariably seen in relation to the model of George Eliot rather than, say, Dostoevsky—even though a novel like *The Princess Casamassima* would seem to bear, at least from certain points of view, as much relation to one like *The Possessed* as it does to one like *Felix Holt*. And although Philip Rahv is undoubtedly correct in observing of James that "there never was a writer so immersed in personal relations," it is important to add that personal relations may (and perhaps invariably do) serve as a medium for the expression of ideas—especially ideas of a political nature. And indeed, James's observant amenuensis makes this aspect of his thinking clear when she notes that "his Utopia was an anarchy where nobody would be responsible for any other human being but only for his own civilized character."

Such ideas are implicit in James's work, but because they are incorporated into the very texture of human relationships there, it is extremely difficult to isolate them. Still, James's preternaturally sensitive recording of the pressure exerted by mind on mind, will on will, is surely not completely disconnected from ideas regarding social order or, indeed, the very nature of life in society. The individual "cases" (to use one of his favorite and most revealing words) which James observed so scrupulously and imagined in such meticulous detail served to confirm his general and somewhat gloomy view of the way of the world and the pitifully small chance for freedom it afforded. Once again, Miss Bosanquet, who was certainly one of James's most astute and sympathetic readers, and who had the advantage of watching his work develop as it were from the inside out, has summarized the matter with admirable economy and clarity. Discounting as mere surface the intensely perceived particulars of James's fiction—those same particulars that would serve as the very stock in trade and almost the total substance of a novelist of manners*—she concludes that now, "with the complete record before us . . . we can understand how little those international relations that engaged Henry James's attention mattered to his genius":

> Wherever he might have lived and whatever human interactions he might have observed, he would in all probability have reached much the same conclusion that he arrived at by the way of America, France, and England. When he walked out of the refuge of his study into the world and looked about him,

* For the sake of perspective here, it is worth bearing in mind Joseph Warren Beach's observation that although James was "writing in the time of Gladstone and Bernard Shaw, [he] seems hardly to have given a thought to the practical consequences and bearings of personal conduct. It is not in the relative terms of cause and effect that he considers human action. He is content, like some visionary Platonist, to refer each item of conduct to an absolute standard of the good and the beautiful." One could wish for no better introduction to the character of Maggie Verver and her predicament.

he saw a place of torment, where creatures of prey perpetually thrust their claws into the quivering flesh of the doomed, defenceless children of light. . . . The essential fact is that wherever he looked Henry James saw fineness apparently sacrificed to grossness, beauty to avarice, truth to a bold front. *He realized how constantly the tenderness of growing life is at the mercy of personal tyranny and he hated the tyranny of persons over each other.* His novels are a repeated exposure of this wickedness, a reiterated and passionate plea for the fullest freedom of development, unimperilled by reckless and barbarous stupidity. [Italics added.]

In sum, the striving to break out of the net of human relations and to experience an existence unmediated by social forms (one's own reality *an sich*)—a striving reflected, for example, in Isabel Archer's attempt to define herself without relation to anyone or anything—is clearly the expression of an idea with the profoundest social and political implications, but it is an idea that does not seem to have been taken very seriously by many academic readers of James. The deep and inevitable tension between the psychic needs of individuals and the demands and pressures of society serves, of course, as Hawthorne's great subject, but if one were to judge Hawthorne's work on the basis of James's treatment of it in 1879, one would be likely to conclude, remembering especially the famous catalogue of all that the country lacks, that American society was something that Hawthorne had to invent for the purposes of fiction. One might begin to explore the implications of such a conclusion by observing that the literature of the Transcendental period in general suggests that the institutional aspects of American life failed to register fully in the literary consciousness and were therefore regarded as having only a questionable existence in reality at the time that Hawthorne was writing books like *The Scarlet Letter*; accordingly, it is possible to argue that he was inescapably driven back into the past to locate a credible setting in which to situate his complex drama of human involvements. Indeed, perhaps the most remarkable (and from certain points of view, surely the most chilling) imaginative achievement of the commanding American writers of the nineteenth century was their almost unprecedented success in virtually willing away the society in which they lived. Their deepest response to the pressures of that society was to become unable, in a certain sense, to feel them. Hawthorne is almost alone in resisting this general drift, and in the end he is even more divided against himself about the emotional consequences of that resistance than Melville; but more than anything else the works of writers like Thoreau and Emerson (as well as those of Emily Dickinson, whose declaration that "the Soul selects her own Society" reveals no trace of irony), indicate that the assumptions that underlie social life had lost their hold on the imaginations of these writers, and that more and more for these Americans who had committed themselves to an ideal of "self-reliance" with a vengeance, the country they lived in (as Quentin Anderson has argued in *The Imperial Self*) came to resemble the imperium of their own imagination. For them, it was no longer the world which set limits on the power of the imagination, but the imagination which, no matter how bleak the appearance of things, could be relied upon, like Thoreau's chanticleer, to call its own triumphant tune.

Some indication of how this breathtaking sense of human possibility clashes with the characteristic European estimate is provided by an observation made by Carlyle in a letter to Emerson dated April 6, 1870. Concluding his remarks on Emerson's *Society and Solitude*, Carlyle notes: "How you go as if altog^r on the 'Over-Soul,' the Ideal, the Perfect or Universal & Eternal in this life of ours; and take so little heed of the frightful quantities of *friction* and perverse *impediment* there everywhere are; the reflections upon wh^h in my own poor life made me now &

then very sad, as I read you. Ah me, ah me; what a vista it is. . . ." Carlyle's retort to Margaret Fuller, which is better known and more succinct, strikes the same note; when told that Miss Fuller had announced: "I accept the universe," Carlyle reportedly replied: "By Gad, she'd better!"

James is no exception to this general Transcendental development, though he shares with Hawthorne the ability to estimate precisely the prodigious weight of those conditions of the real world and of life in society under which the spirit is obliged to labor. But while Hawthorne is ultimately inclined to condemn—at least in principle—the restless striving to be free of such conditions as strengthening a wish to break the links in the chain of common humanity (the ambiguous aspect of this image, which is familiar to all readers of Hawthorne, serves to remind us of the corresponding melancholy insistence on the cost of civilization which connects that author's work with Freud's), for James the individual risks suffocation and extinction unless he can successfully resist the pressures and encroachments of other wills. As a consequence, for James the assertion of individual will becomes synonymous not only with self-definition, but, as will be seen, with survival itself.

Yet although James's concern with the question of individual will may thus be understood in relation to the progress of certain commanding ideas in America, it must also be seen as a response, however complex, to the various deterministic theories—e.g., those of Darwin, Spencer, and the Literary Naturalists—prevalent in Europe during the period of his creative maturity. In the case of William James's intellectual development, this connection is of course explicit: the principles of his pragmatic philosophy, as articulated in such writings as "Great Men and Their Environment" (1880), "The Dilemma of Determinism" (1884), "The Will To Believe" (1896), and *Pragmatism* (1909), were established in clear opposition to the notion, simply put, "that the necessity which some philosophers ascribe to nature be extended to include human nature." Moreover, James's philosophical papers, as Alburey Castell goes on to point out, "express the interests of an alert and sensitive mind during one of the most critical quarter centuries in modern history. Darwin and Spencer, Newman and Huxley, Arnold and Pater, Tolstoy and Dostoievsky, Ibsen and Zola, Marx and Nietzsche, formed the climate of opinion within which James's ideas took shape."

It is equally evident that William James's assertion of the doctrine of free will, far from being an abstract philosophical gesture or a form of intellectual exercise, grew out of intense psychological need; it was first arrived at during a period of mental collapse in 1870—the year of Minny Temple's death, incidentally, which both William and Henry experienced as shattering the sense of virtually boundless possibility that they had invested in her (it represented, in Henry's succinct formulation, "the end of our youth"). William James's descent into desolation that year is summarized, in disguised form, as the transcribed experience of a Frenchman in Lectures VI and VII ("The Sick Soul") of *The Varieties of Religious Experience* (1902). According to this account, during the darkest hours of an unrelenting "panic fear" brought on by a sudden and unkillable awareness of "that pit of insecurity beneath the surface of life," William at last concluded that "in accumulated acts of thought lies salvation . . . ," and he went on to reflect on the possibilities available to him in his present situation:

Hitherto, when I have felt like taking a free initiative, like daring to act originally, without carefully waiting for contemplation of the external world to determine all for me, suicide seemed the most manly form to put my daring into; now, I will go a step further with my will, not only act with it, but believe as well; believe in my individual reality and creative power. My belief to be sure can't be optimistic—but I will posit life, (the real, the good) in the self governing resistance of the ego to the world. . . .

"My first act of free will," he wrote, "shall be to believe in free will." And it seems altogether likely that a remarkably similar determination to "believe in my individual reality and creative power" sustained his brother Henry through some of the grimmest days of his own career, especially after the humiliating failure of his play *Guy Domville* in 1895, which may well have helped to produce the awesome assertions of mastery (from the point of view of content as well as technique) associated with the "major phase."

It is, of course, not without significance that William James's reading during this period should have included works of Schopenhauer and Henry James, Sr. With regard to the latter, Gay Wilson Allen observes that "whether [William] finished his father's works in 1870 is not known, but the barrier which always prevented his finding satisfaction in Henry Sr.'s theology would have been an even greater one during this year of his mental crisis. The basis of his father's faith was the losing of the individual self in the selfhood of God, but William found it necessary to assert his selfhood to survive."

Predictably enough, just as Nietzsche ultimately saw the need to overcome his own attraction to Schopenhauer, so too William James "soon came to hate" that melancholy thinker, whose reasoning arrived at a denial of the will similar to that prescribed by certain eastern religions as the only means of achieving equilibrium and happiness. (According to the testimony of Thomas Sergeant Perry, incidentally, who got to know the Jameses in 1858-59, the year they spent in Newport, both William and Henry were at that time at least vaguely acquainted with some of Schopenhauer's work. Recalling their reading and conversation of that period, Perry wrote to Percy

Lubbock: "We fished in various waters, and I well remember when W.J. brought home a volume of Schopenhauer and showed us with delight the ugly mug of the philosopher and read us amusing specimens of his delightful pessimism.") In a reaction to this general drift of feeling, on January 5, 1870, during the period of crisis, "after reading Plato, [William James] copied, as if making it his motto: 'Ein ganzer Mensch—ein ganzer Wille'—a whole man is a whole will."

The very fact that James should choose to express himself in German on this point seems significant, and his general philosophical shift from denial to affirmation of the will—a shift significantly produced by a text in classical philosophy—would serve to link him with the German philosopher, almost the same age, who is one of the subjects of inquiry in this book. Unlike William James, Nietzsche had begun as a more or less passionately devoted disciple of Schopenhauer, and in the course of time had concluded (characteristically) that his emotional as well as intellectual survival depended on his ability to defy his master's influence insofar as he could detect it in himself. Although the character of William James's motivations was clearly different, there are evident similarities between his thought and Nietzsche's, whether one considers their resistance to all deterministic systems, or compares their ultimate rejection of what is sometimes referred to as the Correspondence Theory of Truth—a rejection which in Nietzsche's case led to a total denial of all forms of external authority. What is perhaps most apparent is the resemblance between Nietzsche's endorsement of only those truths "favorable to life" and William James's pragmatic conception of truth as a function of "the will to believe." Moreover, as Bertrand Russell has pointed out, "pragmatism, in some of its forms, is a power-philosophy."

The points of contact between pragmatism and Nietzschean philosophy would not be very difficult to establish, and it is in any case certain that in later years William James knew Nietzsche's work, since he refers to him at some length in the *Varieties of Religious Experience* (1902). But although such resemblances will be pointed out from time to time in the pages that follow, they are essentially beyond the scope of the present study, which is primarily concerned with certain parallels between the development of Nietzsche's thought and that of the novelist Henry James. These parallels are clustered chiefly, though by no means entirely, around a central belief held increasingly by both the novelist and the philosopher: the belief in art as the sole means of ordering and justifying the chaos of our experience in the world, and of endowing that experience with value. For both Nietzsche and James, the activity of art—or perhaps more precisely, the exercise of taste—becomes a means for the continual reassertion of personality and the mastery of experience. It is seen as a way of preserving the integrity of individual identity, and is consequently valued as the ultimate (and indeed the only) form of power over what would otherwise be simply a meaningless and menacing existence, a chaos threatening the obliteration of individual personality at every moment.

Looking back over his works in the collected New York Edition which incorporated his revisions, James found himself contemplating (in his Preface to *The Golden Bowl*, the last work in the series) the whole question of the "growth of one's 'taste,' as our fathers used to say: a blessed comprehensive name for many of the things deepest in us. The 'taste' of the poet is, at bottom and so far as the poet in him prevails over everything else, his active sense of life: in accordance with which truth to keep one's hand on it is to hold the silver clue to the whole labyrinth of his consciousness." The question is taken up by Nietzsche in Zarathustra's speech "On Those Who Are Sublime": "And you tell me, friends, that there is no disputing of taste and tasting? But all of life is a dispute over taste and tasting. Taste—that is at the same time weight and scales and weigher; and woe unto all the living that would live without disputes over weight and scales and weighers!"

It is to be hoped that a careful consideration of such parallels, whatever else it may suggest, will provide a coherent way of reading James: that it will help to explain some of his apparently contradictory values and serve to establish a plausible view of his development as continuous, rather than broken into "early," "middle," and "later" phases. Lest there be some misunderstanding, however, it should be made clear at this point that this study makes no attempt to establish an "influence" by Nietzsche on the novelist. The notion of "influence" is problematic in any case; in the present circumstances it may be enough to say that while it is certain that William James knew Nietzsche's work (though not, of course, as early as 1870), it hardly follows that Henry did—especially before the writing of *The Golden Bowl*. Still, before proceeding to explore a number of unexpected but significant correspondences between the works of Henry James and those of the German philosopher, it would be useful to consider some of the possible ways in which James might actually have become aware of Nietzsche's work, if only in order to define the general world of ideas in which both men inevitably moved during the last quarter of the nineteenth century.

3. *"Historical"* and *"Inner"* Culture: *Thomas Sergeant Perry's View of Nietzsche*

The first American notice of Nietzsche's work appeared in the July 1875 number of the *North American Review* and was written by James's friend Thomas Sergeant Perry.* It was a review

---

* The reader generally inclined to think of American men of letters in the later nineteenth century as a provincial lot, out of touch with larger currents of ideas, might be interested in perusing the imposing bibliography of

of the second of Nietzsche's *Unzeitgemässe Betrachtungen* ("Untimely Meditations," translated as "Thoughts out of Season" in the Levy edition), which the philosopher had entitled *Vom Nutzen und Nachtheil der Historie für das Leben* ("The Use and Abuse of History," in the Levy translation by Adrian Collins; rendered more accurately by Walter Kaufmann as "Of the Use and Disadvantage of History for Life").

Whether James ever read the review is not recorded in any of the published correspondence between the two friends, but if he had read it a number of Perry's remarks summarizing Nietzsche's critique of modern culture might have intrigued him. "The charges [Nietzsche] brings against modern culture are," Perry noted, "for the most part, well deserved":

> Our culture, [Nietzsche] says, gets no further than thinking and feeling about culture, it never rises to any determination about culture. An ancient Greek would be obliged to confess that a man of to-day has historical culture; but if he were to say that a man might be cultivated so far as possessing education goes, and yet be without inner culture, he would find no one to argue with him. . . . As Nietzsche says, the Greeks learned to "organize chaos," by devoting themselves to cultivating what they had within themselves. . . .

The distinction expressed here between "historical" culture and "inner" culture—culture that presumably involves no historical awareness, manifests no historical self-consciousness—bears an interesting resemblance to James's distinction between the culture of Europe and that of America. For if, in James's terms, culture for the European consists in bringing oneself into

---

writings published by Perry during his lifetime. Among his books are histories of Greek literature and English literature in the eighteenth century; his briefer writings are concerned with contemporary novels and works of nonfiction in numerous languages, and in those essays the range of subjects he considers extends from aspects of primitive culture to the Spanish court at the end of the seventeenth century to the problems of modern capitalism.

a proper relation to the accumulations (both material and spiritual) of the past, for the American it consists essentially in the cultivation of the self, the creation and "rendering" of personality as a work of art. Culture therefore becomes an absorbing form of activity for the American, while for the European it suggests nothing so much as a passive relation—a veritable bondage—to the past, and this distinction probably has a great deal to do with why, in James's "international relation," it is usually the Americans who gain the upper hand—at least from a moral point of view. The European is seen as a kind of empty vessel gradually filled with the rich inheritance of the past: he is nothing in himself, but, like Madame Merle in *The Portrait of a Lady*, exists entirely in his "relations"—with other people and especially with the "things" around him.

It was that same "European" passivity which Nietzsche saw as the predominant characteristic of modern culture, a form of culture which in his judgment had become self-conscious to the point of paralysis. In this regard, summarizing (and in part subscribing to) Nietzsche's view of the presumed effects of "excessive historical training," Perry notes: "If anything is suggested to us, instead of trying to do it, we feel our pulses, look at our tongues, and write accounts of the way the proposal affects us. We have become self-conscious to an extent which was unknown to our ancestors; we demoralize ourselves and those about us by looking at everything in an ironical spirit." And just that passivity in the face of accumulated fact ("the fatal futility of Fact," as James was to call it in his Preface to *The Spoils of Poynton*) which Nietzsche saw as rendering men the prisoners of history, he rejected, as James did, as inimical to life.

4. *James, Bourget, and Nietzsche*

James kept up a correspondence with Perry until the end of his life, and that correspondence, because it was almost invariably filled (presumably on both sides) with news of authors and books, often provides information about James's reading during any given period. In a letter written in March of 1884, for instance, James suggested to Perry that he "try Emile Bourget's *Psychologie Contemporaine* if you haven't already done so," and observed of the book that "it is really almost brilliant." It is clear that James was referring to a book by Paul Bourget (the "Emile" was a slip in all likelihood related to the appearance of the name of Zola one sentence later) entitled *Essais de psychologie contemporaine* (Paris, 1883); that this is so is confirmed by a letter to Perry written a few months later, after James had met Bourget and the Frenchman had become "a great friend of mine."

Although this friendship was to wane somewhat in later years (according to Leon Edel, when Bourget became increasingly reactionary and predictably anti-Dreyfusard), the two writers apparently saw a good deal of each other over the years, and James paid Bourget the very rare compliment of saving all the letters the French novelist had written to him. James never cared much for Bourget's novels (although *Cruelle Enigme*, published in 1885, was dedicated to him), but he once remarked to Edith Wharton that Bourget "was the first, easily, of all the talkers I ever encountered." He offered exactly the same estimate in a letter to Charles Eliot Norton written during the summer of 1892 from Siena, where James and the Bourgets were then staying.

James also wrote, in an essay first published in 1888, that unlike his cruder contemporaries in France (who have "almost nothing to show us in the way of the operation of character, the possibilities of conduct, the part played in the world by the idea. . . ."), Bourget "notes with extraordinary closeness the action of life on the soul," and this observation surely provides some clue as to the intellectual—or "professional"—basis of the relationship between the two writers. Indeed, as I. D. McFarlane has maintained, "it was quite understandable that James should look with approval upon an author who bid fair to lead the reaction against the naturalist novel of Zola and his satellites," though James was to learn eventually that Bourget's rather schematic and deterministic view of human motivation was "in a sense . . . carrying the naturalist technique into the realm of psychology."

Nietzsche was also familiar with Bourget's work, and he alludes to the French author on several occasions (usually in terms of praise) in his own writings. Like James, however, Nietzsche thought that Bourget's novels left a good deal to be desired; in a letter to Hippolyte Taine, for example (apparently his only letter to him), Nietzsche refers to *André Cornelis* (Paris, 1887)—a novel that was dedicated to Taine—and asserts decisively that he does not like the book; he goes on to explain that he finds it marred by defects of a kind "from which, I hope [Bourget's] delicate good taste will hereafter restrain him." "But it seems, does it not," Nietzsche concludes, "that the spirit of Dostoevsky gives this Parisian novelist no peace?"

In one of his last works Nietzsche was to maintain that Dostoevsky was "the only psychologist . . . from whom I had something to learn," but it is clear that his reading of Bourget also proved to be of some use. In his 1883 "Avant-Propos" to the *Essais de psychologie contemporaine*—the book that James recommended to Perry the following year—Bourget acknowledges that what he is attempting is not, properly speaking, literary criticism, and he goes on to indicate that "mon ambition a été de rediriger quelques notes capables de servir à l'historien de la vie morale pendant la seconde moitié du dix-neuvième siècle français." Such an ambition seems entirely consistent with those of Nietzsche, as does the analysis of Flaubert under the aspect of romanticism as well as nihilism. Moreover, the *Essais* contains a chapter entitled *Théorie de la décadence*, to which Nietzsche's own theory on that subject, set forth in *Der Fall Wagner* ("The Case of Wagner," first published in 1888), is significantly indebted. What Nietzsche derived from Bourget was, in René Wellek's words, "his definition of decadence as the anarchy of atoms, the 'disintegration' of the will." Of course, as Wellek goes on to point out, Nietzsche "had described the symptoms many times before under different names," but the obvious affinity between the two writers is worth remarking.

The two men actually met, however briefly, during the summer of 1888—the last summer of Nietzsche's sane life—when both of them were staying at Sils Maria and taking their meals at the same hotel. (In a letter dated October 4 of that year, Nietzsche confesses that he was "disappointed to find [Bourget] not interested in music.") Since Bourget's letters to James have not been published, there is no available evidence to indicate that Bourget ever mentioned the meeting (or meetings) to him, but it is worth keeping in mind that whatever conversation Bourget might have had with Nietzsche took place during the period of closest association between the Frenchman and the American novelist.

5. *James and "Vernon Lee"*

Among their mutual friends in Italy around this time Bourget and James numbered Bernard Berenson (the man responsible for selecting much of what is included in the art collection of Mrs. Isabella Stewart Gardner—"Mrs. Jack"—of whom further mention will be made later) and Violet Paget, "a young Englishwoman of twenty-seven" whose acquaintance James had made in the spring and summer of 1884, about the same time he had first met Bourget. Miss Paget "had lived most of her life in Italy" (largely in Florence), "had known Sargent since her childhood," and "had lately published, under the name of Vernon Lee, volumes entitled *Euphorion* and *Belcaro*." Of this young woman James wrote to T. S. Perry in September 1884 (evidently in response to something Perry had said in his previous letter): "I don't think I think Violet Paget *great*, but I think her a most astounding young female, & *Euphorion* most fascinating & suggestive, as well as monstrous clever. She has a prodigious cerebration." James goes on to record that "she has been in England this summer, & I have seen a good deal of her."

During this same period Vernon Lee dedicated her first attempt at a novel, entitled *Miss Brown*, to James (she had apparently described it to him beforehand as "very radical and atheistic"), and although he considered the book "very bad, *strangely* inferior to her other writing, & . . . painfully disagreeable in tone . . . strangely without delicacy or fineness, & the whole thing without form as art . . . in short a rather deplorable mistake," his harsh judgment (first confided in a letter to Perry) does not seem to have affected their relationship—at least not overtly. It is, however, worth remembering that James was sent a copy of the novel in early December of 1884, and that despite at least one inquiry he delayed for months before he could bring himself to communicate his verdict to the young author; when he finally did so, in mid-May of the following year, although he apologized in his letter for his "dogmatic and dictatorial tone" and assured her that it was "only an extreme indication of interest and sympathy in what you do," his disapproval was, if qualified, unmistakable. (Bourget, who visited Lee in Florence in March of 1885, reviewed her novel two months later in an essay entitled "L'esthéticisme anglais." Although like James he found the book misconceived—"interminable et plein de défauts," according to his latest biographer

—he did not commit his judgment to print, choosing instead to avoid the issue by engaging in a more general speculative discussion.)

The relationship with Vernon Lee lasted through the years of James's closest association with Bourget, and only ended, to all intents and purposes, in early 1893 after she had made the mistake of satirizing James in a story. James subsequently had second thoughts about the suggestion he had made to his brother William that he be sure to call on Lee when he was in Florence during January of that year, and he quickly wrote to warn William that he had better "draw it mild with her on the question of friendship. She's a tiger-cat!" Moreover, her "treachery to private relations" led James to conclude that there was a "great second-rate element in her first-rateness," and despite her eventual profuse apologies and an attempt by a mutual friend to reconcile the two in 1900, James was not to see her again until 1912, and that was in all likelihood the last time they met. Still, despite James's fallen estimation of Miss Paget's character, he confessed his sorrow at losing the "sight and profit of one of the most intelligent persons it had ever been my fortune to know."

6. *"Vernon Lee" and Nietzsche*

At the end of the same year in which James published *The Golden Bowl*, an article by Vernon Lee entitled "Nietzsche and the 'Will to Power'" appeared in the *North American Review* —the same magazine that had carried *The Ambassadors* in twelve monthly installments during the previous year. Whether or not James ever read the article, of course, it could not possibly have affected his writing of *The Golden Bowl*; still, this account of Nietzsche does raise certain issues which will come to bear on our discussion.

In the course of this spirited and often penetrating essay, Vernon Lee makes a number of points intended to establish an emotional perspective into which Nietzsche's philosophy may be placed. To begin with, she asserts that inasmuch as "the appearance of volition exists only in the face of two conceivable modes of action, which imply Consciousness, there can be no will, no choice, in cases where the instincts have the blind, automatic action of reflexes"; but she then goes on to attribute Nietzsche's personal hostility (personal as against philosophical: a distinction out of keeping with the whole thrust of his enterprise) to the varieties of determinism to "the proud and combative and self-centered man's excessive and unphilosophical scorn for anything like habits, blind instincts and reflexes."

Lee proceeds to attack what she regards as one of the central inconsistencies of Nietzsche's thought. Nietzsche, she observes, "was never able to carry his individualism . . . to its logical conclusion of anarchy inside as well as outside the individual"—a judgment which clearly fails to take into account the shattered state of Nietzsche's mind after his collapse in 1888. According to Nietzsche, Vernon Lee argues, the hierarchy of values established by "the Zarathustrian person (to say nothing of the eventually coming 'Über-Mensch')" necessitated a "regime of categorical imperatives" which "was the outcome, solely, of the individual himself"; and this individual "went through this novitiate of purifications, professed this *rule* of vigils and chastenings . . . for the simple gratification of his own fine gentleman's *taste*." "But, if we look at facts," Lee continues, "this superlative Zarathustrian 'good form' (for as such this moral Beau Brummel gives it us), is, like every other kind of *good form*, a product for which no isolated individuality could suffice, and for which no pressure of merely individual preference could originally account. It is essentially an historical, sociological product."

This argument would seem to discount the power of certain world-historical figures (Napoleon, for example, or even the Spanish king for whose sake Castilians allegedly learned to lisp) to impose their sense of "good form" on the world. But that is not Lee's point. If we apply T. S. Perry's useful distinction between "historical" and "inner" culture to her argument, it becomes clear that given the terms of that argument what she is maintaining is that the only possible culture is "historical" culture: the values and discriminations which ultimately govern our behavior—indeed, any values and discriminations—must be seen not only as the complex products of the past, but, perhaps more importantly, as products of life in society, a particular society at a particular moment in time. As a consequence, the prospect of a wholly original, unmediated and detached relation to experience—the relation of the artist to his unformed material—is regarded as altogether illusory. (Just such a relation is, of course, exactly what Emerson advocates in *Nature*, first published in 1836 and almost certainly known to Nietzsche, who in any case regarded the New England Transcendentalist as nothing less than "the author who has been richest in ideas in this century." At the beginning of *Nature*, Emerson asserts: "Our age is retrospective. It builds the sepulchres of the fathers. . . . The foregoing generations beheld God and nature face to face; we, through their eyes. Why should not we also enjoy an original relation to the universe? Why should not we have a poetry and philosophy of insight and not of tradition, and a religion by revelation to us, and not the history of theirs?")

For Vernon Lee, the very existence of values and discriminations presupposes life in society, which is to say the possibility of alternative judgments; the need to determine for oneself what is of value in one's experience would not arise were it not for the pressures exerted by the values and wills of other persons, experienced individually and in their institutional embodiments. Accordingly, the pattern which defines the individual personality, no matter how intricate, is inevitably generated in relation to a preexistent order. "For, if the individual has not grown as a mere random jumble of uncoordinated instincts," Lee asserts, "this is explained by his not existing as an isolated individual, companionless, *in vacuo*. Man is, more or less, a composite and orderly whole because he is an integral part of a whole which can only be composite and orderly. . . ." And she pursues the implications of the point:

> The *law-to-himself* of the finer human being is the expression of a more perfect and well-nigh automatic adaptation to the hierarchy outside. . . . But if there did not exist, if there had not existed for aeons, creatures more or less similar around us, if the universe had cared to produce only isolated higher individuals, or Super-Men, would there have been a need for such a complex form of life; a need for reactions, so intricate and so subordinate to one another; a need for perception, will or thought; an opening, so to speak, for such superfine moral manners?

Although she rejects it, Lee is also aware of the deeper significance of Nietzsche's conception of the exercise of "taste" as a metaphysical activity. This notion is repeatedly expressed by Nietzsche—in *Thus Spoke Zarathustra*, for example, in the assertion that "To esteem is to create. . . . Esteeming itself is of all esteemed things the most estimable treasure. Through esteeming alone is there value: and without esteeming, the nut of existence would be hollow." Indeed, she senses that this activity is at the very heart of his entire philosophical enterprise:

> . . . more than in any other philosopher, we become aware that there is in Nietzsche's mind something round which his system has grown, but which is far more essential and vital to him than his system: something continually alluded to, constantly immanent, round which he perpetually hovers, into which he frequently plunges, on whose bank he erects meta-

physical edifies, lets off fireworks of epigrams, sets holocausts ablaze and sings magnificent dithyrambs; but which remains undefined, a vague *It*. Such an ineffable central mystery exists in the thought of many philosophers . . . ; a whirlpool explaining everything, but never itself explained; called, as the case may be, "Higher Law," "Truth," "Good," sometimes merely "Nature," "God." It is one of Nietzsche's finest and profoundest achievements that he has, once or twice, called this transcending *It* by a new, surprising and, methinks, a correct name, "My Taste."

For Nietzsche, it must be remembered, the death of God alluded to in *Die fröhliche Wissenschaft* ("The Gay Science," first published in 1882) created not what might be called in the language of classified advertising an "unprecedented opportunity," but a terrifying void which made the "revaluation of all values" an immediate and desperate necessity if life was to have any meaning and men were to withstand the terrors of an existence which they could perceive as pointless. Under these circumstances, once Nietzsche saw himself (as he surely came to do), as single-handedly assuming the burden once borne by the living God, it is hardly surprising that he could have cried out as he did: "Give me, ye heavenly ones, give me madness! madness to make me believe at last in myself." (Consider once again the suggestive link with Emerson, who declared in "Self-Reliance": "To believe your own thought, to believe that what is for you in your private heart is true for all men—that is genius. Speak your latent conviction, and it shall be the universal sense; for the inmost in due time becomes the outmost. . . .") To this grimly prophetic prayer Vernon Lee, "in humility and confidence," opposes her own: "Give us, ye Heavenly Ones, Sanity; so that we may believe in all which is not merely our own self."

By reasserting the primacy of the "not-ego," Vernon Lee is reasserting the primacy of an "outside world" in relation to

which we define ourselves and perceive the limits of our powers: a world consisting of material objects, institutions, and
other minds, a world in which we grasp aspects of our own
identity in others and in which we maintain and refine our sense
of ourselves through endless varieties of struggle—a world which
(like its inhabitants) suffers the consequences and enjoys the
benefits of the past, and which is in the end the sole ground of
all our values, the dark wood in which we continually find and
lose our way. Such a view of things represents, in Henry James's
sense of the word, a "European" gesture (an affirmation of the
"historical" culture discussed above); and as we have been seeing in the case of Emerson, Vernon Lee's argument against
Nietzsche might, with some slight modification, be applied
with equal force to the triumphant denial, made by a remarkable number of nineteenth-century American writers, of the notion that human life consists ineluctably—and at its highest—
of life in society.

The notion that "the state or political community" is "the
highest of all [communities]," and that it "embraces all the rest,
aims at good in a greater degree than any other, and at the highest good," is, of course, at least as old as Aristotle's *Politics*; and
although it is no doubt true that that assumption was challenged to a considerable degree by the insistence of Christian-
ity on maintaining a sharp contrast between the claims and re-
wards of this world and those of the next, what is perhaps most
significant about the nineteenth-century American form of the
denial is that it is not justified by a clear affirmation of a higher
form of community. On the contrary, in the view of the writers
we are considering, cultivation of self serves paradoxically as the
highest social good, and must not be compromised in favor of
any other human claims, even those of an obviously philan-
thropic nature: by definition there can be no fixed model, no
clear limits, no established range of obligations imposed upon

this process of individual development. "If a plant cannot live according to its nature," writes Thoreau in "Civil Disobedience," "it dies; and so a man." One may reasonably assume that Thoreau did not have in mind trimmed hedges or roses made to climb a trellis—no matter how healthy such horticultural specimens might actually prove to be.

The example of Thoreau, like that of Emerson, seems very much to the point here, especially if one looks carefully at some of his more familiar declarations in an essay like "Civil Disobedience"—e.g., his pronouncement regarding the American government that "a single man can bend it to his will," his imperative that "you must live within yourself," his assertion that " 'I, Henry Thoreau, do not wish to be regarded as a member of any incorporated society which I have not joined.' . . . I simply wish to refuse allegiance to the State, to withdraw and stand aloof from it effectually. . . . In fact, I quietly declare war with the State, after my fashion, though I still make what use and get what advantage of her I can, as is usual in such cases. . . . However, . . . if a man is thought-free, fancy-free, imagination-free, that which *is not* never for a long time appearing *to be* to him, unwise rulers or reformers cannot fatally interrupt him." The moral implications of this view are expressed by Emerson with characteristically breathtaking simplicity: "From this transfer of the world into the consciousness, this beholding of all things in the mind, follow easily [the Transcendentalist's] whole ethics. It is simpler to be self-dependent."

Lee concludes her own argument with a passage that might serve as a gloss on Emerson's assertion (an even more startling version of which appears as the epigraph to Chapter III below):

We have seen how [Nietzsche's] "Will to Power," remaining consciously such, fails to metamorphose itself into those desires for the not-ego, into that striving after the external-to-oneself, into that thinking and feeling of the outside world, which is the process of exteriorization of the subject into the object, normal and necessary in every healthy soul. We have seen similarly how, despite his extraordinary genius, the vastness of the universe and its complexity and vigor of life entirely escaped Nietzsche, until the world shrank to being little more for him than an inert, almost counterfeit, stage filled up by his own imaginary size and strength; the cooperation of every kind of existence, the give and take of past and present, the ceaseless act of assimilation and reproduction, and their culmination in the immortally living human work, all this accessory, organic, and endlessly complex activity becoming replaced in his mind, by the puny deed of volition of a mere individual Über-Mensch. Nay, we have seen how he gravely asserted that this microscopic human detail could actually accept with a pompous "Yes" the inevitable course of life universal, of which he, his thought and volition, are but as the minutest bubble of froth. . . .

Although this series of harsh judgments (the last of which echoes Carlyle's tart reply to Margaret Fuller's announced acceptance of the existence of the universe), undoubtedly serves to place some of Nietzsche's pronouncements in a certain realistic perspective, the judgments do not provide any significant understanding of what Lee previously refers to as that "emotional condition, organic and permanent" which forms "the living nucleus of all his teaching." Similarly, her attack on Nietzsche's notion of *amor fati* (which she does not name) as being at best a form of what Ibsen called the "vital lie" and at worst merely "a new variety of the doctrine of renunciation" does not sufficiently explore the ambiguous character of this notion or the emotional ground out of which it emerges. Leaving aside the question of philosophical antecedents for the conception (in the Stoic philosophers and Spinoza, for example), let us consider the nature of the problem to which Nietzsche's *amor fati* was an attempted solution, and then go on to determine in what ways this idea resembles some of those of William James.

7. *The Sacred Will:*
Nietzsche, William James, and Emerson

By the time Nietzsche wrote *Thus Spoke Zarathustra* (Parts I and II first published in 1883; Part III in 1884; Part IV—privately—in 1885), the importance of the function of will in his philosophy had been decisively established; will had come to be seen as the very principle by which the character of reality was determined and sustained. Accordingly, once it was claimed that the will of God had ultimately failed—if God is seen as the ultimate external authority and source of order—then it was only through a supreme assertion of individual will that the world could be rendered coherent at all. It is as though all phenomena were conceived as iron filings, and God were the magnet determining their arrangement; once the magnet is withdrawn the pattern vanishes, and what is required is an equivalent magnetic force that is capable of compelling the whole variety of disparate phenomena into an orderly relation— the same relation as before, which constitutes the order of things we recognize as the world. In other words, nothing less than the continued existence of the world as an intelligible phenomenon comes to be dependent on the power of the individual will:

> And what you have called world, that shall be created only by you: your reason, your image, your will, your love shall thus be realized. And verily, for your own bliss, you lovers of knowledge.

The world, which was formerly created in God's image, would now have to be created in one's own image, and the problem was to get the two images to correspond exactly, so that the world would in no way be diminished, but would afford the same richness of possibility. This required finding in oneself everything demanded by the life of the world, since the world had to be the creation of a single will, and that will could not be augmented by the assistance of others. The second creation of the world could no more be a social enterprise than was the first.

But here Nietzsche found that the assertion of the will (which allowed for the conviction that one was actively willing things as they in fact are) had a fixed and unalterable limit: the past. It seemed impossible to exercise the will retroactively, and this limitation served to produce anxiety in the creator, for if the past had been as the past had been without the active participation (that is, the conscious participation) of the creator, then clearly he could not be all-powerful: clearly there were elements of the past surviving in the present for which his act of will was not responsible. And given Nietzsche's reasoning, if the creator was not all-powerful, then he was simply powerless, forced to live in a world he had not created—which he had not deliberately endowed with meaning down to its most minute particular, and which was therefore (as a result of the death of God) wholly meaningless.

In the section entitled "On Redemption" [*Von der Erlösung*] in Part II of *Thus Spoke Zarathustra*, Nietzsche continued to ponder the problem of retroactive assertion of the will and the emotional consequences of the failure of such an assertion (which include self-hatred expressed as a desire for revenge which, when detected, produces in its turn a more intense self-hatred):

> To redeem those who lived in this past and to recreate all "it was" into a "thus I willed it"—that alone should I call redemption. Will—that is the name of the liberator and joy-bringer; thus I taught you, my friends. But now learn this too: the will

itself is still a prisoner. Willing liberates; but what is it that puts even the liberator himself in fetters? "It was"—that is the name of the will's gnashing of teeth and most secret melancholy. Powerless against what has been done, he is an angry spectator of all that is past. The will cannot will backwards; and that he cannot break time and time's covetousness, that is the will's loneliest melancholy. . . . That time does not run backwards, that is his wrath; "that which was" is the name of the stone he cannot move. And so he moves stones out of wrath and displeasure, and he wreaks revenge on whatever does not feel wrath and displeasure as he does. Thus the will, the liberator, took to hurting; and on all who can suffer he wreaks vengeance for his inability to go backwards. This, indeed this alone, is what revenge is: the will's ill will against time and its "it was."

Zarathustra goes on to argue against the "fables of madness" which counsel that no redemption of the past is possible, and then concludes:

I led you away from these fables when I taught you, "The will is a creator." All "it was" is a fragment, a riddle, a dreadful accident—until the creative will says to it, "But thus I willed it." Until the creative will says to it, "But thus I will it, thus I shall will it."

But has the will yet spoken thus? And when will that happen? Has the will been unharnessed yet from his own folly? Has the will yet become his own redeemer and joy-bringer? Has he unlearned the spirit of revenge and all gnashing of teeth? And who taught him reconciliation with time and something higher than any reconciliation? For that will which is the will to power must will something higher than any reconciliation; but how shall this be brought about? Who could teach him also to will backwards?

Nietzsche's attempt to resolve this problem, to find a way of asserting the mind's dominion over all time, eventually resulted in his conception of the doctrine of "eternal recurrence." Although its precise significance in Nietzsche's thought is not established until later, this doctrine is first presented in *Die fröhliche Wissenschaft* (published in 1882, before *Zarathustra*), the book which, significantly enough, also contains the troubling announcement of the death of God. In the section of that work entitled *Das grösste Schwergewicht* (translated as "The Heaviest Burden" in the Levy edition, as "The greatest weight" in Walter Kaufmann's version, from which the following passage is taken), Nietzsche writes:

> What, if some day or night a demon were to steal after you into your loneliest loneliness and say to you: "This life as you now live it and have lived it, you will have to live once more and innumerable times more; and there will be nothing new in it, but every pain and every joy and every thought and sigh and everything unutterably small or great in your life will have to return to you, all in the same succession and sequence—even this spider and this moonlight between the trees, and even this moment and I myself. The eternal hourglass of existence is turned upside down again and again, and you with it, a dust grain of dust." Would you not throw yourself down and gnash your teeth and curse the demon who spoke thus? Or have you once experienced a tremendous moment when you would have answered him: "You are a god, and never have I heard anything more divine." If this thought gained possession of you, it would change you as you are or perhaps crush you. The question in each and every thing, "Do you desire this once more and innumerable times more?" would weigh upon your actions as the greatest weight. Or how well disposed would you have to become to yourself and to life *to crave nothing more fervently* than this ultimate eternal confirmation and seal?

Karl Löwith contends that although in *Zarathustra* "eternal recurrence is the basic inspiration, it is not presented as a hypothesis but as a metaphysical truth," and he goes on to assert that in the passage quoted above, "the idea is introduced . . . not as a metaphysical doctrine but as an ethical imperative: to live *as if* 'the eternal hourglass of existence' will continually be turned, in order to impress on each of our actions the weight of an inescapable responsibility." Kaufmann disputes such an interpretation, which he characterizes as a product of "the mis-apprehension that the recurrence represents an analogy to Kant's Categorical Imperative," and he argues on the basis of Nietzsche's later philosophy that the recurrence must be seen as (in Nietzsche's phrase) "the most extreme form of nihilism." Referring throughout to Nietzsche's formulations in a note (dated June 10, 1887) included in *Der Wille zur Macht*, he concludes:

> "*Duration* coupled with an 'in vain,' without aim and end [*Zeil und Zweck*], is the *most paralyzing* thought." "Let us think this thought in its most terrible form: existence as it is, without sense and aim, but recurring inevitably without a finale of nothingness: 'the eternal recurrence' " (WM 55). The doc-trine means that all events are repeated endlessly, that there is no plan nor goal to give meaning to history or life, and that we are mere puppets in an absolutely senseless play.

The phenomenon described by Nietzsche is of course a form of determinism so extreme that even the slightest gesture of freedom appears to be precluded by it. Under these circum-stances, life would be unthinkable for the conscious man, for he would be required to live at every moment with the intolerable knowledge that nothing he did could possibly have any effect on the course of his life. Faced with this unendurable prospect, what Nietzsche characteristically proceeds to do is to reverse the terms of the situation, to move from one state of affairs to its implied antithesis: for the man who is totally impotent he substitutes the man who is all-powerful. Making the move in imagination from a vision of total enslavement to one of total freedom (given Nietzsche's Heracleitean turn of mind, there are rarely midway points between such polarities), he con-ceives of a being who would literally be a match for the universe. And indeed the workings of that universe, Nietzsche believed, would in the future more and more be shown to be, on the evidence of physical science, a function of deterministic principles of the kind embodied in extreme form in the idea of eternal recurrence (which Nietzsche regarded as "the most *scientific* of all possible hypotheses"). Consequently, just as Nietzsche interpreted Heracleitus to be claiming that since everything contained its opposite within itself, the necessity ruling the universe must imply freedom, so he concluded that the existence of a will without effect in the world implied the possible existence of a will whose effects would be unlimited.

Hence the powerful man, the man powerful enough to impose his own will (in the form of his distinctive values) on the world, came to be regarded by Nietzsche as the only man who could survive the constant, immediate, and total threat of chaos which characterizes the world of the recurrence—a world that is either totally meaningless or totally meaningful, depending solely on the power of the individual will. Such a man, a man of sure and undivided will, would have to possess extraordinary qualities; and perhaps chief among them would be that "Dionysian faith" extolled in *Die Götzen-Dämmerung* ("Twilight of the Idols," published after Nietzsche's collapse in 1889).*

As an exemplar of that faith Nietzsche chooses Goethe,

---

* For the sake of clarity, it should be noted at this point that the term "Dionysian" signifies something very different in the context of the later philosophy from what it signifies in *The Birth of Tragedy*; in the earlier work, the "Dionysian" tendency exists in polar opposition to the "Apollonian," and in Nietzsche's view it is by bringing these antithetical impulses into a tense balance that the finest examples of Greek tragedy—works by Aeschylus and Sophocles—achieve their awesome ordering power. In the later phase of Nietzsche's philosophy, the Dionysian tendency is not conceived in any such opposition, and the term seems to acquire the almost wholly positive and vitalistic associations it is likely to have for the modern reader—the reader of D. H. Lawrence, for example.

whom he presents not only as an incalculably great artist but also as a man of extraordinary personal power who "did not retire from life but put himself into the midst of it; he was not fainthearted but took as much as possible upon himself, over himself, into himself":

> What he wanted was *totality*; he fought the mutual extraneousness of reason, senses, feeling, and will. . . . he disciplined himself to wholeness, he *created* himself. . . . Goethe conceived a human being who would be strong, highly educated, skillful in all bodily matters, self-controlled, reverent toward himself, and who might dare to afford the whole range and wealth of being natural, being strong enough for such freedom; the man of tolerance, not from weakness but from strength, because he knows how to use to his advantage, even that from which the average nature would perish; the man for whom there is no longer anything that is forbidden—unless it be *weakness*, whether called vice or virtue. Such a spirit who has *become free* stands amid the cosmos with a joyous and trusting fatalism, in the faith that only the particular is loathsome, and that all is redeemed and affirmed in the whole—*he does not negate any more*. Such a faith, however, is the highest of all possible faiths: I have baptized it with the name of *Dionysus*.

At the end of this work, moreover, Nietzsche declares that he is "the last disciple of the philosopher Dionysus—I, the teacher of the eternal recurrence," thus indicating that the Dionysian faith was linked in his own mind with the idea of eternal recurrence. The basis of this association seems clear enough: given the eternal recurrence, the affirmation of any moment in time becomes an affirmation of the whole, and by a similar process the affirmation of the cosmos serves as an affirmation of self. In this way existence becomes at last endurable: it is therefore not surprising that Nietzsche should have written, in a note for *Zarathustra*, "*After the vision of the overman*, in a gruesome way the doctrine of the *recurrence*: now bearable!" Indeed, by virtue of this mutual affirmation of self and cosmos, existence becomes (to use a Nietzschean word) "joyful"; will and reality correspond. But in Nietzsche's view this kind of correspondence could occur only in the lives of the greatest human beings, whose active passivity (if it may be so called) in the face of the universe indicated that in the sense of the fullness of their power they could regard it as if it were really an extension of themselves; accordingly, "acceptance" of the cosmos becomes a form of self-acceptance:

> My formula for the greatness of a human being is *amor fati:* that one wants nothing to be different—not forward, not backward, not in all eternity. Not merely bear what is necessary, still less conceal it . . . but *love it.*

A somewhat joyless echo of this notion of *amor fati* may be found in a diary entry (for March 22, 1870) which William James addressed to Minny Temple soon after her death: "By that big part of me that's in the tomb with you," he wrote, "may I realize and believe in the immediacy of death! May I feel that every torment suffered here passes and is as a breath of wind, every pleasure too":

> . . . Minny, your death makes me feel the nothingness of all our egoistic fury. The inevitable release is sure; wherefore take our turn kindly whatever it contain. Ascend to some sort of partnership with fate, & since tragedy is at the heart of us, go to meet it, work it in to our own ends, instead of dodging it all our days, and being run down by it at last. Use your death (or your life, it's all one meaning). . . .

It is significant that Gay Wilson Allen, who quotes more of this passage in his biography of William James, should first perceive an obvious similarity between the sentiments expressed here and those of Marcus Aurelius, and then go on to observe that James's thoughts also "unconsciously echoed Emerson's teaching on 'Fate' (in *The Conduct of Life*, 1851), with which he was familiar: " 'Tis the best use of Fate to teach a fatal courage. . . . For if fate is so prevailing, man is a part of it, and can confront fate with fate.' " As will become apparent, the presence of Emersonian values and assumptions is so pervasive in William James's thinking (not to mention Henry's) that it would have been surprising if those patterns of belief failed to figure in his readings of his own experience. Eloquent testimony to that presence is provided by James himself in the address which he delivered at Concord in 1903 on the occasion of the Centenary of Emerson's birth. Although "the form that so lately moved upon these streets and country roads . . . is now dust," he reflects, "the soul's note, the spiritual voice, rises strong and clear above the uproar of the times, and seems securely destined to exert an ennobling influence over future generations." "Beloved master," he concludes: "As long as our English language lasts men's hearts will be cheered and their souls strengthened and liberated by the noble and musical pages with which you have enriched it."

To say that Nietzsche was also "familiar" with this essay would be a considerable understatement, as Charles Andler and others have noted. Indeed, in considering the general question of Nietzche's affinity to Emerson, it is worth remembering that in a letter to Carl von Gersdorff written in September 1874, Nietzsche confided that he never traveled without packing a copy of Emerson's *Essays* in his suitcase;* moreover, in two significant

---

* Andler also indicates that Nietzsche had certainly read and in some cases frequently reread *Emerson's Essays: First Series* (1856); *The Conduct of Life* (1860); *Society and Solitude* (1870); and *Essays: Second Series* (1876). In addition, citing Arthur Berthold's *Bücher und Wege zu Büchern* (1900), he notes that Nietzsche's library contained German trans-

notes written around the time of *Die fröhliche Wissenschaft* (1881-1882) and published posthumously in the *Nachlass*, Nietzsche described his deep sense of connection with Emerson and his estimate of that author's achievement in terms which could hardly be called equivocal: "Emerson. I have never felt so much at home in a book, so much in my own house as,—I ought not to praise it; it is too close to me." "The author as yet the richest in ideas of this century has been an American (unfortunately clouded by German philosophy). Milky glass." In addition, in her biography of her brother Elisabeth Foerster-Nietzsche asserts that the motto at the beginning of the first edition of *Die fröhliche Wissenschaft*—a book which in any case contains praise for Emerson—represents a quotation from Emerson "a little transformed"; the motto ("To the poet and the sage all things are friendly and sacred, all events profitable, all days holy, all men divine") seems to be a reworking of a sentence in Emerson's essay "History."

There are numerous indications that Nietzsche's interest in Emerson continued all through the productive period of his life, but it is in any case clear that during the writing of *Zarathustra* in late 1884—two years after Emerson's death—the Concord Sage was still on Nietzsche's mind. In a letter written to Overbeck from Nice on December 22, 1884, Nietzsche gave some indication that he was concerned not only with Emerson's specific works, but with his general intellectual development as well:

> . . . I am having translated into German for me (in writing) a longish essay by Emerson, which gives some clarity about his

lations of all of these works except for *Society and Solitude*. Following Eduard Baumgarten's *Der Pragmatismus* (1938), Hermann Hummel produces the same list of three works in German translation, but adds that "from another source we know that [Nietzsche] possessed" Emerson's *Essay ueber Goethe und Shakespeare* (H. Grimm, 1857).

development. If you want it, it is at your disposal and your wife's. I do not know how much I would give if only I could bring it about, *ex post facto*, that such a glorious, great nature, rich in soul and spirit, might have gone through some *strict* discipline, a really *scientific education*. As it is, in Emerson, we have *lost a philosopher*. . . .

As we have seen, like his brother Henry (who in 1887 published a significant essay on the American thinker's life and work), William James had read and reread Emerson, and this might well account for the similarity between some of his reflections and some of Nietzsche's; but in a number of its most striking particulars his thinking seems to bypass that of his countryman and proceed directly to problems of the kind usually associated primarily with Nietzsche. As early as 1868, for instance, William James was recording his conviction that "God is dead or at least irrelevant, ditto everything pertaining to the 'Beyond,' " and then perceiving (as Nietzsche was to do) that the metaphysical problems which emerged as a distressing consequence of this conviction made it imperative "to get at something absolute without going out of your own skin!"

Such thoughts had occurred to William James long before he could possibly have read anything by Nietzsche, but it is interesting that later in his life he should have cited a passage from *Zur Genealogie der Moral* ("On the Genealogy of Morals," published 1887) in his own *Varieties of Religious Experience* (1902). The quotation occurs in Lectures 14 and 15 (on "The Value of Saintliness"), and it would be useful to keep in mind the predicament of the "transfigured victims" (in F. W. Dupee's suggestive phrase) of Henry James's later novels in reflecting on the implications of Nietzsche's remarks and William James's evaluation of them.

William James cites Nietzsche as "the most inimical critic of the saintly impulse whom I know," and in a discussion of the "feud" pursued by "the saintly and the worldly ideal . . . in literature as much as in real life," he quotes the following passage from the *Genealogy* (noting that he has "abridged, and in one place transposed, a sentence"):

> The sick are the greatest danger for the well. The weaker, not the stronger, are the strong's undoing. It is not *fear* of our fellow-man, which we should wish to see diminished; for fear rouses those who are strong to become terrible in turn themselves, and preserves the hard-earned and successful type of humanity. What is to be dreaded by us more than any other doom is not fear, but rather the great disgust, not fear, but rather the great pity—disgust and pity for our human fellows. . . . The morbid are our greatest peril—not the "bad" men, not the predatory beings. Those born wrong, the miscarried, the broken—they it is, the weakest, who are undermining the vitality of the race, poisoning our trust in life, and putting humanity in question. Every look of them is a sigh—"Would I were something other! I am sick and tired of what I am." In this swampsoil of self-contempt, every poisonous weed flourishes, and all so small, so secret, so dishonest, and so sweetly rotten. Here swarm the worms of sensitiveness and resentment; here the air smells odious with secrecy, with what is not to be acknowledged; here is woven endlessly the net of the meanest of conspiracies, the conspiracy of those who suffer against those who succeed and are victorious; here the very aspect of the victorious is hated—as if health, success, strength, pride, and the sense of power were in themselves things vicious, for which one ought eventually to make bitter expiation. Oh, how these people would themselves like to inflict the expiation, how they thirst to be the hangmen! And all the while their duplicity never confesses their hatred to be hatred.

Although James sees "poor Nietzsche's antipathy" as "itself sickly enough," he finds himself obliged to admit that "we all know what he means, and he expresses well the clash between the two ideals." James then proceeds to an analysis of the essentials of the clash, and the language he uses is significant:

The carnivorous-minded "strong man," the adult male and cannibal, can see nothing but mouldiness and morbidness in the saint's gentleness and self-severity, and regards him with pure loathing. The whole feud revolves essentially upon two pivots: Shall the seen world or the unseen world be our chief sphere of adaptation? and must our means of adaptation in this seen world be aggressiveness or non-resistance?

The debate is serious. In some sense and to some degree both worlds must be acknowledged and taken account of: and *in the seen world both aggressiveness and non-resistance are needful.* It is a question of emphasis, of more or less. Is the saint's type or the strong-man's type the more ideal? [Italics added.]

"According to the empirical philosophy," James goes on to observe, "all ideals are matters of relation." Hence, "ideality in conduct is altogether a matter of adaptation."

For his part, James argues, the saint is "entirely adapted" to a "millennial society":* in the abstract, therefore, he is "a higher type of man than the 'strong man,' because he is adapted to the highest society conceivable, whether that society ever be concretely possible or not." In the real world, however, "we find that the individual saint may be well or ill adapted, according to particular circumstances"—as it turns out, according to whether or not his sainthood stops short of nonresistance and he is capable of asserting aggressive impulses ("Christ himself was fierce upon occasion," James points out). In short, to demonstrate his "strength and stature" in the world, the saint must (although this may seem paradoxical) give evidence of a certain worldly mastery and power.

---

* The definition of the saint offered by James here provides an unexpected perspective on Francis Grund's observation that "Americans love their country not, indeed, *as it is;* but *as it will be.* They do not love the land of their fathers; but they are sincerely attached to that which their children are destined to inherit. They live in the future. . . ." Grund's remarks are taken up again in the next chapter, where their implications for our present discussion are developed further.

In general, James concludes, given the limitations imposed by the world on human possibility, we should do our best to be saints; and describing the effect of saints, he writes: "Their sense of mystery in things, their passion, their goodness, irradiate about them and enlarge their outlines while they soften them." This sentence might easily serve as a description of the Jamesian heroine—one thinks of Milly Theale, for instance—and indeed it will presently be seen that the whole line of thinking advanced by William James bears significantly on our understanding of the action of *The Golden Bowl*, a novel which after all seeks to explore the question of precisely what, in worldly terms, one is permitted to do in order to ensure the triumph of the ideal.

As we have observed, whether or not Henry James ever actually read Nietzsche is in no way crucial to the argument developed here; it is, however, evident that the American novelist was at various times of his life close to people who had done so, people whose minds he respected and whose ideas engaged him. Recent studies have made it increasingly clear, moreover, that it would have been very difficult for anyone who moved in the kind of intellectual company James did, or saw the kinds of magazines he would have been likely to see, or knew his brother's lectures on *The Varieties of Religious Experience*, to have remained wholly unaware of the emerging presence of Nietzsche at the turn of the century.

II

The Background of Assumptions

Imagination, which in truth,
Is but another name for absolute power. . . .
WORDSWORTH   The Prelude

Beware when the great God lets loose a thinker on this planet.
Then all things are at risk. It is as when a conflagration has broken
out in a great city, and no man knows what is safe, or where it will
end. There is not a piece of science but its flank may be turned to-
morrow; there is not any literary reputation, not the so-called eternal names of fame, that may not be revised and condemned. The
very hopes of man, the thoughts of his heart, the religion of nations, the manners and morals of mankind are all at the mercy of
a new generalization.   EMERSON   "Circles"

Both Henry James and Nietzsche were above all possessed of
an intense belief in the power of art as an activity that serves to
order and thus give coherence and meaning to experience,
which would otherwise be profoundly inconclusive: essentially
formless, chaotic, and without value. As we shall see, their respective pronouncements along these lines are rich in parallels;
but their thinking corresponds in other related but sometimes
unexpected ways as well. Some of these correspondences will be
considered at length in this chapter, and it is important to note
at the outset something that should become increasingly ap-

parent: namely, that these particular correspondences, far from being isolated and coincidental, derive from aesthetic and general philosophical assumptions which the two men, in their different ways, evidently shared, and which form the basis of many of the theoretical and emotional tendencies we have come to identify with modernism.

Each point of correspondence considered here seems related to a central association of art and power. For both writers, moreover, one of the most vital consequences of that felt association was a recognition that if it is within the artist's power to determine what is "estimable" (to use Nietzsche's word in *Zarathustra*) in experience and what is not, then, given the nature of human relationships, his art will ultimately reveal itself to be a form of power not only over his own experience but over the perceptions of other people with respect to their own experience as well. The far-reaching intellectual implications of this view are suggested by the passage from Emerson's "Circles" which appears as the epigraph to the present chapter. Nietzsche quotes most of this passage with approval near the end of his *Schopenhauer als Erzieher,* and in order to drive home the general philosophical point he emphasizes the continuation of the thought as it appears in Emerson's essay: "The things which are dear to men at this hour," Emerson observes, "are so on account of the ideas which have emerged on their mental horizon, and which caused the present order of things, as a tree bears its apples. A new degree of culture would instantly revolutionize the entire system of human pursuits." In our own discussion, we shall be concerned not only with the larger theoretical significance of this view, but with its immediate emotional consequences. The linking of art and power will be considered in later phases of the present essay, when it has been placed in its proper philosophical context. And it is to that context that we now turn our attention.

A number of the ideas we have been discussing have, of course, figured more or less prominently, and in various guises, in the thought of many writers who have concerned themselves with art as an activity that serves as a means for transcending the limitations of actual experience. To enumerate the diverse appearances and transformations of such ideas from the time of Plato or the pre-Socratics through the so-called "post-modern" period would be considerably beyond the scope of the present study—although we will continue to take note of some of these claims, particularly in their nineteenth-century European and American manifestations, as they come to bear on our immediate discussion. At this point, it may be useful to focus some of the themes we will be following, and to indicate the character of the more immediate literary and philosophical company in which, as theoreticians of art, James and Nietzsche move. In the present context, the most efficient means of suggesting these larger connections would seem to be to trace, if only very briefly, some of the notions shared by the novelist and the philosopher as those notions appear in the thinking of three important figures usually identified with the progress and alleged (though largely unconfirmed) decline of romanticism.

The three are Schiller, Hegel, and Oscar Wilde, and the general term "romanticism," as A. O. Lovejoy would have recognized, is unfortunately much too vague to define the precise range of emphases and values expressed in their works; nor does it go very far toward suggesting the extraordinary power with which they, like James and Nietzsche, invested the activity of art. As a consequence, in order to make clear what it is they have in common, and to show how a number of their aesthetic ideas connect with those of the two authors whose relation forms the subject of this study, we shall need to consider their specific pronouncements in several distinct (if overlapping) areas.

1. *The Notion of Absolute Culture; Art as a Means of Achieving Freedom from the Limitations of Experience*

In the course of his *Letters on the Aesthetic Education of Man* (1795), a work significantly influenced by Fichte and conceived in large part as an attempt to reconcile the subject-object dualism posited by Kant, Schiller makes the assertion that "it is only through Beauty that man makes his way to Freedom"; accordingly, in order for a solution to be found to that political problem, man "will have to approach it through the problem of the aesthetic." Although Schiller acknowledges that "the artist is indeed the child of his age," and that "his theme he will, indeed, take from the present," he goes on to insist that "his form he will borrow from a nobler time, nay, from beyond time altogether, from the absolute, unchanging, unity of his being. Here, from the pure aether of his genius, the living source of beauty flows down, untainted by the corruption of the generations and ages wallowing in the dark eddies below."

Beauty for Schiller consists in the revelation of the timeless within the conditions imposed by time; because it speaks to the soul and the senses simultaneously, it provides man with a means of achieving the infinite through the finite realm. In the experience of artistic beauty, Schiller maintains, abstract and sensuous elements serve to generate and reinforce one another; just as the sensuous experience leads to a recognition of the abstract idea existing beyond time, so too the abstract idea realizes itself in the material world through the concrete artistic form. This process is described by Schiller in relation to the aesthetic contemplation of a statue of a goddess dating from classical antiquity:

> While the woman-god demands our veneration, the god-like woman kindles our love; but even as we abandon ourselves in ecstasy to her heavenly grace, her celestial self-sufficiency makes

us recoil in terror. The whole figure reposes and dwells in itself, a creation completely self-contained, and, as if existing beyond space, neither yielding nor resisting; here is no force to contend with force, no frailty where temporality might break in. Irresistibly moved and drawn by those former qualities, kept at a distance by these latter, we find ourselves at one and the same time in a state of utter repose and supreme agitation, and there results that wondrous stirring of the heart for which mind has no concept nor speech any name.

Thus, within the closed circle of aesthetic contemplation, inconclusive temporal experience is exchanged for the comprehensive calm of eternal form: at the same time, reason takes on the aspect of sensuousness, and the abstract form is made concrete and vibrant with the immediacy of the moment. The transformation thus effected through the medium of art enables the perceiver to reach beyond the particular conditions of his own existence; as a consequence, Schiller concludes that the capacity for perceiving beauty cannot simply be determined by the historical conditions obtaining at a particular time and place. For if the sense of beauty is to serve as the instrument of liberation, the means of ennobling man and freeing him from all the limitations and restrictions imposed by his otherwise inescapable environment, then it must exist as an "instrument not provided by the State," and one which will never fail to "open up living springs which, whatever the political corruption, would remain clear and pure." Hence, Schiller argues, what is required is a conception of beauty that is independent of time and "derived from a source other than experience, since by means of it we are to decide whether that which in experience we call beautiful is justly entitled to the name":

> This pure rational concept of Beauty, if such could be found, would therefore—since it cannot be derived from any actual case, but rather itself corrects and regulates our judgment of every actual case—have to be discovered by a process of abstrac-

tion, and deduced from the sheer potentialities of our sensuo-rational nature. In a single word, Beauty would have to be shown to be a necessary condition of Human Being.

As a consequence of such convictions, Schiller is moved to an exhortation which might well serve as a defense of James's mode of characterization, particularly in the novels of the so-called "major phase":

> From now on, then, we must lift our thoughts to the pure concept of human nature; and since experience never shows us human nature as such, but only individual human beings in individual situations, we must endeavour to discover from all these individual and changing manifestations that which is absolute and unchanging, and, by the rejection of all contingent limitations, apprehend the necessary conditions of their existence. True, this transcendental way will lead us out of the familiar circle of phenomenal existence, away from the living presence of things, and cause us to tarry for a while upon the barren and naked land of abstractions. But we are, after all, struggling for a firm basis of knowledge which nothing will shake. And he who never ventures beyond actuality will never win the prize of truth.

Proceeding along the same line of thought in his *Philosophy of Fine Art* (first published in 1835)—a work in which he pays significant homage to Schiller as a precursor—Hegel places art in "the realm of *absolute Spirit*," and declares that "we are justified in associating it with the self-same province which belongs to religion and speculative philosophy":

> In every direction in which Mind or Spirit becomes identical with the absolute Mind it frees itself from the restricting limits of its positive existence, and, while liberating itself from the contingent relations, which pertain to it in its temporal existence, and the finite content of its objects and interests, is made aware of and discloses the entire wealth of reality it contains.

Thus, in Hegel's view, "on the finite plane of determinate existence, and under the restricting conditions of its externality and necessity," Spirit is prevented from "rediscovering the immediate vision and enjoyment of its freedom." As a result, it is "driven by its absence to seek that vision in a higher sphere." And "that sphere," Hegel asserts, "is art, and its realization is the Ideal."

For Hegel, then, it is the craving of the Spirit which produces art, and "the defects of immediate reality which drive us forward inevitably to the idea of the beauty of art." Seeking to grasp truth absolutely, truth "lifted up from its environment of temporary conditions, from its running to and fro among the whirl of finite particularity," Spirit ultimately discovers what it seeks in art, where it has attained repose in "an external form, from which the hunger of Nature and the prose of life no longer stare at us." Consequently, in the deepest contemplation of art, consciousness is able to divest itself of the limitations imposed on it by a particular state or a particular culture, and Spirit succeeds at last in embracing its own likeness in what Hegel terms "that region of more essential reality":

> . . . the fundamental *principle*, for the realization of which the State exists, and wherein the individual man finds his satisfaction as a citizen, is, despite all the variety of that life, all the manifold differentiation of class within itself and as related to the world without, still a whole that is *one-sided*. . . . It is, in short, only the national life, and further, the life of a *particular* nation; a life, moreover, in which freedom is realized in a particular sphere of existence as individualized reality. And on this account it is that we are necessarily conscious, that rights and obligations in the mere bounds of civic existence, on the plane, that is to say, of merely this world's or temporal existence, do not discover the absolute satisfaction we are seeking. . . . What mankind, pressed on all sides by the boundaries of his purely terrestrial life, in fact requires is that

region of more essential reality, in which every opposition and contradiction is overcome, and freedom can finally claim to be wholly at peace with itself. And this is, of course, nothing other than absolute Truth itself, no merely relative Truth. In the Truth, according to its highest notion, all must be brought home to one unity. In it there can be no opposition between freedom and necessity, Spirit and Nature, knowledge and the object of knowledge, law and impulse, between whatever form, in fact, the opposition of these contradictory phenomena may assume.

Oscar Wilde, a figure often taken to be lacking in true seriousness (on the basis of the largely mistaken conventional identification of seriousness and solemnity),* proceeds from assumptions similar to Hegel's—assumptions which he may have derived from Pater—in the enormously influential collection of his critical essays entitled *Intentions* (1891). In one of the four discourses on aesthetic matters that make up that volume, he declares that art, far from mirroring the limitations and immediate conditions of the age in which it is produced, "never expresses anything but itself." Indeed, Wilde goes on to assert, art "has an independent life, just as Thought has, and develops purely on its own lines"; hence, "the only history it preserves

* The situation here calls to mind John Ashbery's telling observation (in an appreciation of Saul Steinberg) regarding the work of Erik Satie: it makes one wonder what everyone else was so serious about. Richard Ellmann develops a similar point in relation to Wilde's misleading reputation: "In protesting the independence of criticism," he maintains, "Wilde sounds like an ancestral Northrop Frye or Roland Barthes. These portentous comparisons do indeed claim virtue by association, and such claims may be broadened. André Gide found Nietzsche less exciting because he had read Wilde, and Thomas Mann in one of his last essays remarks almost with chagrin on how many of Nietzsche's aphorisms might have been expressed by Wilde, and how many of Wilde's by Nietzsche. What I think can be urged for Wilde then, is that for his reasons and in his own way he laid the basis for many critical positions which are still debated in much the same terms, and which we like to attribute to more ponderous names."

for us is the history of its own progress." As a result, he concludes that "all beautiful things belong to the same age."

In Wilde's estimation, moreover, the critical spirit (which he regards as the most significant legacy of the ancient Greeks, that "nation of art-critics") represents nothing less than the highest development of the artistic spirit, and for him "the Critical Spirit and the World-Spirit are one." This is, of course, another way of expressing the Hegelian view that "the realm of Fine Art is the realm of *absolute spirit*,"* but Wilde follows out the implications of this notion in a way that Hegel did not, making extravagantly clear what it might actually mean for one to free oneself of the limitations of one's age and culture by achieving that absolute culture which corresponds to the realm of absolute Spirit:

> The culture that this transmission of racial experience makes possible [Wilde has just remarked that imagination "is simply concentrated race-experience"] can be made perfect by the critical spirit alone, and indeed may be said to be one with it. For who is the true critic but he who bears within himself the dreams, and ideas, and feelings of myriad generations, and to whom no form of thought is alien, no emotional impulse obscure? And who the true man of culture, if not he who by fine scholarship and fastidious rejection has made instinct self-conscious and intelligent, and can separate the work that has

---

* Similarly, Schiller's view of the synthetic character of the aesthetic emotion finds a more or less adequate paraphrase in Wilde's assertion that art "addresses itself, not to the faculty of recognition nor to the faculty of reason, but to the aesthetic sense alone, which, while accepting both reason and recognition as stages of apprehension, subordinates them both to a pure synthetic impression of the work of art as a whole. . . ." In a related passage which appears further on in Part II of "The Critic as Artist," Wilde combines Schiller's notion with Hegel's conception of the operation of spirit. "Just as Nature is matter struggling into mind," Wilde writes, "so Art is mind expressing itself under the conditions of matter, and thus, even in the lowliest of her manifestations, she speaks to both sense and soul alike."

distinction from the work that has it not, and so by contact and comparison makes himself master of the secrets of style and school, and understands their meanings, and listens to their voices, and develops that spirit of disinterested curiosity which is the real root, as it is the real flower, of the intellectual life, and thus attains to intellectual clarity, and, having learned "the best that is known and thought in the world," lives—it is not fanciful to say so—with those who are the Immortals. Yes, . . . the contemplative life, the life that has for its aim not *doing* but *being*, and not *being* merely, but *becoming*—that is what the critical spirit can give us. The gods live thus: either brooding over their own perfection, as Aristotle tells us, or, as Epicurus fancied, watching with the calm eyes of the spectator the tragi-comedy of the world they have made. We, too, might live like them, and set ourselves to witness with appropriate emotions the varied scenes that man and nature afford. . . . From the high tower of Thought we can look out at the world. Calm, and self-centred, and complete, the aesthetic critic contemplates life, and no arrow drawn at a venture can pierce between the joints of his harness. He at least is safe. He has discovered how to live.

And indeed, according to Wilde, the man in possession of this absolutely free and unconstrained critical spirit which signifies the highest stage of culture will retire from the strife of human activity and, Buddha-like, "sit contended 'in that deep, motionless, quiet which mortals pity, and which the gods enjoy.' He will look out upon the world and know its secret. By contact with divine things, he will become divine. His will be the perfect life, and his only."

2. *The Prerogatives of Divinity; the Artist as Superman*

One of Schiller's most celebrated pronouncements in the *Aesthetic Letters* is that "man only plays when he is in the fullest sense of the word a human being, and he is only fully a human being when he plays." Significantly, it is just this capacity for

disinterested play which is described, in the same passage, as
the characteristic portion of the gods of antiquity:

> . . . it was long ago alive and operative in the art and in the
> feeling of the Greeks, the most distinguished exponents of
> both; only they transferred to Olympus what was meant to be
> realized on earth. Guided by the truth of that same proposi-
> tion, they banished from the brow of the blessed gods all the
> earnestness and effort which furrow the cheeks of mortals, no
> less than the empty pleasures which preserve the smoothness
> of a vacuous face; freed those ever-contented beings from the
> bonds inseparable from every purpose, every duty, every care,
> and made idleness and indifferency the enviable portion of
> divinity—merely a more humane name for the freest, most
> sublime state of being.

By freeing man from the constraints imposed upon his development by both sensuousness and rationality—the two
realms in which he is bound to live simultaneously—the play
impulse alive in the aesthetic disposition serves to restore to him
"the highest of all bounties, . . . the gift of humanity itself":
paradoxically, then, full humanity may only be achieved to the
extent that human limitations are overcome. Once this ideal
condition has been attained, "from being a slave of nature,
which he remains as long as he merely feels it, man becomes its
lawgiver from the moment he begins to think it."

The assumption of power thus begins, in Schiller's view, with
"contemplation (or reflection)," which may be regarded as "the
first liberal relation which man establishes with the universe
around him." As a consequence of this new relation, "as soon as
she becomes his thought," nature, "that which hitherto merely
dominated him as force, now stands before his eyes as object":

> Whatsoever is object for him has no power over him; for in
> order to be object at all, it must be subjected to the power
> that is his. To the extent that he imparts form to matter, and
> for precisely as long as he imparts it, he is immune to its effects;

for spirit cannot be injured by anything except that which robs
it of its freedom, and man gives evidence of his freedom precisely by giving form to that which is formless. Only where
sheer mass, ponderous and inchoate, holds sway, its murky
contours shifting within uncertain boundaries, can fear find its
seat; man is more than a match for any of nature's terrors once
he knows how to give it form and convert it into an object of
his contemplation. Once he begins to assert his independence
in the face of nature as phenomenon, then he also asserts his
dignity *vis-à-vis* nature as force, and with noble freedom rises in
revolt against his ancient gods. Now they cast off those ghastly
masks which were the anguish of his childhood and surprise
him with his own image by revealing themselves as projections
of his own mind. The monstrous divinity of the Oriental,
which rules the world with the blind strength of a beast of
prey, shrinks in the imagination of the Greeks into the friendly
contours of a human being. The empire of the Titans falls,
and infinite force is tamed by infinite form.

Thus, in his capacity as artist—that capacity which serves as the
defining condition of his essential humanity—man "gives form
to matter when he annuls time again, when he affirms persist-
ence within change, and subjugates the manifold variety of the
World to the unity of his own Self." What is even more significant is that far from being arbitrary, the form which is thus
imposed on matter by man is ultimately indistinguishable from
the shape of reality itself; indeed, that form must finally be regarded as a revelation of the very nature of reality, an expression
of the highest laws which govern its existence. For "where
. . . the formal drive holds sway," Schiller observes, "and the
pure object acts within us, we experience the greatest enlargement of being: all limitations disappear, and from the mere
unit of quantity to which the poverty of his senses reduced him,
man has raised himself to a unity of ideas embracing the whole
realm of phenomena." "During this operation," Schiller concludes, in a passage evocative of Emerson, "we are no longer in

time; time, with its whole never-ending succession, is in us. We are no longer individuals; we are species. The judgment of all minds is expressed through our own, the choice of all hearts is represented by our action."

Similarly, Hegel declares that "man is under an obligation to make himself at peace and at home in the environment of the world; or, to put it rather differently, his individuality must live itself into Nature and all the conditions of that external world, and by doing so assert its freedom visible." In this way, man comes to perceive that his most individual inner life is really one with the external world in the continuum of spirit, spirit in the ceaseless process of its awakening. As a result, the opposition between the forms generated by the mind and the intractable material of the external world ceases to exist:

> . . . these two related factors, that is, on the one side, the entirety of his inward life and the character it possessses or displays in all conditions or actions whatsoever, and, on the other, that objective entirety of external existence which confronts him, must wholly lose the appearance of two worlds which are either indifferent to or not homogeneous with each other, and forthwith proclaim themselves as harmoniously related and identical in substance. This externally objective world must, in so far as it is the reality of the Ideal, surrender the semblance of its own objective self-subsistency and stubbornness, in order that its fundamental unity with that to which it supplies the external and particular embodiment may be exhibited in truth.

In Hegel's view, just as all matter strives toward consciousness and form, so too it is the nature of spirit to free itself from the limitations of its particular formal manifestation; to the extent that it succeeds in freeing itself from such limitations, it approaches the realm of absolute spirit. For Wilde, in this connection, freedom from the limitations imposed by one's historical situation implies a corresponding freedom from the moral restrictions which govern the behavior of men trapped within such limitations. Hence, the moral categories applicable to the behavior of ordinary men become null and void in the case of the extraordinary critical spirit who has achieved transcendent or "true" culture; the only law he is obliged to obey is that of his own development:

> . . . when we reach the true culture that is our aim, we attain to that perfection of which the saints have dreamed, the perfection of those to whom sin is impossible, not because they make the renunciations of the ascetic, but because they can do everything they wish without hurt to the soul, and can wish for nothing that can do the soul harm, the soul being an entity so divine that it is able to transform into elements of a richer experience, or a finer susceptibility, or a newer mode of thought, acts or passions that with the common would be commonplace, or with the uneducated ignoble, or with the shameful vile.

"Is this dangerous?" Wilde goes on to ask rhetorically in the character of one of the participants in his dialogue. "Yes; it is dangerous—all ideas, as I told you, are so."

3. The Self as a Work of Art

As might be expected, Schiller, Hegel, and Wilde all regard human personality in its unconscious, natural state as a chaotic ground of blind potentialities seeking to be realized in form. Indeed, in his Third Letter, Schiller observes that it is just this impulse on the part of man to see himself as material to be redeemed by art that "makes him Man." for "he does not stop short at what Nature herself made of him, but has the power of retracing by means of Reason the steps she took on his behalf, of transforming the work of blind compulsion into a work of free choice, and of elevating physical necessity into moral necessity." Similarly, Hegel remarks that man "will not permit" his natural form "to remain as he finds it; he alters it deliberately. This is the rational ground of all ornament and decoration. . . ." And Wilde, of course, again and again emphasizes the importance of artificiality and conscious style, arguing that these qualities serve to exalt behavior and experience by endowing them with the unmistakable impress of deliberate design.

To re-create oneself under the conditions of art is, ideally, to bring to consciousness all of one's experience as material and to realize it entirely in form. The full attainment of such a state Schiller is inclined to reserve for divinity, but he is quick to note that "a disposition to the divine man does indubitably carry within him, in his Personality": for "we must surely call divine any tendency which has as its unending task the realization of that most characteristic attribute of Godhead, viz., absolute manifestation of potential (the actualization of all that is possible), and absolute unity of manifestation (the necessity of all that is made actual)." Arguing along similar lines, Hegel suggests that the activity of the artist corresponds in essence to the striving of the spirit to realize itself completely in the world; hence, the artist succeeds in his enterprise only insofar as he is able to externalize his inner life in powerful and vivid forms:

> In conformity, then, with the notion of the Ideal, we may conclude that even when we are dealing with the mere expression of emotional life, we shall never fully establish our title to truly objective art so long as any part of all that is comprised in the subject-matter, which stirs an artistic inspiration, remains still wrapped up within the soul that seeks to express itself; rather all that lies there should be completely unfolded. . . . For that which is highest and most excellent is not by any means that we are unable to express, as though the poet contained in himself still greater depths than those expressed on the face of his work. The work of an artist is the consummate fruit of that artist, and reflects precisely what he is, and all that remains behind in the temple of his soul is a naught or nothing.

And indeed, it is just this impulse to empty the temple of the soul entirely, to extend the domain of art into every chamber of one's being, that Thomas Mann came to see as linking Wilde with Nietzsche. "Rebels in the name of beauty," he termed the two, "for all that the German iconoclast's rebellion went tremendously deeper and cost tremendously more in suffering, renunciation, and self-conquest. . . ." In Mann's view, the "major premise" of Nietzsche's philosophy—"namely, that life can be justified only as an aesthetic phenomenon"—"applies exactly to himself, to his life, his thinking, and his writing. . . . Consciously, down to his self-mythologizing in his last moment, down to madness, this life was an artistic production, not only in terms of its wonderful expressiveness, but in terms of its innermost nature. It was a lyric, tragic spectacle, and one of utmost fascination."

James, too, was stirred by the ultimate promise of art, the promise that one may achieve complete possession of oneself by becoming the author of one's own being; but unlike Wilde, who was ultimately forced to recognize the limitations of his own artistic power in the world and was shattered by the recognition, and unlike Nietzsche, who seems almost to have chosen to go mad rather than face the possibility of such limitations, the American novelist came to see that he would have to yield to the restless, chaotic, random world of experience that portion of his life that was its due, if only, ironically, to ensure that that area existing beyond his direct control would always remain available as the unfailing source of sustenance for his all-consuming art.

III

American Identity, Universal Culture, and the Unbounded Self

I believe America is the new World. Europe is a lost name, like Nineveh or Palenque. There is no more Europe, only a mass of ruins from the Past.   D. H. LAWRENCE

The Americans of all nations at any time upon the earth have probably the fullest poetical nature. The United States themselves are essentially the greatest poem. . . . The American poets are to enclose old and new for America in the race of races. Of them a bard is to be commensurate with a people. To him the other continents arrive as contributions . . . he gives them reception for their sake and his own sake. . . . Of all mankind the great poet is the equable man. Not in him but off from him things are grotesque or eccentric or fail of their sanity. . . . He bestows on every object or quality its fit proportions neither more nor less. He is the arbiter of the diverse and he is the key. . . . Obedience does not master him, he masters it. High up out of reach he stands turning a concentrated light . . . he turns the pivot with his finger. . . . His brain is the ultimate brain. He is no arguer . . . he is judgment. He judges not as the judge judges but as the sun falling around a helpless thing.

WALT WHITMAN

1. *"The Man without a Country"*

We have already considered William James's definition of the saint as someone "entirely adapted" to a "millennial society" in relation to certain characters in Henry James's later fiction; but it may now be useful to apply that definition to the novelist himself. If we do so, we may begin to grasp the force of Theodora Bosanquet's observation (briefly alluded to earlier in our discussion) that her employer's "Utopia was an anarchy where nobody would be responsible for any other human being but only for his own civilized character." "His circle of friends," she then concludes her reminiscences, "will easily recall how finely Henry James had fitted himself to be a citizen of this commonwealth." By definition, then, the commonwealth to which James had so admirably fitted himself did not exist; and of one thing Miss Bosanquet is certain: that in the existing nations of this world James was never completely at home. Again and again, throughout her record of the time she spent in his employ, she conveys her impression that he was somehow never wholly a citizen of any existing country. He was, in a way, at home in England, but even his decision to assume the citizenship of that adopted country, which he seems to have done largely on moral grounds having to do with the apparent reluctance of the United States to enter the First World War, struck him as in essence nothing more than a confirmation of a long association, not something that altered in any fundamental way his own conception of himself: "I was really too associated before for any nominal change to matter. The process has only shown me that I virtually *was*—so that it's rather disappointing in respect to acute sensation. I *haven't* any." The implication here is that for the artist whose work represents an attempt to be free of the limitations of the past (the "nets" in Joyce's *A Portrait of the Artist as a Young Man* by which the soul may be ensnared), the matter of specific national identity becomes purely nominal—or "titular," in Thoreau's word. A similar view of national identity seems to assert itself in the lives and works of some of the commanding exiles of modernism: Beckett and Nabokov most notably, and to some extent Graves, Huxley, Hemingway, and Lawrence, not to mention numerous contemporary authors of Latin American origin.

"James was never really English or American," Miss Bosanquet remarks, "or even"—she adds in a fine discrimination to which he would surely have assented—"Cosmopolitan." It was precisely such national categories, no matter how general (and "Cosmopolitan," after all, indicates a category which may itself presuppose a recognition of the preeminence of national claims in the definition of one's identity), that from a certain point of view James sought to avoid all his life. Of this refusal (or inability, as some critics have maintained) to define himself according to the standards of any particular nationality—or even of all nationalities put together—his secretary was very much aware; just as she recalls that Jacques-Émile Blanche, when he was endeavoring to paint The Master's portrait, "declared it to be a hard task to isolate the individual character of the model," so too she herself was inclined to wonder: "Would it have been possible to fit him into any single category? He had reacted with so much success against both the American accent and the English manner that he seemed only doubtfully Anglo-Saxon."

That successful reaction against national entanglement seems to have been to a considerable extent the product of deliberate choice on James's part; but it must be acknowledged that the question is not a simple one, and that significant testimony to the contrary also exists. In general, this testimony is concerned with the effects (usually regarded as profoundly unfortunate, for one reason or another) of James's expatriation, and it tends to elaborate upon the various aspects of his estrangement—

which is seen as having starved his art—from the mainstream of social life in both America and Europe. The critical tendency which derives from this interpretation of the relation between James's life and work reached its fullest (though by no means its most extreme) expression in Van Wyck Brooks's famous and vaguely influential polemic, *The Pilgrimage of Henry James* (1925), but the general line may be found in cruder versions (notably in V. L. Parrington's "Henry James and the Nostalgia of Culture"—Parrington's two-page acknowledgment and lament of James's existence in the posthumously published third volume of his *Main Currents in American Thought* (1930); and Thomas Wentworth Higginson's "Henry James, Jr., in *Short Studies of American Authors* (published by Ticknor and Fields in 1880), as well as richer and more interesting variations (e.g., Herbert Croly's "Henry James and His Countrymen," which appeared in 1904, and Ferner Nuhn's *The Wind Blew from the East*, published in 1942).

Moreover, the view that James eventually became "a man without a country," a man who had lost his moorings in the world (who, like Winterbourne in *Daisy Miller*, "had been too long in Europe") and therefore had very little left to sustain him besides the unrelenting exercise of art—this view has hardly been limited to James's critics. On the contrary, in addition to sympathetic readers like Edna Kenton ("Henry James in the World," 1934), such sensitive and understanding personal friends of the author as Edmund Gosse and (in a more imaginative and convincing way) Percy Lubbock have stated or implied as much, and Edith Wharton—herself an expatriate whom James accused, after his return to England from a trip to America in 1904, of lacking "a Country of your Own (comme moi, par exemple!)," he of course meaning England—predictably sidesteps the entire question when she asserts: "The truth is that he belonged irrevocably to the old America out of which I also came, and of which—almost—it might paradoxically be said that to follow up its last traces one had to come to Europe. . . ."

Very likely defending herself as much as James, Mrs. Wharton is concerned with refuting "the nonsense talked by critics of a later generation, who never knew James, much less the world he grew up in, about his having thwarted his genius by living in Europe, and having understood his mistakes too late. . . ." "As a witness of his long sojourns in America . . . ," Mrs. Wharton advises these critics, "I can affirm that he was never really happy or at home there." Yet there are no decisive indications that James was ever really happy or completely at home in England, either. Indeed, in his *Roadside Meetings* (1931), Hamlin Garland recounts the following confession allegedly made by James when Garland was visiting him at Rye, probably in 1906 or 1907:

> "If I were to live my life over again," he said in a low voice, and fixing upon me a sombre glance, "I would be an American. I would steep myself in America, I would know no other land. I would study its beautiful side. The mixture of Europe and America which you see in me has proved disastrous. It has made of me a man who is neither American nor European. I have lost touch with my own people and I live here alone. My neighbours are friendly but they are not of my blood, except remotely. As a man grows old he feels these conditions more than when he is young. I shall never return to the United States, but I wish I could."*

One may well doubt the accuracy of this transcription (where are the characteristic Jamesian cadences and hesitations? where

* It is interesting to consider these remarks in relation to the condition of unending exile depicted in Edward Everett Hale's "The Man without a Country" (a work first published immediately after the Civil War); indeed the very phrase that Hale takes as his title is applied to James by no less discriminating a friend than Edmund Gosse, in the passage from his retrospective essay on James presented below.

is the Jamesian vocabulary?), especially if one takes into account the fact that these remarks are being recollected, presumably after a considerable passage of time, by a man usually associated with populist sentiments, and that the account is included in a book first published six years after Van Wyck Brooks's book on James. But even so, the general sense of regret expressed seems more or less plausible. Moreover, it is a sentiment which is strongly hinted at if not actually confirmed by one of James's closest friends, Edmund Gosse, in his 1920 review of Percy Lubbock's edition of James's letters; referring specifically to the period following James's return from the United States in 1883, after the death of his father, Gosse writes:

> When he returned to Bolton Street . . . he had broken all the ties which held him to residence in America, a country which, as it turned out, he was not destined to revisit for more than twenty years. By this means Henry James became a homeless man in a peculiar sense, for he continued to be looked upon as a foreigner in London, while he seemed to have lost citizenship in the United States. It was a little later than this that that somewhat acidulated patriot, Colonel Higginson, in reply to someone who said that Henry James was a cosmopolitan, remarked, "Hardly! for a cosmopolitan is at home even in his own country!" This condition made James, although superficially gregarious, essentially isolated, and though his books were numerous and were greatly admired, they were tacitly ignored alike in summaries of English and of American current literature. There was no escape from this dilemma. Henry James was equally determined not to lay down his American birthright and not to reside in America. Every year of his exile, therefore, emphasized the fact of his separation from all other Anglo-Saxons, and he endured, in the world of letters, the singular fate of being a man without a country.

Gosse's observations provide a convincing summary account of the nature of James's "international" predicament—especially as that predicament was reflected in his uncertain status as a man of letters—and unlike Garland's anecdote they also serve to give some indication of the part played in the situation by James's own determination to resist the various demands (no doubt experienced as real encroachments) made by both England and America, to assert his own independence and to define himself essentially without relation to either nation-state.

But although there can be little doubt that his position was to a considerable extent a matter of his own choosing, the apparent freedom implied by such a lack of firm national connection evidently had for James a sometimes painfully ambiguous character (clearly emphasized by Gosse's use of such words as "exile" and "separation" in describing James's life in England). Of the painful aspect of that ambiguity no one was more thoroughly aware than Percy Lubbock, one of James's most acute and sympathetic critics. In his admirable Introduction to his edition of James's letters, Lubbock demonstrates his precise understanding of James's decision, and then goes on to explain how James succeeded—with great effort—in converting the consequences of that choice to his own artistic advantage:

> His decision to settle in Europe, the great step of his life, was inevitable, though it was not taken without long reflection; but it was none the less a decision for which he had to pay heavily, as he was himself very well aware. If he regarded his own part as that of an onlooker, the sense in which he understood observation was to the highest degree exacting. . . . It would be useless for him to live where the human drama most attracted him unless he could grasp it with an assured hand; and he could never do this if he was to remain a stranger and a sojourner, merely feeding on the picturesque surface of appearances. To justify his expatriation he must work his own life completely into the texture of his new surroundings, and the story of his middle years is to be read as the most patient and laborious of attempts to do so. Its extraordinary success need hardly be insisted on; its failure, necessary and foredoomed, from certain points of view, is perhaps not less obvious. But the great fact of interest is the sight of him taking up the task,

with eyes, it is needless to say, fully open to all its demands, and never resting until he could be certain of having achieved all that was possible.

Lubbock concludes that James "could never forget that he had somehow to make up to himself for arriving as an alien from a totally different social climate," and notes that "it remained true, none the less, that with much that is common ground among educated people of our time and place he was never really in touch. One has only to think of the part played, in the England he frequented, by school and college, by country-homes, by church and politics and professions, to understand how much of the ordinary consciousness was closed to him."

These remarks make it clear how little those who understood him most completely (e.g., Lubbock and Theodora Bosanquet) found it possible to regard James as a novelist of manners. Moreover, the (perhaps unintentionally) ironic force of Lubbock's account of James's relative remoteness from the particularities of English social life makes itself felt if one considers that the list of aspects of that life which, he claims, were "closed" to James significantly echoes the novelist's own legendary inventory of all that was lacking in the United States of Hawthorne's time. As a consequence of such deprivations, James argues in his *Hawthorne* (1879), the earlier author was starved of those materials—those complex institutional configurations and dense tissues of social circumstance—required to make a successful novelist and for which James himself had presumably moved to Europe, that "rich, dark hive," where such elements of social life were thought to be fairly palpable. Reflecting on "the items of high civilisation, as it exists in other countries, which are absent from the texture of American life," James enumerates the following:

> No State, in the European sense of the word, and indeed barely a specific national name. No sovereign, no court, no personal loyalty, no aristocracy, no church, no clergy, no army, no diplo-

matic service, no country gentlemen, no palaces, no castles, nor manors, nor old country houses, nor parsonages, nor thatched cottages, nor ivied ruins; no cathedrals, nor abbeys, nor little Norman churches; no great Universities or public schools—no Oxford, nor Eton, nor Harrow. . . . no political society, no sporting class—no Epsom nor Ascot! Some such list as that might be drawn up of the absent things in American life—especially the American life of forty years ago.

But "some such list as that" is just what Lubbock provides when he wishes to indicate those aspects of English social life which were unavailable to James. Their very unavailability to such a passionately inquiring spirit should, however, give us pause, for it suggests the possibility that James might have been essentially indifferent to such matters, as indifferent as Melville or Hawthorne himself might have been. For in the great American novels of the nineteenth century—and this is at once their most liberating and most vexing achievement—character is not seen as continuous with social circumstances. Indeed, the central characters of such works, "isolatoes" all—Natty Bumppo, Hester Prynne, Ishmael, Ahab, Huckleberry Finn, Isabel Archer —move uncomfortably on the social stage, almost as if under compulsion; they seek to define themselves in a kind of cosmic isolation, the possibility of which may be associated with solitary reveries, or with the trackless wilderness, the desultory movement of the raft on the river which allows one to lie back and take in the stars, or the *Pequod* hurtling "further and further into the blackness of the sea and the night."

Like the characters in the great Russian novels of this period, particularly those of Dostoevsky and Tolstoy, the characters in the "classic" American fiction we are describing seem less concerned with success or even survival in social terms than they do with salvation—and this distinguishes them decisively from characters in Balzac or Dickens or George Eliot. For the most part, moreover, they are intent on taking their salvation neat; and although Hawthorne and James may be critical of this impulse (in part because it seems to take so little account of what is referred to in *The Portrait of a Lady* as the "artillery" of this world), they are hardly won over by the compelling moral authority of existing social institutions. Indeed, even in *The Scarlet Letter* Hawthorne's moral allegiance is not so much to an actual society—the society he is concerned with exists significantly in the past, at a considerable distance from his own—as to the idea of society itself.

The inevitable clash, perceived by all these writers, no matter what the character of their response, between concrete social institutions and a vision of individual freedom which refuses to be bounded by such forms, is characteristically presented in its most extreme terms by Thoreau, who begins his essay on "Walking" (first published after his death in 1862) with the following announcement to the reader:

> I wish to speak a word for Nature, for absolute freedom and wildness, as contrasted with a freedom and culture merely civil,—to regard man as an inhabitant, or a part and parcel of Nature, rather than a member of society. I wish to make an extreme statement, if so I may make an emphatic one, for there are enough champions of civilization: the minister and the school-committee and every one of you will take care of that.

Oppositions of this sort, often associated with a central antagonism between society (regarded as an area of inevitable compromise) and nature (envisioned as an area permitting total freedom and the full perfection of the self), weigh heavily on the American imagination. From Lubbock's point of view, however, the causes of the estrangement, the perpetual homelessness in the world, which he perceived in Henry James, seemed to have less to do with James's general moral assumptions, or even the actual facts of the novelist's life in Europe, his actual social situation, than they did with what Lubbock could surmise of the complicated circumstances of his childhood. Indeed, "it is impossible," Lubbock asserts, "to say these limitations were imposed on him only because he was a stranger among strangers; they belonged to the conditions of his being from much further back. They were implied in his queer unanchored youth, in which he and his greatly gifted family had been able to grow in the free exercise of their talents without any of the foundations of settled life." And later, to reinforce his conclusions about the endlessly unsettling life of the Jameses—a matter that has not, incidentally, received the careful attention it deserves—Lubbock notes, with perceptible heat, that "the children's extraordinarily haphazard and promiscuous education went forward under various teachers, their father's erratic rule having apparently but one principle, that they should stay nowhere long enough to receive any formal imprint."

Although this general explanation of James's apparent sense of homelessness is not without its merits, its emphasis on the eccentricities of his upbringing tends to obscure the continuities between the values evident in that upbringing and the larger cultural assumptions manifest in the work of a writer like Thoreau—for instance, in the scornful reference to "the school-committee" which appears in the passage previously quoted. As a consequence of this tendency to neglect the connections between Jamesian idiosyncrasy and more immediately familiar attitudes, Lubbock's view seems too limited a way of understanding James's apparent cultural isolation. Another way, as we have seen, is offered by Theodora Bosanquet, when she observes of the novelist that "wherever he might have lived and whatever human interactions he might have observed, he would in all probability have reached much the same conclusion that he arrived at by the way of America, France, and England. When he walked out of the refuge of his study into the world and looked about him, he saw a place of torment, where creatures of prey perpetually thrust their claws into the quivering flesh of the doomed, defenceless children of light." Such observations point to the inclination to regard distinct social particulars as elements of *psychomachia* which has figured in American imaginative life at least since the Puritans; that inclination (as Miss Bosanquet's language itself suggests) would go far toward explaining those unmistakable aspects of gothic melodrama which may be perceived throughout his work, and which, for all his alleged commitment to the principles of literary realism, link him decisively with Hawthorne.

In his later years, after his brother William's death, James wrote a memorable letter to his sister-in-law Alice declining her invitation to spend the summer with her and the children in Cambridge; in that letter, he expressed himself as follows on the question of returning to the place where he had spent so much of his youth:

> Dearest Alice, I could come back to America (could be carried back on a stretcher) to die—but never, never to live. To say how the question affects me is dreadfully difficult because of its appearing so to make light of you and the children—but when I think of how little Boston and Cambridge were of old ever *my* affair, or anything but an accident, for me, of the parental life there to which I occasionally and painfully and losingly sacrificed, I have a superstitious terror of seeing them at the end of time again stretch out strange inevitable tentacles to draw me back and destroy me. . . .

2. *"The Heir of All the Ages"*

However one may finally be inclined to see the origin of James's feelings of essential unrelatedness, there can be no doubt that, following the family rule, he converted necessity into virtue and resolved (as he indicated in a letter written to his brother William in 1888) that his identity as a writer would be consciously, even aggressively, ambiguous: "I have not the least hesitation," James wrote, "in saying that I aspire to write in such a way that it would be impossible to an outsider to say whether I am at a given moment an American writing about England or an Englishman writing about America (dealing as I do with both countries,) and so far from being ashamed of such an ambiguity I should be exceeding proud of it, for it would be highly civilized."

In a suggestive passage in the second volume of his biography of James, Leon Edel has described the general ambition expressed here (which he sees as related in part to James's lingering impressions of imperial Rome) in the following terms:

> He would do more than achieve greatness. He would create a kind of imperium of letters, annex Europe to his native American domain, achieve a trans-Atlantic empire larger than that of other novelists. And like Marcus Aurelius he would offer the world the countenance of a conqueror who was, as Arnold said, tender and blameless—*tendentemque manus ripae ulterioris amore.*

And, indeed, an ambition almost as grandiose as the one imagined here by Edel is articulated by James in a letter he wrote when he was twenty-four to Thomas Sergeant Perry. In that letter, James confessed that "deep in the timorous recesses of my being is a vague desire to do for our dear old English letters and writers *something* of what Ste. Beuve and the best French critics have done for theirs." "For one of my calibre," he continues, "it is an arrogant hope. *Aussi* I don't talk about it." A few sentences later, however, James comes back to the idea and reveals the full dimensions of his ambition:

When I say that I should like to do as Ste. Beuve has done, I don't mean that I should like to imitate him, or reproduce him in English: but only that I should like to acquire something of his intelligence & his patience and vigour. One feels—I feel at least, that he is a man of the past, of a dead generation; and that we young Americans are (without cant) men of the future. . . . We have exquisite qualities as a race, and it seems to me that we are ahead of the European races in the fact that . . . we can deal freely with forms of civilization not our own, can pick and choose and assimilate and in short (aesthetically &c), claim our property wherever we find it. To have no national stamp has hitherto been a regret & a drawback, but I think it not unlikely that American writers may yet indicate that a vast intellectual fusion and synthesis of the various National tendencies of the world is the condition of more important achievements than any we have seen.

So much for James's aspirations, which are obviously considerably in excess of those of the novelist of manners. What is also worth remarking in this passage is the conception of the American as a work of art: "the heir of all the ages," a being whom all the divergent tendencies and cultures of Europe have labored to produce. More precisely, the American is represented here as the master of history, a person who is by definition (that is, to the extent that he is an American) not imprisoned by the past but perfectly free to construct himself deliberately, who "can deal freely with forms of civilization not [his] own, can pick and choose and assimilate and in short (aesthetically &c,) claim [his] property wherever [he] finds it." In sum, being an American is predicated on the assumption that it is possible to free oneself from the past, and the more absolute that freedom the more secure one's identity as an American will be. One does not become an American simply by being born in America, but by choosing that identity, which requires that one see one's life as a continual effort to escape from the bondage of the past—one's own or any other.

Just as the nation itself comes into being by throwing off the weight of the past, so too the individual American realizes his own identity. Thus, the American is true to his exacting national identity only to the extent that he is true to his distinctive personal identity. What makes him an authentic American is his ability to regard himself as free to correct the accidents of birth and circumstance and to reemerge, like Fitzgerald's Gatsby, as it were from his own "Platonic idea" of himself, his personality an ideal and necessarily ever-changing composite of all those qualities he finds most admirable.

This insistence on the liberation from the conditions of history as the defining element of American identity takes us back to the Puritans, whose "city upon a hill" could never be envisioned as another one of the kingdoms of this earth; it also takes us into the very heart of Transcendentalist belief (particularly in the case of Emerson and Thoreau) in the mid-nineteenth century. In our own time, such assumptions, often unrecognized and unacknowledged, reveal themselves in a somewhat different form, as in Robert Jay Lifton's ambitious essay on "Protean Man" (first published in 1967).

Lifton introduces his essay with the "claim that certain contemporary historical trends, acting upon universal psychological potential (within many divergent cultures), have become sufficiently powerful and novel to create a new kind of man." This new kind of man, he goes on to indicate, arrives at his sense of his own identity through a "protean style of self-process," which is "characterized by an interminable series of experiments and explorations—some shallow, some profound—each of which may be readily abandoned in favor of still new psychological quests." One of the consequences of this "protean style of self-process," in Lifton's view, is the disappearance of "the classical superego, the internalization of clearly defined criteria of right and wrong transmitted within a particular culture by parents to their children. Protean man," Lifton continues, "requires freedom from precisely that kind of superego—he requires a symbolic fatherlessness—in order to carry out his explorations." And finally, Lifton asserts, we must understand that "protean man's affinity for the young—his being metaphorically and psychologically so young in spirit—has to do with his never-ceasing quest for the imagery of rebirth. He seeks such imagery from all sources. . . ."

Now all of this will seem perfectly familiar—even commonplace—to the reader of nineteenth-century American literature. Notions of this sort turn up with legendary frequency in the writings of the period, whether poetry or prose—in works by Melville and Mark Twain as well as Whitman. But it is clearly in Emerson and Thoreau that such patterns of assumptions are most pronounced, as the merest smattering of quotations serves to indicate: "Whoso would be a man, must be a nonconformist. He who would gather immortal palms must not be hindered by the name of goodness, but must explore if it be goodness. Nothing is at last sacred but the integrity of your own mind. . . . No law can be sacred to me but that of my nature. Good and bad are but names very readily transferable to that or this; the only right is what is after my constitution; the only wrong what is against it." (Emerson, "Self-Reliance.") And from Thoreau's *Walden* (1854): "I left the woods for as good a reason as I went there. Perhaps it seemed to me that I had several more lives to live, and could not spare any more time for that one." On youth and age:

What old people say you cannot do, you try and find that you can. Old deeds for old people, and new deeds for new. Old people did not know enough once, perchance, to fetch fresh fuel to keep the fire a-going; new people put a little dry wood under a pot, and are whirled round the globe with the speed of birds, in a way to kill old people, as the phrase is. Age is no

> better, hardly so well, qualified for an instructor as youth, for
> it has not profited so much as it has lost. One may almost
> doubt if the wisest man has learned anything of absolute value
> by living. Practically, the old have no very important advice to
> give the young, their own experience has been so partial, and
> their lives have been such miserable failures, for private rea-
> sons, as they must believe; and it may be that they have some
> faith left which belies that experience, and they are only less
> young than they were. I have lived some thirty years on this
> planet, and I have yet to hear the first syllable of valuable or
> even earnest advice from my seniors. They have told me noth-
> ing, and probably cannot tell me anything to the purpose. Here
> is life, an experiment to a great extent untried by me; but it
> does not avail me that they have tried it. If I have any experi-
> ence which I think valuable, I am sure to reflect that this my
> Mentors said nothing about.

This passage also incidentally speaks to Lifton's contention that
"technology (and technique in general), together with science,
have special significance for protean man." Finally, with respect
to the commitment to the "imagery of rebirth" that characterizes "protean man," we have in Thoreau's *Walden* not only the
author's repeated allusions to himself as Chanticleer, the crow-
ing cock, but numerous assertions like the following, which
bring the work to its majestic close: "Only that day dawns to
which we are awake. There is more day to dawn. The sun is but
a morning star."

It might just as easily be argued that one could wish for no
more precise embodiment of the "polymorphous versatility" to
which one of Lifton's patients, "a gifted young teacher," refers
than the "I" of Whitman's "Song of Myself," that elusive
principle of identity that seems to flow like water from occupation to occupation and place to place ("The life in us," Thoreau observes, "is like the water in the river"). These works first
appeared well over a century ago, and the fact that Lifton apparently does not perceive them as precedents for his own

notions is significant. It may be taken as an indication of how thoroughly such assumptions have been incorporated into our patterns of thinking about the conditions of self-definition, and as a testimony to a conception of American identity that requires that one arrive at one's conclusions about the present for oneself, without drawing on the experience of others in the past: that one perceive the world afresh as the first settlers on these shores were inclined to do, as a New World to be inhabited by "a new kind of man" (in Lifton's phrase, a phrase which itself echoes Crèvecœur's famous question of 1782, "What, then, is the American, this new man?")—a man whose conception of himself would not be bounded by his own past or that of any nation.

The view of all Europe (and ultimately America as well, insofar as that name may be taken to signify an actual geographical rather than an exclusively moral state) as a *means* for the perfection of the American—or, from a slightly different point of view, for the creation of an unlimited ideal of human excellence out of actual available but limited human possibilities—recalls the distinction discussed in the previous chapter between "historical" and "inner" culture, and the corresponding distinction in James's own work between "European" and "American." The relevance of these distinctions in the present context becomes clear as one perceives that in the letter to Perry under scrutiny, when James declares, "I think that to be an American is an excellent preparation for culture," despite the initial appearance of the remark, he is far from being ironic. In James's view, culture (in the sense of "historical" culture) can and should be acquired by the American for the sake of his full refinement and development, but that culture hardly serves to exhaust his sense of the available possibilities for self-definition. The case of the European in this regard is significantly different. Indeed, one has only to recall the famous debate on "things" which takes place between Madame Merle and Isabel Archer in *The Portrait of a Lady*, and the matter becomes plain.

Isabel has just indicated that she would not care in the slightest what kind of house her prospective husband might own, and Madame Merle replies:

> "That's very crude of you. When you've lived as long as I you'll see that every human being has his shell and that you must take the shell into account. By the shell I mean the whole envelope of circumstances. There's no such thing as an isolated man or woman; we're each of us made up of some cluster of appurtenances. What shall we call our 'self'? Where does it begin? where does it end? It overflows into everything that belongs to us—and then it flows back again. I know a large part of myself is in the clothes I choose to wear. I've a great respect for *things!* One's self—for other people—is one's expression of one's self; and one's house, one's furniture, one's garments, the books one reads, the company one keeps—these things are all expressive."

> This was very metaphysical; not more so, however, than several observations Madame Merle had already made. Isabel was fond of metaphysics, but was unable to accompany her friend into this bold analysis of the human personality. "I don't agree with you. I think just the other way. I don't know whether I succeed in expressing myself, but I know that nothing else expresses me. Nothing that belongs to me is any measure of me; everything's on the contrary a limit, a barrier, and a perfectly arbitrary one. Certainly the clothes which, as you say, I choose to wear, don't express me; and heaven forbid they should!"

> "You dress very well," Madame Merle lightly interposed.

> "Possibly; but I don't care to be judged by that. My clothes may express the dressmaker, but they don't express me. To begin with it's not my own choice that I wear them; they're imposed upon me by society."

> "Should you prefer to go without them?" Madame Merle enquired in a tone which virtually terminated the discussion.

It is important not to be misled by James's irony here. The fact is that in the scene described, as in the novel as a whole, despite what may be taken as Isabel's engaging naïveté, she holds all the moral cards. As is usually the case in James, American moral vivaciousness is contrasted here with the moral exhaustion, produced by continual compromise, of the European. And indeed, a series of assertions which may be regarded as a perfectly adequate gloss on the passage quoted appears in James's 1887 essay on Emerson: "The genius itself," he writes, "it seems to me impossible to contest—I mean the genius for seeing character as a real and supreme thing. . . . no one has had so steady and constant, and above all so natural, a vision of what we require and what we are capable of in the way of aspiration and independence. With Emerson it is ever the special capacity for moral experience—always that and only that. We have the impression, somehow, that life had never bribed him to look at anything but the soul; and indeed in the world in which he grew up and lived the bribes and lures, the beguilements and prizes, were few. He was in an admirable position for showing, what he constantly endeavoured to show, that the prize was within." The ironic balance which is essential to James's estimate is made apparent in his wonderfully wry observation, in the book on Hawthorne, that "the doctrine of the supremacy of the individual to himself, of his originality, and, as regards his own character, *unique quality*, must have had a great charm for people living in a society in which introspection—thanks to the want of other entertainment—played almost the part of a social resource." But here again, the irony must be perceived within the larger perspective of James's ultimate assent to Emersonian values. In the world of Isabel Archer, "the bribes and lures, the beguilements and prizes," may be many, but the prize is still "within."

For the European, the things of this world are seen as an end in themselves, and they serve to define with great precision the real and inescapable limits of one's identity and expectations; for the American, on the other hand, "things," if they serve for anything at all, serve merely as a means of achieving a higher sense of being in the world—or more precisely, they are seen as that class of worldly particulars about which one must obtain a thorough knowledge in order to take an accurate measure of the renunciations required by one's ideals, that class of particulars which one is continually attempting to transcend and which is ultimately rejected as incommensurate with the more exalted and demanding terms of one's own ideal self-definition.

Thus, the American, unlike the European, appears to be possessed of a standard for estimating the value of his experience which precedes that experience and is not derived from it: in short, he refuses to be defined by his experiences in the world but insists instead on seeing himself always in terms of his indestructible ideals and aspirations. He continually reaffirms his ideal distance from his actual experience, and in this way he becomes (in a sense) invulnerable to his own experience, at least to the extent that that experience is rendered powerless to change or challenge seriously his ideal conception of himself. For the edges of self-definition of the American (unlike those of the European) are not worn smooth by life in society and the compromise and ambiguity, the acknowledged and unacknowledged forms of error, the deception of self and others which are, always and everywhere, essential features of that life; instead, unaltered by time and ordinary human conditions, those edges remain, for the American, knife-like, clear, and hard.

In the present context, when James sets out to articulate exactly what it is that the American begins with and never loses, and that the European perpetually lacks, he observes that "we must of course have something of our own—something distinctive & homogeneous—& I take it that we shall find it in our moral consciousness, our unprecedented spiritual lightness and vigour." The profound significance of this "unprecedented spiritual lightness" referred to by James was vividly expressed thirty years before by Francis J. Grund, a German nobleman who in the course of his travels through the United States was so taken with the country that he eventually settled here and became a citizen. Grund produced a study entitled *The Americans, in Their Moral, Social, and Political Relations* (1837), a work which surely deserves to be much better known than it is at present. In that work, which first appeared at just about the same time as Tocqueville's *Democracy in America* (1835; first American edition, 1838)—to which it provides an important and very interesting contrast—he asserts:

> America is to [the American] but the physical means of establishing a moral power, the medium through which his mind operates—the local habitation of his political doctrines. His country is in his understanding; he carries it with him wherever he goes, whether he emigrates to the shores of the Pacific or the Gulf of Mexico; his home is wherever he finds minds congenial with his own.

Despite the conventional rhetoric which at certain points tends to obscure the extraordinary implications of the view emerging here, Grund's formulation clearly suggests something rather different from the notion of a British Empire on which the sun never sets, for the empire he has in mind is one whose limits are not (and could not be) defined in any worldly geography. Unlike the empires of this earth, this empire of the moral imagination can never fall or be destroyed, because it can never be fully realized in the realm of fact: if it were fully realized, that would signify that history had come to an end and the millennium had arrived. The America described here is an idea which has no particular home in the world; indeed, the world is seen in relation to it merely as the "medium" in which the idea may manifest itself (imperfectly, to be sure), the "local habitation" of an ultimately unrealizable ideal of unlimited personal freedom and perfectibility.

It is useful at this point to recall William James's definition (discussed in the previous chapter) of the saint as someone "entirely adapted" to a "millennial society" in an "unseen world," someone whose true home would be "the highest society conceivable, whether that society ever be completely possible or not." Clearly such a definition corresponds to Grund's view of the American, whom he regards as unshakably committed to an idea of his country, essentially adapted to an unseen and ideal society: a society perpetually coming into being but never arriving at the point of existence, a state which seems always beyond reach, like that "green light" pursued by Jay Gatsby, that "orgiastic future that year by year recedes before us." "The Americans love their country," Francis Grund observes, "not, indeed, *as it is*; but *as it will be*. They do not love the land of their fathers; but they are sincerely attached to that which their children are destined to inherit. They live in the future, and *make* their country as they go on."

3. *"Der gute Europäer"*

The general aspiration which we have been considering is expressed by James in the letter to Perry as a wish for "a vast intellectual fusion and synthesis of the various National tendencies of the world"—a fusion and synthesis embodied by definition in the American, "the heir of all the ages," who would preside over this new empire of the mind. A strikingly similar wish appears to lie at the heart of Nietzsche's conception of the "Good European." This term is first introduced in Volume I of *Menschliches, Allzumenschliches* ("Human, All-Too-Human," Volume I published in 1878; Volume II, *Vermischte Meinungen und Sprüche*—"Mixed Opinions and Maxims"—1879), a work written soon after the break with Wagner, during a period of despair and self-doubt, and later described by Nietzsche as "the history of an illness and a convalescence." In a section of that work entitled "The European man and the abolition of nations," Nietzsche makes the following assertions:

> Trade and industry, books and letters, the way in which all higher culture is shared, the rapid change of house and scenery, the present nomadic life of everyone who is not a landowner— these circumstances necessarily produce a weakening, and finally the abolition, of nations, at least in Europe; and as a consequence of continual intermarriage there must develop a mixed race, that of the European man. . . . It is not the interest of the many (of peoples), as is often claimed, but above all the interest of certain royal dynasties and also of certain classes in commerce and society, that drives to nationalism. Once one has recognized this, one should declare oneself without embarrassment as a *good European* and work actively for the amalgamation of nations. . . .

In the course of his later writings it becomes clear that there are two aspects to Nietzsche's idea of the "good European." The first is related to his conviction that the process of European fusion which he is describing is historically inevitable; in this sense, what he is envisioning is not very startling: it is a kind of cultural Common Market, a Pan-European confederation whose citizens would be by definition cosmopolitan. And indeed, in some passages where it occurs Nietzsche appears simply to be using the term "good European" to mean something very much like "cosmopolitan," as opposed to "provincial" or "parochial." Consider, for example, the following paragraph from the "Peoples and Fatherlands" section (Part Eight) of *Jenseits von Gut und Böse* ("Beyond Good and Evil," first published in 1886):

> We "good Europeans"—we, too, know hours when we permit ourselves some hearty fatherlandishness, a plop and relapse

into old loves and narrownesses . . . hours of national agita-
tions, patriotic palpitations, and various other sorts of archaiz-
ing sentimental inundations. More ponderous spirits than we
are may require more time to get over what with us takes only
hours and in a few hours has run its course: some require half
a year, others half a life, depending on the speed and power of
their digestion and metabolism. Indeed, I could imagine dull
and sluggish races who would require half a century even in our
rapidly moving Europe to overcome such atavistic attacks of
fatherlandishness and soil addiction and to return to reason,
meaning "good Europeanism."

To the extent that the "good European" has achieved a sense
of his identity which, although historically inevitable, is still
far from the consciousness of the majority of his contemporaries, it is of course perfectly logical for Nietzsche to see him
as a man of the future, one of "those rarer and rarely contented
human beings who are too comprehensive to find satisfaction
in any fatherlandishness and know how to love the south in
the north and the north in the south—the born Midlanders,
the 'good Europeans.' " This particular formulation is reminiscent of the definition of artistic sensibility which emerges later
in the works of Thomas Mann, especially in a work like "Tonio
Kröger" (1903), in which "north" and "south" function (as
they do in Nietzsche) as metaphorical directions signifying the
polarity between the intellect and the senses, the spirit and the
flesh. Tonio Kröger is represented as embodying the type of
the artist, and the uneasiness reflected in his very name suggests
that the type may be regarded as the issue of an ambiguous mar-
riage of north and south (just as the name "Stephen Dedalus"
in Joyce's *Portrait*, insofar as it is intended as a generic name
for the artist, suggests a similar mingling of apparently antago-
nistic traditions):

. . . "I call you Kröger because your first name is so crazy.
Don't mind my saying so, I can't do with it at all. Tonio—why,

what sort of name is that? Though of course I know it's not
your fault in the least. . . ."

"Yes, it's a silly name—Lord knows I'd rather be called Heinrich or Wilhelm. It's all because I'm named after my mother's
brother Antonio. She comes from down there, you know. . . .*

But Nietzsche makes it abundantly clear elsewhere that what
he has in mind as the culmination of the process to which he
keeps alluding is considerably more remarkable than European
cosmopolitanism or a wedding of bourgeois and artistic values.
The "free, *very* free spirits" described as "good Europeans" in
the preface to *Beyond Good and Evil* (dated June 1885), or
those grandly addressed in the second volume of *Human, All-
Too-Human* (dated September 1886), as "you men of destiny,
triumphant, conquerors of time, the healthiest and the strongest, you *good Europeans!*" appear to be creatures of another
human order entirely. And the larger possibilities to which
Nietzsche has been alluding at last begin to reveal themselves
more fully in a memorable passage in *Beyond Good and Evil:*

> Call that in which the distinction of the European is sought
> "civilization" or "humanization" or "progress" or call it sim-
> ply—without praise or blame—using a political formula, Eu-
> rope's democratic movement: behind all the moral and politi-
> cal foregrounds to which such formulas point, a tremendous
> *physiological* process is taking place and gaining momentum.
> The Europeans are becoming more and more similar to each
> other; they become more and more detached from the condi-
> tions under which races originate that are tied to some climate
> or class; they become increasingly independent of any *determi-
> nate* milieu that would like to inscribe itself for centuries in

---

* What happens, in Mann's view, when the tense ironic balance which
defines the artistic temperament gives way, is of course clearly illustrated
by the disintegration of Aschenbach's personality in "Death in Venice"
(1911), a later novella which may be read as a gloss on the artistic ambition and the sense of emotional possibility (however precarious) articulated in the first.

body and soul with the same demands. Thus an essentially supra-national and nomadic type of man is gradually coming up, a type that possesses, physiologically speaking, a maximum of the art and power of adaptation as its typical distinction.

The tempo of this process of the *"evolving European"* may be retarded by great relapses, but perhaps it will gain in vehemence and profundity and grow just on their account: the still raging storm and stress of "national feeling" belongs here, also that anarchism which is just now coming up. But this process will probably lead to results which would seem to be least expected by those who naïvely promote and praise it, the apostles of "modern ideas." *The very same new conditions that will on the average lead to the leveling and mediocritization of man— to a useful, industrious, handy, multi-purpose herd animal—are likely in the highest degree to give birth to exceptional human beings of the most dangerous and attractive quality.*

To be sure, that power of adaptation which keeps trying out changing conditions and begins some new work with every generation, almost with every decade, does not make possible the *powerfulness* of the type, and the over-all impression of such future Europeans will probably be that of manifold, garrulous workers who will be poor in will, extremely employable, and as much in need of a master and commander as of their daily bread. But while the democratization of Europe leads to the production of a type that is prepared for *slavery* in the subtlest sense, in single, exceptional cases the strong human being will have to turn out stronger and richer than perhaps ever before— thanks to the absence of prejudice from his training, thanks to the tremendous manifoldness of practice, art, and mask. *I meant to say: the democratization of Europe is at the same time an involuntary arrangement for the cultivation of tyrants— taking the word in every sense, including the most spiritual.*

This passage is echoed by a section added in 1887 to the second edition of *Die fröhliche Wissenschaft.* Entitled "We who are homeless," this section celebrates the strength of those Europeans (and "there is no lack" of them) "who are entitled to call themselves homeless in a distinctive and honorable sense"; these "children of the future" are, "in one word—and let this be our word of honor—*good Europeans*, the heirs of Europe, the rich, oversupplied, but also overly obligated heirs of thousands of years of European spirit." It is to such figures, avowed enemies of "the religion of pity" and what is judged to be the general leveling tendency of modern society, that Nietzsche addresses himself:

> . . . it is to them that I especially commend my secret wisdom and *gaya scienza*. For their fate is hard, their hopes are uncertain; it is quite a feat to devise some comfort for them—but what avail? We children of the future, how *could* we be at home in this today? We feel disfavor for all ideals that might lead one to feel at home even in this fragile, broken time of transition; as for its "realities," we do not believe that they will *last*. The ice that still supports people today has become very thin; the wind that brings the thaw is blowing; we ourselves who are homeless constitute a force that breaks open ice and all other too thin "realities."
>
> We "conserve" nothing; neither do we want to return to any past periods; we are not by any means "liberal"; we do not work for "progress"; we do not need to plug up our ears against the sirens who in the market place sing of the future; their song about "equal rights," "a free society," "no more masters and no servants" has no allure for us. We simply do not consider it desirable that a realm of justice and concord should be established on earth (because it would certainly be the realm of the deepest leveling and *chinoiserie*); we are delighted with all who love, as we do, danger, war, and adventures, who refuse to compromise, to be captured, reconciled, and castrated; we count ourselves among conquerors; we think about the necessity for new orders, also for a new slavery—for every strengthening and enhancement of the human type also involves a new kind of enslavement. Is it not clear that with all this we are bound to feel ill at ease in an age that likes to claim the distinction of being the most humane, the mildest, and the most righteous age that the sun has ever seen?

First impressions notwithstanding, what is at issue in passages of this kind is considerably more than a premonition of the emergence of Nazism. The characteristically paradoxical situation that Nietzsche is describing is not produced by a clash of values, but by the most profound commitment to the preeminent value of individualism in all its refinements, as the history of Greece (with which it is hardly necessary to say Nietzsche was familiar) serves to indicate. It is helpful to keep in mind that that culture which is generally credited with the development of democracy has periodically, throughout the course of its history, fallen subject to tyranny: what is significant in this context is that these apparently antithetical political situations may both be regarded as consequences of an insistence on the power and supremacy of the individual.

For our present purposes, it is enough to remark how the impulse to achieve a self-definition independent of one's national or class origins, the impulse to be free of the limitations imposed by a particular time and place, feeds a larger, more abstract, more far-reaching impulse: the impulse to transcend all human limitations. What is involved here is a wish to achieve an absolute condition of freedom (which is regarded not only as an index of individuality, but of full humanity), in favor of which, in one's emotional life, any qualified condition of freedom is rejected, precisely because it is experienced as an intolerable manifestation of slavery.* As a consequence, there

---

* To grasp the implications of this habit of mind in nineteenth-century America, a nation obsessed with "the slavery issue" in more ways than one, we need only consider the deceptively humorous observations of Ishmael in *Moby-Dick* as an implicit commentary on Ahab's monomaniacal need to assert an independence which knows no bounds: "What of it," Ishmael says, "if some old hunks of a sea-captain orders me to get a broom and sweep down the decks? What does that indignity amount to, weighed, I mean, in the scales of the New Testament? Do you think the archangel Gabriel thinks anything the less of me, because I promptly and respectfully obey that old hunks in that particular instance? Who aint a slave? Tell me that. Well, then, however the old sea-captains may order me about—however they may thump and punch me about, I have the satisfaction of know-

is in Nietzsche's thought a perfectly consistent development from the conception of the "supra-national" "good European" to the superman, the ultimate "man of the future," in whom the limited condition of humanity is itself overcome. The logic of this development has been traced with great clarity and sensitivity by Leo Strauss, who derives it from an analysis of the speech entitled "On the Thousand and One Goals" in Part I of *Thus Spoke Zarathustra*. The "goals" in question are those embodied by various nations or cultures, and Strauss is concerned with two of these in particular: that of the Greeks and that of the Hebrews, seen from Nietzsche's point of view as mutually exclusive and antithetical.* Nietzsche finds the chief imperatives governing the characteristic direction of each of these cultures (as well as some of the imperatives gov-

---

ing that it is all right; that everybody else is one way or other served in much the same way—either in a physical or metaphysical point of view, that is; and so the universal thump is passed round, and all hands should rub each other's shoulder-blades, and be content."

A corresponding sentiment is expressed by Father Mapple in more explicitly anti-Emersonian terms, terms which do not identify assertions of individual will as the only true celebrations of the Deity; here divinity is not (as in Emerson) located within man. Accordingly, Father Mapple observes that "if we obey God, we must disobey ourselves; and it is in this disobeying ourselves, wherein the hardness of obeying God consists." Consider, in this context, Ahab's perception of the ultimate challenge to the supremacy of his will: "Is Ahab Ahab? Is it I, God, or who, that lifts this arm? But if the great sun move not of himself; but is as an errand-boy in heaven; nor one single star can revolve, but by some invisible power; how then can this one small heart beat; this one small brain think thoughts; unless God does that beating, does that thinking, does that living, and not I."

* The opposition between "Jerusalem and Athens," "Hebraism and Hellenism," is of course not unfamiliar in the later nineteenth century, and it serves to link Nietzsche's concerns significantly with those of such writers as Arnold and Pater. A fuller account of this connection is provided in the Notes.

erning other cultures) undoubtedly great and praiseworthy, but because he cannot agree to abide by the one without implicitly rejecting the other—indeed, without rejecting all the others— his conception of himself demands that he refuse to be bound by either. Strauss proceeds to reconstruct the stages of Nietzsche's thinking on this subject, and then goes on to indicate the ultimate significance of Nietzsche's conclusions:

> Nietzsche's reverence for the sacred tables of the Hebrews, as well as for those of the other nations in question, is deeper than that of any other beholder. Yet since he too is only a beholder of these tables, since what one table commends or commands is incompatible with what others command, he himself is not subject to the commandments of any. This is true also and especially of the tables, or "values," of modern Western culture. But according to him, all scientific concepts, and hence in particular the concept of culture, are culture-bound; the concept of culture is an outgrowth of 19th-century Western culture; its application to the "cultures" of other ages and climates is an act stemming from the spiritual imperialism of that particular culture. There is, then, for Nietzsche, a glaring contradiction between the claimed objectivity of the science of cultures and the subjectivity of that science. To state the case differently, one cannot behold—i.e., truly understand—any culture unless one is firmly rooted in one's own culture or unless one belongs, in one's capacity as a beholder, to some culture. But if the universality of the beholding of all cultures is to be preserved, the culture to which the beholder of all cultures belongs must be the universal culture, the culture of mankind, the world culture; the universality of beholding presupposes, if only by anticipating, the universal culture which is no longer one culture among many. Nietzsche sought therefore for a culture that would no longer be particular and hence in the last analysis arbitrary. The single goal of mankind is conceived by him as in a sense super-human: he speaks of the super-man of the future. The super-man is meant to unite in himself, on the highest level, both Jerusalem and Athens.

The distinction here between Jerusalem and Athens would seem to correspond in essence to James's distinction between "Europe" and "America"—if that distinction is seen as reflecting the contrast between "historical" and "inner" culture which we have already considered, and if it is noted that for James the transcendence of "historical" culture and the attainment of "inner" culture functions (as they do for Emerson and Thoreau) as moral imperatives. In other words, one's moral stature becomes a function of one's ability to separate oneself from the past: the intensity of the assertion of one's distinctive individuality becomes the chief index of one's moral worth (and, as indicated earlier, one's fidelity to the ideal embodied in the very notion of America—which helps to explain why, in James's work, Americans almost invariably have the moral edge in "the international relation"). It is important in this context to bear in mind that in his summary of the implications of the contrast between Jerusalem and Athens in the section of *Zarathustra* on which he focuses, Strauss points out that Nietzsche judged the defining characteristic of the Hebrew culture to be "the utmost honoring of father and mother," while for the Greek culture it was "the full dedication of the individual to the contest for excellence, distinction, supremacy."

Even if one does not choose to pursue these parallels, it seems evident that James's conception of the American writer of the future—the master of experience whose cultural identity would represent a powerful amalgamation of various national tendencies—parallels in its fundamental intention and implication Nietzsche's idea of the "good European" as that idea emerges in its fullest aspect. Nor does the parallel appear coincidental, an odd quirk of the *Zeitgeist* which is of debatable significance and only incidental interest: for as will be seen, this is not the only point at which James's ideas and those of Nietzsche coincide.

4. The "Highest Specimens" of Humanity

The powerful synthetic figure projected by Nietzsche is liberated from the defining limitations of his own place and time, and ultimately from all historical conditions; he is therefore able to achieve a condition of supreme detachment which represents a leap to the superhuman. Another perspective on this achievement is suggested by several of Nietzsche's observations regarding nineteenth-century men who in his judgment had approached at least world-historical magnitude. Included in a list of such men would be Goethe, for example ("not a German event, but a European one"), and, of course, Napoleon; about such extraordinary figures Nietzsche asserts:

> In all the more profound and comprehensive human beings of this century, the total tendency underlying the enigmatic workings of their soul was, at bottom, to prepare the way for this new synthesis and to anticipate, experimentally, the European of the future. Only in their foregrounds or in weaker hours, as in old age, they belonged to the "fatherlandish" ones—they were merely taking a rest from themselves when they became "patriots." I am thinking of human beings like Napoleon, Goethe, Beethoven, Stendhal, Heinrich Heine, and Schopenhauer.

Nietzsche's remarks about Napoleon are worth particular attention here, for although (like Emerson) he was inclined to regard the limited personality of the French conqueror himself with mixed feelings (in a note for *The Will to Power* written during the summer or fall of 1883, he observes that Napoleon "had been corrupted by the means he *had* to employ, and had *lost* the *nobility* of his character," and in the *Genealogy of Morals* he condemns him as a "synthesis of the *inhuman* and *superhuman*" [*Unmensch* and *Übermensch*]), his view of the significance of the military aspect of Napoleon's career remained undivided and affirmative: he regarded Napoleon's imperial efforts as an attempt to achieve, in the external, military sphere, that same international synthesis that his own powerful man of the future would embody in his own nature:

> . . . When Napoleon wanted to bring Europe into an association of states (the only human being who was strong enough for that!), they botched everything with their *"Wars of Liberation"* and conjured up the misfortune of the insanity of nationalities (with the consequence of race fights in such long-mixed countries as Europe!).

Such observations make it clear that Nietzsche's admiration for Napoleon is not simply a consequence of the latter's enormous importance in the history of Europe—i.e., his "historical importance," as defined by his role in an unfolding drama with a beginning, a middle, and an end (all variable and dependent upon the observer's point of view). For Nietzsche, the central meaning of Napoleon's career is not to be found in what he actually achieved or failed to achieve, but in the impulse which his life expressed: the impulse of the "Dionysian" man described in *Twilight of the Idols* (and exemplified there by Goethe), who by an act of will is able to overcome the obstacles placed in the way of his realization of his vision of himself by the actual conditions of his existence. By seizing the accidental materials of history and compelling them to obey the logic of his own self-conception, the exemplary figure makes of his experience a drama in which he figures as the hero: through a transcendent act of imagination (which might, under certain circumstances, be very difficult to distinguish from madness) he becomes his own fiction, a work of art created in his own image, and as a consequence succeeds in tearing himself out of the process of history.

Such a man is regarded as having freed himself from history because he has taken his life into his own hands: his existence is no longer a product of blind, external forces, but of conscious, subjective will. If it has a meaning, it is the meaning that he himself has given it. Consequently, the value of his life is no longer relative: it is not determined by his function in any given society, or by the part he may play in a particular historical development. His value is conceived as absolute, and (by a familiar Nietzschean process of reversal) it becomes the standard by which events in the external world are measured. In short, the powerful man is no longer subject to the limitations imposed on his will by the external world: instead, that world has become (in ways that will become clear presently) subject to him.

This general line of thinking is revealed in Nietzsche's remarks about Napoleon in the section of *Twilight of the Idols* entitled "My conception of genius." In that section, Nietzsche declares that "great men . . . are explosives in which a tremendous force is stored up" ("I am no man, I am dynamite," he once said of himself), and he goes on to observe that once such a man appears in the world, "What does the environment matter then, or the age, or the 'spirit of the age,' or 'public opinion'!" Nietzsche then considers "the case of Napoleon" in relation to the dominant human "type" produced by revolutionary and prerevolutionary France, and he concludes that "Because Napoleon was *different*, the heir of a stronger, older, more ancient civilization than the one which was then perishing in France, he became the master there, he *was* the only master." Nietzsche then proceeds to elaborate on the relationship between the great man and the age he usually comes to dominate:

> Great men are neccssary, the age in which they appear is accidental; that they almost always become masters over their age is only because they are stronger, because they are older, because for a longer time much was gathered for them. The rela-

tionship between a genius and his age is like that between strong and weak, or between old and young: the age is relatively always much younger, thinner, more immature, less assured, more childish.

The surprising juggling of youth and age in conjunction with strength and weakness here would appear to be of some psychological significance, but that is not our most immediate concern. What we do need to remark is the notion (suggested by the use of such adjectives as "necessary" and "accidental" in this passage) that it is the great man who in a sense defines the age: it is in relation to him that the age is judged, and not vice versa, for he serves as the "necessary" standard of value in an "accidental" age, and it is his existence alone which ultimately has the power to "justify" the existence of the age. Were it not for the fact that he distinguished it, the age would, as one might say, have no point. This view is stated explicitly, if somewhat flamboyantly, in part of a late note (1887-1888) for *The Will to Power* (a note which, incidentally, taken in its entirety, is extremely important to a full understanding of the psychological substructure of much of Nietzsche's thought): "The revolution made possible Napoleon: that is its justification. For a similar prize one should have to desire the anarchical crash of our entire civilization."

For Nietzsche, a society or an epoch is redeemed from mediocrity and weakness only to the extent that it is able to produce men of such magnitude and energy; but men of this type may not be judged in relation to their usefulness in preserving or strengthening any existing society, since in Nietzsche's view "the value of a man . . . does not reside in his utility; for it would continue to exist even if there were no one to whom he could be of any use. And why could not precisely that man who produced the most disastrous effects be the pinnacle of the whole species of man: so high, so superior that everything would perish from envy of him?" Accordingly, such commanding figures cannot be judged on the basis of their historical consequences—which may be most unfortunate—inasmuch as their essential value resides precisely in their ability to overcome historical conditions. Such figures exemplify what Nietzsche refers to as "supra-historical" values in the second of his *Unzeitgemässe Betrachtungen*, published in 1874, *Vom Nutzen und Nachtheil der Historie für das Leben* ("Of the Use and Disadvantage of History for Life")—the work reviewed by T. S. Perry in 1875. In that work, Nietzsche makes a distinction between the "historical" and the "supra-historical" point of view which is worth examining here.

For the "historical" man (who is, in Nietzsche's view, a casualty of the lamentable influence of Hegel, not to mention the vaguely Darwinian belief in evolution as a synonym for progress) the meaning of existence reveals itself progressively, in stages: it unfolds like a story, with a beginning, a middle, and an end. According to Nietzsche, such men "believe that the meaning of existence will become ever clearer in the course of its evolution"; consequently, they must look to the future to endow the present with meaning. The "supra-historical" man, on the other hand, is defined as the man "who does not envisage salvation in the process but for whom the world is finished in every single moment and its end [*Ende*] attained. What could ten new years teach that the past could not teach?" The "supra-historical" figure thus functions as an exemplar of values which are in a sense beyond the reach of history, values which are not simply derived from history (for if they were so derived they might very well be superseded in time once they came to be seen as merely relative to a particular time and place), but which are conceived as existing absolutely, independent of history.

Nietzsche's effort here would seem to be generated by his perception of the moral void left by the death of God; what he is attempting is to rescue values from the rush of time and to reestablish them—as Plato and his Christian followers also sought to do—on some secure, unchanging ground accessible to persons capable of detaching themselves from their immediate historical circumstances and of seeing those circumstances at a distance, from the perspective of the ideal. The problem Nietzsche is addressing is, as Kaufmann aptly observes, a problem "of supreme importance and actually nothing less than *the* problem of *Historismus,* which was later to be developed by Ernst Troeltsch, Benedetto Croce, and Friedrich Meinecke"; it is a problem "in which philosophy of history and theory of values meet," for what Nietzsche is finally asking is "whether there are genuinely supra-historical values or whether all values are merely historical phenomena which are valid only in a certain place and time."

In this early essay on history, Nietzsche concludes that human existence is endowed with meaning and value only by those exceptional human beings who are able to establish themselves beyond historical conditions, those powerful natures who, by wrenching themselves free of historical limitations ("Only strong personalities can endure history," Nietzsche observes; "the weak are extinguished by it") have managed to become the measure of themselves, and by extension the standard against which the rest of humanity is judged: for such natures exemplify the human potential fully realized, and their lives represent historical events "elevated" and "intensified" into "comprehensive symbols."* Indeed, Nietzsche asserts, these

---

* Not surprisingly, Nietzsche's assertions here are reminiscent of a passage in Emerson's "Self-Reliance": "Ordinarily, every body in society reminds us of somewhat else, or of some other person. Character, reality, reminds you of nothing else; it takes place of the whole creation. . . . Every man is a cause, a country, and an age; requires infinite spaces and numbers and time fully to accomplish his thought; —and posterity seem to follow his steps as a procession. . . . all history resolves itself very easily into the biography of a few stout and earnest persons. . . ."

exemplary beings "form a sort of bridge over the wan stream of becoming. They may not perhaps continue a process, but they live out of time, as contemporaries" and call to one another "across the waste spaces of time." And because these human beings who serve as the measure of humanity do not represent the outcome of a single, continuous process of historical development, but are rather, at all times, "apparently scattered and accidental existences" (as they are characterized in Part Six of *Schopenhauer als Erzieher*, also published in 1874), Nietzsche ultimately concludes that "The *goal of humanity* cannot lie in the end [*Ende*] but only in its highest specimens."

5. The "Vessel of Consciousness"

Nietzsche came to see these "highest specimens" of humanity as serving an ultimate moral function as exemplary embodiments of human values and potentialities which would otherwise be subject to the pressures of history, determined exclusively by the vagaries of the historical moment. Realized in persons defined by their success in overcoming the limitations (and, significantly, the judgments) of their own time, such values are rescued from the historical process and rendered absolute: they become the values according to which human beings always and everywhere are to be judged. Since they have not, in Nietzsche's view, been generated by the historical process, they cannot be undone by it, and they remain undiminished in force or applicability regardless of the general character of the actual human "specimens" which mankind might have to offer at any particular time—flawed and disappointing as these might be.

In a remarkably similar way, Henry James came to regard his own "supersubtle fry" as making available certain moral alternatives to the range of possibilities for human character fixed by historical circumstances in any given epoch. Looking back over a lifetime's work in fiction when he was writing the extraordinary Prefaces for the collected New York edition (published 1907-1909), James defended himself against the accusation made by some of his contemporaries that he had seriously violated the principles of realistic fiction (as opposed to romance)—principles to which these contemporaries had been led to believe he gave his undivided allegiance—by centering his attention on exceptional, unrepresentative cases, characters thought to have no counterparts in the actual life of the times in which they were supposed to live. To this particular charge James replied with considerable agitation in his Preface to the volume which takes its title from "The Lesson of the Master." Asked by an anonymous "friend" "where on earth, where roundabout us at this hour," he had " 'found' " his "eminent cases," James tells us that he responded promptly and unapologetically: "If the life about us for the last thirty years refuses warrant for these examples, then so much the worse for that life. The *constatation* would be so deplorable that instead of making it we must dodge it: there are decencies that in the name of the general self-respect we must take for granted, there's a kind of rudimentary intellectual honor to which we must, in the interest of civilization, at least pretend."

"But I must really reproduce the whole passion of my retort," he continues:

> What does your contention of non-existent conspicuous *exposures*, in the midst of all the stupidity and vulgarity and hypocrisy, imply but that we have been, nationally, so to speak, graced with no instances of recorded sensibility fine enough to react against these things?—an admission too distressing. What one would accordingly fain do is to baffle any such calamity, to *create* the record, in default of any other enjoyment of it; to imagine, in a word, the honourable, the producible case. What better example than this of the high and helpful public and, as it were, civic use of the imagination?—a faculty for the possible

fine employments of which in the interest of morality my esteem grows every hour I live. How can one consent to make a picture of the preponderant futilities and vulgarities and miseries of life without the impulse to exhibit as well from time to time, in its place, some fine example of the reaction, the opposition or the escape? One does, thank heaven, encounter here and there symptoms of immunity from the general infection; one recognises with rapture, on occasion, signs of protest against the rule of the cheap and easy; and one sees thus that the tradition of a high aesthetic temper needn't, after all, helplessly and ignobly perish. These reassurances are one's warrant, accordingly, for so many recognitions of the apparent doom and the exasperated temper—whether with the spirit and the career fatally bruised and finally broken in the fray, or privileged but to gain from it a finer and more militant edge. I have had, I admit, to project *signal* specimens—have had, naturally, to make and to keep my cases interesting; the only way to achieve which was to suppose and represent them eminent. In other words I was inevitably committed, always, to the superior case; so that if this is what you reprehensibly mean, that I have been thus beguiled into citing celebrities without analogues and painting portraits without models, I plead guilty to the critical charge. Only what I myself mean is that I carry my guilt lightly and have really in face of each perpetrated licence scarce patience to defend myself.

James's insistence here on his "high and helpful public and, as it were, civic use of the imagination" makes it clear that the imaginary figures he is projecting are meant to be understood as exemplary spiritual figures: that is to say, they are offered to us as the embodiment of spiritual alternatives to the present as it is. Such a function has most often been associated with the exemplary figures of traditional religion, but as the work of Matthew Arnold would suggest, the increasing dimness of contemporary religious experience (institutionally and doctrinally defined) produces a need to locate these possibilities of transcendence in works of the imagination, where they are thought to survive with undiminished vigor. The logic of this development is articulated by Yeats in a memorable passage in the second volume of his *Autobiography* (*The Trembling of the Veil*, 1922):

> I was unlike others of my generation in one thing only. I am very religious, and deprived by Huxley and Tyndall, whom I detested, of the simple-minded religion of my childhood, I had made a new religion, almost an infallible church of poetic tradition, of a fardel of stories, and of personages, and of emotions, inseparable from their first expression, passed on from generation to generation with some help from philosophers and theologians. I wished for a world, where I could discover this tradition perpetually, and not in pictures and in poems only, but in tiles round the chimney-piece and in the hangings that kept out the draft. I had even created a dogma: "Because those imaginary people are created out of the deepest instinct of man, to be his measure and his norm, whatever I can imagine those mouths speaking may be the nearest I can go to truth." When I listened they seemed always to speak of one thing only: they, their love, every incident of their lives, were steeped in the supernatural.

Like Nietzsche's "highest specimens," the symbolic personages described here by Yeats combine the functions of the artist, the philosopher, and the saint; and linked with one another they form a "tradition" of expressions of "the deepest instinct of man," a tradition of essential being which serves (to use Nietzsche's phrase) as "a sort of bridge over the wan stream of becoming."

The decisive, even defiant tone of James's Preface is especially significant in this larger context; it is the tone of a writer convinced of the moral authority of his fiction—an authority which is not simply that associated with the presumed mission of literary realism in this period. The writer who is speaking here, far from being a man who failed to come to terms with the ordinary life of his own time (as the stereotype of James would have it), is a man actively and unequivocally engaged in what he sees as a continual combat against the disheartening limitations of the actuality he faces daily—or, as he refers to the enemy in another Preface, "the fatal futility of Fact." In this respect, James clearly resembles the "virtuous man" depicted by Nietzsche in the Meditation on History considered earlier, the man who "will always rise against the blind force of facts, the tyranny of the actual, and submit himself to laws that are not the fickle laws of history." And just as James regards his "signal specimens" as an implicit reproach directed against contemporary society, so too Nietzsche sees the "highest specimens" selected from the past (Goethe, for example) as representatives of a standard of human excellence against which men of the present are measured and found severely wanting: "How few living men have a right to live, as against those mighty dead!" Nietzsche declares, and he goes on to praise "the memory of the great 'fighters against history,' that is, against the blind power of the actual," "men who troubled themselves very little about the 'thus it is,' in order that they might follow a 'thus it must be' with greater joy and greater pride." It is just such a conflict that James is describing, and he observes in addition that in the clash between the ideal and the actual, if the ideal is not overwhelmed and destroyed it will indeed prevail and ultimately gain in power: for that is surely what he is implying when he asserts that "the spirit and the career" of those "signal specimens" who embody the "high aesthetic temper" will either be "fatally bruised and finally broken in the fray, or privileged but to gain from it a finer and more militant edge." Moreover, the conviction expressed here (and elsewhere as well) by James that adversary relationships ultimately either destroy or strengthen has numerous parallels in Nietzsche's thought, ranging from the latter's conception of a powerful, synthetic European culture created by the union of disparate and warring elements, to his characteristic assertion that "What does not destroy me, makes me stronger."

In the course of development of James's fictional technique, the "signal specimen" comes more and more to be employed as the "vessel of consciousness," focusing the range of proliferating implications of the story in which he figures, and that story comes more and more to be the record of his own dawning awareness, the chronicle of his efforts to comprehend the full significance of the situation in which he finds himself. As a result, the action of the story is increasingly conceived as a "process of vision" (as James observed in his Preface to *The Ambassadors*), and James is finally convinced of "the unreality of the sharp distinction, where the interest of observation is at stake, between doing and feeling."

Many of James's readers, of course—not all of them hostile or superficial—have pointed to the relative lack of recognizable dramatic action in the later fiction as an enervating refinement which diminishes the impact of the human situations depicted by making it difficult to locate the characters in relation to their specific material circumstances, or to arrive at a precise sense of the actual temporal duration of their elliptical conversations (especially when, as if by design, dialogue and internal monologue become more and more difficult to distinguish). In works like *The Beast in the Jungle* (1903), for instance, it may be argued that the general presence of the physical world is virtually eliminated; and indeed, in such works the weight of that world is felt only insofar as particular material objects may be seen as possessing symbolic value, reflecting on an external plane the essential situation of the characters:

> He had been standing by the chimney-piece, fireless and sparely adorned, a small, perfect old French clock and two morsels of rosy Dresden constituting all its furniture. . . .

The physical objects here tell the whole story of the relationship between John Marcher and May Bartram—a story in which two highly polished and immobile figures face one another in a fireless room while a clock ticks off the hours they spend in the isolation of each other's company.

It is clear that in works of this kind the physical world no longer serves as a hard, factual alternative to a fluid psychological state: on the contrary, the external world has a tendency to mirror the preoccupations of the character, and everything perceived seems to reduce itself into an inventory of the contents of his mind. If his mind is narrow, then, so much the worse for him, for so much more meager will the world appear. Thus, in *The Beast in the Jungle*, the combined sense of emptiness and suffocation which pervades the narrative is produced by the inability of the central character to break through the wall of his own egotism and recognize the existence in the world of the rich variety of persons and things which do not merely serve his own conception of himself.

The general point to be grasped here is that many of the objections to James's later style fail to take adequate account of the continuity between that style and the human predicaments—all having to do with limitations of vision—it attempts to explore. In the later James, characters are no longer defined and evaluated according to what they do, or even what they say: they tell us who they are through what they see. Accordingly, the drama in these works has been moved from the plane of explicit action to what James regards as the more fundamental plane of perception; and so far as James is concerned, this shift does not involve the slightest diminution of moral seriousness, or the slightest reduction of concern for concrete human consequences, since it may well be argued that what one sees—or fails to see—in other people has everything to do with how one behaves toward them and with how one's behavior must ultimately be judged.

This line of reasoning, which associates the ultimate morality with depth of vision (no matter how apparently demonic the possessor of such vision may be), leads us directly to the paradoxical aspect of Maggie Verver's triumph in *The Golden Bowl*—a triumph which has been seen by a number of critics as a manifestation of an essential brutality masked as high civilization. The terms of such a paradox will be as familiar to readers of Nietzsche as to those who have reflected on the meaning of Kurtz's savagery in Conrad's *Heart of Darkness*, a work which obliges us to consider whether the ultimate act of civilization, the ultimate self-recognition which leads to the achievement of complete awareness and the loss of all illusions, might not require—on grounds of conscience, as it were—a descent into barbarism. It is in the context of such vexing concerns as these, concerns which also manifest themselves in works like Yeats's "The Second Coming" and in the doctrine of the mask which he elaborates in *A Vision*, that the achievements of James's "major phase" must be located. Failure to take in this context may lead us to mistake those novels for supreme refinements of Howellsian realism which declare their allegiance to the familiar moral and aesthetic values which underlie such accounts of experience; seen in those terms, the novels which James wrote at the turn of the century must appear simply bewildering.

The drama in those late works—most notably *The Wings of the Dove* and *The Golden Bowl*—results from the continuous conflict between the comprehensive view of the situation which the highly conscious person at the center of the story is struggling to achieve, and the partial, superficial views represented by those persons of limited intelligence and sensibility by whom he is surrounded—"the tangle, the drama, the tragedy and comedy of those who appreciate consisting so much of their relation with those who don't." As against these superior persons, "every one else shows for comparatively stupid"; other persons James regards as being, to one degree or another, "fools," but he considers them essential to the drama: "verily even, I think," he observes, "no 'story' is possible without its fools."

These specimens of ordinary (or inferior: the distinction collapses for James, as it does for Nietzsche) humanity serve as the human setting for a jewel of great price, the fine central intelligence of the story; defined by the quality and intensity of their feelings rather than by their actions *per se*, these ordinary persons are judged to be, in relation to the "large lucid reflector," creatures of "a denser and duller, a more vulgar and more shallow capacity" for appreciation of the various facets, the nuances and intricacies of the situation. But since the story is, in James's terms, "a case of feeling," there is room in it for "ever so many possible feelings, stretched across the scene like an attached thread on which the points of interest are strung." "There are threads shorter and less tense," James goes on to observe, "and I am far from implying that the minor, the coarser and less fruitful forms and degrees of moral reaction, as we may conveniently call it, may not yield lively results. They have their subordinate, comparative, illustrative human value— that appeal to the witless which is often so penetrating." The general thrust and tone of these remarks hardly require commentary, but it is important to point out that James seems to regard the predicament of superior persons—those possessed of "the power to be finely aware and richly responsible"—marooned among "persons of markedly limited sense" as essentially tragic; the point is made explicit when, in the Prefaces, he identifies his "signal specimens" with Hamlet and Lear, whom he evidently takes to be exemplars of the type:

> Their being finely aware—as Hamlet and Lear, say, are finely aware—*makes* absolutely the intensity of their adventure, gives the maximum of sense to what befalls them. We care, our

curiosity and our sympathy care, comparatively little for what happens to the stupid, the coarse, and the blind; care for it, and for the effects of it, at the most as helping to precipitate what happens to the more deeply wondering, to the really sentient. Hamlet and Lear are surrounded, amid their complications, by the stupid and the blind, who minister in all sorts of ways to their recorded fate.

This may seem a curious way of understanding *Lear*, but that is not the main point to be remarked; it is evident that James is chiefly concerned here with making a fundamental distinction between two classes of persons, "the more deeply wondering" and "deeply sentient" on the one hand, and "the stupid, the coarse and the blind" on the other. Between these two classes lies a gulf so immeasurably wide that the difference between them seems to be perceived not simply as a difference of degree but one of kind. There is, moreover, a very powerful suggestion in this passage (and elsewhere in James's writings) that awareness is valued as that quality which defines full humanity: it would follow from this premise that those persons not capable of fine awareness could not be (by definition) fully human. The apparently paradoxical assumptions underlying James's insistence on an all but supernatural degree of awareness as a criterion for full humanity will be considered in the next section of the present chapter; it is worth remarking at this point, however, that the reiterated demand for such a stringent criterion might help to account for the unsettling remark made by Sherwood Anderson—a writer essentially concerned with characters who have been broken and blinded by circumstances, with the confused and hurt and inarticulate, toward whom he is inclined to express a kind of helpless, agonized compassion—that James was "the novelist of those who hate."

And indeed, it is as though those characters in James's fiction who lack the capacity for rich, deep comprehension exist in another dimension entirely: they are deficient, incomplete, and they derive their chief—perhaps their only—value from their subordinate relation to those "signal specimens" who occupy James's most scrupulous attention:

> I confess I never see the *leading* interest of any human hazard but in a consciousness (on the part of the moved and moving creature) subject to fine intensification and wide enlargement. It is as mirrored in that consciousness that the gross fools, the headlong fools, the fatal fools play their part for us—they have much less to show us in themselves. The troubled life mostly at the centre of our subject—whatever our subject, for the artistic hour, happens to be—embraces them and deals with them for its amusement and its anguish: they are apt largely indeed, on a near view, to be all the cause of its trouble.

The precise nature of the "trouble" that James alludes to here will be an object of speculation later, when the question of the significance of clashing "points of view" in James's fiction is taken up in some detail; for the moment, it is sufficient to observe that the representatives of ordinary, unredeemed humanity—"the gross fools, the headlong fools, the fatal fools"—are endowed with value only to the extent that they are reflected in the lively consciousness of the "large lucid reflector" in their midst.

6. The "Human, Superhuman" Paradox

James's sharp distinction between "signal specimens" and "fools" bears a significant resemblance to the distinction made by Nietzsche between mankind's "highest specimens" and what he was inclined to call—with great melodramatic deliberateness and in full awareness of the implications of the term—"the herd." But Nietzsche begins from a somewhat different premise: for him, humanity in general is essentially without value, since man as such appears to occupy a position in the scheme of things which is only slightly (and hardly decisively) above that of the animals. Indeed, Nietzsche seems to be convinced that in most respects it is impossible to make a significant distinction between men and animals, and to this extent at least he shows the influence of those evolutionary ideas—often incompletely understood—which came to dominate the imagination of his age. The background of Nietzsche's thinking on this point is summarized efficiently by Kaufmann. "If the teaching of evolution is correct and man is not essentially different from the apes," he observes, then from Nietzsche's point of view it would follow that "no quantitative addition, either of more and more human beings or of more and more intelligence (which man is supposed to share with the chimpanzee, though he has more of it), can give man the unique dignity which the Western tradition has generally conceded him":

> What is worthless to start with, cannot acquire value by multiplication. If man's value is zero, no addition of such zeros will ever lead to any value. A steady increase of intelligence through history, even if it could be demonstrated, would not change this picture. If man is to have any worth, there must be a "qualitative leap," to use Hegel's apt expression.

Significantly enough, Nietzsche envisions just such a leap in his early *Schopenhauer als Erzieher* (1874), the third of the *Unzeitgemässe Betrachtungen*. In that work, Nietzsche ponders the question of how men may be lifted from the level of animality to that of essential humanity (which is conceived as a potentiality never realized by the mass of men); and he concludes, much as he did in the preceding Meditation on History, that the unique value of mankind may be glimpsed only in its "highest specimens," who are now defined as "those true *men, those no longer animals, the philosophers, artists and saints.*" "With their appearance," Nietzsche continues, "nature, who never jumps, makes her only jump, and it is a *jump for joy. . . ."*

In short, for Nietzsche, the gulf separating the mass of humanity from its "highest specimens" is as great as—indeed, in the last analysis, is the same as—the gulf separating animals from men. For in Nietzsche's terms the human condition is essentially that of "the herd": most men never exceed the limitations of their animal aspect. To become a "truly *human* being," therefore—to realize the higher potentiality (a potentiality defined by the ability to create values) inherent in humanity—one must somehow succeed in transcending "the herd." But this means that, in a sense, one must transcend the human condition itself, "leap," like the "highest specimens," to a level of absolute values above nature. Consequently, once he has rejected the "human, all-too-human" as the essentially animalistic, Nietzsche arrives at the paradox of the "human, superhuman": to become fully human, one must actually become superhuman.

A remarkably illuminating discussion of this paradox occurs in what may seem an unexpected place: the works of F. W. H. Myers, one of the founders (in 1882) of the Society for Psychical Research and a thinker for whom William James had the profoundest respect.† In the chapter on "Genius" in his

* James W. Hillesheim and Malcolm R. Simpson, the translators of *Schopenhauer as Educator*, provide a useful explanatory note for this passage: "In *The Origin of the Species* [*sic*] (Chap. VI, 'Difficulties of the Theory') Darwin refers to 'that old, but somewhat exaggerated, canon in natural history of *"Natura non facit saltum."*' That is, nature does nothing by leaps. But, might not one ask, 'Why should not Nature take a sudden leap from structure to structure?' Darwin's reply is that, 'On the theory of natural selection, we can clearly understand why she should not; for natural selection acts only by taking advantage of slight successive variations; she can never take a great and sudden leap, but must advance by short and sure, though slow steps.'"

† James's formal tribute, delivered on March 8, 1901, after Myers's death, is included under the title "Frederick Myers's Services to Psychology" in

study of *Human Personality and Its Survival of Bodily Death* (originally published in two volumes in 1903), Myers observes:

> . . . I shall suggest . . . that Genius . . . if that vaguely used word is to receive anything like a psychological definition—should . . . be regarded as a power of utilising a wider range than other men can utilise of faculties in some degree innate in all;—a power of appropriating the results of subliminal mentation to subserve the supraliminal stream of thought;—so that an "inspiration of Genius" will be in truth a *subliminal uprush*, an emergence into the current of ideas which the man is consciously manipulating of other ideas which he has not consciously originated, but which have shaped themselves beyond his will, in profounder regions of his being. I shall urge that there is here no real departure from normality; no abnormality, at least in the sense of degeneration; but rather a fulfillment of the true norm of man, with suggestions, it may be, of something *supernormal*;—of something which transcends existing normality as an advanced stage of evolutionary progress transcends an earlier stage.

For Myers, as for Nietzsche and Henry James, the essential character of humanity ("the true norm of man," in Myers's formulation) is not a given but something that remains to be realized: it is a condition of supreme awareness toward which human beings as they are continually strive, an absolute condi-

---

Memories and Studies (1911), but his letters also provide evidence of the nature and extent of his admiration. A few quotations will suffice to make the point: "I seriously believe that the general problem of the subliminal, as Myers proposed it, promises to be one of the *great* problems, possibly even the greatest problem, of psychology . . ." (letter of March 3, 1901, to James Sully); "He 'looms' upon me after death more than he did in life, and I think that his forthcoming book about 'Human Personality' will probably rank hereafter as 'epoch-making' " (letter of June 26, 1901, to Charles Eliot Norton); "Fifty or a hundred years hence, people will know better than now whether his instinct for truth was a sound one; and perhaps will then pat me on the back for backing him" (letter of July 10, 1901, to Frances R. Morse).

tion which exists beyond the bounds of actual human possibility but which reveals itself in some degree to every human being. For all three of these authors, and for William James as well, it is the power of consciousness that defines full humanity. But the closer one comes to achieving complete or unbounded consciousness, the closer one will be to a condition usually associated with divinity, and the further away from the human condition if that condition is conceived as essentially one of limitation.

The "human, superhuman" paradox at which Nietzsche arrives accordingly reveals itself in the thought of all these writers, and it is not surprising that they all should have projected figures who seemed actually to embody or at least to prefigure that future condition of absolute consciousness which would collapse the distinction between man and God. To the extent that they were able to realize that potentiality in themselves by achieving higher and higher levels of awareness, such figures would have to be seen as living in the future—from which they might, as if from a great height, regard the experience of the present. Once again, it is useful here to recall William James's definition of the saint as someone "entirely adapted" to a "millennial society." The definition suggests the moral authority which is achieved by the person who is able to live in relation to an ideal moral future: the saint is a citizen of a world which has not yet come into being, and he serves to remind us that it could. A similar exemplary authority is possessed by Myers's "Genius" and Henry James's "vessel of consciousness," but the ultimate ambition underlying these conceptions is most fully articulated in Nietzsche's superman. Combining in himself the functions of the philosopher, the artist, and the saint, he prefigures a world entirely intelligible, entirely beautiful, and entirely noble.

Like the other authors we have been considering here, Nietzsche assumes that true humanity consists in the ability to transcend human limitations; but unlike those authors, he refuses to entertain the possibility of relative transcendence, and that refusal is clearly related to the endless process of self-accusation which may be an inevitable component of any attempt at self-improvement but which in his case often reached a near-hysterical pitch and surely helped to produce the tragedy of his life. It is not possible, in Nietzsche's view, for a man to transcend only some limitations and thus rise at least to that extent above "the herd": he must either overcome all such limitations or be subjected to them all, for with respect to the conditions of existence he can be only master or slave.

To the extent that it is possible to detect any traces whatsoever of the herd in himself, he is a slave, guilty of inadequacy and weakness; in order to achieve any sense of freedom, therefore, he must eradicate all such traces of dependency or subjection—that is, he must become a superman. The remarkable parallel between this predicament and that of Melville's Ahab (which we considered earlier in another context, on page 90n above) is worth some attention here.

Another perspective on this line of reasoning comes into focus when one remembers that for Nietzsche, "in man there is both *creator* and *creature*." By overcoming the creature in himself (the natural aspect, the "slave" aspect, that which is acted upon and is therefore to that degree the product of external and unconscious forces, that which is subject to limitation, change, and decay), the "highest specimen" achieves the status of a pure creator. As a result, he is no longer simply another one of the things in this world (just as the universal culture is not simply another historical culture among many), subject, like them, to an unrelenting, melancholy process of deterioration: instead, he has become the source of the standards by which the things of this world are to be measured. And in this sense his very existence confers meaning on the world, for all things are now seen to derive whatever value or significance they may have only from their relation to him: they possess value only to the degree that he "esteems" them. In the same way, because he remains able at every moment to give form to the accidental materials of his own life, he comes to represent the ideal against which all humanity is judged: all men are now defined by the degree to which their lives reveal (or fail to reveal) the same talent for endless self-transformation, and to which they themselves demonstrate the same ability to liberate themselves from the crushing logic of their own personalities, and in the end from their own most persistent desires and needs.

It is no wonder, then, that the powerful man, the artist of self-overcoming, should be filled with a sudden surge of power by the conviction that the "slovenly wilderness" of the world (in Wallace Stevens's memorable phrase) has miraculously organized itself around him, like a picture around its center, rationally and harmoniously.* Like a prisoner who has escaped an intolerable fate, he is all at once free to rejoice in his assurance that the natural process of mutability and its corollary in the shifting and uncertain nature of human relationships no longer have any power over him.

Accordingly, it seems consistent that the conception of the "overman" which finally emerges in *Zarathustra* should have crystallized for Nietzsche at least partly as a result of the working of intense personal pressures on him during a particularly

---

* Nietzsche's characteristic tendency to represent the invigorating effects of art primarily in physiological terms, which is evident even in *The Birth of Tragedy*, is also illustrated by such later observations as the following (from a note of Spring Fall 1887 in *The Will to Power*): "Art reminds us of states of animal vigor; it is on the one hand an excess and overflow of blooming physicality into the world of images and desires; on the other, an excitation of the animal functions through the images and desires of intensified life;—an enhancement of the feeling of life, a stimulant to it."

agonizing period of his life: he was working feverishly on the book at a time when, according to his own account, his "lack of confidence" was "immense—everything I hear makes me feel that people despise me." His troubled relationship with Lou Andreas-Salomé was then, as he believed, "in its final and most painful throes," and it is evident that "the winter of 1882/83, when the first part of *Zarathustra* was written in Rapallo, and the summer of 1883, when he wrote Part II, in Sils Maria, were among the loneliest and most desperate periods in [Nietzsche's] life." A glimpse of Nietzsche's emotional state during this period is provided by a revealing letter of February 19, 1883, to Peter Gast, which reads in part as follows:

> This winter was the worst in my life; and I regard myself as the victim of a disturbance in *nature*. The old Europe of the Great Flood will kill me yet. . . . The enormous burden which lies on me as a result of the weather (even Etna is beginning to erupt!) has transformed itself into thoughts and feelings whose pressure in me was *terrible*; and from the sudden *shedding* of this burden, as a result of ten absolutely clear and fresh January days, my "Zarathustra" came into being, the most *liberated* of all my productions.

Like James's "lucid reflector," Nietzsche's "highest specimen" comes to occupy the center of his own world: as a result, everything in that world is, in one way or another, subordinated to him, and he possesses the power to confer significant value on persons and experiences which in themselves reveal none. The meaning of the world therefore becomes, to a remarkable extent, a function of his "taste" ("a blessed comprehensive name," in James's words, "for many of the things deepest in us"): his perceptions, discriminations, and evaluations establish the categories according to which the world must be understood. Its meaning is determined in relation to his own preferences. But though the world, on all its levels, is consequently envisioned as striving to fulfill his wishes, this way of seeing things, because it possesses no external metaphysical sanction, is not secure; it may be threatened at any moment by other points of view.

To the precise nature of this threat (which represents, to borrow one of James's favorite phrases in his later years, "the other side of the medal") and to some of its far-reaching consequences we now turn. But we may pause here long enough to note that the experience that both James and Nietzsche were describing (though in somewhat different ways) was the experience of ordering the world like God, who suffers in His profound, unending, matchless solitude the failure of humanity to reach that goal of total consciousness and responsibility which by definition He embodies and toward which (again by definition) it continually strives. Some of the darker strains concealed in this analogy may be detected in Zarathustra's speech "Upon the Blessed Isles." "But let me reveal my heart to you entirely, my friends," the exemplary philosopher observes: "*if* there were gods, how could I endure not to be a god! *Hence* there are no gods. Though I drew this conclusion, now it draws me."

IV
"Point of View" and Perspectivism

People who speak in this way have not learnt to understand you,
Wisdom of God, Light of our minds. They do not yet understand how the things are made which come to be in you and
through you. Try as they may to savour the taste of eternity,
their thoughts still twist and turn upon the ebb and flow of
things in past and future time. But if only their minds could be
seized and held steady, they would be still for a while and, for
that short moment, they would glimpse the splendour of eternity which is for ever still. They would contrast it with time,
which is never still, and see that it is not comparable. They
would see that time derives its length only from a great number
of movements constantly following one another into the past,
because they cannot all continue at once. But in eternity nothing
moves into the past: all is present. Time, on the other hand, is
never all present at once. The past is always driven on by the
future, the future always follows on the heels of the past, and
both the past and the future have their beginning and their end
in the eternal present. If only men's minds could be seized and
held still! They would see how eternity, in which there is neither
past nor future, determines both past and future time. Could
mine be the hand strong enough to seize the minds of men?
Could any words of mine have power to achieve such a task?

ST. AUGUSTINE   Confessions

1.

Over the years, much has been made of James's use of the "point of view" as an element of structure in his fiction, but discussions of this important matter have usually taken place in the context of more or less uncritical celebrations of James's impressive technique—which is seen to be on a par with his "symbolism," "imagery," "rhetoric," "irony," and "ambiguity"—and that technique, like many other aspects of this novelist's art, has unfortunately very often been considered *in vacuo*, as if it were somehow in itself a good thing to have, like one's health or money in the bank. Even so intelligent a treatment of James as that of Wayne C. Booth in his widely respected study of *The Rhetoric of Fiction* has at its heart a kind of deadness resulting from a general failure to take into account what might be called the philosophical content of the technique under examination: as a result of this failure, the discussion, which is clear and convincing in most other respects, is significantly lacking in a sense of the lively interaction between technical possibilities and the novelist's intention seen in its larger philosophical context, between the execution and the idea, between the various strategies and elements of technique adopted by the novelist and the underlying conception of experience which leads him to adopt them and which may then in its turn be reinforced by his having done so. While a particular style, for example, will tend to produce a certain way of looking at the world (one has only to think of the case of Hemingway in this connection), it is equally true that a certain way of looking at the world will result in a certain style—or at least a certain range of possible styles: technique and conception, in other words, often seem to generate and reinforce one another, and in the work of the most accomplished authors, technique may be seen to reflect—indeed almost to enact—the vision that it serves.

For Booth, however, the elements of fictional technique are pure and isolate and easily distinguishable, like the colors of the spectrum, and the way in which the range of these colors may be limited, the way in which they may be modified and combined in the palette of any particular artist, does not appear to be of much interest to him. As a consequence, his explanation of the function of any specific element of fictional technique is likely to resemble an obviously painstaking but finally rather bewildering attempt to describe a piece of ordinary furniture—a chair, say—to a visitor from another planet: one seems, that is, to be overhearing the description, and all at once one becomes aware of how much it diminishes his own experience of various kinds of chairs and the many unofficial uses to which they may be put in the world (by the lion tamer or the torturer or the political speechmaker, for instance)— some of which may be associated with pleasure or pain, to suggest only two of the most general contradictory possibilities. There is, moreover, a real question about the ultimate usefulness of such descriptions, especially if one is inclined to think that observing that Kafka's story "The Metamorphosis" affords an example of a narrator "more or less distant from the reader's own norms" (in this case "physically and emotionally" distant)—if this does not represent a studied ironic understatement—is a bit like saying that what distinguishes a Rembrandt masterpiece is the presence of the color brown.

It seems clear that the use of what is ostensibly the same technique by different artists—especially artists separated by a considerable distance in time—involves enormous changes in emphasis and implication: for example, the mosaics at Ravenna as well as many of the paintings of Manet contain central figures who fix the observer with their gaze, but the significance of that particular element of composition could hardly be said to be the same in both cases, since each of these artistic products is embodied in a context of motives (and expectations which, like motives, are to some extent also defined by the pressures of the historical moment) vastly different from that of its presumed counterpart, a context which is, in the last analysis, part of its meaning, and in relation to which all the separate elements of the composition must be seen if the precise significance of any one of them is to become clear. In short, the fact that an artist employs a particular technique is neither here nor there: what is significant is what he means by it.

Any reader familiar with more than a few of his works must come to realize that James's increasing reliance, especially in his later fiction, on "the register, ever so closely kept, of the consciousness" of a particular "signal specimen" as the center around which to organize the story, reflects some of the novelist's deepest concerns. Indeed, James himself attributed his frequent use of this "fine central intelligence" (as R. P. Blackmur calls it) to an "instinctive disposition" on his part; it was, he revealed, a method of composition to which he was powerfully drawn despite his clear awareness of the fact "that the novelist with a weakness for that ground of appeal is foredoomed to a well-nigh extravagant insistence on the free spirit. . . ." The person "affected with a certain high lucidity" eventually became for James not simply an exceptionally intelligent and sensitive fictional character with "a value intrinsic," but "a compositional resource . . . of the finest order." From the point of view of structure, placing such a character and the play of his impressions and reactions at the very center of the story obviously made for a unity and an intensity of focus which could not easily have been achieved by other means. But James's interest in such characters clearly extended beyond their structural uses, and it is highly significant that he ultimately came to see the "large lucid reflector" as no less than "the most polished of possible mirrors of the subject." The implications of this description will soon become apparent, but it is worth remarking at this point that the process of composition which corresponds to such a view of the "intense perceiver" consists essentially "in placing advantageously, placing right in the middle of the light" that most polished—and therefore most inclusive —of reflectors.

As a consequence of this method, the novelist, with "that magnificent and masterly *indirectness* which means the *only* dramatic straightness and intensity," appears to withdraw from the action, thus allowing the "intense perceiver" to discover the subject for himself and, in the process, to reveal it to the reader. The function of such characters as Lambert Strether, therefore ("*he* a mirror verily of miraculous silver" in James's estimation), is to create the story out of its particulars by gradually perceiving the full significance of the events in which he is involved; in this way he serves as that "central light" which brings out the full range of "values" (James often uses this term as a painter would in speaking of color) of the subject:

> To lift our subject out of the sphere of anecdote and place it in the sphere of drama, liberally considered, to give it dignity by extracting its finest importance, causing its parts to flower together into some splendid special sense, we supply it with a large lucid reflector, which we find only . . . in that mind and soul concerned in the business that have at once the highest sensibility and the highest capacity, or that are, as we may call it, most admirably agitated.

The degree to which the "lucid reflector" is actually to be "concerned in the business" James specifies in his Preface to *The Golden Bowl*, when he remarks upon "my preference for dealing with my subject-matter, for 'seeing my story,' through the opportunity and the sensibility of some more or less detached, some not strictly involved, though thoroughly interested and intelligent, witness or reporter, some person who contributes to the case mainly a certain amount of criticism and interpretation of it." Moreover, looking back over his collected works, he acknowledges that more often than not "the shorter things in especial that I have gathered into this Series have ranged themselves not as my own impersonal account of the affair in hand, but as my account of somebody's impression of it—the terms of this person's access to it and estimate of it contributing thus by some fine little law to intensification of interest."

The lucid reflector's gradually dawning awareness of the precise nature of his predicament thus becomes the central experience of James's fiction, and in this regard Morris Roberts is surely correct when he observes that "the lucid reflector is no mere technical device but the very substance of James's art." "It is," Roberts explains, "a character who is 'richly responsible' as well as 'finely aware,' the chief person in the story, and by the same stroke a triumph of method and a triumph of value. Its fineness creates the predicament upon which the story hangs, and in dealing with this predicament the character's lucidity and passion play upon and intensify each other. . . ." But the full implications of James's "mode of treatment"—the content, as it were, of his technique—are best grasped by R. P. Blackmur, who is frequently one of James's most brilliant (if at times also one of his most bewildering) interpreters. In his Introduction to the collected Prefaces, Blackmur elucidates with elegant economy and unusual directness James's seizure of "the possibility, which belonged to the novel alone, of setting up a fine central intelligence in terms of which everything in it might be unified and upon which everything might be made to depend":

> No other art could do this; no other art could dramatise the individual at his finest; and James worked this possibility for all it was worth. It was the very substance upon which the directed attention, the cultivated appreciation, might be concentrated.

And this central intelligence served a dual purpose, with many modifications and exchanges among its branches. It made a compositional centre for art such as life never saw. If it could be created at all, then it presided over everything else, and would compel the story to be nothing but the story of what that intelligence felt about what happened. This compositional strength, in its turn, only increased the value and meaning of the intelligence *as* intelligence, and *vice versa*.

Blackmur goes on to point out that "the plea for the use of such an intelligence as both an end and a means is constant throughout the Prefaces—as the proudest end and as the most difficult means." In sum, the "lucid reflector" in James's fiction represents, to Blackmur's mind, the simultaneous embodiment of end and means: seen with respect to its technical function, it is a means, a device which allows for the unfolding of the story with maximum effect, intensity, and energy; but it must also be seen as an end to the extent that it represents the ideal of intelligent perception in relation to which the lesser perceivers in the story are judged. In this sense, James's fiction actually does what it says, for the values it endorses are the same as those according to which it is constructed. The very process of reading the fiction therefore serves as an initiation into the reading of experience itself, and in both cases the only reader whose view is sufficiently deep and comprehensive is the "one on whom nothing is lost."

A word of qualification is necessary here, however. In "The Turn of the Screw," when the governess hands Mrs. Grose a letter explaining that Miles is not being invited back to school, that simple soul declines to take it, and observes, "Such things are not for me, Miss." What she means, of course, is that she can't read, and the clear implication is that she is incapable of grasping the amazing possibilities (whether they are illusory or not) that the governess sees in the situation. The governess reads very well; and as a consequence the reader of the tale, so carefully singled out and flattered in the framing sequence which precedes the presentation of the manuscript proper ("You'll understand. *You* will."), is inevitably engaged with her in the attempt to fathom the true character of the elusive experience. But it is possible that the governess's ability to read the world like a literary text full of hidden clues and concealed relationships is simply obsessive, leading her to see dark meanings in events and utterances that never conclusively lose their innocent aspect. And if her habit of mind is being criticized in this way, then so too is that of the clever reader: seen from this perspective, the story may be read as a cautionary tale which illustrates the potentially disastrous consequences of a pursuit of symbolic significance so intense that it looks right through the face of appearances in order to grasp a reality presumed to be hidden from view. A similar destructive possibility is represented in *The Beast in the Jungle*, in which John Marcher spends most of his time staring his fate (in the person of May Bartram) in the face and failing to get the point precisely because it is so apparent.

The critique of the potential misuses of the symbolic imagination which is suggested by these stories may be seen in a longer perspective if one views them in relation to Hawthorne's "Young Goodman Brown," a work in which the actual world loses its immediacy and is in effect exchanged for a shadowy vision of a witches' sabbath in which the most respected members of the community are imagined to participate. In both Hawthorne and James, there is a persistent fear that the tendency to read experience (individual or collective) like a text in order to extract symbolic meanings from it—a habit of mind ultimately associated with Puritanism—will become so all-consuming that the most pressing realities of one's existence, the nearest possibilities, will be rendered insubstantial and ungraspable. And it is worth remembering that in James's work failure to get the point that confronts one directly is often a matter of life and death (consider, in addition to the outcome in the works already touched on briefly here, the fate of the characters in "Daisy Miller" and "The Pupil").

2.

As we have seen, a good deal of the drama in James's fiction results from the conflict between the "lucid reflector" and that "penumbra" of persons "of comparative stupidity" surrounding him. Once the story is conceived as the demonstration of a "process of vision" (as James described *The Ambassadors*), the distinction between doing and seeing inevitably collapses and the struggle between the "intense perceiver" and the "fools" is moved, as might be expected, almost entirely to the level of perception. (Accordingly, as one of James's recent critics has pointed out, the novelist's "conviction that 'seeing' [an activity which is regarded as involving such qualities as a "reflective nature, sensitivity to impressions, analytical turn of mind, speculative propensities, and, above all, insatiable curiosity and capacity for appreciation"] could be an authentic rather than merely a vicarious form of 'being'—a form more intense and more valuable than any other—makes the observer a major Jamesian type.") Consequently, personal identity, which is usually defined through an overt clash of wills, is now defined through more complex acts of awareness. But it would be a serious mistake to suppose that the resulting perceptual struggle has become any less vehement or urgent: as will soon become clear, the act of perception was for James essentially an act of will, and what he saw as ultimately at stake in this struggle which for a lifetime consumed his finest energies was nothing less than the survival of individual personality.*

* Significantly, although James was theoretically inclined to grant the artist his own subjects and his own view of the world, in the case of his friend Paul Bourget it was precisely the novelist's vision that he attacked,

For if the individual personality is defined as a function of its perceptions of the world, which reflect its most characteristic instincts and inclinations, then the surrender of those perceptions becomes synonymous with the extinction of personality. ("Tell me what the artist is," James once observed, "and I will tell you of what he has been conscious"; the reverse, of course, is also true, and the relevance of the remark becomes apparent when one calls to mind Blackmur's important assertion that "as the artist is only a special case of the man, so his vision is only an emphatic image of the general human vision.") As a consequence, no matter how genteel and rarefied its outward forms, the continual conflict of "points of view" which occupies James's attention and is manifested by his technique has in the end all the force of a life and death struggle, and this surely helps to account for those apparently disproportionate energies which mysteriously break through the surface of exquisitely modulated Jamesian conversations every now and then, as well as that unmistakable air of menace, almost palpable at times, which may be detected as one character's "taste" (which James significantly defined as no less than the "active sense of life") clashes with that of another. And indeed, in James's view just as the self had to be defined (and defended) against the rush of undifferentiated experience by the ceaseless exercise of "taste," the activity of fine discrimination and evaluation which amounted to a continual reassertion of personality, so too one's

---

and his remarks in this connection are revealing: "I absolutely don't like this work. It's a pity—such a pity—she's a whore!—your manner of wishing to incarnate yourself each time in a prostitute—and to see men only as little hysterical, angry types who beat women with whom they sleep (and who deceive for them either husbands or lovers), or who try, like your detestable poet, to disfigure them. I speak with no false delicacy or hypocrisy; but your out-and-out eroticism displeases me as well as this exposition of dirty linen and dirty towels. In a word, all this is far from being life as I feel it, as I see it, as I know it, as I wish to know it."

own way of seeing the world had to be protected from what might be regarded as the onslaught of other, less comprehensive minds. (Percy Lubbock's observations about James's "adventures of perception and discrimination" are surely pertinent in this regard, and it seems especially significant that "not long before [James's] death he confessed that at last he found himself too much exhausted for the 'wear and tear of discrimination' "; "the phrase," as Lubbock is well aware, "indicates the strain upon him of the mere act of living.")

In the exemplary drama of perception imagined by James, then, the perceptions of the "lucid reflector" are continually threatened by opposing "points of view," and although that most unremittingly intelligent and sensitive of characters "almost demonically both sees and feels, while the others but feel without seeing," those others, coarser, shallower, more limited, apparently have—at least potentially—the power to "possess" him:

> Thus we get perhaps a vivid enough little example, in the concrete, of the general truth, for the spectator of life, that the fixed constituents of almost any reproducible action are the fools who minister, at a particular crisis, to the intensity of the free spirit engaged with them. The fools are interesting by contrast, by the salience they acquire, and by a hundred other of their advantages; and the free spirit, always much tormented, and by no means always triumphant, is heroic, ironic, pathetic or whatever . . . only through having remained free.

"Remaining free" in this context seems to involve successfully resisting the encroachments of others, or resisting what James, echoing Emerson, described early in his career as "the detestable tendency toward the complete effacement of privacy in life and thought everywhere so rampant with us nowadays." The "free spirit," that is to say, attempts to maintain his own ideas and ideal expectations, his own view of the world and the possibilities for personal development that it offers, in defiance of the cynical or ignorant debasement of values which in this view is indicated by complicity in the brutal way of the world. (This is, of course, the characteristic attitude of much of the nineteenth-century literature associated with Transcendentalism.) For in the world, all that is rare and fine is liable to be crushed by overpowering mindlessness, vulgarity, and grossness. By pitting himself against that world, the "free spirit," in James's view, is signifying his refusal to accept the conditions for "success" or even, as in the case of Milly Theale, survival—laid down by "the stupid, the coarse, and the blind." This is, as James was well aware, a very risky business, and the categorical refusal of the "free spirit" to demand any less of life than what is at any moment indicated by his own sense of its finest possibilities frequently results in his undoing: his growing melancholy, sometimes undeniably painful awareness of the exact costs entailed by his holding out for the ideal.

But no matter what its consequences, the effort of the "free spirit" is not, in James's estimation, futile and pathetic; it is never regarded simply as a hopeless flourish of nobility in the face of overwhelming vileness. Nor is it seen essentially as a pale and timorous gesture of self-protection, comparable to the warding off of an unavoidable and very likely mortal blow. On the contrary; for James the effort, despite its possibly misleading contrary appearance at times, represents a kind of *non serviam* hurled in the very teeth of actuality, a clear rejection of the dreary estimates of human possibility and the valueless prospects of the life lived from day to day in quiet desperation by the mass of men. What the "free spirit" wants instead is something "splendid" and "distinguished" (to use two of James's most characteristic words), and he will settle for nothing less. Quentin Anderson's observations linking James's recollections of his cousin Minny Temple with fictional heroines like Milly Theale are very much to the point here. "What is most striking about Minny as she appears in the reminiscences," Anderson remarks, "is her power, not her pathos, her unmeasured demand on life, not the shortness of her span. The pathos, the short run, these are treated as they are in Milly and Maggie, who, like Minny, are somehow life incarnate."

And indeed, although the "free spirit" may often be defeated in worldly terms, his values invariably emerge triumphant, for those values serve as the standard by which the apparent victors are judged and finally condemned. Even in the case of Milly Theale, the heroine of *The Wings of the Dove*, who is, as Blackmur observes, "actually killed by the conditions of life," the values of the "free spirit" come to dominate the shabby characters who have been circling her like birds of prey, ultimately souring their life together and turning the prize which they have sought for so long so unscrupulously to ashes in their mouths. In the end, both Merton Densher and Kate Croy stand deeply compromised and dishonored in their own eyes, for Milly has "stretched out her wings, and it was to *that* they reached. They cover us." Her values, in short, her exemplary qualities of heart and mind, provide the moral standard in relation to which Densher and Kate must come to measure and see themselves at last; and in this way those values, which have survived the assault of the two predators, survive death as well.

Moreover, when its language is understood in relation to the concluding scene of *The Wings of the Dove*, an extraordinary passage from one of James's strangest and most suggestive essays —and one of his most pertinent in the present context—assumes an unexpected significance. The essay, a contribution to a 1910 symposium on immortality, had been very little read and never reprinted until F. O. Matthiessen included it in his indispensable "group biography" and selection of writings from *The*

James Family in 1947; entitled "Is There a Life after Death?"
the essay closes with the following words:

> If I am talking, at all events, of what I "like" to think I may,
> in short, say all: I like to think it open to me to establish specu-
> lative and imaginative connections, to take up conceived pre-
> sumptions and pledges, that have for me all the air of not being
> decently able to escape redeeming themselves. And when once
> such a mental relation to the question as that begins to hover
> and settle, who shall say over what fields of experience, past
> and current, and what immensities of perception and yearning,
> it shall *not* spread the protection of its wings? No, no, no—I
> reach beyond the laboratory-brain.

That the values of the "free spirit"—e.g., exceptional intelligence, sensitivity to nuance, openness to impressions, curiosity,
great expectations—should be made to prevail no matter what
the fate of the particular character who embodies those values
is ensured by both the conception and the technical execution
of those numerous examples of James's fiction in which such
characters figure prominently. For just as the story is conceived
essentially as that of a distinguished person who is in many ways
really "too good for this world" (this phrase is actually applied
by James to young Morgan Moreen in "The Pupil"), a person
of remarkable discernment and high lucidity who is, like Fitzgerald's Gatsby with his "incorruptible dream," judged in relation to the other characters as "worth the whole damn bunch
put together," so too that story takes the form of a gradual un-
veiling to the discerning eye of what James once referred to as
"the full ironic truth" about the situation. Thus, the consciousness of the "lucid reflector" comes to serve a double function:
as we have seen, it is both end (the embodiment and source of
those exemplary values in relation to which the events and
characters of the fiction must be judged) and means (the process of continual implicit judgment by which those exemplary
values are revealed).

We may now observe that the two aspects of the "lucid reflector" bear a significant resemblance to the two fundamental aspects of the human being as Nietzsche conceived him: creature and creator, that which is subject to human limitations and that which is capable of transcending such limitations. To the extent that the "lucid reflector" is actually implicated in the human action of the story, he is continually threatened by the awareness that his "point of view" may simply be one of many possible (the nature of this threat, as has been suggested previously, is related to the fear of extinction of personality) and he is consequently involved in an ongoing struggle with other persons which involves his attempting, usually indirectly, often through innuendo, to get his "point of view," his construction of the situation, to prevail. But it is, after all, the characteristic vision of the "lucid reflector" which is wholly in control of the story, and he is therefore above the arena to the extent that he is not simply an actor but also the "vessel of consciousness" in which the action is contained. By definition, then, his evaluation is not simply one of many possible legitimate evaluations of the action; since he feels, sees, and understands so much more than anyone else his is the only finally comprehensive (the most "moral," if one applies this description in the sense that James is using it when he speaks of "the perfect dependence of the 'moral' sense of a work of art on the amount of felt life concerned in producing it"), the deepest construction possible of that particular combination of events and characters which constitutes the story in which he figures.

It is consequently possible, though no doubt excessively reductive, to view the Jamesian fiction as an elaborate mechanism for ensuring the eventual definitive triumph (in one form or another) of the "signal specimen" over that circle of the simple-minded and unappreciative in whose midst in actuality he is imprisoned; such a view might help at least to explain why James (a writer notoriously misunderstood and neglected by the general public, especially in his later life, as any cursory perusal of the sales figures for his books during this period—including *The Ambassadors, The Golden Bowl,* and finally the entire collected New York Edition—makes only too apparent) observed in himself such a growing sense of "authority," as well as "an immense increase—a kind of revelation—of freedom" whenever he engaged in the composition of fiction. But in the present context what is most important to remark about the "lucid reflector" is that whatever may happen to him in his "creature" aspect, his status as "creator" remains assured: his "point of view," that is, is not conceived by James as merely arbitrary; it is not simply one of the possible ways of seeing the story.

As James's notebook ruminations (as well as his formal recollections in the Prefaces) indicate, the unique relationship between the "lucid reflector" and the particular body of experience articulated in the story is essential to his conception. Indeed, "throughout the Prefaces," as Blackmur has noted, "the plea for the use of such [a fine central] intelligence . . . is constant," and again and again in the Notebooks James records his efforts at defining that single character of all the characters involved in the action of the particular story who would be capable of appreciating its implications fully. Finding that central intelligence which would correspond to the story to be told, which would capture all its nuances and gradually explore its buried revelations, thus became for James one of the chief problems to be resolved in the preliminary stages of composition, and it is to this initial process of testing and discovery that James is referring in his Preface to *The Princess Casamassima,* when, after distinguishing between the respective functions of the "consciousness . . . subject to fine intensification and wide enlargement" and "the gross fools, the headlong fools, the fatal fools," he observes:

This means, exactly, that the person capable of feeling in the given case more than another of what is to be felt for it, and so serving in the highest degree to *record* it dramatically and objectively, is the only sort of person on whom we can count not to betray, to cheapen or, as we say, give away, the value and beauty of the thing. By so much as the affair matters *for* some such individual, by so much do we get the best there is of it, and by so much as it falls within the scope of a denser and duller, a more vulgar and more shallow capacity, do we get a picture dim and meagre.

What is perhaps most striking about this passage is James's unexpected appeal to the notion of objectivity in a context in which he would seem to be describing a highly subjective view of "the given case." For James, as for Emerson, the more comprehensive and objective vision is achieved, paradoxically, through the most profound commitment to one's own distinctive subjectivity: the "full measure of truth" residing in a particular experience, far from revealing itself to detached and disinterested observation, can only be achieved through a profoundly interested relation, an intense form of "appreciation" which may be either pleasurable or painful but which is in any case available only to that person for whom the experience may be seen to count most.* This notion of "objectivity,"

* The bewildering moral difficulties produced by such a belief were clearly recognized by Conrad, who managed them with genius through a continual but subtle shifting of perspective. For Conrad, the profound gulf between the interested moral actor and the disinterested judge could never be bridged; there was no "objective" account of the experience to which both parties could agree, and this is of course what accounts for that extraordinarily revealing outburst which occurs near the beginning of *Lord Jim* (1900). Brought up before an official board of Inquiry "in the police court of an Eastern port," Jim takes in the scene: "The face of the presiding magistrate, clean shaved and impassable, looked at him deadly pale between the red faces of the two nautical assessors. The light of a broad window under the ceiling fell from above on the heads and shoulders of the three men, and they were fiercely distinct in the half-light of the big

which is clearly at odds with the basic impulse and theoretical pronouncements of literary realism and naturalism, is related to James's definition of the "lucid reflector" as that "most polished of possible mirrors of the subject," but it now becomes plain that for James the image of the subject thus projected is one in which "picture" and "idea" are "interfused"; the experience, that is, is not simply a preexistent given which is explored in all its aspects, but is in fact brought into being and rendered apprehensible by passing through the medium of the reflector's lively consciousness and taking on the colors and shades of his own deepest concerns. Experience fills the "vessel of consciousness" in the same way that water takes the shape of the container into which it is poured.

The consciousness of the "lucid reflector" as James conceives it is therefore both active and passive (just as the "lucid reflector" himself functions as both end and means): it creates as it records by ceaselessly weighing, selecting, and organizing the various aspects of the experience. As a consequence, what the consciousness serves "in the highest degree to *record*," it records—in James's significant formulation—both "dramatically and objectively," receiving impressions and working them into art by giving them distinctive form. But although it is fairly certain that it is to some such process as this that James is referring when he speaks of a consciousness which "records" experience "dramatically," his unusual use of the word "objectively" in this context, almost as it were in apposition to "dramatically," remains vaguely problematic and mysterious.

The mystery begins to clear somewhat when one consults a remarkably similar passage in Nietzsche's Meditation on History (the second of the *Unzeitgemässe Betrachtungen*) in

---

court-room where the audience seemed composed of staring shadows. They wanted facts. Facts! They demanded facts from him, as if facts could explain anything!"

which he expresses his views on a related point—the presumed "objectivity" of the historian (the novelist, James once maintained, must see himself "as an historian and his narrative as history"):

> Might not an illusion lurk in the highest interpretation of the word objectivity? We understand by it a certain standpoint in the historian, who sees the procession of motive and consequence too clearly for it to have an effect on his own personality. We think of the aesthetic phenomenon of the detachment from all personal concern with which the painter sees the picture and forgets himself, in a stormy landscape, amid thunder and lightning, or on a rough sea: and we require the same artistic vision and absorption in his object from the historian. But it is only a superstition to say that the picture given to such a man by the object really shows the truth of things. Unless it be that objects are expected in such moments to paint or photograph themselves by their own activity on a purely passive medium!
>
> But this would be a myth, and a bad one at that. One forgets that this moment is actually the powerful and spontaneous moment of creation in the artist, of "composition" in its highest form, of which the result will be an artistically but not an historically true picture. To think objectively, in this sense, of history is the work of the dramatist: to think one thing with another, and weave the elements into a single whole; with the presumption that the unity of plan must be put into the objects if it be not already there. So man veils and subdues the past, and expresses his impulse to art—but not his impulse to truth and justice. Objectivity and justice have nothing to do with each other. There could be a kind of historical writing that had no drop of common fact in it and yet could claim to be called in the highest degree objective.

At times the precise intent of Nietzsche's formulations here is difficult to grasp, but it seems clear enough that in the main what he is suggesting is that history, like art, is an activity involving "composition," and that the value of historical writing is therefore not solely a function of its thoroughness and accuracy—at least not in the ordinary use of those terms. The distressing implications of this general line of thinking become only too clear when one calls to mind the politically inspired wish-fulfillments which often present themselves as history in our time, not to mention the notorious "subjective" historiography of the Nazi era; and although Kaufmann characteristically attempts to exonerate Nietzsche on this latter score as well as on many others by protesting—with considerable justice, of course—that the philosopher's ideas were distorted and torn out of context, it is nevertheless significant, as the Harvard philosopher Stanley Cavell has remarked, that the Nazis did not become noticeably attached to the writings of John Stuart Mill.*

As the interesting fate in the world of ideas associated with Rousseau, Marx, Darwin, and Freud—as well as the New Testament—would appear to suggest, the abuses apparently invited by a particular body of ideas are often highly revealing; indeed, careful consideration of such abuses may be as essential to a complete understanding of the significance of a specific line of thought as is a detailed analysis of those texts in which the line of thought is first presented and developed. There is, moreover, no doubt that Nietzsche was well aware of the potentially dangerous character of his ideas from very early on: indeed, he took pride in their threatening aspect. In *Schopenhauer als Erzieher* (1874), quoting a passage from Emerson's "Circles" regarding the effect of revolutionary thinkers (the passage which appears in part at the head of the preceding chapter), Nietzsche observes: "If such thinkers are dangerous, it is clear why our academic thinkers are not dangerous; for their thoughts grow as peacefully in the fields of tradition as

* For further elaboration of the controversy involved here, the reader is directed to the Notes.

any tree ever bore its apples. They do not scare [*erschrecken*], they do not turn things upside down; and one could apply to all their strivings and efforts the words Diogenes used when someone praised a philosopher: 'What great achievements has he to show, he who has been philosophizing so long and has never *hurt* anybody?' The epitaph of university philosophy should read: 'It never hurt anybody.' "

In Nietzsche's view, the historian, if he is to be something more than an antiquarian collector, if he is to demonstrate his power to order experience, must extricate himself from an enormously burdensome relationship of passive fidelity to accumulated facts: beginning with "the presumption that the unity of plan must be put into the objects if it is not already there," the historian must go on to appropriate the past as the material out of which he creates a work of art. Only then, in Nietzsche's judgment, is it possible for the historian to achieve true objectivity, which is conceived as the result of his having deliberately infused the isolated facts with a coherent meaning, thereby raising past events to the level of general, exemplary significance. (The novelist, as James observes in a related context, "must know *man* as well as *men*, and to know man is to be a philosopher"; moreover, should the novelist be lacking in that philosophical capacity he will be "unable to prosecute those generalizations in which alone consists the real greatness of a work of art.")

Particular attention should be paid here to the fact that both Nietzsche and James associate "objectivity" with dramatic representation, for that association is obviously crucial to an understanding of their shared sense of the quality in question. James's devotion to dramatic values in his fiction is of course very well known, as is the fact that that devotion eventually led to the humiliating failure of *Guy Domville*, his last major attempt at writing for the stage. Not without reason, certainly, did Ezra Pound consider James "the victim and the votary of the 'scene' "; the Prefaces seem positively to ring with appeals for dramatic intensity, and Wayne Booth is undoubtedly right when he asserts that "there are times when we might, with Lubbock, think him entirely interested in the dramatic for its own sake, so often does he repeat his formula, 'Dramatize, dramatize!' " Flushed with the apparent provincial success of his dramatized version of *The American* and consequently feeling as though he had just "tasted blood," in 1891 (four years before his crushing theatrical failure) James himself announced to his brother William that he was finally sure of himself and now "c'est une rage (of determination to *do*, and triumph, on my part,) for I feel at least as if I had found my *real* form, which I am capable of carrying far, and for which the pale little art of fiction, as I have practised it, has been, for me, but a limited and restricted substitute. The strange thing is that I always, universally, knew *this* was my more characteristic form. . . ." And it is not until James comes to record his thoughts about *The Ambassadors* that he achieves the conviction that he has at last, in that novel, surpassed what he has always thought of as "the sum of all intensities": "the book," he asserts, "gathers an intensity that fairly adds to the dramatic . . . or that has at any rate nothing to fear from juxtaposition with it. I consciously fail to shrink in fact from that extravagance. . . ."

James's high valuation of dramatic technique is related to the possibilities which it affords for the direct presentation of events: in the dramatic scene experience appears unmediated and thus "the illusion of life," which James considered "the beginning and the end of the art of the novelist" and which he strove unremittingly to convey, is achieved with a singular economy and power. For him, as for Nietzsche, dramatic representation consists in the vivid bodying forth of a complex of relations which may be grasped immediately, a bright image of potential meanings completely realized, completely externalized by having been discharged, as it were, in the world of concrete physical appearances. In other words, more immediately than any other form, drama succeeds in revealing the general through the particular: it seizes the essential character and coherence of what may seem like ordinary isolated (and therefore by implication valueless) experiences and transforms those experiences before the beholder's eyes by intensifying them and endowing them with the aura of events enacted in the imagination. Like all fiction, then, but with greater immediacy because it presents us with actual persons visible before our eyes who are simultaneously apprehended as imaginary personages, drama succeeds in raising isolated, inconclusive experiences to the level of representative significance by converting commonplace facts into compelling metaphors.

So far as Nietzsche is concerned, the "real value" of history has to do with its ability to accomplish similar results, but he is quick to point out that what he has in mind is not simply the production of abstractions and general propositions of a kind that might bear the same relation to the record of events as the moral does to the end of a cautionary tale. Indeed, "if the value of a drama lay merely in its final scene," Nietzsche asserts, "the drama itself would be a very long, crooked and laborious road to the goal: and I hope history will not find its whole significance in general propositions, and regard them as its blossom and fruit." "On the contrary," he continues, "its real value lies in inventing ingenious variations on a probably commonplace theme, in raising the popular melody to a universal symbol and showing what a world of depth, power and beauty exists in it." But the ability to effect such a transformation presupposes an observer who stands at an ideal aesthetic distance from the experience he describes—that is, an observer who somehow remains above the experience without being altogether detached from it, a profoundly interested observer whose imagination is engaged by an event, not one who seeks to demonstrate his indifference to it:

> But this requires above all a great artistic faculty, a creative vision from a height. . . . Objectivity is so often merely a phrase. Instead of the quiet gaze of the artist that is lit by an inward flame, we have an affectation of tranquillity; just as a cold detachment may mask a lack of moral feeling. In some cases a triviality of thought, the everyday wisdom that is too dull not to seem calm and disinterested, comes to represent the artistic condition in which the subjective side has quite sunk out of sight. Everything is favoured that does not rouse emotion, and the driest phrase is the correct one. They go so far as to accept a man who is *not affected at all* by some particular moment in the past as the right man to describe it. This is the usual relation of the Greeks and the classical scholars. They have nothing to do with each other—and this is called "objectivity"!

For Nietzsche, then, as for James, the depth and comprehensiveness of the depiction are entirely dependent upon the quality of the recording consciousness; it is not surprising, then, that Nietzsche should go on to caution the reader not to "believe any history that does not spring from the mind of a rare spirit," thus echoing James's "axiom" for the aspiring young artist in fiction that "no good novel will ever proceed from a superficial mind." In this context, the more general conviction which follows for James deserves careful attention:

> There is one point at which the moral sense and the artistic sense lie very near together; that is in the light of the very obvious truth that the deepest quality of a work of art will always be the quality of the mind of the producer. In proportion as that intelligence is fine will the novel, the picture, the statue partake of the substance of beauty and truth.

The ultimate moral implications of James's evident identification of beauty and truth here will be considered presently; at
this point we may leave off with the observation that the view
expressed in this passage is intimately related to James's un-
abashed assertion that "as the picture is reality, so is the novel
history," and to his unyielding insistence that "literature is an
objective, a projected result; it is life that is the unconscious,
the agitated, the struggling, floundering cause."

3.

Ideally, in the vision of James's "lucid reflector," that "most
polished of possible mirrors of the subject" whose consciousness
serves to record "dramatically and objectively" all the nuances
of "the given case," things would appear exactly as they are:
their meaning, that is to say, would be at any given moment
fully revealed. In this respect, the "lucid reflector" corresponds
closely to Nietzsche's "supra-historical" man (discussed earlier),
"for whom the world is finished in every single moment and its
end attained." Moreover, just as Nietzsche soon came to realize
that the way of seeing things which he was proposing required
qualities that were ultimately superhuman, so too James recognized that for the "lucid reflector" really to see things as they
are would mean that he would have to grasp them in their past,
present, and future aspects simultaneously.

Though it has often been emulated by novelists, it is significant that such omniscience has traditionally been regarded in
the world of actual experience as a possibility available only to
God, in whose eternal vision, as Saint Augustine observes, "all
is present":

> It is in this way, then, that you mean us to understand your
> Word, who is God with you, God with God. . . . For your
> Word is not speech in which each part comes to an end when
> it has been spoken, giving place to the next, so that finally the

whole may be uttered. In your Word, all is uttered at one and the same time, yet eternally. If it were not so, your Word would be subject to time and change, and therefore would be neither truly eternal nor truly immortal. . . . For we know, O Lord, that the extent to which something once was, but no longer is, is the measure of its death; and the extent to which something once was not, but now is, is the measure of its beginning. Your Word, then, in no degree either gives place to anything or takes the place of anything, because it is truly immortal and eternal. Therefore it is by a Word co-eternal with yourself that you say all that you say; you say all at once and the same time, yet you say all eternally; and it is by this Word that all things are made which you say are to be made. You made them by your Word alone and in no other way. Yet the things which you create by your Word do not all come into being at one and the same time, nor are they eternal.

Among the effects produced by a passage of this kind is an emergent suspicion that the familiar convention of the "omniscient author" in fiction may require deeper analysis than it has usually received. Indeed, it is possible to argue that this authorial stance necessarily has religious implications, and that significant changes in its use (the various ways of limiting or undermining the authority of the narrator, for example), may accordingly serve as a valuable index of shifts in religious sensibility as well as in the area of more general philosophical belief.

For our present purposes, however, it is enough to observe that James's recognition of the fact that in a realistic fiction the presence of a totally lucid character (one whose perception of the situation would be, by implication, superhuman) would make for serious problems is not only of interest from the technical standpoint; it also serves to indicate James's clear desire to reserve, like God, certain prerogatives for himself as an author whose larger vision would inevitably exceed and frame that of his characters, no matter how lucid they might be.

It is in this way, in James's view, that the novelist maintains

his crucial "intellectual superiority" to those "elementary passions" in which his characters are embroiled and by means of
which they define themselves. Unlike his characters, "the author must understand what he is talking about," and it is finally
only he who possesses the vision of the whole. Indeed, just as
God and only God, all-perceiving and all-knowing, is in secure
possession of the secrets of the universe which He has made by
His "Word alone and in no other way," so too by virtue of his
perfect knowledge does the novelist rule over his own fictional
creation:

> . . . a large part of the very source of interest for the artist . . .
> resides in the strong consciousness of his seeing all for himself.
> He has to borrow his motive, which is certainly half the battle;
> and this motive is his ground, his site and his foundation. But
> after that he only lends and gives, only builds and piles high,
> lays together the blocks quarried in the deeps of his imagina-
> tion and on his personal premises. He thus remains all the
> while in intimate commerce with his motive, and can say to
> himself—what really more than anything else inflames and sus-
> tains him—that he alone has the secret of the particular case,
> he alone can measure the truth of the direction to be taken by
> his developed data. There can be for him, evidently, only one
> logic for these things; there can be for him only one truth and
> one direction—the quarter in which his subject most completely
> expresses itself. The careful entertainment of how it shall do
> so, and the art of guiding it with consequent authority—since
> this sense of "authority" is for the master-builder the treasure
> of treasures, or at least the joy of joys—renews in the modern
> alchemist something like the old dream of the secret of life.

Thus, the "intense perceiver" ultimately comes to be regarded as "the impersonal author's concrete deputy or delegate,
a convenient substitute or apologist for the creative power otherwise so veiled and disembodied." And indeed, the point is
driven home by the very nature of the language usually em-

ployed by James in describing the activity of the artist in fiction: whether he is referring to "the artist, the divine explanatory genius" or speaking of the "muffled majesty of authorship," perceiving "by the light of a heavenly ray" that "the province of art is all life, all feeling, all observation, all vision . . . all experience," or asserting his "power to guess the unseen from the seen, to judge the implication of things, to judge the whole piece by the pattern," the assumption of supernatural authority and cogency remains apparent. In terms only slightly less exalted, the artist is conceived by James to be the very type of the person "on whom nothing is lost," the person for whom "experience is never limited, and . . . never complete; it is an immense sensibility, a kind of huge spider web of the finest silken threads suspended in the chamber of consciousness, and catching every air-borne particle in its tissue. It is the very atmosphere of the mind; and when the mind is imaginative—much more when it happens to be that of a man of genius—it takes to itself the faintest hints of life, it converts the very pulses of the air into revelations."

The "triumph" of vision for such a person, as R. P. Blackmur has pointed out, consists "in the gradual inward mastery of the outward experience": he seeks to master his experience, that is, by bringing it fully into consciousness, and as a result he becomes increasingly involved in efforts to achieve the ultimate refinement of perception, "a view of *all* the dimensions." Indeed, as James observes of his own "incorrigible taste for gradations and super-positions of effect," he is virtually "addicted to seeing 'through'—one thing through another, accordingly, and still other things through *that*," so that finally, "he takes, too greedily perhaps, on any errand, as many things as possible by the way. It is after this fashion that he incurs the stigma of labouring uncannily for a certain fulness of truth—truth diffused, distributed and, as it were, atmospheric." No doubt it is this relentless pursuit of the horizon of consciousness that prompted A. R. Orage's significant remark that James "was in love with the next world, or the next state of consciousness; he was always exploring the borderland between the conscious and the super-conscious."

James himself more than once confesses his extreme delight with the pursuit of suggestions and hints of far-reaching significance occasionally let slip inadvertently by reality; in the Preface to *The Ambassadors,* for instance, he observes: "No privilege of the teller of tales and the handler of puppets is more delightful, or has more of the suspense and the thrill of a game of difficulty breathlessly played, than just this business of looking for the unseen and the occult, in a scheme half-grasped, by the light or, so to speak, by the clinging scent, of the gage already in hand. No dreadful old pursuit of the hidden slave with bloodhounds and the ray of association can ever, for 'excitement,' I judge, have bettered it at its best." And yet to the "constant and vast majority of men," in James's estimation, life "in the way of intelligible suggestion says nothing."

Still, there are "persons of a fine sensibility . . . whose innermost spirit, experience has set vibrating," and the function of such persons in the world is regarded as unique. For it is precisely on account of the existence of such persons that James pronounces it "conceivable that the possibility" of personal immortality "may vary from man to man, from human case to human case, and that the quantity or the quality of our practice of consciousness may have something to say to it"; indeed, he goes on to conclude (numbering himself, not unexpectedly, among such persons) that "in proportion as we (of the class I speak of) enjoy the greater number of our characteristic inward reactions, in proportion as we do curiously and lovingly, yearningly and irrepressibly, interrogate and liberate, try and test and explore, our general productive and, as we like conveniently to say, creative awareness of things . . . in that proportion does our function strike us as establishing sublime relations."

In all likelihood, William James would have been entirely in agreement with such pronouncements and would have shared the sense that immortality may be a function of the power of consciousness (which helps to explain his increasing interest in psychic phenomena); and significantly, both brothers would have been able to cite precedents in Emerson for their beliefs. In 1903, on the occasion of the centenary of Emerson's birth, William James delivered an address at Concord in the course of which he observed of his mentor that "through the individual fact there ever shone for him the effulgence of the Universal Reason. The great Cosmic Intellect terminates and houses itself in mortal men and passing hours. Each of us is an angle of its eternal vision, and the only way to be true to our Maker is to be loyal to ourselves. . . . If the individual open thus directly into the Absolute, it follows that there is something in each and all of us, even the lowliest, that ought not to consent to borrowing traditions and living at second hand. . . . In seeing freshly," James went on, "and not in hearing of what others saw, shall a mind find what truth is. . . . 'Other world! there is no other world.' All God's life opens into the individual particular, and here and now, or nowhere, is reality. . . . Be how it may, then," he concludes, "this is Emerson's revelation: The point of any pen can be an epitome of reality; the commonest person's act, if genuinely actuated, can lay hold on eternity. This vision is the headspring of all his outpourings; and it is for this truth, given to no previous literary artist to express in such penetratingly persuasive tones, that posterity will reckon him a prophet. . . . His life was one long conversation with the invisible divine, expressing itself through individuals and particulars: 'So nigh is grandeur to our dust, so near is God to man!' "

For his own part, Henry James is fully aware of the fact that the "creators" he has in mind (to use the Nietzschean term for persons possessing such ultimately superhuman potentialities) would be something of an anomaly in the terms of realistic fiction, and accordingly he recognizes in his own preferred treatment of character "the danger of filling too full any supposed and above all any obviously limited vessel of consciousness." It is therefore in the interest of preserving the indispensable "air of reality," "the illusion of life," that James is obliged to place limits on the awareness of his "intense perceivers":

> If persons either tragically or comically embroiled with life allow us the comic or tragic value of their embroilment in proportion as their struggle is a measured and directed one, it is strangely true, none the less, that beyond a certain point they are spoiled for us by this carrying of a due light. They may carry too much of it for our credence, for our compassion, for our derision. They may be shown as knowing too much and feeling too much—not certainly for their remaining remarkable, but for their remaining "natural" and typical, for their having the needful communities with our own precious liability to fall into traps and be bewildered.

As we have seen, however, the very process of ordering the fiction is a recurring triumph over the possibilities of bewilderment. In this way, the author is able to maintain at all times his superiority over even the most lucid of his characters, and his relationship to them consequently reflects a sustained dramatic irony: he is always far ahead of them, more fully conscious of the nature of the circumstances in which they are (to varying degrees) "embroiled." No doubt this accounts for the reader's occasionally vexing sense that there is nothing in the story which is beyond the author's understanding or control; but the scheme has a more far-reaching significance. For as James conceives the novel, the author's comprehensive awareness serves as the larger frame within which the account of the more or less unsuccessful efforts of individual characters to unravel the tangle of their lives is finally placed. As a consequence, there is a continuous implicit comparison between the limited "points of view" of particular persons and what may be characterized as the impersonal, all-inclusive point of view, which does not simply exemplify one of the degrees of lucidity represented as humanly possible by the story—for it lies always just beyond the reach of the capacities of even the most intense perceiver—but which remains at all times an unattainable ideal of total clarity and refinement of perception. In its own terms, then, the story represents the transcendence over personal limitations of vision even as it demonstrates that such transcendence is humanly impossible.

The celebrated technical achievement of the Jamesian novel thus reveals itself to be an essential function of the novel's philosophical import, for by suggesting, if only by implication, that the ideal goal of "a view of *all* the dimensions" of the situation has been attained at least by the author, who remains in precise control of all the movements of his characters—movements which he not only fully understands but which, indeed, form the very basis of his "demonstration" (consider, by way of contrast here, the examples of Thomas Hardy and Dostoevsky)—James is able to overcome and augment the partial views available to the individual characters; consequently, the novel finally succeeds in justifying itself to the extent that it "does attempt to represent life" in its most complete aspect, an endeavor that James regarded as "the only reason for the existence of a novel," and which in his view served to make it "under the right persuasion, the most independent, most elastic, most prodigious of literary forms."

4.

The development of James's thinking on the general matter of literary perspective is worth some attention, and his remarks on Maupassant (contained in an essay on that author first published in the *Fortnightly Review* for March of 1888 and reprinted later in the same year in *Partial Portraits*) are particularly instructive here. Reflecting on Maupassant's "little disquisition on the novel in general, attached to that particular example of it which he has just put forth [*Pierre et Jean*, 1888]," James makes the observation that no single literary form can be regarded as in itself possessing any absolute validity—much less an automatic superiority over other forms—inasmuch as "there are simply as many different kinds [of fiction] as there are persons practising the art, for if a picture, a tale, or a novel be a direct impression of life (and that surely constitutes its interest and value), the impression will vary according to the plate that takes it, the particular structure and mixture of the recipient." James makes essentially the same point elsewhere, perhaps most fully in his Preface to *The Portrait of a Lady*, written for the New York Edition some twenty years after the Maupassant essay:

> The house of fiction has . . . not one window, but a million—a number of possible windows not to be reckoned, rather; every one of which has been pierced, or is still pierceable, in its vast front, by the need of the individual will. These apertures, of dissimilar shape and size, hang so, all together, over the human scene that we might have expected of them a greater sameness of report than we find. They are but windows at the best, mere holes in a dead wall, disconnected, perched aloft; they are not hinged doors opening straight upon life. But they have this mark of their own that at each of them stands a figure with a pair of eyes, or at least with a field-glass, which forms, again and again, for observation, a unique instrument, insuring to the person making use of it an impression distinct from every other. *He and his neighbours are watching the same show, but one seeing more where the other sees less, one seeing black where the other sees white, one seeing big where the other sees small, one seeing coarse where the other sees fine.* And so on, and so on;

there is fortunately no saying on what, for the particular pair of eyes, the window may *not* open; "fortunately" by reason, precisely, of this incalculability of range. The spreading field, the human scene, is the "choice of subject"; the pierced aperture, either broad or balconied or slit-like and low-browed, is the "literary form"; but they are, singly or together, as nothing without the posted presence of the watcher—without, in other words, the consciousness of the artist. Tell me what the artist is, and I will tell you of what he has *been* conscious. Thereby I shall express to you at once his boundless freedom and his "moral" reference. [Some italics added.]

At first glance, these remarks, taken in their broadest sense, appear to suggest that there is no "objective" way of verifying the accuracy of any impression of "the spreading field" of reality; but if we examine the passage more closely it becomes clear that such a view is significantly undercut by James's evident conviction that one artist—the type of the person of high consciousness and refined sensibility—by virtue of the intensity of his perceptions succeeds in seeing more than his squinting neighbors do (presumably from their "slit-like and low-browed" apertures) of what is in fact actually and demonstrably out there, apprehensible in one degree or another to them all. This extremely important contradiction is reflected precisely in the inconsistent series of contrasts provided by James between the person "seeing more where the other sees less, one seeing black where the other sees white, one seeing big where the other sees small, one seeing coarse where the other sees fine": "black" and "white" are surely qualities which differ in kind from "more" and "less," in the same way that "big" and "small" differ from "coarse" and "fine." The opposition between these two kinds of qualities is ultimately related to that between the two conflicting conceptions of the relationship of art to truth maintained by both James and Nietzsche; for our purposes at the moment, however, it is enough to perceive that the contradiction which surfaces in the passage cited is mirrored by the characteristic divided intention—or double impact—of James's style. That style, very much like that of the painter Sargent, his contemporary, occupies a middle ground between the cultivation of stylistic particularity and the attempt at absolute fidelity to a reality of things undeniably *there* ("The real," James once observed, "represents to my perception the things we cannot possibly *not* know, sooner or later, in one way or another"): it is a style which strives for impersonality even as it strives to be an unmistakable, inimitable expression of a distinctive sensibility, a style at once realistic and insistently inventive. To the extent that concrete realities (like physical objects of specifiable colors and dimensions) are taken to exist "out there," the style presents itself as passive, a faithful record of the ways of the world of external phenomena; but to the extent that what is out there is regarded as a function of the contents of the particular consciousness, the style takes on the aspect of an assertion of imaginative power.

The issue here—and it is one to which we shall be returning—is perhaps best articulated by William James in an unforgettable passage in an essay of 1878 entitled "Remarks on Spencer's Definition of Mind as Correspondence"; in that essay, the American philosopher asserts:

I, for my part, cannot escape the consideration, forced upon me at every turn, that the knower is not simply a mirror floating with no foot-hold anywhere, and passively reflecting an order that he comes upon and finds simply existing. The knower is an actor, and coefficient of the truth on one side, whilst on the other he registers the truth which he helps to create. Mental interests, hypotheses, postulates, so far as they are bases for human action—action which to a great extent transforms the world—help to *make* the truth which they declare. In other words, there belongs to mind, from its birth upward, a spontaneity, a vote. It is in the game, not a mere looker-on; and its judgments of the *should-be*, its ideals, cannot be peeled off from the body of the *cogitandum* as if they were excrescences, or meant, at most, survival. We know so little about the ultimate nature of things, or of ourselves, that it would be sheer folly dogmatically to say that an ideal rational order may not be real. *The only objective criterion of reality is coerciveness, in the long run, over thought.* [Italics added.]

Neither Henry James nor Nietzsche would have been deaf to the challenge implicit in that concluding sentence; and that William James was himself inclined to consider the possibility of a test of strength between consciousness and the presumably irresistible facts of material existence is suggested by his own later preoccupation with psychic phenomena and the question of personal immortality. But in our immediate context what is perhaps most compelling about the observations quoted is their general applicability to the novelistic enterprise as conceived by Henry James. In the Jamesian novel, the view of reality available to even the most lucid of reflectors is determined by his own limitations: what he takes in is a reflection of his particular situation in the world, an image which is to a considerable extent produced by his own strengths and inadequacies. But the novelist himself stands above such limitations and potential illusions, and his view of things—in contrast to that of his characters—is not simply a function of his temperament, no matter how rich and comprehensive. To the extent that he succeeds, in James's terms, the novelist presents us with a complete and unobstructed vision of nothing less than the world as it is, the world as it would be apprehended by the ultimate perceiver, God. This world reveals itself to be a perfect mirror-image of the supremely powerful consciousness, and (as in Emerson) consciousness comes to be regarded as the spiritual analogue of the material world.

Although James indicates in his essay on Maupassant that

he is willing to assent to the French writer's contention "that any form of the novel is simply a vision of the world from the stand-point of a person constituted after a certain fashion, and that it is therefore absurd to say that there is, for the novelist's use, only one reality of things," he goes on to qualify his assent by noting that this claim "seems to me commendable, not as a flight of metaphysics, hovering over bottomless gulfs of controversy, but, on the contrary, as a just indication of the vanity of certain dogmatisms." James is here understandably assimilating Maupassant's position to his own familiar argument that the individual artist be allowed his characteristic view of the world, for in his judgment it is not the nature of the particular impression of life which should be at issue for the critic; instead, the critic's business should begin with an acknowledgment of the proposition that "the value of the artist resides in the clearness with which he gives forth that impression." Summarizing Maupassant's position in his own language, James affirms that "the particular way we see the world is our particular illusion about it . . . and this illusion fits itself to our organs and senses; our receptive vessel becomes the furniture of *our* little plot of the universal consciousness." (This last is an impressively Emersonian formulation, especially if one remembers that for Emerson consciousness is finally indivisible, and each individual has his own distinctive access to the universal mind.) James then goes on to quote, with evident approval, the following significant passage from Maupassant:

> How childish, moreover, to believe in reality, since we each carry our own in our thought and in our organs. Our eyes, our ears, our sense of smell, of taste, differing from one person to another, create as many truths as there are men upon earth. And our minds, taking instruction from these organs, so diversely impressed, understand, analyse, judge, as if each of us belonged to a different race. Each one of us, therefore, forms

for himself an illusion of the world, which is the illusion poetic, or sentimental, or joyous, or melancholy, or unclean, or dismal, according to his nature. And the writer has no other mission than to reproduce faithfully this illusion, with all the contrivances of art that he has learned and has at his command. The illusion of beauty, which is a human convention! The illusion of ugliness, which is a changing opinion! The illusion of truth, which is never immutable! The illusion of the ignoble, which attracts so many! The great artists are those who make humanity accept their particular illusion. Let us, therefore, not get angry with any one theory, since every theory is the generalized expression of a temperament asking itself questions.

Although it is unlikely that he knew this passage, the assertions contained within it correspond at so many points to Nietzsche's own expressed convictions that it might be of some use in helping to explain Nietzsche's singling out of Maupassant (in *Ecce Homo*) as "one of the strong race, a genuine Latin toward whom I am well disposed."

For his part, James observed of the passage that what was most interesting about it was "not that M. de Maupassant happens to hold that we have no universal measure of the truth," but rather that his assertions constituted "the last word on a question of art from a writer who is rich in experience and has had success in a very rare degree." And although James considers it "of secondary importance that our impression should be called, or not called, an illusion"—a judgment in which both William James and Nietzsche would surely have concurred—he is nevertheless grateful for the clarity of Maupassant's affirmation of the notion that the artist's "particular organism constitutes a case, and the critic is intelligent in proportion as he apprehends and enters into that case." Proceeding to suggest a calculus of critical judgments corresponding to that premise, James declares that "a case is poor when the cluster of the artist's sensibilities is small, or they themselves are wanting in keenness, or else when the personage fails to admit them—either through ignorance, or diffidence, or stupidity, or the error of a false ideal—to what may be called a legitimate share in his attempt."

It is significant that the artistic limitations sketched out by James here correspond to limitations which define individual characters in his fiction. The notion of the "case," in James's own literary theory and practice, usually applies to that character whose instincts and predispositions, strengths and weaknesses of perception, combine most effectively to bring out the potential complications and "values" of the chosen subject. In the fully developed novel as James conceives it—in contrast to the "tale," which is intended as a more limited form of "demonstration"—there may be numerous such "cases," of course, persons of differing constitution whose conceptions of the world (as indicated by their divergent estimates and expectations regarding the particular situation in which they find themselves) are in essential conflict; indeed, that conflict usually serves as the central issue of the fiction, which may thus in itself be seen as exemplifying a relentless pursuit and process of refinement of its own implications. But it is essential to keep in mind that the partial views of the situation which are achieved by the particular "cases" attempting to grasp it in its full dimensions are not simply combined in that vision of the whole which is available to the author. His vision finally represents more than a composite of the limited views of the characters: it not only exceeds theirs, but is of another order entirely.

As a consequence, it is not surprising that James eventually comes to regard the novel as the only literary form which is able to transcend its own limitations, for as he conceives it, the novel fulfills its grandest function and succeeds in working its finest meaning to the extent that it embodies a movement from the potential chaos of clashing perspectives available to individual persons "constituted after a certain fashion"—a fashion which determines to a considerable degree their view of their situation—to the essential, unchallengeable unity and wholeness of vision possessed by an author somehow finally removed from the arena of perceptual struggle. And indeed it is to just such a triumph of vision that James is referring (in his Preface to *The Portrait of a Lady*) when he speaks of "the high price of the novel as a literary form—its power not only, while preserving that form with closeness, to range through all the differences of the individual relation to its general subject-matter, all the varieties of outlook on life, of disposition to reflect and project, created by conditions that are never the same from man to man (or, so far as that goes, from man to woman), but positively to appear more true to its character in proportion as it strains, or tends to burst, with a latent extravagance, its mould."

5.

James's conception of the novel thus manifests an intense concern with the precise rendering of human particularities and characteristics of personality at the same time as it reflects a striving to exceed the limits of individual personality and to be free of personal identity entirely. This fusion of apparently contradictory concerns calls to mind William James's assertion with respect to Emerson that "his life was one long conversation with the invisible divine, expressing itself through individuals and particulars," as well as Henry James's related allusion to "the curiously generalized way, as if with an implicit protest against personalities, in which [Emerson's] intercourse, epistolary and other, with his friends was conducted." Significantly, a similar combination of impulses appears to be common to all the writing Jameses, whose powerful (if occasionally indi-

rect) assertions of selfhood—manifested by an underlying fero-
cious insistence on distinctive qualities of temperament and
sensibility—are matched by equally powerful yearnings for an
ideal selflessness. (F. W. Dupee's summation of the peculiar
moral policy of the family with respect to individual identity
seems very much to the point here. "An experiment in the nurture of a radical morality," Dupee observes, "the family discipline consisted in cultivating ego and conscience simultaneously.") This alternation between self-assertion and self-denial
often reveals itself in unexpected and unsettling remarks, and
it may surface in any one of a variety of ways. At times, for instance, it takes the form of a tendency to regard other members
of the family as secret enemies whose achievements constitute
acts of aggression, indeed threats directed against one's very
life; in this case, feelings of hostility are turned inward against
oneself and then expressed, as in the following passage from
the diary of that extraordinary invalid Alice James, with characteristic irony (predictably the family mode):

> Within the last year [Henry] has published *The Tragic Muse*,
> brought out *The American* [as a drama], and written a play,
> *Mrs. Vibert* . . . and his admirable comedy; combined with
> William's *Psychology*, not a bad show for one family! especially
> if I get myself dead, the hardest job of all. . . .

At other times, however, this alternation—which is paral-
leled by the swing from feelings of supreme confidence to feelings of utter helplessness and despair periodically experienced
by all the members of the family—appears in expressions of
deep personal animus which are all the more remarkable for
being couched in language directly antithetical to their sense.
Consider, in this context, the following observations from a
valuable essay by Cushing Strout on "William James and the
Twice-Born Sick Soul":

The sickness in this family [Strout is here referring to the tendency to hypochondria as well as other ailments with apparent
psychological components] gives deeper meaning to [Ralph
Barton] Perry's innocent remark about the James household
that "the region of family life was not empty, but was charged
with palpable and active forces." There is a strong hint of sup-
pressed hostility in Alice James's confession that in her hysteria
she sometimes felt "a violent inclination" to throw herself out
of the window or "knock . . . off the head of the benignant
Pater, as he sat, with his silver locks, writing at the table." The
same point could be made of the benign father's remark to
Emerson that he "wished sometimes that lightning would
strike his wife and children out of existence, and he should suffer no more from loving them."

The full significance of the curious linguistic form of such
remarks as those cited here by Strout will be the subject of some
speculation in the concluding sections of this study; at this
point, however, it may prove useful to juxtapose these remarks
of Alice James and Henry James, Sr. with two observations by
Nietzsche which seem to engage the issue. The first is from
a section of *The Gay Science* (1882) entitled "In Honour of
Shakespeare," and it is concerned with Nietzsche's startlingly
unorthodox reading of the character of Brutus in the play *Julius Caesar:*

> The best thing I could say in honour of Shakespeare *the man,*
> is that he believed in Brutus, and cast not a shadow of suspi-
> cion on the kind of virtue which Brutus represents! It is to him
> that Shakespeare consecrated his best tragedy—it is at present
> still called by a wrong name,—to him, and to the most terrible
> essence of lofty morality. Independence of soul!—that is the
> question at issue! No sacrifice can be too great there: one must
> be able to sacrifice to it even one's dearest friend, although he
> be the grandest of men, the ornament of the world, the genius
> without peer,—if one really loves freedom as the freedom of
> great souls, and if *this* freedom be threatened by him:—it is
> thus that Shakespeare must have felt! The elevation in which

he places Caesar is the most exquisite honour he could confer upon Brutus; it is thus only that he lifts into vastness the inner problem of his hero, and similarly the strength of soul which could cut this knot!—

It will be useful to recall the sentiments expressed here later, when the time comes to trace out some of the underlying assumptions of *The Golden Bowl*.

The second passage bearing on the present point is from *The Case of Wagner* (1888), and it contains some of Nietzsche's most penetrating and unsettling reflections on the character of love. As he is careful to indicate, what Nietzsche has in mind here is "love translated back into nature"—love of that agonistic variety which may be discerned as an element deeply and actively involved in the Heraclitean strife of nature. "Not the love of a 'higher virgin'!" Nietzsche declares, "but love as *fatum*, as fatality, cynical, innocent, cruel—and precisely in this a piece of nature. That love which is war in its means, and at bottom the deadly hatred of the sexes!" He then proceeds to a series of assertions regarding Bizet's *Carmen*, an opera to which he was passionately attached:

> I know no case where the tragic joke that constitutes the essence of love is expressed so strictly, translated with equal terror into a formula, as in Don José's last cry, which concludes the work:
>   "Yes, *I* have killed her,
>   I—my adored Carmen!"
> Such a conception of love (the only one worthy of a philosopher) is rare: it raises a work of art above thousands. For on the average, artists do what all the world does, even worse—they misunderstand love. . . . They believe one becomes selfless in love because one desires the advantage of another human being, often against one's own advantage. But in return for that they want to *possess* the other person.—Even God does not constitute an exception at this point. He is far from thinking, "What is it to you if I love you?"—he becomes terrible when

one does not love him in return. *L'amour*—this saying remains true among gods and men—*est de tous les sentiments le plus égoiste, et par conséquent, lorsqu'il est blessé, le moins généreux.* (B. Constant.)

To grasp some of the emotional implications of such a view, as well as the kinds of irony it is likely to produce, one has only to recall Ralph Barton Perry's splendid observation that the "amiable ferocity" of Henry James, Sr. "was an exercise in contempt for selfhood, on his own part and in behalf of others."

The tangled, shifting relationship of selfhood, selfishness, and selflessness remains one of Nietzsche's most compelling concerns throughout his effective career, and it is important to remember that that same relationship serves as the central focus of all three of the novels of James's so-called "major phase." The subject first emerges for Nietzsche as one requiring sustained investigation in *The Birth of Tragedy* (1872), the earliest work of his maturity. In that work, questions related to personal identity and the potential loss of self are addressed to the experience of Greek tragedy, which produces in the spectator a response in which joy and terror mingle. Confronted by that overpowering drama, as Nietzsche conceives it, the spectator finds himself temporarily swept up in that Dionysian *Rausch* which represents the obliteration of the *principium individuationis*, the extinction of individual personality; he is seized by a rapture which involves "the annihilation of ordinary bounds and limits of existence." Accordingly, in Nietzsche's view, "the most immediate effect of the Dionysian tragedy" is "that the state and society and, quite generally, the gulfs between man and man, give way to an overwhelming feeling of unity leading back to the very heart of nature."

A remarkably similar experience is described by Emerson in

a stunning formulation added to his first book, *Nature* (1836), in its second version (1847): "Crossing a bare common, in snow puddles, at twilight, under a clouded sky, without having in my thoughts any occurrence of special good fortune, I have enjoyed a perfect exhilaration. I am glad to the brink of fear." And Emerson goes on to specify the implications of such experiences in terms highly reminiscent of those employed by Nietzsche: "Standing on the bare ground—my head bathed by the blithe air and uplifted into infinite space—all mean egotism vanishes. I become a transparent eyeball; I am nothing; I see all; the currents of the Universal Being circulate through me; I am part or parcel of God. The name of the nearest friend sounds then foreign and accidental: to be brothers, to be acquaintances, master or servant, is then a trifle and a disturbance. I am the lover of uncontained and immortal beauty. In the wilderness, I find something more dear and connate than in streets and villages."

To drive home his point regarding the escape from personal identity, Nietzsche goes on to cite a tradition, which he regards as "undisputed," that "Greek tragedy in its earliest form had for its sole theme the sufferings of Dionysus and that for a long time the only stage hero was Dionysus himself." Such a tradition, he argues, may be taken as evidence for his claim that the intense preoccupation with the torn and dismembered god suggests, among other things, "that this dismemberment, the properly Dionysian *suffering,* is like a transformation into air, water, earth, and fire, and that we are therefore to regard the state of individuation as the origin and primal cause of all suffering, as something objectionable in itself." Nietzsche then evokes the hope of a "rebirth of Dionysus, which we must now dimly conceive as the end of individuation," and insists that "it is this hope alone that casts a gleam of joy upon the features of a world torn asunder and shattered into individuals." And "this view of things," Nietzsche concludes, "already provides us with all the elements of a profound and pessimistic view of the world, together with the *mystery doctrine of tragedy*: the fundamental knowledge of the oneness of everything existent, the conception of individuation as the primal cause of evil, and of art as the joyous hope that the spell of individuation may be broken in augury of a restored oneness."

The judgment of individuation as "the primal cause of evil" is, of course, qualified to a considerable degree even in *The Birth of Tragedy* by Nietzsche's conception of the complementary relationship in the emerging drama between the Apollonian *principium individuationis*, the "form-giving" power which succeeds in establishing—among other things—the limits by which we define ourselves, and the Dionysian energy erupting in a frenzy of overreaching. Similarly, in the later philosophy the lament over individuation appears to be counterbalanced by the celebration of the powerful individual, the superman. These disjunctive estimates, however, are not as contradictory as they might at first appear. The question here would seem to be one of emphasis: in the later works, Nietzsche still clearly accepts unequivocally the view of the world as a place of strife and dismemberment through individuation, only now, given that state of affairs, he is attempting to envision a human creator who would be emotionally comprehensive and commanding enough to compel the world into oneness. Indeed, even in *The Birth of Tragedy* Nietzsche makes this point when he pays homage to "the heroic effort of the individual to attain universality, in the attempt to transcend the curse of individuation and to become the *one* world-being. . . ."

It is clear, therefore, that from first to last Nietzsche regards individuation (especially in relation to personal identity) as a painful burden, for each thing in the world "has to suffer for its individuation, being merely a single one beside another." What

is most significant, however, is how at various stages in his philosophical development Nietzsche imagines that it may be possible to overcome this fundamental limitation and achieve at
last the feeling (familiar to readers of Emerson) that it is one's
own heart and no other that beats at the very center of the cosmos. In his later works, he maintains the possibility of achieving
such a conviction by projecting varieties of the superman, the
individual of supremely powerful will capable of serving as the
focus around which the universe, as if obeying an unspoken
wish, comes to organize itself. In *The Birth of Tragedy*, however, it is not the supreme assertion of selfhood but the "shattering of the individual" which is regarded as the means to the
same end; in this case, the extinction of personal identity results in a "fusion with primal being" which ultimately leads to
the experience of "the metaphysical comfort that life is at the
bottom of things, despite all the changes of appearances, in-
destructibly powerful and pleasurable. . . ."

Certain aspects of William James's thinking are instructive
here—his notion of "indeterminism," for example. That pluralistic notion, as it is expressed in the essay entitled "The Dilemma of Determinism" (1884), "represents the world as vulnerable, and liable to be injured by certain of its parts if they
go wrong." The precise details of James's theory need not
be enumerated for the purposes of our present discussion,
but it is surely important to note that the theory, in James's
words, "gives us a pluralistic, restless universe, in which no
single point of view can ever take in the whole scene; and to a
mind possessed of the love of unity at any cost, it will, no doubt,
remain forever inacceptable. A friend with such a mind once
told me that the thought of my universe made him sick, like
the sight of the horrible motion of a mass of maggots in their

carrion bed." Pursuing this analogy, James goes on to assert that "the indeterminism with its maggots, if you please so to speak about it, offends only the native absolutism of my intellect—an absolutism which," he adds significantly, "after all, perhaps, deserves to be snubbed and kept in check."

The "love of unity at any cost" which William James refers to here, that striving for an ultimate point of view which could "take in the whole scene," certainly possessed the mind of his brother Henry, though the novelist was inclined to reveal this ambition in such a way as to make it seem an exclusively technical one. Thus, in discussing the composition of his fiction James alludes again and again to "the effort of the artist to preserve for his subject that unity, and for his use of it (in other words for the interest he desires to excite) that effect of a *centre*, which most economise its value." How much was actually invested in this struggle to achieve a center begins to emerge when one remembers that despite James's familiar declaration that in contemplating the opportunities afforded by a story he was capable of seeing "dramas within dramas . . . and innumerable points of view," the novelist, far from welcoming the prospect of divergent points of view endowed with roughly the same weight within a single story, confesses that he "had a mortal horror" of the possibility of even "two stories, two pictures in one." The main ground of his fear in this regard, as he goes on to suggest, is his sense of the inevitable "loss of authority" which would result from such a division of perspective:

> The reason of this was the clearest—my subject was immediately, under that disadvantage, so cheated of its indispensable centre as to become of no more use for expressing a main intention than a wheel without a hub is of use for moving a cart. It was a fact, apparently, that one *had* on occasion seen two pictures in one; were there not for instance certain sublime Tintorettos at Venice, a measureless Crucifixion in especial,

which showed without loss of authority half a dozen actions separately taking place? Yes, that might be, but there had surely been nevertheless a mighty pictorial fusion, so that the virtue of composition had somehow thereby come all mysteriously into its own. . . . A picture without composition slights its most precious chance for beauty, and it is moreover not composed at all unless the painter knows *how* that principle of health and safety, working as an absolutely premeditated art, has prevailed.

But the final impossibility of achieving, despite all the accomplishments of art, a perfectly secure and unchallengeable position in relation to the world as one experiences it, the inevitable human failure to attain that central position which would assure one's ultimate "health and safety" by affording "a view of *all* the dimensions" of one's situation, produces in the artist the dilemma of "the aesthetic consciousness, proud of its conquests and discoveries, and yet trying, after all, as with the vexed sense of a want, to look through other windows and eyes." In this way, the artist—the artist in fiction in particular—attempts to overcome the limitations of his own vision; by seeking "to live the life of others" ("let anyone feel the urge to transform himself," Nietzsche observes, "and to speak out of other bodies and souls, and he will be a dramatist"), he is engaging in a ceaseless effort to obtain a unified and comprehensive view of an inexhaustible reality to which his own direct access must remain forever limited.

In a sense, William James, too, following the lead of Emerson (which did not require that he cease to snub "the native absolutism of [his] intellect") eventually came to acknowledge his own "love of unity at any cost," his own desire for "a view of *all* the dimensions," seen and unseen, of our experience. He did so by envisioning a kind of afterlife which exists in the present just beyond the reach of our minds, "a continuum of cosmic consciousness" in which everything that seems partial in this life is rendered whole, and in which a vast meeting of all individual striving souls takes place and they are reconciled at last. ("Ah! seest thou not, O brother," Emerson writes, "that we thus part only to meet again on a higher platform, and only be more each other's because we are more our own?") James's thinking on this point is crystallized in an unmistakably Emersonian passage in his "Final Impressions of a Psychical Researcher" (1909):

> Out of my experience, such as it is (and it is limited enough) one fixed conclusion dogmatically emerges, and that is this, that we with our lives are like islands in the sea, or like trees in the forest. The maple and the pine may whisper to each other with their leaves, and Conanicut and Newport hear each other's foghorns. But the trees also commingle their roots in the darkness underground, and the islands also hang together through the ocean's bottom. Just so there is a continuum of cosmic consciousness, against which our individuality builds but accidental fences, and into which our several minds plunge as into a mother-sea or reservoir. Our "normal" consciousness is circumscribed for adaptation to our external earthly environment, but the fence is weak in spots, and fitful influences from beyond leak in, showing the otherwise unverifiable common connection. Not only psychic research, but metaphysical philosophy, and speculative biology are led in their own ways to look with favor on some such "panpsychic" view of the universe as this.*

Citing the conclusion of *The Varieties of Religious Experience* (1902) in this general context, Matthiessen observes that

---

* Compare Emerson in *Nature:* "We learn . . . that . . . the Supreme Being does not build up nature around us, but puts it forth through us, as the life of the tree puts forth new branches and leaves through the pores of the old. As a plant upon the earth, so a man rests upon the bosom of God; he is nourished by unfailing fountains, and draws at his needs inexhaustible power. Who can set bounds to the possibilities of man? . . . Man has access to the entire mind of the Creator, is himself creator in the finite. . . ."

William James "left the question of immortality open, but he was by now thoroughly convinced that 'the world of our present consciousness is only one out of many worlds of consciousness that exist.'" And Matthiessen goes on to point out that James "took the pluralistic view that God was not necessarily one nor infinite but simply '*something* larger than ourselves' in whose support we could find help."

When Henry James contemplated the prospect of immortality, he found that he could not finally conceive of it in terms other than those relating to the continuation of personal identity. Indeed, for him, as has already been observed, the possibility of a life after death is seen to increase in direct proportion to the quality of individuality—evidenced by one's powers of consciousness and discrimination—achieved in this life. Moreover, James observes that the "most general effect" of the question of immortality takes "mostly either one of two forms; the effect of making us desire death, and for reasons, absolutely *as* welcome extinction and termination; or the effect of making us desire it as a renewal of the interest, the appreciation, the passion, the large and consecrated consciousness, in a word, of which we have had so splendid a sample in this world":

> Either one or the other of these opposed states of feeling is bound finally to declare itself, we judge, in persons of a fine sensibility and whose innermost spirit experience has set vibrating at all; for the condition of indifference and of knowing neither is the condition of living altogether so much below the human privilege as to have little right to pass for unjustly excluded or neglected in this business of the speculative reckoning.

As is usual in James, who follows the tradition which extends at least as far back as Schiller, it is a question here whether persons not possessed "of a fine sensibility"—persons whose poor apprehension of life falls "so much below the human privilege"

—should really be regarded as having realized in themselves the condition of full humanity. Indeed, James asserts, "it may very well be asked in their behalf whether they are distinguishable as 'living' either before or after"; and he continues: "How *can* there be a personal and a differentiated life 'after,' it will then of course be asked, for those for whom there has been so little of one before?"

The association of vitality, full humanity, and intense individuality, familiar to readers of Emerson, also occurs with great regularity in D. H. Lawrence, as in the following characteristic passage from "Reflections on the Death of a Porcupine" in which Lawrence sets down "the inexorable law of life":

1. Any creature that attains to its own fullness of being, its own living self, becomes unique, a nonpareil. It has its place in the fourth dimension, the heaven of existence, and there it is perfect, it is beyond comparison.

2. At the same time, every creature exists in time and space. And in time and space it exists relatively to all other existence, and can never be absolved. Its existence impinges on other existences, and is itself impinged upon. And in the struggle for existence, if an effort on the part of any one type or species or order of life, can finally destroy the other species, then the destroyer is of a more vital cycle of existence than the one destroyed.

3. The force which we call *vitality*, and which is the determining factor in the struggle for existence, is, however, derived also from the fourth dimension. That is to say, the ultimate source of all vitality is in that other dimension, or region, where the dandelion blooms, and which men have called heaven, which is only a way of saying that it is not to be reckoned in terms of space and time.

4. The primary way, in our existence, to get vitality, is to absorb it from living creatures lower than ourselves. It is thus transformed into a new and higher creation. (There are many ways of absorbing: devouring food is one way, love is often another. . . .)

The Nietzschean aspect of these pronouncements is striking, but no less striking is the sense that they serve to link Lawrence with William James as well as Emerson—though like Carlyle, and for similar reasons, Lawrence ultimately parts company with these "extreme" Americans who seem to recognize no obstacle to the triumph of their imaginations. Still, the assumptions revealed in this passage, which underlie the intense and often violent struggles between characters in novels like *Sons and Lovers* and *Women in Love*, may also have a great deal to do with the essential nature, if not the outward appearance, of the struggles depicted in James's later novels.

Although he shared the Emersonian sense of another, wider dimension of experience which remained accessible to the individual consciousness even under the limited conditions of this life, Henry James does not seem to have been very much attracted to the idea of a continuum of "cosmic consciousness" in which individual personalities would at last be joined. For him, individual personality was so intensely conceived and completely articulated, so powerfully sustained by consciousness, that he tended to think of it as virtually indestructible, and found it hard to imagine its inability to survive even death. Moreover, so far as he was concerned, that reconciliation of all clashing viewpoints was taking place continually in the consciousness of the artist; and it was the artist's ability to achieve, under any circumstances, a "view of *all* the dimensions," a wholeness which would finally unify the world of his experience, that assured his ultimate "health and safety."

6.

For Nietzsche, the possibility of ultimate absorption into the *Ur-Ein*, the primal womb of being described in *The Birth of Tragedy*, appears as terrifying as it is seductive, for although such an absorption may be imagined as affording the deeply reassuring and ineffable experience of union with the ceaseless process of the universe, it is also imagined to be irreversible: moreover, it clearly involves the total extinction of personal identity and thus represents, to Nietzsche's mind, a form of death (the degree of individuality being, for both Nietzsche and James, the index for determining to what extent a person may be said to be alive, not to say human—a participant in divinity, in Emersonian terms). As will soon become apparent, Nietzsche views the universe as an arena of endless struggle in which "every center of force" is alternately expanding and contracting, seeking to dominate and being dominated by others; everything is therefore literally fighting for its life, and as a consequence individuality becomes a function of resistance to the encroachments of others. Hence, "in the end," as Walter Kaufmann has observed, Nietzsche's "emphasis on individuality led him to the conception of a vast plurality of individual wills to power, and culminated in a monadological pluralism that shows many interesting parallels to that of Whitehead and, it would seem, of modern physics." Nietzsche elaborates on the "necessary perspectivism" that emerges from this view in an occasionally puzzling note of March-June 1888 included in *The Will to Power:*

> Physicists believe in a "true world" in their own fashion: a firm systematization of atoms in necessary motion, the same for all beings—so for them, the "apparent world" is reduced to the side of universal and universally necessary being which is accessible to every being in its own way (accessible and also already adapted—made "subjective"). But they are in error. The atom they posit is inferred according to the logic of the perspectivism of consciousness—and is therefore itself a subjective fiction. This world picture that they sense differs in no essential way from the subjective world picture: it is only construed with more extended senses, but with *our* senses nonetheless—And in any case they left something out of the constellation without

knowing it: *precisely this necessary perspectivism by virtue of which every center of force—and not only man—construes all the rest of the world from its own viewpoint, i.e., measures, feels, forms, according to its own force—*They forgot to include this perspective-setting force in "true being"—in school language: the subject. . . .

Perspectivism is only a complex form of specificity. *My idea is that every specific body strives to become master over all space and to extend its force (—its will to power:) and to thrust back all that resists its extension. But it continually encounters similar efforts on the part of other bodies* and ends by coming to an arrangement ("union") with those of them that are sufficiently related to it: thus they conspire together for power. And the process goes on—[Italics added.]

The significance of the notion of perspectivism and its place in the general scheme of Nietzsche's philosophy are matters discussed with notable clarity by Arthur C. Danto in the chapter entitled "Perspectivism" in his *Nietzsche as Philosopher* (1965). After expressing his conviction that Nietzsche "advanced a pragmatic criterion of truth: p is true and q is false if p works and q does not,"* Danto argues that when Nietzsche "proclaims time and time again that everything is false," what he means is "that there is no order in the world for things to correspond to; there *is* nothing, in terms of the Correspondence Theory of Truth, to which statements can stand in the required relationship in order to be true."

A view of the "creative possibilities" afforded by this position is again provided by William James, who asserts of pragmatism

---

* Cf. William James: "Any idea upon which we can ride, so to speak; any idea that will carry us from one part of our experience to any other part, linking things satisfactorily, working securely, simplifying, saving labor; is true for just so much, true in so far forth, true *instrumentally*. This is the 'instrumental' view of truth taught so successfully at Chicago, the view that truth in our ideas means their power to 'work,' promulgated so brilliantly at Oxford."

that "it converts the absolutely empty notion of a static relation of 'correspondence' . . . between our minds and reality,
into that of a rich and active commerce (that any one may follow in detail and understand) between particular thoughts of
ours, and the great universe of other experiences in which they
play their parts and have their uses." Henry James's reference
to "the state of private poetic intercourse with things, the kind
of current that in a given personal experience flows to and fro
between the imagination and the world" is also worth remarking in this context. Danto goes on to explore the implications of
this line of thought in Nietzsche's work, finally showing how
it inevitably issues in the "tragic" perception (as that perception is exemplified by the wisdom of Silenus in *The Birth of
Tragedy*) "that life is devoid of meaning and that the world is
only emptiness."

For Nietzsche, Danto argues, there is no possible way of
claiming greater validity for one view of reality than for another; under these circumstances, both the opponents and the
adherents of the common sense view in philosophy, for example, must be regarded as putting forth equally empty claims
(though they may still possess some "instrumental" value in a
particular situation) since "the would-be opponents and depre-
cators of the categories of common sense are shown . . . to
have no better grounds for claiming authoritativeness than it
has, while common sense itself is shown to have no basis at all
in reality and not the slightest claim to truth." Similarly, Danto
goes on to observe of Euclidian geometry that it "is but one of
an infinite number of possible geometries," just as common
sense is "but one of a number of possible interpretations of the
world"; he then proceeds to outline what follows from this position for Nietzsche:

The question sometimes arises as to which of these geometries
correctly describes the geometry of the physical world; a Nietzschean answer would be that not one of them does, for the

world has no geometry to describe. So with philosophies, including that of common sense. There is no real world structure *of* which each of these is an interpretation, no way the world really is in contrast with our modes of interpreting it. There are only rival interpretations: "There are no facts [*Tatsachen*], only interpretations." And accordingly no *world in itself* apart from some interpretation—"as though there would be a world left over once we subtracted the perspectival!" We cannot even speak of these interpretations as "distorting" reality, for there is nothing that counts as a veridical interpretation relative to which a given interpretation could distort: or every interpretation is a distortion, except that there is nothing for it to be a distortion of. To revert to the analogy with geometries, if we decide that Euclidean geometry is "true," this will be because it has worked for us for a long time as an instrument in surveying, triangulation, and other metrical activities.

The world is thus conceived as a vast uncreated void, a *tabula rasa* whose meaning, for each person or nation, is one that has been imposed upon it as a consequence of certain needs. And just as those needs will differ from person to person and nation to nation, so too will conceptions of the world differ; there is therefore no human way of arriving at a unified view of the world *as it is*, beneath all its aspects (it is important to recall William James's "indeterminism with its maggots" in this connection), for as Danto remarks, quoting Nietzsche, "the world is in fact only a 'relation-world: it has a different aspect from every point, its being is essentially different at every point.'" Moreover, it is impossible to take all of these divergent, fragmentary perspectives into account and then proceed to construct the whole through a process of addition, since "one cannot say that the world is . . . the sum of these perspectives: 'for these in any case are altogether incongruent.' This means, then, that the only world we can significantly speak of is the world from where we are."

As we have already observed, particularly in our discussion of the notion of "universal culture," Nietzsche's profound frustra-

tion with the human inability to transcend such inevitable limitations of vision, a frustration expressed by his desire to achieve
"the eye of Zarathustra, an eye that beholds the whole fact of
man at a tremendous distance—below," leads inexorably to his
conception of the superman. Danto provides a different (though
finally complementary) analysis of the matter, emphasizing the
logical emergence of the will to power in a situation in which
no perspective can be regarded as necessarily superior to any
other; he summarizes his argument as follows:

> The doctrine that there are no facts but only interpretations
> was termed *Perspectivism*. To be sure, we speak of seeing the
> same thing from different perspectives, and we might allow
> that there is no way to see the thing *save* through a perspective,
> and finally, that *there is no one perspective which is privileged
> over any other*. These would be logical features of the concept
> of perspective itself. The only difficulty here is in talking about
> the "same thing" on which there are distinct perspectives. . . .
> Certainly we cannot say what *it* is except from one or another
> perspective, and we cannot speak about it as it is in itself. . . .
> We can meaningfully say nothing, then, about whatever it is
> on which these are perspectives. *We cannot speak of a true per-
> spective, but only of the perspective that prevails. Because we
> cannot appeal to any fact independently of its relation to the
> perspective it is meant to support, we can do little more than
> insist on our perspective, and try, if we can, to impose it on
> other people. Common sense constitutes one perspective among
> many. And it, no less than the others, seeks to impose itself
> where it can; it is the metaphysics of the masses or, as Nietz-
> sche will say, of the herd.* [Italics added.]

In sum, in the absence of a metaphysical principle of authority to which one might appeal in order to determine the
relative legitimacy of any particular way of seeing things, all
questions concerning the final validity of any human perspective ultimately reduce themselves to questions of power. For
inasmuch as it is clear that Nietzsche's nihilism, as Danto

notes, consists in his maintaining that "the world is made up of points of origin for perspectives," and equally clear that Nietzsche "goes still further and sees these points as occupied by active powers, wills, each seeking to organize the world from its perspective, each locked in combat with the rest," one is bound to conclude that this line of thinking indeed represents "the beginning of [Nietzsche's] notorious and utterly misunderstood doctrine of Will-to-Power." Hence, alluding later to Nietzsche's own observation regarding the striving of "every specific body . . . to become master over all space and to extend its force (—its will to power:) and thrust back all that resists its extension," an observation contained in the note on perspectivism cited previously from *The Will to Power*, Danto suggests that the "'First Law' of Nietzsche's theory" might be formulated as follows: "A force will tend to move outward forever until some external force impedes its dilation"; consequently, "were it not resisted, a body (force) would occupy the whole of space." (It is perhaps not too farfetched to think of the Prince's enigmatic last remark to Maggie at the conclusion of *The Golden Bowl* in this connection: "'See'? I see nothing but *you*.")

Given Nietzsche's view of the universe as an eternal battleground in which each element strives for dominance over the others, it follows that "a philosophical problem is a question not to be answered but to be overcome," since behind each such problem is "a will to impose its own order." Nietzsche himself is quite explicit on the implications of this point in Part One of *Beyond Good and Evil*, where he observes that inasmuch as each philosophy (and the mode of formulating any specific philosophical problem and of establishing its relation to other problems in the end implies an entire philosophy) represents an attempt—a literal attempt, to Nietzsche's mind—to conceive the world, all philosophies strive to assume the role of the ultimate creator, God:

. . . what formerly happened with the Stoics still happens to-day, too, as soon as any philosophy begins to believe in itself. It always creates the world in its own image; it cannot do other-wise. Philosophy is this tyrannical drive itself, the most spirit-ual will to power, to the "creation of the world," to the *causa prima.*

Accordingly, Nietzsche concludes that to maintain one's indi-vidual identity and remain free one must successfully resist enslavement by another man's conception of the world. More-over, pursuing this line of reasoning still further, he arrives at the conclusion that true freedom, paradoxically, may be the most exacting master of all, for it requires that one overcome not only the convictions and ideals of others but ultimately one's own convictions and ideals as well ("What? A great man?" Nietzsche asks in this regard: "I always see only the actor of his own ideal"). This point is developed at some length in a passage from *The Antichrist:*

Freedom from all kinds of convictions, to be able to see freely, is part of strength. . . . Conviction as a *means.* . . . Great passion uses and uses up convictions, it does not succumb to them—it knows itself sovereign. Conversely: the need for faith, for some kind of unconditional Yes and No, this Carlylism, if one will forgive me this word, is a need born of *weakness.* The man of faith, the "believer" of every kind, is necessarily a de-pendent man—one who cannot posit *himself* as an end, one who cannot posit any end at all by himself. The "believer" does not belong to himself, he can only be a means, he must be *used up,* he requires somebody to use him up. . . . The be-liever is not free to have any conscience at all for questions of "true" and "untrue": to have integrity on *this* point would at once destroy him. The pathological condition of his perspective turns the convinced into fanatics—Savonarola, Luther, Rous-seau, Robespierre, Saint-Simon: the opposition-type of the strong spirit who has *become* free. . . . the grand pose of these sick spirits, these epileptics of the concept. . . .

Seen in its simplest aspect, what Nietzsche is explicitly concerned with here is the cultivation of what might be called critical detachment, the effort to liberate oneself from one's most cherished assumptions and beliefs; but the full dimensions of the enterprise which he is recommending only begin to emerge after one considers Zarathustra's speech "On Self-Overcoming." "Whatever I create and however much I love it," Zarathustra declares in the course of that speech, "soon I must oppose it and my love: thus my will wills it." For the final independence of soul that Nietzsche has in mind demands an ongoing process of ruthless self-scrutiny, a process which in principle can never be allowed to result in the attainment of a position of psychic security and rest, for even the desire for such a position is rejected as a sign of weakness, an expression of the instinct of the "herd."

As Nietzsche comes to recognize, the cost of such independence is very high indeed, for it requires not only estrangement from the mass of men but continual war with oneself: the overcoming of one personal limitation leads to the establishment of another, which must in its turn be overcome. (Consider Nietzsche's observation in an 1883 letter to Overbeck: "Meanwhile I am still the incarnate wrestling match, so that your dear wife's recent requests made me feel as if someone were asking old Laocoön to set about it and vanquish his serpents.") Hence, like a master waiting in the darkness for the reappearance of a recalcitrant—and in his view a potentially murderous—slave, Nietzsche uneasily watches the intricate workings of his personality with an eye to apprehending the slightest element of thought or feeling that betrays a quality of "slavishness"; continually on guard against what he regards as human failings, he seeks to surprise and overwhelm every impulse that does not come up to his standard for "nobility." But paradoxically, he must be willing to sacrifice even the ideal of nobility in the interest of the free development of the self, for once that ideal threatens to become an end in itself it becomes an end beyond the self and therefore its master.

Whether or not one wishes to regard this unending process of self-overcoming as a striving to be superhuman, it is undeniably clear that as a result of it Nietzsche is able to achieve an almost preternatural awareness of the possibilities for subtle tyranny by one aspect of the self over another: forms of tyranny, varieties of self-deception and bad faith, which may result in one's becoming merely the representative of one's ambitions, the actor of one's own life. Indeed, no one who has ever read Nietzsche's *Ecce Homo*, that *sui generis* autobiography of his works which is possessed of a lucidity finally so cruel and self-corrosive that it reaches into madness, could fail to understand the force of Freud's remark—a remark which he is said to have repeated on a number of occasions—that Nietzsche "had a more penetrating knowledge of himself than any other man who ever lived or was likely to live."

In relation to himself and others Nietzsche evidences a positively Jamesian obsession with discovering the motive behind the motive, and like James he is "addicted to seeing 'through' —one thing through another, accordingly, and still other things through *that*. . . ." In the case of the philosopher, this process of unremitting perception is suggested by a difficult and frequently exhausting prose style in which each sentence—indeed, each phrase—tends to leap beyond itself and proceed with almost blinding speed to further reaches of the subject, further questions arising out of the questions; but the process occasionally manifests itself in a more static form in reverberating aphorisms, such as this one entitled "Honest toward Honesty" from Volume Two of *Human, All-Too-Human*: "One who is openly honest towards himself ends by being rather conceited about this honesty. He knows only too well why he is honest—

for the same reason that another man prefers outward show and hypocrisy." Thus, for Nietzsche (as for James) the process of thought takes on the appearance of an endless succession of perspectives, each of which dissolves—or "sees through"—the one preceding it.

In this way, the will-to-power is internalized: the divergent perspectives of Nietzsche's doctrine are moved inward, and out of their ceaseless conflict the self is continually reborn at a higher level of strength and consciousness. And just as the world is regarded as possessing no fixed and final form, in the same way the self is conceived as endlessly coming into be-ing, a dynamic image of life itself (life seen under the aspect of will-to-power); for the secret which life confides to Zara-thustra is this: "Behold . . . *I am that which must always overcome itself.* Indeed, you call it a will to procreate or a drive to an end, to something higher, farther, more manifold: but all this is one. . . ." The means of this self-overcoming, this power to give form to oneself which is ultimately identified with the power to give form to the world, is the endless activity of art, the appropriation of all reality as material, the subjugation of actuality to idea, the imposition of pattern on the fluidity of experience. And it is for this reason that Nietzsche concludes that "the phenomenon 'artist' is still the most transparent:—to see through it to the basic instincts of power, nature, etc.!"

V

The Artist of the Real

I dreamed that I floated at will in the great Ether, and I saw this world floating also not far off, but diminished to the size of an apple. Then an angel took it in his hand and brought it to me and said, "This thou must eat." And I ate the world.

EMERSON Journals

1.

"We need 'unities,' " Nietzsche maintains, "in order to be able to reckon," but "that does not mean we must suppose that such unities exist. We have borrowed the concept of unity from our 'ego' concept—our oldest article of faith. If we did not hold ourselves to be unities, we would never have formed the concept 'thing.' Now, somewhat late, we are firmly convinced that our conception of the ego does not guarantee any actual unity." Yet even if no such unity exists, in order for man to survive at all it is necessary that that "fiction" (as Nietzsche calls it) be imposed upon the world, along with related "fictions" like "the concept of activity (separation of cause from effect)" and "the concept of motion (sight and taste)," all of which serve to compel fluid experience into distinguishable, manageable shapes. That such "lies are necessary in order to live," Nietzsche observes, "is itself part of the terrifying and questionable character of existence," and it is important to recall that Nietzsche provides one explanation for the title of his *Beyond Good and Evil* in relation to this general line of reasoning: "We are

fundamentally inclined to claim," he asserts, "that the falsest
judgments . . . are the most indispensable for us; that without
accepting the fictions of logic, without measuring reality against
the purely invented world of the unconditional and self-
identical, without a constant falsification of the world by means
of numbers, men could not live—that renouncing false judgments would mean renouncing life and a denial of life. To recognize untruth as a condition of life—that certainly means resisting accustomed value feelings in a dangerous way; and a
philosophy that risks this would by that token alone place itself
beyond good and evil."

In this view, the conceptions according to which experience
is generally ordered possess a purely "instrumental" value. They
function neither as descriptions nor as explanations, for there is
literally nothing in the world they could describe or explain. Indeed, as has already been noted, so far as Nietzsche is concerned
the view "that things possess a constitution in themselves quite
apart from interpretation and subjectivity, is a quite idle hypothesis: it presupposes that interpretation and subjectivity are
not essential, that a thing freed from all relationships would still
be a thing."

Once the existence of things is conceived wholly as a function
of subjectivity, it follows for Nietzsche that the creation of the
self as a work of art is a means of accomplishing nothing less
than the creation of the world. "The world that we have not
reduced to terms of our own being, our own logic, our psychological prejudices and presuppositions," he declares, "does not
exist as a world at all." The world is thus brought into being in
the image of the creator: it corresponds exactly to the dimensions of the self. As a result, it will possess richness and variety,
harmony and beauty, only to the extent that these qualities are
possessed by the creator himself; hence, it is only through a
process of cultivation of consciousness combined with rigorous

self-discipline that the world can finally be endowed with order and value. Such is the significance of Zarathustra's speech "On the Gift-Giving Virtue," in which he describes the "thirst" of the creator to share the plenitude of his being with the finite world:

> Verily, I have found you out, my disciples: you strive, as I do, for the gift-giving virtue. What would you have in common with cats and wolves? This is your thirst: to become sacrifices and gifts yourselves; and that is why you thirst to pile up all the riches in your soul. Insatiably your soul strives for treasures and gems, because your virtue is insatiable in wanting to give. You force all things to and into yourself that they may flow back out of your well as the gifts of your love. Verily, such a gift-giving love must approach all values as a robber; but whole and holy I call this selfishness.

Similarly, in order for the world to be brought into unity, it is necessary for the creator to have "disciplined himself"— like Goethe, in Nietzsche's judgment—"to wholeness." In that process, the impulse to art is turned inward, and all that is fragmentary and discordant in the personality is subordinated to an ideal conception of the self. Nietzsche finds an extremely compelling (albeit to his sense misguided) version of this effort to achieve perfection in the practice of Christian piety, "the 'life in God,'" which he regards as "the subtlest and final offspring of the *fear* of truth, as an artist's worship and intoxication before the most consistent of all falsifications, as the will to the inversion of truth, to untruth at any price." Still, such a model, Nietzsche indicates, has had its uses, for "it may be that until now there has been no more potent means for beautifying man himself than piety: it can turn man into so much art, surface, play of colors, graciousness that his sight no longer makes one suffer.—"

What Nietzsche has in mind here is developed further in a

significant passage in the Second Essay of *The Genealogy of Morals;* here the process of self-conquest is understood as a function of "bad conscience" [*schlechtes Gewissen*], that condition of division within the self which in a somewhat bizarre analogy he describes as "an illness, there is no doubt about that, but an illness as pregnancy is an illness":

> One should guard against thinking lightly of this phenomenon merely on account of its initial painfulness and ugliness. For fundamentally it is the same active force that is at work on a grander scale in those artists of violence and organizers who build states, and that here, internally, on a smaller and pettier scale, directed backward, in the "labyrinth of the breast," to use Goethe's expression, creates for itself a bad conscience and builds negative ideals—namely, the *instinct for freedom* (in my language: the will to power); only here the material upon which the form-giving and ravishing nature of this force vents itself is on man himself, his whole ancient animal self—and not, as in that greater and more obvious phenomenon, some *other* man, *other* men. This secret self-ravishment, this artists' cruelty, this delight in imposing a form upon oneself as a hard, recalcitrant, suffering material and in burning a will, a critique, a contradiction, a contempt, a No into it, this uncanny, dreadfully joyous labor of a soul voluntarily at odds with itself that makes itself suffer out of joy in making suffer—eventually this entire *active* "bad conscience"—you will have guessed it—as the womb of all ideal and imaginative phenomena, also brought to light an abundance of strange new beauty and affirmation, and perhaps beauty itself.—After all, what would be "beautiful" if the contradiction had not first become conscious of itself, if the ugly had not first said to itself: "I am ugly"?

Proceeding through successive stages of painful internal contradiction and cruelty unleashed against the self, moving from recognition of the threat of ugliness and weakness to mastery of these aspects of the personality, engaging in a war of total conquest in which the self is reconsolidated after every victory at a further stage of beauty and wholeness, the Nietzschean artist of self-overcoming, the "Dionysian man" exemplified by Goethe in *Twilight of the Idols,* succeeds at last in imposing his own ideal form upon himself. In the course of that process, moreover, the ideal form may be seen to gain in value and power in direct proportion to its increasing ability to turn the aimless ugliness of the actual to its own advantage: the actual, that is, is converted into a means ultimately working in the service of the ideal, and the ideal is continually renewed and strengthened by its successful subjugation of the actual. (For James, it will be recalled, the ideal is similarly hardened by the ceaseless testing of the actual, and if it is not in the end destroyed by that intense and unrelenting pressure it is sure to emerge from it with "a finer and more militant edge.") The beauty of the ideal form, in short, is regarded as a function of its power to harness the wildness that threatens it: consequently, the deeper the perception of adversary forces, the greater the awareness of the menace against the conception of the self, the more intense the potential experience of panic and despair if the willed form should give way and one be left with nothing but the chaos of experience, by so much the more powerful must be the vision of wholeness which arises in opposition. "How much did this people have to suffer," Nietzsche observes of the creators of Greek tragedy in this regard, "to be able to become so beautiful!" Consequently, it is understandable that Nietzsche should be scornful of those who "want, if possible—and there is no more insane 'if possible'—*to abolish suffering,*" for he regards human suffering as an indispensable stimulus to perfection:

> The discipline of suffering, of *great* suffering—do you not know that only *this* discipline has created all enhancements of man so far? That tension of the soul in unhappiness which cultivates its strength, its shudders face to face with great ruin, its inventiveness and courage in enduring, persevering, interpreting, and

exploiting suffering, and whatever has been granted to it of
profundity, secret, mask, spirit, cunning, greatness—was it not
granted to it through suffering, through the discipline of great
suffering? In man *creature* and *creator* are united; in man there
is material, fragment, excess, clay, dirt, nonsense, chaos; but in
man there is also creator, form-giver, hammer hardness, spectator divinity, and seventh day: do you understand this contrast?
And that *your* pity is for the "creature in man," for what must
be formed, broken, forged, torn, burnt, made incandescent, and
purified—that which *necessarily* must and *should* suffer? And
our pity—do you not comprehend for whom our *converse* pity
is when it resists your pity as the worst of all pamperings and
weaknesses?

The emotional ground out of which such assertions arise is
clearly indicated in one of Nietzsche's letters to Franz Overbeck. The letter, postmarked Rapallo, December 25, 1882, was
written during one of the darkest and most desolate periods of
Nietzsche's life, just after he had spent an agonizing summer
caught in a triangular relationship with Paul Rée and Lou
Andreas-Salomé, and just before he had begun to regain some
sense of well-being by losing himself in the writing of the first
part of *Thus Spoke Zarathustra*; it reads in part as follows:
"This last *bite of life* was the hardest I have chewed yet, and it
is still possible that I may *suffocate* on it. I have suffered of
the ignominious and tormenting memories of this summer as
of a madness. . . . I tense every fiber of my self-overcoming—but I have lived in solitude too long, living off 'my own
fat,' so that now, more than anyone else, I am being broken
on the wheel of my own feelings. If only I could sleep! But the
strongest doses of my opiates help me no more than my six-to-
eight hour marches. If I do not discover the alchemists' trick of
turning even this—filth into *gold*, I am lost.—Thus I have the
most beautiful opportunity to prove that for me 'all experiences
are useful, all days holy, and all human beings divine!!!!! All

human beings divine." But he continues: "My suspicion has now become very great: in everything that I hear I feel contempt for me. . . . Yesterday I broke off my correspondence with my mother, too: it had become unendurable. . . . My relationship with Lou is in its final and most painful throes: at least it seems that way to me today. Later—if there is any later—I'll say a word about that too. *Pity*, my friend, is a kind of hell—whatever the adherents of Schopenhauer may say. I am not asking you: 'what am I to do?' A few times I thought of renting a small room in Basel, visiting you now and then, and attending lectures. A few times I also thought of the opposite: driving my solitude and renunciation to its ultimate point and— Well, let that be. . . ."

For Nietzsche, the subordination of the "creature" element to the "creator" element in man represents a triumph of consciousness over actual (and often painful) experience, and it is therefore regarded as a form of liberation. Through consciousness the Nietzschean creator is able to free himself from subjection to blind impulse: he himself calls into being all that he is and he alone possesses the power to command and give form to himself. Like Zarathustra, he has been struck by the knowledge that "whatever lives, obeys," and that "he who cannot obey himself is commanded. That is the nature of the living."

Accordingly, for the man who has come into full possession of himself, who has, indeed, become a world unto himself, there is only one law left to obey (in Nietzsche's terms conceivably the most exacting and paradoxical of all laws, as has already been suggested): that of his own free development. And in Nietzsche's view it is the continuous discovery of that law, followed by a rigorous adherence to it, which serves as the basis for that process of self-definition in which the creator must at all times be engaged, that process of " 'giving style' to one's character—a great and rare art!" which is described in *The Gay Science*:

It is practiced by those who survey all the strengths and weaknesses of their nature and then fit them into an artistic plan
until every one of them appears as art and reason and even
weaknesses delight the eye. Here a large mass of second nature
has been added; there a piece of original nature has been removed—both times through long practice and daily work at it.
Here the ugly that could not be removed is concealed; there it
has been reinterpreted and made sublime. . . . It will be the
strong and domineering natures that enjoy their finest gaiety in
such constraint and perfection under a law of their own; the
passion of their tremendous will relents in the face of all styl-
ized nature, of all conquered and serving nature. . . . Conversely, it is the weak characters without power over themselves
that *hate* the constraint of style. . . .

By becoming a law unto himself, the powerful man also establishes the law of his own development as that law which is binding on all men. "To believe your own thought," Emerson declares in "Self-Reliance," "to believe that what is true for you in
your private heart is true for all men,—that is genius"; and
Nietzsche, almost as if glossing that sentence, asserts: "The
noble type of man experiences *itself* as determining values; it
does not need approval; it judges, 'what is harmful to me is
harmful in itself'; it knows itself to be that which first accords
honor to things; it is *value-creating.* Everything it knows as part
of itself it honors: such a morality is self-glorification." (Another
passage from "Self-Reliance"—though as we have seen it would
be possible to isolate many more such passages in Emerson's
writings which find an echo in the writings of Nietzsche—only
serves to underscore the obvious and powerful affinity between
the two writers on this score: "On my saying, What have I to
do with the sacredness of tradition, if I live wholly from within?"
Emerson declares, "my friend suggested,—'But these impulses
may be from below, not from above.' I replied, 'They do not
seem to me to be such; but if I am the devil's child, I will live
then from the devil.' No law can be sacred to me but that of

my nature. Good and bad are but names very readily transferable to that or this; the only right is what is after my constitution; the only wrong what is against it.")

With his characteristic combination of unsettling boldness and unexpected delicacy, aggressive plain talk and extraordinary subtlety of perception, Nietzsche sketches out some of the implications of this general line of thinking:

> At the risk of displeasing innocent ears I propose: egoism belongs to the nature of a noble soul—I mean that unshakable faith that to a being such as "we are" other beings must be subordinate by nature and have to sacrifice themselves. The noble soul accepts this fact of its egoism without any question mark, also without any feeling that it might contain hardness, constraint, or caprice, rather as something that may be founded in the primordial law of things: if it sought a name for this fact it would say, "it is justice itself." Perhaps it admits under certain circumstances that at first make it hesitate that there are some who have rights equal to its own; as soon as this matter of rank is settled it moves among these equals with their equal privileges, showing the same sureness of modesty and delicate reverence that characterize its relations with itself—in accordance with an innate heavenly mechanism understood by all stars. It is merely another aspect of its egoism, this refinement and self-limitation in its relations with its equals—every star is such an egoist—it honors *itself* in them and in the rights it cedes to them. . . .

Just as the work of art, for Nietzsche, is conceived on an aristocratic model as a hierarchy of means subordinated to a single, all-embracing end, so too society is regarded as a mechanism for the production of those "higher specimens" discussed earlier: indeed, as we have seen, that is society's sole justification. And in order that such types of the noble soul—the soul which *"knows itself to be at a height"*—may be produced, certain human sacrifices become necessary. "Ordinary human beings," therefore, "the vast majority who exist for service and the general advantage, and who *may* exist only for that," those "ever-toiling" representatives of man in his "creature" aspect who are characterized by their distinctive "lowliness" and the "half-brutish poverty of their souls," must be made to serve as beasts of burden in order to facilitate the creation of conditions favorable to the cultivation of the noble soul. To that end, in short, ordinary human beings must be considered no more than a means. Nietzsche is perfectly clear on this point, and he is careful to insist that the transcendent beings he has in mind—like those "highest specimens" described in the Meditation on History—are not to be regarded as possessing merely "instrumental" value as a stay against anarchy, a way of preserving social stability:

> The essential characteristic of a good and healthy aristocracy . . . is that it experiences itself *not* as a function (whether of the monarchy or the commonwealth) but as their *meaning* and highest justification—that it therefore accepts with a good conscience the sacrifice of untold human beings who, *for its sake,* must be reduced and lowered to incomplete human beings, to slaves, to instruments. Their fundamental faith simply has to be that society must *not* exist for society's sake but only as the foundation and scaffolding on which a choice type of being is able to raise itself to its higher task and to a higher state of being—comparable to those sun-seeking vines of Java—they are called *Sipo Matador*—that so long and so often enclasp an oak tree with their tendrils until eventually, high above it but supported by it, they can unfold their crowns in the open light and display their happiness.

It is possible to regard the Jamesian technique of subordinating the shallow, fragmentary "fools" in a story to the full development of the "signal specimen" in the light of notions such as those articulated here by Nietzsche in what is perhaps their most extreme and unequivocal form; more important, however, is the evident parallel between Nietzsche's sense of the relation between extraordinary individuals and the society which serves to produce them and James's view of the matter with respect to his own American heroines. For in James's view, American society is ultimately vindicated of the many charges lodged against it (which include pushiness, coarseness, and want of culture)—it is, in Nietzsche's formulation, "justified"—only by its ability to produce human specimens of such inexhaustible vitality and exquisite sensitivity as those who figure as the central focus of much of his own fiction, characters whose energy in "affronting" their destinies (to use the word that James applies to Isabel Archer) serves as a sharp judgment on the relative moral indifference or exhaustion which is most often seen as characterizing the European relation to experience.

A striking passage in Paul Bourget's *Outre-Mer* (1894), a book about America that he published after a year of traveling around the country, speaks unexpectedly but distinctly to this point. Bourget is here describing a portrait which he claims is "that of a woman whom I do not know"; but there is little doubt that the portrait in question is one of Isabella Stewart Gardner executed by John Singer Sargent, a portrait Bourget "could have seen only at Mrs. Gardner's house":

> It is a portrait such as fifteenth century masters painted. . . . The woman is standing, her feet side by side, her knees close together, in an almost hieratic pose. Her body, rendered supple by exercise, is sheathed—you might say molded—in a tight-fitting black dress. Rubies, like drops of blood, sparkle in her shoes. Her slender waist is encircled by a girdle of enormous pearls. . . . The head, intellectual and daring, with a countenance as of one who has understood everything, has for a sort of aureole, the vaguely gilded design of one of those Renaissance stuffs. The rounded arms are joined by the clasped hands—firm hands . . . which might guide four horses with the precision of an English coachman. It is the picture of an energy, at once

deliberate and invincible, momentarily in repose, and all the
Byzantine Madonna is in that face, with its wide-open eyes.
Yes, this woman is an idol, for whose service man labors, which
he has decked with the jewels of a queen, behind each of
whose whims lie days and days spent in the ardent battle of
Wall Street. Frenzy of speculation in land, cities undertaken
and built by sheer force of millions, trains launched at full
speed over bridges built on a Babel-like sweep of arch, the
creaking of cable cars, the quivering of electric cars, sliding
along their wires with a crackle and a spark, the dizzy ascent of
elevators in buildings twenty stories high. . . . these are what
have made possible this woman, this living orchid, unexpected
masterpiece of this civilization.

It would be worthwhile to recall the force of the associations
made in this passage in contemplating the world of *The Golden
Bowl* later in our discussion; for our purposes at present it is
enough to observe that given the general view of the function
of society expressed implicitly by Bourget (as well as James), it
follows that a particular society is ultimately judged by its
ability to produce such human "masterpieces" as he is describing.

Nietzsche, for his part, has no doubt whatsoever about what
is required for the production and cultivation of such persons:
all other considerations must be subordinated to that end, and
all the lesser creatures in the society must be made to serve it.
For this is, in Nietzsche's view, no more than the nature of
things. "Here we must beware of superficiality and get to the
bottom of the matter," he observes, "resisting all sentimental
weakness: life itself is *essentially* appropriation, injury, overpowering of what is alien and weaker; suppression, hardness,
imposition of one's own forms, incorporation and at least, at
its mildest, exploitation. . . ."

It may be remarked that Nietzsche's account here of the activity which defines the process of life itself corresponds closely

to his description of the activity of art: and indeed, in his view the process of art and the process of life itself are identical, or at least indistinguishable. The artist and the world, that is to say, generate one another, and their mutual efforts close in a perfect circle: for just as the world strives to create the artist in order to realize itself, so too does the artist strive to create the world by giving it form. More precisely, just as the world—seen in microcosm in the form of a particular society—labors to produce something beyond itself, that noble soul who somehow exceeds all limitations of time and place, so too that creator confers honor on the world and endows it with value by acknowledging himself to be its "masterpiece"; and in this way, by revealing himself to be its ultimate purpose, the Nietzschean creator, assuming the prerogatives of God, out of "the feeling of fullness of power that seeks to overflow, the happiness of high tension, the consciousness of wealth that would give and bestow," imposes his own wholeness on the world.

2.

It is therefore to such noble personages as these, as Nietzsche declares in his Meditation on Schopenhauer, that "the whole of nature is impelled for its redemption." "And when the whole of nature is impelled toward man," he explains, "she indicates that he is necessary for her redemption from the curse of animal life, and that finally, in him, existence holds a mirror up to itself in which life appears no longer senseless but in its metaphysical significance." Consequently, it is only with the appearance of "those true men, *those no longer animals, the philosophers, artists and saints*" (three functions which, as suggested previously, are combined in the superman) that nature "feels [herself] for the first time to be at her goal." For without these transcendent beings nature is imagined as suffering from a painful awareness of her own meaninglessness; powerless to conceive a clear purpose for her own existence, blindly "she fulfills her ends in a general and clumsy manner, whereby she sacrifices too much energy." Thus, "nature's procedure," in Nietzsche's view, "appears wasteful; yet this is not the wastefulness of a criminal luxuriance but of inexperience. It is to be assumed that if she were human, she would never cease to be annoyed at herself for her lack of skill." In sum, although "nature always wishes to be useful to all, . . . she cannot find the best and most adapted ways and means for this purpose. That is the cause of her great suffering and melancholy. It is certain that nature, with her compulsive need for redemption, wishes to make existence explicable and meaningful by the production of the philosopher and the artist. . . ."

These types of the noble soul have, in Nietzsche's estimation, risen above their "disgust at the valuelessness of [their] existence," and have at last succeeded in giving meaning to that existence by imposing upon it "a high and transfiguring overall goal: to win power in order to come to the help of nature [*physis*], and to correct her foolishness and clumsiness a little." The creator thus serves to bring nature to consciousness, "at first, admittedly, solely for [him]self"—by means of a rigorous process of self-perfection during which " 'blind instinct' " is replaced "by conscious will"—"but eventually for everybody." The general means of achieving this larger goal is, according to Nietzsche, what we call "culture." For just as nature strives toward something beyond itself which will serve to give it a higher meaning, so too "every man is used to finding a limitation within himself, both of his talent and his moral will, which fills him with longing and melancholy; and as he, out of a sense of sin, yearns for the Holy, so he also, as an intellectual being, has a deep desire for the 'genius' [*Genius*] within himself. Here are the roots of all true culture, and by this I mean the longing of man to be reborn as saint and 'genius.' " As a consequence,

Nietzsche concludes, "the goal of all culture" may be seen as nothing less than "the production of 'genius' ":

> This is the fundamental idea of culture, insofar as it sets but one task for each of us: *to further the production of the philosopher, of the artist and of the saint within us and outside us, and thereby to work at the consummation of nature.* Just as nature needs the philosopher, so she also needs the artist for a metaphysical purpose, namely, for her own self-enlightenment so that she may at last see as a clear and distinct image what she never sees in the flux of becoming—and thus reach self-knowledge. It was Goethe who remarked, in presumptuous but profound words, that all nature's attempts are only valuable insofar as the artist finally guesses the meaning of her stammering, meets her half way and expresses the real intention of her attempts. "I have often said," he once exclaimed, "and will often say it again, the *causa finalis* of the affairs of men and the world is dramatic poetry. For the stuff is otherwise completely useless." And thus nature finally needs the saint in whom the individual ego is entirely melted away and who feels his suffering life as an identity, affinity and unity with all that is living: the saint in whom that wonder of transformation occurs, upon which the play of becoming never changes, that final and highest becoming-human after which the whole of nature strives for its redemption from itself.

Something of what Nietzsche means by his well-known but somewhat puzzling dictum (set forth in *The Birth of Tragedy*) that "it is only as an *aesthetic phenomenon* that existence and the world are eternally *justified*" is suggested by his quotation from Goethe in this passage, but to that question—as well as to the conception of the saint advanced here by Nietzsche—it will be necessary to return; what is most important to remark in our present context is that the process of culture as Nietzsche envisions it ultimately results in the production of the superman, that man who has at last succeeded in freeing himself from every human limitation. For culture, in Nietzsche's view,

"is the child of every individual's self-knowledge and inadequacy. Everyone who possesses culture is, in fact, saying: 'I see
something higher and more human than myself above me.
Help me, all of you, to reach it, as I will help every person who
recognizes the same thing and suffers the same thing, so that
finally the man may again come into being who feels himself
infinite in knowing and loving, in seeing and ability, and who
with all his being is a part of nature, as judge and criterion of
things.' "

"Creation—," Zarathustra asserts in his speech "Upon the
Blessed Isles," "that is the great redemption from suffering.
. . . Whatever in me has feeling, suffers and is in prison; but
my will always comes to me as my liberator and joy-bringer.
. . . Away from God and gods this will has lured me; what
could one create if gods existed?" Accordingly, the Nietzschean
creator, who begins by looking "upon himself as a miscarried
work of nature, but at the same time as evidence of the greatest and most wonderful intentions of this artist," succeeds in
time in executing these intentions to perfection in himself by
disciplining "himself to wholeness, . . . [creating] himself";
he then turns to the world once more with "the deepest conviction that we meet nature almost everywhere in her need, as she
strives toward man, as she painfully feels that her work has
again failed, as she nevertheless succeeds in producing the most
wonderful beginnings, outlines and forms, so that the people
with whom we live resemble the most valuable sculptural fragments which call out to us: 'Come, help, complete, combine
that which belongs together! We have an immeasurable longing
to become whole!' "

And indeed it is to this plea that the creator, the "Dionysian
man" possessed of "the highest of all possible faiths"—the
faith that "all is redeemed and affirmed in the whole"—it is
to this plea that he seeks ultimately to respond. "I walk among

men as among the fragments of the future—that future which
I envisage," Zarathustra declares in his speech "On Redemption." "And this is all my creating and striving, that I create
and carry together into One what is fragment and riddle and
dreadful accident. And how could I bear to be a man if man
were not also a creator and guesser of riddles and redeemer of
accidents?" In this way, the Nietzschean creator comes to assume the role of the artist whose material is man, and significantly the instrument which is regarded as most appropriate
for his task is at once that of creation and destruction, as Nietzsche suggests in the ambiguous subtitle for his self-consciously
"iconoclastic" *Twilight of the Idols:* "How One Philosophizes
with a Hammer." "But my fervent will to create," Zarathustra
announces, "impels me ever again toward man":

> . . . thus is the hammer impelled toward the stone. O man, in
> the stone there sleeps an image, the image of my images. Alas,
> that it must sleep in the hardest, the ugliest stone! Now my
> hammer rages cruelly against its prison. Pieces of rocks rain
> from the stone: what is that to me? I want to perfect it; for a
> shadow came to me—the stillest and lightest of all things once
> came to me. The beauty of the overman came to me as a
> shadow. O my brothers, what are the gods to me now?

It is important to recognize that the vision of wholeness
which the Nietzschean creator seeks to realize is derived from
his conviction that the will which manifests itself in the workings of the universe is essentially that of the artist. Thus, when
Nietzsche declares in *The Birth of Tragedy* that "existence and
the world seem justified only as an aesthetic phenomenon,"
what he has in mind is related to his conception of the continual process of art in life, that ceaseless working of the dia-
lectic by means of which life perpetually overcomes itself. Consequently, evoking Heraclitus ("That which is in opposition
is in concert, and from things that differ comes the most beau-

tiful harmony"), Nietzsche observes that one of the chief functions of the tragic myth is to "convince us that even the ugly
and disharmonic are part of an artistic game that the will in
the eternal amplitude of its pleasure plays with itself." "This
primordial phenomenon of Dionysian art," Nietzsche explains,
may be understood as analogous to "the wonderful significance
of *musical dissonance*"—that is, to dissonance "artistically employed." For just as every dissonance implies a new and larger
harmony of which it forms a part and toward which it consequently serves as a means, so too does every form reach for a
form beyond itself, a form which exceeds its present limitations
and therefore defines a new and more inclusive whole. This
longing, carried to infinity, constitutes for Nietzsche the essence
of "the tragic effect":

> For we now understand what it means to wish to see tragedy
> and at the same time to long to get beyond all seeing: referring
> to the artistically employed dissonances, we have to characterize
> the corresponding state by saying that we desire to hear and at
> the same time long to get beyond all hearing. That striving for
> the infinite, the wing-beat of longing that accompanies the
> highest delight in clearly perceived reality, reminds us that in
> both states we must recognize a Dionysian phenomenon: again
> and again it reveals to us the playful construction and destruc-
> tion of the individual world as the overflow of a primordial de-
> light. Thus the dark Heracleitus compares the world-building
> force to a playing child that places stones here and there and
> builds sand hills only to overthrow them again.

In Nietzsche's view, therefore, just as form ultimately strives
toward formlessness, toward the destruction of the limitations
inherent in all forms, so at the same time does formlessness desire resolution into form. This notion is related to the conception of perpetual "exchange" suggested by fragment 90 of
Heracleitus: "All things are an Exchange for Fire, and Fire for
all things, just as goods for gold and gold for goods." And in-

deed, commenting upon the transformations of this living fire conceived by Heracleitus to be the very substance of the cosmos, which "was ever and is and shall be ever-living Fire, kindled in measure and quenched in measure," in one of his earliest works Nietzsche observes that ". . . just as the child and the artist play, the eternally living fire plays, builds up and destroys, in innocence . . . like a child he piles heaps of sand by the sea, piles up and demolishes; from time to time he recommences the game. A moment of satiety, then again the desire seizes him, as desire compels the artist to create. Not wantonness, but the ever newly awakening impulse to play, calls into life other worlds. . . ."* It is in this way, finally, that "existence and the world are eternally *justified*," in Nietzsche's view, "only as an aesthetic *phenomenon*"; for the entire cosmos is seen as taking on meaning only by virtue of its ceaselessly giving form to itself—ever new forms to itself—through the process of art. Consequently, art for Nietzsche comes to be regarded as the ultimate value-creating activity, providing us with a joyful vision of the inevitably benign and inexhaustibly productive aspect of nature, and of all of our experience. By offering itself as a model for the playful activity of the whole universe, and therefore for all human activity, it enables us to see an unending process of liberation in what might otherwise be apprehended as nothing more than a spectacle of continual chaos, disintegration, and loss.

3.

An argument for the necessity of redeeming life through art which is similar in many ways to the one outlined by Nietzsche

---

* Compare Santayana on Emerson: "He was like a young god making experiments in creation: he blotched the work, and always began on a new and better plan. Every day he said 'Let there be light,' and every day the light was new. His sun, like that of Heraclitus, was different every morning."

in his Meditation on Schopenhauer (particularly in its insistence on the blindness and aimlessness of nature) is advanced
by James throughout the Prefaces. Speaking, for example, of
his own inveterate tendency in conceiving his fiction to seize
upon the most infinitesimal "germ of a 'story,' . . . a single
small seed, a seed . . . minute and wind-blown" which may
have taken the form of "a mere floating particle in the stream
of talk," James explains that the nature of this "precious particle—reduced, that is, to its more fruitful essence," is such that "at
touch of [it] the novelist's imagination winces as at the prick
of some sharp point. . . ." The "virtue" of "the stray suggestion, the wandering word, the vague echo" for the imaginative
author "is all in its needle-like quality, the power to penetrate
as finely as possible. This fineness it is that communicates the
virus of suggestion, anything more than the minimum of which
spoils the operation." Consequently, inasmuch as "one's subject is in the merest grain, the speck of truth, of beauty, of
reality, scarce visible to the common eye," James concludes that
"the first thing to be done for the communicated and seized
idea is to reduce almost to nought the form, the air as of a mere
disjoined and lacerated lump of life, in which we may have happened to meet it."

The reason for James's insistence on this precaution is not
difficult to fathom. The particle must be torn out of the actual
circumstances in which it appeared before those circumstances
have worked to limit the range of its suggestiveness, before it
has become impossible to perceive it in any other relation.
Moreover, in his view, the more complete the information the
novelist is given about the actual outcome of the particular incident or situation which has captured his creative interest, the
more precise the details he is provided with about the real-life
event, the less there is left to his imagination; as a result, he is
prevented from freely constructing the whole form which the

fragment in itself suggests to him, and is instead reduced to the melancholy contemplation of "clumsy life again at her stupid work." And indeed, like Wilde, James hardly troubles to conceal his scorn for life's ineptitude in this regard, for it is his firm conviction that under actual circumstances the finest possibilities for the interesting and illuminating development of any situation will almost invariably be left unrealized or destroyed:

> For the action taken, and on which my friend, as I knew she would, had already begun all complacently and benightedly further to report, I had absolutely, and could have, no scrap of use; one had been so perfectly qualified to say in advance: "It's the perfect little workable thing, but she'll strangle it in the cradle, even while she pretends, all so cheeringly, to rock it; wherefrom I'll stay her hand while yet there's time." I didn't, of course, stay her hand—there never *is* in such cases "time"; and I had once more the full demonstration of the fatal futility of Fact. The turn taken by the excellent situation—excellent, for development, if arrested in the right place, that is in the germ—had the full measure of the classic ineptitude; to which with the full measure of the artistic irony one could once more, and for the thousandth time, but take off one's hat. It was not, however, that this in the least mattered, once the seed had been transplanted to richer soil; and I dwell on that almost inveterate redundancy of the wrong, as opposed to the ideal right, in any free flowering of the actual, by reason only of its approach to calculable regularity.

James confesses that besides eliciting such wonderfully measured expressions of profound impatience from him—impatience to the point of downright exasperation—it "amuses him again and again to note how, beyond the first step of the actual case, the case that constitutes for [the novelist] his germ, his vital particle, his grain of gold, life persistently blunders and deviates, loses herself in the sand." For life, possessing no clear sense of the aristic goal which would endow the chain of experience with

its finest meaning, wanders aimlessly; and since it "has no direct
sense whatever for the subject" perceived by the artist, it "is
capable, luckily for us, of nothing but splendid waste." This
"splendid waste" represents that supply of human experience
which is available for the artist to salvage; hence, James asserts,
because "waste is only life sacrificed and thereby prevented from
'counting,' I delight in a deep-breathing economy and an organic form." Indeed, in James's view it is not only the function
but also the responsibility of the artist to conserve the fund of
human experience which life is so often inclined to squander, to
reclaim experience from worthlessness and to make it reusable,
as it were, by endowing it with clear purpose and illustrative
value ("the general and the only source of success of a work of
art," James maintains in "The Art of Fiction," is "that of being
illustrative") : "Hence the opportunity for the sublime economy
of art, which rescues, which saves, and hoards and 'banks,' in-
vesting and reinvesting these fruits of toil in wondrous useful
'works' and thus making up for us, desperate spendthrifts that
we all naturally are, the most princely of incomes."

For James, therefore, art is profoundly "useful" in the conduct of one's life; indeed, as he asserts of literature in particular
in an angry letter to H. G. Wells (written when James was
seventy-two, partly in response to "a devastating lampoon upon
himself and his literary method expressed through the lips of
the author's fictional hero" in Wells's 1915 novel, *Boon*), "I
regard it as relevant to a degree that leaves everything else behind." In an earlier letter to James, Wells had attempted to
justify his attack on him by relating it to what he claimed was
"a real and very fundamental difference in our innate and developed attitudes toward life and literature." "To you," Wells
had maintained, "literature like painting is an end, to me literature like architecture is a means, it has a use." James's reply to
this assertion was decisive and unequivocal. "There is no sense

in which architecture is aesthetically 'for use' that doesn't leave any other art whatever exactly as much so," he wrote: "It is art that *makes* life, makes interest, makes importance, for our consideration and application of these things, and I know of no substitute whatever for the force and beauty of its process." Significantly, in a further letter to James on this subject (dated July 13, 1915), Wells noted, with his usual combination of irritating literalness and undeniable acuteness: "When you say 'it is art that *makes* life, makes interest, makes importance,' I can only read sense into it by assuming that you are using 'art' for every conscious human activity. I use the word for a research and attainment that is technical and special. . . ." With respect to a similar conflation of meanings on Nietzsche's part, Arthur Danto observes that " 'Art' . . . has both a wide and narrow use in Nietzsche's writings, and the wide use takes its meaning from the narrow one. Because we know what artists in the narrow sense distinctively do, we are able to see how we, in other activities, are artists as well." Hence, Danto concludes, "Nietzsche . . . means to claim that our original and most fundamental involvement with experience is artistic and transforming, that we spontaneously seek to express, in images and apposite cadences, the way in which we feel and perceive the world."

Of the artistic process, James observes elsewhere that "it prolongs, it preserves, it consecrates." Indeed, "in literature," he contends, "we move through a blest world in which we know nothing except by style, but in which also everything is saved by it, and in which the image is thus always superior to the thing itself." For in his "attempt to render the look of things, the look that conveys their meaning," the artist wrests his material out of the grip of the actual; seeking to construct an "illusion of life" that parallels the actual but in which meaning has been realized, "it is here in very truth that he competes with life." In a famous passage in his Preface to *The Ambassadors,* James elaborates upon the nature of this process:

> Art deals with what we see, it must first contribute full-handed that ingredient; it plucks its material, otherwise expressed, in the garden of life—which material elsewhere grown is stale and uneatable. But it has no sooner done this than it has to take account of a *process*—from which only when it's the basest of the servants of man, incurring ignominious dismissal with no "character," does it, and whether under some muddled pretext of morality or on any other, pusillanimously edge away. The process, that of expression, the literal squeezing-out, of value, is another affair—with which the happy luck of mere finding has little to do.

The competition between art and life therefore centers on the revelation of value, and in James's view the final superiority of art in this respect consists in its ability to appropriate specific experiences and reconstruct them according to that principle of conversion by which the accidental is made to yield the necessary, the random the purposeful, the individual the representative; as a result, the work of art succeeds in generating and preserving meanings which extend beyond its own particulars. "Life being all inclusion and confusion," James observes, "and art being all discrimination and selection, the latter, in search of the hard latent *value* with which alone it is concerned, sniffs round the mass as instinctively and unerringly as a dog suspicious of some buried bone." Carefully qualifying the metaphor, however, he concludes by asserting that "while the dog desires his bone but to destroy it, the artist finds in *his* tiny nugget, washed free of awkward accretions and hammered into a sacred hardness, the very stuff for a clear affirmation, the happiest chance for the indestructible."

In a similar way, the conception of the self as an ever-emerging work of art seems to have provided both Nietzsche and James with an ongoing assurance of what can only be regarded as a form of immortality. For in their shared vision, the self is continuously defined and redefined as new values and truths latent in experience are raised to consciousness, requiring in their turn new definitions of the self; in principle, this process never ends, for it is never possible to reach a point at which it would make sense to say that the self had achieved completion. And indeed the artistic process in general, for both Nietzsche and James, though it may resolve itself momentarily into fixed forms, consists essentially in the ceaseless sloughing off of older and narrower forms in favor of newer and more inclusive ones. Similarly, out of new perceptions, the self is endlessly born anew, and the whole world with it.

Hence James, in his seventieth year, writes to Henry Adams advising him to cultivate his consciousness as a way of overcoming the inveterate gloominess of his temperament (James is replying to a "melancholy outpouring" which he has recently received from Adams, and which he confesses he knows not "how better to acknowledge . . . than by the full recognition of its unmitigated blackness"). For his own part, James maintains, "I still find my consciousness interesting—under *cultivation* of the interest"; and he continues: "You see I still, in presence of life (or of what you deny to be such,) have reactions—as many as possible—and the book I sent you [*Notes of a Son and Brother*, which had just been published] is a proof of them. It's, I suppose, because I am that queer monster, the artist, an obstinate finality, an inexhaustible sensibility. Hence the reactions—appearances, memories, many things, go on playing upon it with consequences that I note and 'enjoy' (grim word!) noting. It all takes doing—and I *do*. I believe I shall do yet again—it is still an act of life." Thus, just as Nietzsche insists that there is finally no clear distinction between the process of art and the process of life itself, so too James, as

F. R. Leavis has perceived, "in many ways . . . expresses his charged sense that the creativity of art is the creativity of life—that the creative impulsion *is* life, and could be nothing else."

4.

Insofar as art for James involves what R. P. Blackmur has called—in a deceptively simple phrase—"the imaginative representation of life," it consists in appropriating actual experience as material and "imposing on it the form of the imagination, the acutest relevant sensibility, which felt it." Accordingly, in discussing the character of Henry St. George in his Preface to *The Lesson of the Master*, James is careful to "maintain his situation to have been in *essence* an observed reality," but he is no less emphatic in asserting that "I should be utterly ashamed, I equally declare, if I hadn't done quite my best for it." James then goes on to suggest the nature of the transformation which takes place as the "observed reality" passes through the medium of the artist's sensibility and its "truth" is, as a consequence, revealed:

> It was the fault of this notable truth, and not my own, that it too obscurely lurked—dim and disengaged; but where is the work of the intelligent painter of life if not precisely in some such aid given to true meanings to be born? He must bear up as he can if it be in consequence laid to him that the flat grows salient and the tangled clear, the common—worst of all!—even amusingly rare, by passing through his hands.

The characteristically ironic apology offered here for the artist's imaginative "gifts"—the very word is revealing—is reminiscent of Wilde, and the passage as a whole serves to remind us of how little patience both men had for what they regarded as the unimaginative and essentially servile practice of literary realism in their own time. (Needless to say, Nietzsche shared this view.) As much of our previous discussion suggests, it

would be possible to cite numerous pronouncements from the
critical writings of these two authors in which they appear to
echo one another's judgments, values, and theoretical assumptions; here, for our present limited purposes, are a handful from
Wilde's "The Decay of Lying":

> The only real people are the people who never existed, and if a
> novelist is base enough to go to life for his personages he
> should at least pretend that they are creations, and not boast of
> them as copies. The justification of a character in a novel is not
> that other persons are what they are, but that the author is
> what he is.

> As the inevitable result of [the] substitution of an imitative for
> a creative medium, [the] surrender of an imaginative form, we
> have the modern English melodrama. The characters in these
> plays . . . are taken directly from life and reproduce its vul-
> garity down to the smallest detail . . . they would pass unno-
> ticed in a third-class railway carriage. And yet how wearisome
> the plays are! They do not succeed in producing that impres-
> sion of reality at which they aim, and which is their only reason
> for existing. As a method, realism is a complete failure.

> We have mistaken the common livery of the age for the ves-
> ture of the Muses, and spend our days in the sordid streets and
> hideous suburbs of our vile cities when we should be out on the
> hillside with Apollo. Certainly we are a degraded race, and
> have sold our birthright for a mess of facts.

As the second of these quotations makes especially clear, for
Wilde, as for James, "the illusion of reality" after which the
artist strives cannot simply be produced by a commitment to
literary realism as a systematic method of representation. The
larger implications of this issue are too involved to enter into
here, but it is important to remember that the fact that an author rejects the current prescribed method of realism (a historically identifiable phenomenon in this context) in no way

signifies that he has abandoned his commitment to the principle of literary realism.

If "the illusion of life" is to be preserved—and in James's view it must be preserved at all costs—the transmutation that his account suggests must be extremely subtle; indeed, it requires a kind of artistic sleight-of-hand to convince the reader that the sequence of experiences to which he is a witness is taking place within the limits of the actual at the same time as those experiences are being refined and intensified before his very eyes so as to yield what James significantly calls "the *best* residuum of truth"—a commodity not regularly available under the conditions of everyday life.

By way of contrast, James's remarks on "romance" (contained in his Preface to *The American*) should be taken into account here: "The only general attribute of projected romance that I can see," he writes, "the only one that fits all the cases, is the fact of the kind of experience with which it deals—experience liberated, so to speak; experience disengaged, disembroiled, disencumbered, exempt from the conditions that we usually know to attach to it and, if we wish so to put the matter, drag upon it, and operating in a medium which relieves it, in a particular interest, of the inconvenience of a *related*, a measurable state, a state subject to all our vulgar communities. The greatest intensity may be so arrived at evidently—when the sacrifice of community, of the 'related' sides of situations, has not been too rash. It must to this end not flagrantly betray itself; we must even be kept if possible, for our illusion, from suspecting any sacrifice at all. The balloon of experience," James continues, "is in fact of course tied to the earth, and under that necessity we swing, thanks to a rope of remarkable length, in the more or less commodious car of the imagination; but it is by the rope we know where we are, and from the moment that cable is cut we are at large and unrelated: we only swing apart from the globe—though remaining as exhilarated, naturally, as we like, especially when all goes well. The art of the romancer is, 'for the fun of it,' insidiously to cut the cable, to cut it without our detecting him."

Unlike the romancer, the literary realist possessed of the kind of moral seriousness that James regards as essential to the novel at its most ambitious and worthwhile is not at liberty to allow experience to drift free of its entanglements in actual conditions; for his work to provide an image of experience which is effectively exemplary, it must maintain continuity with the actualities of existence.

It is in this context that one must understand James's otherwise perplexing remark that the truest realism is "the real most finely mixed with life, which *is* in the last analysis the ideal." Similarly, in praise of Alphonse Daudet he observes: "It is the real—the transmuted real—that he gives us best; the fruit of a process that adds to observation what a kiss adds to a greeting."

Significantly, but not surprisingly, Nietzsche expresses correlative views on the matter of artistic representation. In a passage from *Twilight of the Idols*, reflecting on the "physiological condition" of "frenzy" which he considers "indispensable" "if there is to be any aesthetic doing and seeing," he observes that "what is essential in such frenzy is the feeling of increased strength and fullness"; it is this feeling, in Nietzsche's view, which ultimately issues in the impulse to transform reality:

> Out of this feeling one lends to things, one *forces* them to accept from us, one violates them—this process is called *idealizing*. Let us get rid of a prejudice here: idealizing does not consist, as is commonly held, in subtracting or discounting the petty and inconsequential. What is decisive is rather a tremendous drive to bring out the main features so that others disappear in the process.

> In this state one enriches everyone out of one's own fullness: whatever one sees, whatever one wills, is seen swelled, taut, strong, overloaded with strength. A man in this state transforms things until they mirror his power—until they are reflections of his perfection. This *having to* transform into perfection is—art. Even everything that he is not yet, becomes for him an occasion of joy in himself; in art man enjoys himself as perfection.

Although the implications of aggression here may tend to cloud the issue somewhat, it is clear that what Nietzsche is affirming, albeit in an extreme form, is the artist's conviction that art achieves its mastery over reality by deliberately imposing meaning and value on the things of this world. Zarathustra's speech "On the Gift-Giving Virtue" strikes the same note; in that speech the prophet says of his disciples, "You force all things to and into yourself that they may flow back out of your well as the gifts of your love." In a remarkably similar way, Percy Lubbock, with characteristic sureness of perception, remarks of James that "he did not scruple to claim that except through art there is no life that can be known or appraised. It is the artist who takes over the deed, so called, from the doer, to give it back again in the form in which it can be seen and measured for the first time; without the brain that is able to close round the loose unappropriated fact and render all its aspects, the fact itself does not exist for us."

Nietzsche's insistence upon "frenzy" as a necessary precondition for the process of artistic creation would seem to be related to a growing and unkillable suspicion on his part that no matter how much reality may be transformed in imagination, in the world in which we are all forced to live things are still as they are. The awareness of such a possibility he must have experienced as intolerable, for in his view such a state of affairs would have reflected the ultimate impotence of the artistic will, the transforming imagination; only a sustained frenzy could blot out the recognition of such an overwhelming failure. To James, on the other hand, the disjunction between the imagined and the actual did not appear threatening. In his view, the more fact there was, the greater the world that lay open to artistic conquest; the imagination never ceased to need the actual, the allegedly intractable material, in order to maintain a sense of its own power to transform it into vision, into the stuff of dreams.

But whatever their ultimate differences, it is important for us to remember at this point that it was as a consequence of their general shared belief in the indispensable power of art that both Nietzsche and James opposed the two prevailing schools of thought in the literature of their own day: "naturalism," on the one hand, and "art for art's sake" on the other.

5.

James's refusal to be bound by the tyranny of actuality, his rejection of "the fatal futility of Fact," has already been considered at some length. The position taken by Nietzsche is obviously similar, and even in a work as early as *The Birth of Tragedy* he contends that "art is not merely imitation of the reality of nature but rather a metaphysical supplement of the reality of nature, placed beside it for its overcoming." And in *Twilight of the Idols* he makes his opposition to naturalism entirely explicit (for example, in the epigram characterizing the art of Zola as "the delight in stinking"), and goes on to advance an argument against what he takes to be the underlying assumption of this literary practice. Comparing the "born psychologist" in literature with the "born painter," Nietzsche observes that neither of these investigators of the structure of reality ever "works 'from nature'; he leaves it to his instinct, to his *camera obscura*, to sift through and express the 'case,' 'nature,' that which is 'experienced' ":

What happens when one proceeds differently? For example, if, in the manner of the Parisian novelists, one goes in for back-stairs psychology and deals in gossip, wholesale and retail? Then one lies in wait for reality, as it were, and every evening one brings home a handful of curiosities. But note what finally comes of all this: a heap of splotches, a mosaic at best, but in any case something added together, something restless, a mess of screaming colors. The worst in this respect is accomplished by the Goncourts; they do not put three sentences together without really hurting the eye, the psychologist's eye. Nature, estimated artistically, is no model. It exaggerates, it distorts, it leaves gaps. Nature is *chance*. To study "from nature" seems to me a bad sign: it betrays submission, weakness, fatalism; this lying in the dust before *petits faits* is unworthy of a *whole* artist.

The *"whole* artist," in Nietzsche's view, is one who is secure in his conviction that in relation to experience what is preeminently important is that "one must know *who* one is": "to see *what* is," on the other hand, "that is the mark of the anti-artistic, the factual." Nietzsche develops this distinction further in one of the notes (dated Spring-Fall 1887; revised Spring-Fall 1888) for *The Will to Power.* "The belief that the world as it ought to be *is*, really exists," he declares, "is a belief of the unproductive who do *not desire to create a world* as it ought to be. They posit it as already available, they seek ways and means of reaching it." Hence, " 'will to truth,' " Nietzsche concludes, "*as the impotence of the will to create.*"

On the question of "art for art's sake," Nietzsche and James are again in substantial agreement: for both, this popular notion involves an implicit denial of the essential power and value of art. Hence, in a relatively early essay on Baudelaire (1876), James deplores this tendency to diminish the effective range of art, a tendency which in his judgment betrays shallowness of mind no less than immaturity of spirit on the part of many of its most vigorous advocates. "To deny the relevancy of subject-matter and the importance of the moral quality of a work of art," James declares, "strikes us as, in two words, very childish." Indeed, in his judgment, "the crudity of sentiment of the advocates of 'art for art' is often a striking example of the fact that a great deal of what is called culture may fail to dissipate a well-seated provincialism of spirit." For the adherents of this conception of art, James asserts, "talk of morality as Miss Edgeworth's infantine heroes and heroines talk of 'physic'—they allude to its being put into and kept out of a work of art, put into and kept out of one's appreciation of the same, as if it were a coloured fluid kept in a big-labelled bottle in some mysterious intellectual closet."

Eight years later, in his important essay on "The Art of Fiction," James once again insists on the implicit moral force of the whole artistic enterprise. "It is still expected," he writes there, "though perhaps people are ashamed to say it, that a production which is after all only a 'make-believe' (for what else is a 'story'?) shall be in some degree apologetic—shall renounce the pretension of attempting really to represent life":

> This, of course, any sensible, wide-awake story declines to do, for it quickly perceives that the tolerance granted to it on such a condition is only an attempt to stifle it disguised in the form of generosity. The old evangelical hostility to the novel, which was as explicit as it was narrow and which regarded it as little less favourable to our immortal part than a stage-play, was in reality far less insulting.

For Nietzsche, similarly, the critical error made by the advocates of "art for art's sake" consists in their attempting to drive traditional moral purpose out of the province of art at any cost—even at the cost of denying that their work possesses any purpose or authority whatsoever. Thus, in *Twilight of the Idols*, he observes that "the fight against purpose in art is always a

fight against the moralizing tendency in art, against its subordination to morality. *L'art pour l'art* means, 'The devil take morality!' " "But," Nietzsche goes on to point out, "even this hostility still betrays the overpowering force of the prejudice." In
other words, under these circumstances, even in its resistance to
domination by morality art remains enslaved by the conventional sense of its necessary moral purpose, for in rejecting that
purpose it comes to regard itself as having none at all. But simply because "the purpose of moral preaching and of improving
man has been excluded from art," Nietzsche argues, "it still
does not follow by any means that art is altogether purposeless,
aimless, senseless—in short, *l'art pour l'art*, a worm chewing its
own tail." "Rather no purpose at all than a moral purpose!"—
so Nietzsche summarizes the attitude of the "art for art's sake"
advocates, and "that," he concludes, "is the talk of mere passion." For in his own estimation, "art is the great stimulus to
life: how could one understand it as purposeless, as aimless, as
l'art pour l'art?"

6.

Just as Nietzsche and James share in their thinking an unwa-
vering opposition to any tendency which in their judgment
would have the effect of diminishing the province or the power
of art, so too they are united in their inclination to regard the
artistic product in itself as much less valuable and significant
than the activity which brings it into being. Thus, in the section of *Human, All-Too-Human* entitled "Against the Art of
Works of Art," Nietzsche argues for the superiority of the
process to its works:

> Art is above all and first of all meant to embellish life, to make
> us ourselves endurable and if possible agreeable in the eyes of
> others. With this task in view, art moderates us and holds us in
> restraint, creates forms of intercourse, binds over the unedu-

cated to laws of decency, cleanliness, politeness, well-timed speech and silence. Hence art must conceal or transfigure everything that is ugly—the painful, terrible, and disgusting elements which in spite of every effort will always break out afresh in accordance with the very origin of human nature. Art has to perform this duty especially in regard to the passions and spiritual agonies and anxieties, and to cause the significant factor to shine through unavoidable or unconquerable ugliness. To this great, super-great task the so-called art proper, that of works of art, is a mere accessary.

Similarly, even James, whose unremitting care and devotion to his craft was legendary, in reflecting on no less an artistic achievement than *The Ambassadors*, a work which he himself was "able to estimate . . . as, frankly, quite the best, 'all round,' of my productions," found himself obliged to admit his feeling once again "that one's bag of adventures, conceived or conceivable, has been only half-emptied by the mere telling of one's story." This may seem an extraordinary admission coming from a writer for whom "the mere telling" of the story was everything, but James goes on to explain that that "depends so on what one means by that equivocal quantity. There is the story of one's hero, and then, thanks to the intimate connexion of things, the story of one's story itself." Weighing the possibilities of illustrative value afforded by each, "I blush to confess it," James concludes, "but if one's a dramatist one's a dramatist, and the latter imbroglio is liable on occasion to strike me as really the more objective of the two."

And indeed, exactly what was at stake for James in the artistic process, that process which served to renew and refresh him whenever he engaged himself in it, is revealed in all its secret fullness by Percy Lubbock in the course of his luminous Introduction to James's letters. "In outward manners," Lubbock observes, James "was constantly haunted by anxiety and never looked forward with any confidence"; but "it was very different

in the presence of his work," for it was finally there, in "the inner shrine of his labour," that he lived both "most intensely
and most serenely," and "there he never knew the least failure
of assurance." Hence, according to Lubbock, James threw his
full weight on the belief . . . in the sanctity and sufficiency of
the life of art," and that belief "supported him and it was never
shaken":

> Henry James never took anything as it came; the thing that
> happened to him was merely the point of departure for a delib-
> erate, and as time went on a more and more masterly, creative
> energy, which could never leave a sight or sound of any kind
> until it had been looked at and listened to with absorbed at-
> tention, pondered in thought, linked with its associations, and
> which did not spend itself until the remembrance had been
> crystallized in expression, so that it could then be appropriated
> like a tangible object. To recall his habit of talk is to become
> aware that he never ceased creating his life in this way as it was
> lived; he was always engaged in the poetic fashioning of experi-
> ence, turning his share of impressions into rounded and lasting
> images. From the beginning this had been his only method of
> dealing with existence. . . .

Accordingly, it was by making of his life a work of art that
James came to possess himself wholly at last, for "his life," as
Lubbock acutely observes, "was no mere succession of facts,
such as could be compiled and recorded by another hand; it
was a densely knit cluster of emotions and memories, each one
steeped in lights and colors thrown out by the rest, the whole
making up a picture that no one but himself could dream of
undertaking to paint."

To become aware of the full, the almost unimaginable depth
of James's absorption in the processes of art would seem to require that we have access to a vision of the workings of his creative personality at once so intensely private and particular, so
unguardedly intimate, and yet of such radiant "objective" clar-

ity, that its realization seems beyond the power of words. For James, however, nothing was beyond that power, and he has in fact provided just such a vision in the form of "certain pencilled pages, found among his papers, in which he speaks with only himself for listener." From these pages, "which belong to the same order as the notes for the unfinished novels, but . . . are even more informal and confidential," Lubbock has selected a group of passages which reveal James in rapt communication with his deepest self. He is perceived at just that moment when he "surrenders to the awe and wonder of finding himself again, where he has so often stood before, on the threshold and brink of creation" ("It was absolute for him," Lubbock has previously remarked with breathtaking matter-of-factness, "that the work of the imagination was the highest and most honourable calling conceivable, being indeed nothing less than the actual creation of life out of the void"), and "it is as though for once, at an hour of midnight silence and solitude, he opened the innermost chamber of his mind and stood face to face with his genius." Indeed, Lubbock affirms, "there is no moment of all his days in which it is now possible to approach him more closely." The document which Lubbock then places before the reader is without doubt one of the most singular in all of literature; as will be seen, any attempt to annotate it would be an impertinence:

> I take this up again after an interruption—I in fact throw myself upon it under the *secousse* of its being brought home to me even more than I expected that my urgent material reasons for getting settled at productive work again are of the very most imperative. Je m'intends—I have had a discomfiture (through a stupid misapprehension of my own indeed;) and I must now take up projected tasks—this long time *entrevus* and brooded over, with the firmest possible hand. I needn't expatiate on this—on the sharp consciousness of this hour of the dimly-dawning New Year, I mean; I simply make an appeal to all the powers

and forces and divinities to whom I've ever been loyal and who haven't failed me yet—after all: never, never yet! Infinitely interesting—and yet somehow with a beautiful sharp poignancy in it that makes it strange and rather exquisitely formidable, as with an unspeakable deep agitation, the whole artistic question that comes up for me in the train of this idea . . . of the *donnée* for a situation that I began here the other day to fumble out. I mean I come back, I come back yet again and again, to my only seeing it in the dramatic way—as I can only see everything and anything now; the way that filled my mind and floated and uplifted me when a fortnight ago I gave my few indications to X. Momentary side-winds—things of no real authority—break in every now and then to put their inferior little questions to me; but I come back, I come back, as I say, I all throbbingly and yearningly and passionately, oh mon bon, come back to this way that is clearly the only one in which I can do anything new, and that will open out to me more and more, and that has overwhelming reasons pleading all beautifully in its breast. What really happens is that the closer I get to the problem of the application of it in any particular case, the more I get *into* that application, so that the more doubts and torments fall away from me, the more I know where I am, the more everything spreads and shines and draws me on and I'm justified of my logic and my passion. . . . Causons, causons, mon bon—oh celestial, soothing, sanctifying process, with all the high sane forces of the sacred time fighting, through it, on my side! Let me fumble it gently and patiently out—with fever and fidget laid to rest—as in all the old enchanted months! It only looms, it only shines and shimmers, *too* beautiful and too interesting; it only hangs there too rich and too full and with too much to give and to pay; it only presents itself too admirably and too vividly, too straight and square and vivid, as a little organic and effective Action. . . .

Thus just these first little wavings of the oh so tremulously passionate little old wand (now!) make for me, I feel, a sort of promise of richness and beauty and variety; a sort of portent of the happy presence of the elements. The good days of last August and even my broken September and my better October come back to me with their gage of divine possibilities, and I

welcome these to my arms. I press them with unutterable tenderness. I seem to emerge from these recent bad days—the fruit
of blind accident—and the prospect clears and flushes, and my
poor blest old Genius pats me so admirably and lovingly on the
back that I turn, I screw round, and bend my lips to passionately, in my gratitude, kiss its hands.

7.

In his book on Nietzsche, Arthur Danto contends that "although he had developed a pragmatic theory of truth, he often
spoke in an idiom more congenial to the *Correspondence* Theory of Truth which he was trying, not always and perhaps not
ever in the awareness that he was doing so, to overcome." By
way of developing his point, Danto goes on to express it in the
form of an attractive though debatable analogy: "Like many
innovators," he asserts, Nietzsche "was not quite sure of the
theory he invented or perhaps that he had even invented a new
theory. So the reader finds odd dissonances in his writing, somewhat like architectural disharmonies in a transitional church,
where the style being groped toward has not yet emerged, and
the architect might not even be sure that he is groping toward
a new style at all." "The inconsistency," Danto therefore concludes, "is not in his thought so much as in his language." But
this does not seem at all to be the case, for the contradiction
between two conceptions of truth which is perceived by Danto
remains at the center of Nietzsche's thinking from first to last;
indeed, he deals with it explicitly on numerous occasions, and
in the present context it may be seen as accounting for his al-
ternations between affirmation and denial of the ultimate power
of art to master a shapeless and empty reality by making it over
in its own image of harmony and inexhaustible fullness.

Thus, when Nietzsche declares that "truth is the kind of error without which a certain species of life could not live. The
value for *life* is ultimately decisive," what he has in mind is
clearly the "pragmatic" or "instrumental" conception of truth.

The same general criterion is involved in his assertion that truth is proved "by the feeling of enhanced power—by utility—by indispensability—in short, by advantages . . ."; but no sooner has he made this claim (in an 1888 note for *The Will to Power*) than he turns on it and, characterizing those "advantages" to which he has just alluded as "presuppositions concerning what truth *ought* to be like for us to recognize it," he concludes that any conception arrived at on the basis of such presuppositions is merely "a prejudice: a sign that truth is not involved at all—." Nietzsche is now evidently conceiving of the truth as an order of things which exists apart from and often despite human desires and needs, a reality upon which men are finally not free to impose their own preferred meaning; he is therefore consciously and deliberately pitting one sense of "truth" against the other. And indeed, the same opposition between provisional, pragmatic truth, the lie which is beneficial to life, and the inescapable reality of man's position in the world is reflected in Nietzsche's observation in *Beyond Good and Evil* that "something might be true while being harmful and dangerous in the highest degree." Under these circumstances, Nietzsche asserts, "it might be a basic characteristic of existence that those who would know it completely would perish, in which case the strength of a spirit should be measured according to how much of the 'truth' one could still barely endure—or to put it more clearly, to what degree one would *require* it to be thinned down, shrouded, sweetened, blunted, falsified." Consequently, as he reveals in a sequence of notes written in the 1880's for a Preface to a new edition of *The Birth of Tragedy*, it is Nietzsche's deep conviction that in the end there is only one "truth," one reality of things, "there is only *one* world, and this is false, cruel, contradictory, seductive, without meaning— A world thus constituted is the real world."

But Nietzsche finds such a conclusion sickening and ultimately unendurable, and he is therefore led to the affirmation of art as a means of constructing an illusion (a "lie," as he often calls it) powerful enough to protect us from the "truth." "*We have need of lies*," he insists, "in order to *live*." In this regard, "metaphysics, morality, religion, science" represent for Nietzsche ways of thinking that "merit consideration only as various forms of lies"; "with their help," however, "one can have faith in life." For such lies provide a means of concealing the hideous void which might otherwise be perceived at the very heart of existence. " 'Life *ought* to inspire confidence': the task thus imposed is tremendous," Nietzsche declares. "To solve it, man must be a liar by nature, he must be above all an *artist*." It is against this background that Nietzsche's conception of art as "the *good-will* to illusion" must be understood; the notion is set forth in a section of *The Gay Science* entitled "Our Ultimate Gratitude to Art":

> If we had not approved of the Arts and invented this sort of cult of the untrue, the insight into the general untruth and falsity of things now given us by science—an insight into delusion and error as conditions of intelligent and sentient existence—would be quite unendurable. *Honesty* would have disgust and suicide in its train. Now, however, our honesty has a counterpoise which helps us to escape such consequences;—namely, Art, as the good-will to illusion. We do not always restrain our eyes from rounding off and perfecting in imagination. . . . As an aesthetic phenomenon existence is still *endurable* to us; and by Art, eye and hand and above all the good conscience are given to us, *to be able* to make such a phenomenon out of ourselves. We must rest from ourselves occasionally by contemplating and looking down upon ourselves, and by laughing or weeping *over* ourselves from an artistic remoteness. . . . we need all arrogant, soaring, dancing, mocking, childish and blessed Art, in order not to lose the *free dominion over things* which our ideal demands of us. . . .

In Nietzsche's view, therefore, art serves as "the great means of making life possible, the great seduction to life, the great

stimulant to life," for inasmuch as it involves a process of re-
ordering and transforming experience in accordance with some
pattern of meaning it inevitably represents human existence as
possessing purpose and coherence. Hence the artist, in Nietzsche's account, at heart "cannot endure reality, he looks away
from it, back: he seriously believes that the value of a thing resides in that shadowy residue one derives from colors, form,
sound, ideas. . . ." Indeed, the artist's essential activity must
be regarded as a product of his will "to lie, to flight from
'truth,' to *negation* of truth." For as Nietzsche asserts in a famous dictum, "Truth is ugly. We possess *art* lest we *perish of
the truth*"—a notion clearly echoed in James's observation that
art "muffles the ache of the actual."

For Nietzsche, then, it is precisely because the truth about
human existence is menacing and ugly that the artist is necessary to convert actual experience into beautiful and ultimately
reassuring forms. And those forms, as he suggests in *The Birth
of Tragedy*, will grow in beauty and inclusiveness exactly in
proportion to the magnitude of the threat of meaninglessness
and metaphysical nausea against which they present themselves
as our only protection. Consequently, the more powerful the
form, the greater the work of art and the deeper the reassurance
of ultimate redemption it provides; in this way, man is "de-
ceived" by art, and that deception finally enables him to overcome his sense of utter powerlessness and fear in the face of his
bewildering experience, so that once again "he believes in life:
oh how enraptured he feels! What delight! What a feeling of
power! How much artists' triumph in the feeling of power!" By
participating in the transformation of reality, "man has once
again become master of '*material*'—master of truth!" He has
thus become secure in his conviction that (to borrow James's
formulation) "expression is creation and makes the reality."

This line of reasoning brings Nietzsche to the general, all-
embracing conclusion that "whenever man rejoices, he is al-

ways the same in his rejoicing: he rejoices as an artist, he enjoys himself as power, he enjoys the lie as his form of power.—" Consequently, man's well-being in this world is conceived entirely as a function of his ability to become a *"genius in lying,"* to construct and maintain illusions so powerful that they finally become invulnerable to the assaults of reality. Indeed, in Nietzsche's view such assaults must themselves serve to provide new "material" to be incorporated into the illusion, to be refined, given shape, and made beautiful; unceasingly, they offer new fuel for the hungry processes of art. Thus, " 'beauty' is for the artist something outside all orders of rank, because in beauty opposites are tamed; the highest sign of power, namely power over opposites; moreover, without tension:—that violence is no longer needed; that everything follows, obeys, so easily and so pleasantly—that is what delights the artist's will to power."

In sum, for Nietzsche (as well as for James), art thrives by feeding on all that opposes it: it is strengthened by the opposition of the actual, and indeed it requires that continual opposition to provide it with living material to be transformed. It therefore works its will by converting to its own advantage whatever is formless, painful, and chaotic; as a result, the more intractable experience it succeeds in assimilating and transmuting, the more actuality it is able to appropriate and make over in its own ideal image, the more powerful it becomes. And herein lies the essential paradox of art: for although its process is dialectical and its very existence therefore dependent on that of a real world in opposition to it, by its very nature it seeks to conquer and possess that world completely. Hence, since the ultimate goal of art is nothing less than the redemption of all experience, the transformation of the entire world, it follows that the further the range of its conquests may be made to extend, the more whole the world will begin to appear, and the richer and more coherent will seem the life of the man endowed with the artistic faith.

And indeed, as a consequence of the commitment of one's deepest energies to this all-consuming process of imaginative possession and transfiguration, it becomes possible to strengthen the illusion of artistic control to such a point that at last nothing seems beyond it: at this point, the subjugation of the real appears complete. There is no longer any opposition to the artist's efforts to realize his vision, no hostile reality left to be mastered; the world has been unified under the sign of his will, and he can imagine nothing beyond his creative power.

8.

In different ways, and with different immediate consequences (as we shall see), both James and Nietzsche eventually approached just such a point. And for both men, achieving that state of strange and absolute security seems to have required all along a fundamental conviction of the necessity for loneliness as a precondition for creative work, and a correspondingly deep inner isolation and estrangement from the everyday concerns of men. (James's frequently lamented but essentially misunderstood inability to grasp in his fiction the "downtown" realities of making money would appear to constitute an instance of such estrangement, and the reader will recall Percy Lubbock's observation that "with much that is common ground among educated people of our time and place he was never really in touch.") In Nietzsche's case especially the feeling of solitude seems to have been so intense that it could only be made bearable by being regarded as entirely self-imposed.

Thus, in the spring of 1883, after a preceding summer and winter characterized by nightmarish desolation, he writes to Gersdorff: "Ah, how much there is still hidden in me waiting to be expressed in words and form! There is no limit to the quiet, the altitude, the solitude I need around me in order to hear my inner voices." Elevating his predicament into a metaphorical condition, "I am *solitude* become man," Nietzsche observes of himself elsewhere; but in an 1888 letter to Malwida von Meysenbug he reveals the darker, more immediate side of his emotional state: "there is indeed a great *emptiness* around me," he writes. "Literally, there is no one who could understand my situation. The worst thing is, without a doubt, not to have heard for ten years a single word that actually *got through* to me—and to be understanding about this, to understand it as something necessary!" Similarly, the preceding fall he had written to Erwin Rohde: "Has anyone ever had an inkling of the real cause of my long sickness, which I have perhaps mastered now, in spite of everything? I have forty-three years behind me, and am just as alone as when I was a child."

In James's case, solitude was experienced in the very midst of society, for as Lubbock points out, "much as he always delighted in sociable communion, citizen of the world, child of urbanity as he was, all his friends must have felt that at heart he lived in solitude. . . ." ("The great man," Emerson observes in "Self-Reliance," "is he who in the midst of the crowd keeps with perfect sweetness the independence of solitude.") For James's life "within" was, according to Lubbock, "a cycle of vivid and incessant adventure, known only to himself except in so far as he himself put it into words"; these internal adventures culminated in "the daily drama of his work, with all the comfort and joy it brought him," and it was finally in this "inner shrine of his labour" that "he lived most intensely and most serenely." ("Do your work," Emerson asserts, "and you shall reinforce yourself.")

A charming reminiscence of James by Logan Pearsall Smith reminds us, however, to take into account those aspects of intense imaginative activity which are less easily sustained:

> About the profession of letters in general, the desire to do the best one could with one's pen—and this I confessed was my ambition—he made one remark which I have never forgotten.

"My young friend," he said, "and I call you young—you are disgustingly and, if I may be allowed to say so, nauseatingly young—there is one thing that, if you really intend to follow the course you indicate, I cannot too emphatically insist on. There is one word—let me impress upon you—which you must inscribe upon your banner, and that," he added after an impressive pause, "that word is *Loneliness*."

Visiting Lamb House (where Henry James now generally resided and which he was about to purchase) in early 1900, William James wrote to a friend that "its host, soon to become its proprietor, leads a very lonely life but seems in perfect equilibrium therewith, placing apparently his interest more and more in the operations of his fancy." Exactly how much interest Henry James had come to place in such operations he himself explicitly reveals in a remarkable passage in his essay on immortality (written ten years later). Reflecting on his attempts "to take the measure of my consciousness," James observes:

I had learned, as I may say, to live in it more, and with the consequence of thereby not a little undermining the conclusion most unfavorable to it. I had doubtless taken thus to increased living in it by reaction against so grossly finite a world—for it at least *contained* the world, and could handle and criticise it, could play with it and deride it; it had *that* superiority: which meant, all the while, such successful living that the abode itself grew more and more interesting to me, and with this beautiful sign of its character that the more and the more one asked of it the more and the more it appeared to give. I should perhaps rather say that the more one turned to it, as an easy reflector, here and there and everywhere over the immensity of things, the more it appeared to take; which is but another way of putting, for "interest," the same truth.

In the light of such disclosures as these, it is not entirely surprising that when James came to reveal some of the contents of his unguarded mind during the period of delirium and men-

tal confusion which preceded his death, he should have done
so in part by dictating two letters in the character of Napoleon
Bonaparte.

9.

James's fascination with the figure of Napoleon evidently went
back many years, perhaps to the novelist's adolescence, when
he had been seized with a perception of the glory of the Second Empire. At the age of seventeen James had found himself
one morning looking out upon the unforgettable spectacle of
Paris, the city of light, from the balcony of his fifth-floor room
in a hotel in the Rue de Rivoli. Below him, as Edel has noted,
"there was the wide, open Place du Palais Royal with a ceaseless swarming movement in it. . . . Across the way loomed the
new wing of the Louvre. Against the great palace wall were the
statues of Napoleon's young generals—Hoche, Marceau, Desaix." Recreating the moment years later, James recalled those
statues and observed that "what it somehow came to was that
here massed itself the shining second Empire, over which they
stood straight aloft and on guard, like archangels of the sword,
and that the whole thing was a high-pitched wonder and splendour, which we had already, in our small gaping way, got into
a sort of relation with":

> It meant, immensely, the glittering régime, and that in turn,
> prodigiously something that would probably never be meant
> quite to any such tune again: so much one positively and how-
> ever absurdly said to one's self as one stood up on the high
> balcony to the great insolence of the Louvre and to all the his-
> tory, all the glory again and all the imposed applause, not to
> say worship, and not to speak of the implied inferiority, on the
> part of everything else, that it represented.

However one may estimate the effect of this experience on
the young novelist, the majestic language which James uses to

describe it in his later years (*Notes of a Son and Brother*, from which the passage is taken, was published in 1914) is surely worth remarking; moreover, it is significant that "in later years [James] was to read avidly in Napoleonic lore and to count among his acquaintances Bonapartists and Bonaparte Princesses." Indeed, "in his library, at his death, bound in red morocco—a binding he accorded exclusively to his most valued books—were nine volumes of Napoleonic reminiscences and anecdotes which he purchased and devoured during the 1890's." Included in this collection were "the memoirs of Napoleon's General Marbot—a three-volume work popular in England throughout the 1890's," when, according to Edel, "the flood tide of Napoleonic memoir-writing was at its height; old diaries were being found; old memories were being searched." James appears to have become so enthusiastic about the three volumes of Marbot that copies "were dispatched in haste for [Robert Louis] Stevenson's enjoyment"; moreover, the three volumes that James himself "read in their French original have survived in their expensive bindings, and they disclose in their marked pages what James felt when he spoke of 'fascinated perusal.'"

It is against this background of associations that James's last dictations must be understood, but a clear idea of the specific circumstances under which those dictations were recorded is also essential. On the morning of December 2, 1915, apparently while he was dressing, James suffered a stroke (the novelist "was reported to have told his friend Howard Sturgis that his thought as he collapsed was: 'So here it is at last, the distinguished thing'"). Later in the day, fully conscious, he explained to his secretary that "he had had a stroke 'in the most approved fashion,'" and then proceeded to dictate a cable to this effect to his nephew in New York. Significantly, "on the next day he hunted in a thesaurus to find a word describing his condition—the word 'paralytic' did not satisfy him." (The ex-

traordinary investment in the power of words indicated here is
so characteristic as to require no elaboration, but it is important
that we remember that the ability to find the word which
would reflect the precise character of the experience would signify that the experience had been taken fully into consciousness, where it could be refined, seen in its various relations, and
endlessly reworked. As will become apparent, so all-consuming
was James's consciousness that the experience of his last days,
no matter how painful and elusive, does not appear ever to have
been completely beyond his powers of articulation.)

According to H. Montgomery Hyde, that night James sustained "a second stroke, which caused further paralysis." From
this time on, his mental confusion appears to have grown progressively more intense. On December 8 he called for his secretary, explaining that he wished her to transcribe his dictation,
and "Miss Bosanquet, who took the dictation directly on the
typewriter—as was James's custom" later recalled that "the
sound of the familiar machine, and the ability to ease his mind,
had helped soothe the novelist in his feverish moments." Moreover, the December 8 dictation contains assertions which would
appear to have been brought to mind by the novelist's struggling against his wounded condition (it is worth noting that although "his mind wandered on far-away places and things," the
power of James's "will to live and to do" is indicated by the fact
that he survived this assault of increasingly grave illness until
the end of February 1916); his remarks suggest an attempt to
convert his actual circumstances to some ultimate advantage.
Thus, "I find the business of coming round," he begins by asserting, "about as important and glorious as any circumstances
I have had occasion to record," and after going on to complain
of the wearying and apparently all too familiar task of discovering "within one's carcase new resources for application," he
nonetheless declares that "I feel sure I shall discover plenty of

fresh worlds to conquer, even if I am to be cheated of the amusement of them."

Within two days of this dictation, embolic pneumonia had developed and James's condition had grown considerably worse: "Mind clouded this morning," Miss Bosanquet noted in her diary for December 10, "and he has lost his own unmistakable identity—is just a simple sick man." On December 11 his condition appears to have improved somewhat, and although evidently incoherent he proceeded to dictate again; the dictation for that day reads in part as follows:

> Wondrous enough certainly to have a finger in such a concert and to feel ourselves touch the large old phrase into the right amplitude. It had shrunken and we add to its line—all we can scarce say how, save that we couldn't have left it. We simply shift the sweet nursling of genius from one maternal breast to the other and the trick is played, the false note averted. Astounding little stepchild of God's astounding young stepmother!
>
>   . . . mere patchwork transcription becomes of itself the high brave art. . . . The fault is that they had found themselves too easily great, and the effect of that, definitely, had been, within them, the want of long provision for it. It wasn't why *they* [were] to have been so thrust into the limelight and the uproar, but why they [were] to have known as by inspiration the trade most smothered in experience. They go about shivering in the absence of the holy protocol as in the—they dodder sketchily about—as in the betrayal of the lack of early advantages; and it is upon *that* they seem most to depend to give them distinction—it is upon that, and upon the *crânerie* and the *rouerie* that they seem most to depend for the grand air of gallantry. They pluck in their terror handfuls of plumes from the imperial eagle, and with no greater credit in consequence than that they face, keeping their equipoise, the awful bloody beak that he turns round upon them. We see the beak sufficiently directed in that vindictive intention, during these days of cold grey Switzerland weather, on the huddled and

hustled campaigns of the first omens of defeat. Everyone looks haggard and our only wonder is that they still succeed in "look-ing" at all. It renews for us the assurance of the part played by that element in the famous assurance [divinity] that doth hedge a king.*

The following day, apparently attempting to pick up the theme of the previous afternoon's dictation, James began again, and in the course of his remarks he said, "Next statement is for all the world as if we had brought it on and had given our push and our touch to great events"; he then proceeded:

The Bonapartes have a kind of bronze distinction that extends to their finger-tips and is a great source of charm in the women. Therefore they don't have to swagger after the fact; fortune has placed them too high and anything less would be trivial. You can believe anything of the Queen of Naples or of the Princess Caroline Murat. There have been great families of tricksters and conjurors; so why not this one, so pleasant withal? Our ad-mirable father keeps up the pitch. He is the dearest of men. I should have liked above all things seeing our sister pulling her head through the crown; one has that confident—and I should have had it most on the day when most would have been asked. But we jog on very well. Up to the point of the staircase where the officers do stand it couldn't be better, though I won-der at the *souffle* which so often enables me to pass.

The disordered but evidently growing theme was finally real-ized in a distinct form later that same day, when, according to Miss Bosanquet's account, "after luncheon [James] wanted me again and dictated, perfectly clearly and coherently, two letters from Napoleon Bonaparte to one of his married sisters—I sus-pect they weren't original composition, but subconscious mem-ory—one letter about the Tuileries and the other about some grand opportunity being offered them which they mustn't fall

* *Crânerie* (n.): pluck, swagger; *rouerie* (n.): piece of trickery, knavery, sharp practice.

below the level of. After he had finished the second letter, he seemed quite satisfied not to do any more and fell into a peaceful sleep." Edel points out that "actually the first letter was the Bonaparte letter," and that although "the second has the sharpness of tone, the 'military eloquence' of Napoleon's dictation," significantly "the novelist signed this one with his own name." In Edel's view, James "seems to have thought he was writing to his brother William and his sister-in-law Alice," but it is worth remarking that the form of address in both letters ("Dear and most esteemed brother and sister," "My dear brother and sister,") is ambiguous, and that there was another Alice in the James family.

The first of the letters reads as follows:

Dear and most esteemed brother and sister,
    I call your attention to the precious enclosed transcript of plans and designs for the decoration of certain apartments of the palaces, here, of the Louvre and the Tuileries, which you will find addressed in detail to artists and workmen who are to take them in hand. I commit them to your earnest care till the questions relating to this important work are fully settled. When that is the case I shall require of you further zeal and further taste. For the present the course is definitely marked out and I beg you to let me know from stage to stage definitely how the scheme promises, and what results it may be held to inspire. It is, you will see, of a great scope, a majesty unsurpassed by any work of the kind yet undertaken in France. Please understand I regard these plans as fully developed and as having had my best consideration and look forward to no patchings nor perversions, and with no question of modifications either economic or aesthetic. This will be the case with all further projects of your affectionate

                                                            NAPOLEONE

In one of the passages singled out by James in Marbot's memoirs, the general recalls the Emperor's remarking to him (with what intent seems clear, nor is it difficult to imagine with what effect): "Note that I do not give you an order; I merely express a wish"; and indeed James's second letter, which strikes a noticeably more domineering note, reveals a truly magisterial impatience:

> My dear brother and sister,
>   I offer you great opportunities in the exchange for the exercise of great zeal. Your position as residents of our young but so highly considered Republic at one of the most interesting minor capitals is a piece of luck which may be turned to account in the measure of your acuteness and experience. A brilliant fortune may come to crown it and your personal merit will not diminish that harmony. But you must rise to each occasion; the one I now offer you is of no common cast, and please remember that any failure to push your advantage to the utmost will be severely judged. I have displayed you as persons of great taste and great judgment. Don't leave me a sorry figure in consequence but present me rather as your very fond but not infatuated relation able and ready to back you up, your faithful brother and brother-in-law
>
>   HENRY JAMES

Sometime later, exactly when is not clear, certain other fragments were transcribed (according to Edel, "mostly by James's niece"); among these the following seem relevant in the present context:

> across the border
> all the pieces
> Individual souls, great . . . of [word lost]
> on which great perfections are
> If one does . . . in the fulfilment with the neat and pure and perfect—to the success or as he or she moves through life, following admiration unfailing [word lost] in the highway—Problems are very sordid.
>   . . . These final and faded remarks all have some interest and some character—but this should be extracted by a highly competent person only—some such, whom I don't presume to

name, will furnish such last offices. In fact I do without names not wish to exaggerate the defect of their absence. Invoke more than one kind presence, several could help, and many would but it all better too much left than too much done. I never dreamed of such duties as laid upon me. This sore throaty condition is the last I ever invoked for the purpose.

His biographer characterizes these last utterances as possessing "an extraordinary vitality, an Olympian world weariness"; this second phrase would seem to be a sufficiently apt characterization of the tone of James's discontinuous remarks, but a more precise echo suggests itself. It may seem presumptuous to venture a literary parallel for utterances made under such painful circumstances, but James's concluding assertions in the passages quoted seem so reminiscent of Lear's "They told me I was everything. 'Tis a lie—I am not ague-proof" that a comparison is difficult to resist. For in their slow, majectic cadences and air of undiminished dignity, James's broken sentences, even in their moving pauses, evoke the closing speeches of King Lear:

> I am mightily abused. I should e'en die with pity
> To see another thus. I know not what to say.
> I will not swear these are my hands. Let's see—
> I feel this pin prick. Would I were assured
> Of my condition. . . .
> . . . to deal plainly,
> I fear I am not in my perfect mind.
> Methinks I should know you, and know this man;
> Yet I am doubtful, for I am mainly ignorant
> What place this is; and all the skill I have
> Remembers not these garments; nor I know not
> Where I did lodge last night. . . .

The imperial character of James's final words was confirmed by the novelist's physical appearance. After James's death (as H. Montgomery Hyde has pointed out), "several people who had seen the Master in his coffin were struck by the likeness of the face to Napoleon, which seemed to Theodora Bosanquet 'certainly great,' though Mrs [William] James thought that it was more like the head of Goethe."

10.

The last period of Nietzsche's active life is similarly instructive. In what becomes in retrospect a tragically prophetic letter written to Carl Fuchs in December 1887, he notes that he finds himself "almost without willing it so, but in accordance with an inexorable necessity, right in the midst of settling my accounts with men and things and putting behind me my whole life hitherto." Thus, he goes on, "almost everything that I do now is a 'drawing-the-line under everything.' The vehemence of my inner pulsations has been terrifying, all through these past years; now that I must make the transition to a new and more intense form, I need, above all, a new estrangement, a still more intense *depersonalization*." Within a year, the dark significance of these assertions has fully emerged.

Nietzsche's final transformation begins decisively when he moves to Turin in the fall of 1888. At that point, as Werner Dannhauser has observed in a penetrating essay, "a new note appears in the letters. At first it may strike us as merely an unexpectedly cheerful note. Nietzsche has regained his health and has finally found a place in which he can live permanently. The homeless wandering from city to city has ceased and the dichotomy between his work and his happiness has been abolished. But as gaiety yields to exuberance and exuberance to abandon, the note gradually and inexorably becomes ominous to our ears." And indeed, this period in Nietzsche's life does resemble the strange calm before the storm; or more precisely, that final stage of consumption when the bloom of health appears to have returned. Thus, at the end of October, Nietzsche writes to his friend Peter Gast: "I have just seen myself in the mirror—

never have I looked so well. In exemplary condition, well nourished and ten years younger than I should be." In his eyes, Turin has become the perfect city; he cannot seem to praise it
enough:

> . . . since choosing Turin as my home, I am much changed in
> the honors I do myself—I rejoice, for example, in an excellent
> tailor, and set value on being received everywhere as a dis-
> tinguished foreigner. I have succeeded amazingly well in this.
> In my *trattoria* I receive without any doubt the best there is:
> they call my attention to things, and this is especially a success.
> Between ourselves, I have never known till now what it means
> to enjoy eating—also what I need to keep up my strength. My
> criticism of the winters in Nice is now very stringent; an inade-
> quate and, especially for me, quite intolerable diet. The same,
> perhaps more so, is true, I am sorry to say, of your Venice. I
> eat here with the serenest disposition of soul and stomach.
> . . . In other ways too Nice was *pure foolery*. The Turin land-
> scape is so much more congenial to me than this chalky, tree-
> less, and stupid bit of Riviera that I am thoroughly annoyed
> at having been so late in putting it behind me. I shall say
> nothing of the contemptible and venal kind of people there—
> not excluding the foreigners. Here day after day dawns with
> the same boundless perfection and plenitude of sun: the
> glorious foliage in glowing yellow, the sky and the big river
> delicately blue, the air of the greatest purity—a Claude Lorrain
> such as I never dreamed I would see. Fruits, grapes in the
> brownest sweetness—and cheaper than in Venice! In every way,
> life is worth living here. The coffee in the best cafés, a small
> pot of remarkably good coffee, even the very best quality, such
> as I never found before, twenty centimes—and in Turin one
> does *not* pay a tip. My room, *best* position in the center, sun-
> shine from early morning until afternoon. . . .

Nietzsche goes on to suggest what would seem to be the chief
source of his growing joy and confidence when he confesses to
Gast that "I sometimes look at my hand now with some dis-

trust, because I seem to have the destiny of mankind 'in the palm of my hand.' "*

It is perhaps his acceptance of this awesome imagined responsibility that leads him to the conviction that he is now everywhere acknowledged as a distinguished personage. "All in all," he writes to his mother around Christmas, "your old creature is now an immensely famous person," and he goes on to explain that his "admirers are all very *exclusive* natures, all prominent and influential people, in St. Petersburg, in Paris, in Stockholm, in Vienna, in New York. Ah, if you knew with what words the *foremost* personages express their devotion to me, the most charming women. . . ." His intellectual preeminence is now assured: "I have real geniuses among my admirers—today no other name is treated with so much distinction and reverence as mine." And he concludes by indicating that there is finally no one in Turin who does not treat him with extraordinary respect and affection. "You see," he observes, "that is the best trick of all: without a name, without rank, without wealth, I am treated here like a little prince, by everyone, down to my peddler woman, who will not rest until she has found the sweetest of all her grapes for me."

Moreover, as Dannhauser observes, "it is not only the right place for Nietzsche; it is the right time"; and he goes on to summarize with great exactness and economy Nietzsche's precise state of mind as it is revealed in the last letters:

> All things happen in the right order for him, so that he can write to August Strindberg on December 7, 1888, that "there are no more coincidences in my life." Around Christmas, he repeats this to Overbeck and adds: "I need only to think of somebody and a letter from him comes politely through the door. . . ." The will is now supreme; everything is possible.

* Compare Lear's antithetical response to Gloucester's "O, let me kiss that hand": "Let me wipe it first; it smells of mortality."

He is convinced that *Ecce Homo* will sell more copies than *Nana*. He knows he is "strong enough to break the history of mankind in two"; he knows that "in two months I shall be the foremost name on earth." He is more than a mere man; he has become a destiny.

In a draft for a letter to his sister, Elisabeth, Nietzsche complains that she has "not the remotest conception of what it means to be most closely related to the man and to the destiny in whom the question of millennia has been decided," and repeating the remark he previously made to Gast, he insists, "I hold, quite literally, the future of mankind in the palm of my hand." And of that terrible responsibility he now asserts that "the task which is imposed *upon* me is, all the same, my nature—so that only now do I comprehend what was my predestined good fortune. I play with the burden which would crush any other mortal." Accordingly, although the assumption of such a burden is seen to involve enormous self-sacrifice and self-denial, Nietzsche now perceives that burden as nothing more or less than his very nature: his own nature, that is, has become indistinguishable from the nature of things.

The notion of selflessness that is involved here is one that is related to Nietzsche's conception of the saint as "the riddle of self-conquest and deliberate final renunciation"; Nietzsche elaborates upon this notion, it will be recalled, in the early Meditation on Schopenhauer, where he asserts that "nature finally needs the saint in whom the individual ego is entirely melted away and who feels his suffering life as an identity, affinity and unity with all that is living: the saint in whom that wonder of transformation occurs, upon which the play of becoming never changes, that final and highest becoming-human after which the whole of nature strives for its redemption from itself." To reach this point, a point at which "we no longer understand the word 'I,'" requires the ultimate sacrifice of "creature" to "creator," the denial of the self that is of this world in favor of the self that is beyond it. And as a result of this final conquest over all that is "particular" and "accidental," all that is "coinciden-tal," in the human personality, it becomes possible to effect a complete identification between the processes of self and the processes of the living cosmos. This state of total identification between world and self, a state in which there is no longer any way of distinguishing between the two realms, is depicted by Nietzsche in a memorable note for *The Will to Power*:

And do you know what "the world" is to me? Shall I show it to you in my mirror? This world: a monster of energy, without beginning, without end; a firm, iron magnitude of force that does not grow bigger or smaller, that does not expend itself but only transforms itself; as a whole, of unalterable size, a house-hold without expenses or losses, but likewise without increase or income; enclosed by "nothingness" as by a boundary; not something blurry or wasted, not something endlessly extended, but set in a definite space as a definite force, and not a space that might be "empty" here or there, but rather as force throughout, as a play of forces and waves of forces, at the same time one and many, increasing here and at the same time de-creasing there; a sea of forces flowing and rushing together, eternally changing, eternally flooding back, with tremendous years of recurrence, with an ebb and a flood of its forms; out of the simplest forms striving toward the most complex, out of the stillest, most rigid, coldest forms toward the hottest, most turbulent, most self-contradictory, and then again returning home to the simple out of this abundance, out of the play of contradictions back to the joy of concord, still affirming itself in this uniformity of its courses and its years, blessing itself as that which must return eternally, as a becoming that knows no satiety, no disgust, no weariness: this, my *Dionysian* world of the eternally self-creating, the eternally self-destroying, this mystery world of the twofold voluptuous delight, my "beyond good and evil," without goal, unless the joy of the cradle is itself a goal; without will, unless a ring feels good will toward itself—do you want a *name* for this world? A *solution* for all its riddles? A *light* for you, too, you best-concealed, strongest, most intrepid, most midnightly men?—*This world is the will to power—and nothing besides!* And you yourselves are also this will to power—and nothing besides!

At this point it would be useful to take into account some observations concerning Napoleon made by the French historian Albert Guérard. In the case of that remarkable figure, Guérard maintains, "we come to the paradoxical conclusion that the will to dominate . . . had absorbed even [Napoleon's] desire to be himself." Thus, " 'The greater a man,' [Napoleon] wrote, 'the less is the province of his *will*: he is dependent upon events and circumstances. . . . I am bound above all other men. My master is pitiless, for that master is the nature of things.' " And Guérard goes on to assert that "the obliteration of Self for the realization of absolute egotism, the abdication of the will as a condition of supreme energy: these contradictions are absurd only in the eyes of shallow logicians." "For the slavery that is irksome and degrading," he concludes, "is the petty slavery to the caprice of individuals. He who abandons himself consciously to an irresistible transcendent force is emancipated thereby from all human doubts and fears."

The "transcendent force" to which Nietzsche ultimately gives himself up, though it demands the total surrender of a coherent personality, seems to him to be nothing but his own highest destiny; and by fulfilling that destiny, he arrives at that *amor fati*, that love of his own fate, of which he writes on more than one occasion. As a consequence, he is transported beyond pointless suffering, beyond resistance to the painful conditions of his life; he seems to have achieved at last the superhuman "eye of Zarathustra," and "for such a goal—what sacrifice wouldn't be fitting? what 'self-overcoming' what 'self-denial'?"

It is in this relation, finally, that Nietzsche's last letter must be perceived. The letter is one of several written just after Nietzsche had entered that condition of hopeless insanity in which, as Dannhauser points out, he was to remain, growing "steadily more docile, silent, comatose," until his "second death" more than ten years later; postmarked January 5, 1889, the letter is addressed to the great historian Jakob Burckhardt, who had once been his colleague at Basel, and it begins with what may well be the most chilling assertion of "selflessness" ever recorded: "Actually I would much rather be a Basel professor than God," Nietzsche writes, "but I have not ventured to carry my private egoism so far as to omit creating the world on this account."

VI
The Alchemy of Opposites

"Fair and foul are near of kin,
And fair needs foul," I cried.
W. B. YEATS

The way in which dreams treat the category of contraries and contradictories is highly remarkable. It is simply disregarded. "No" seems not to exist so far as dreams are concerned. They show a particular preference for combining contraries into a unity or for representing them as one and the same thing. Dreams feel themselves at liberty, moreover, to represent any element by its wishful contrary; so that there is no way of deciding at first glance whether any element that admits of a contrary is present in the dream-thoughts as a positive or as a negative.
FREUD *The Interpretation of Dreams*

1.

The sense of sureness and well-being which it is possible for artists to achieve derives, in Nietzsche's view, from their "knowing only too well that precisely when they no longer do anything 'voluntarily' but do everything of necessity, their feeling of freedom, subtlety, full power, of creative placing, disposing, and forming reaches its peak—in short, that necessity and 'freedom of the will' then become one in them." At the very moment of creation, the dialectical process of art appears suspended, for

243

the artist comes to regard his will as an expression of the nature of reality itself. Accordingly, although the act of artistic creation necessarily involves the imposition of form on a resistant material, the form that the artist seeks to impose does not appear to him to be merely an arbitrary one: in his view, that form corresponds (in the particular case) to the discovered structure of reality itself, and that structure, that pattern of meaning toward which the reality appears to strive but which, lacking consciousness, it is incapable of attaining, ultimately enlists the artist as the agent of its realization. Like the sculptor who has glimpsed the figure in the stone, he must obey that form which represents itself as necessary, and as a consequence the reality he labors to bring into being seems to him far more than his personal fabrication: for him, it is ultimately the world itself which is his handiwork, and he seems to have no choice but to yield to its plea for existence.

In *The Golden Bowl*, Maggie Verver reveals a similar double aspect, for in the troubling circumstances in which she finds herself she seems to be both victim and victor, both selfless and self-assertive, and her triumph consists first and last in her emergent ability to do exactly what the situation demands; indeed, it is only by so doing that she is able to avert personal disaster and achieve what both she and her billionaire father regard as ultimate "success." Moreover, Maggie's double aspect—as well as that of the other major characters in this spellbinding novel in which every emotion and act seems to tremble at every moment on the edge of its opposite—must be related to James's implicit conviction that the power of the free spirit to prevail and not simply survive in the real world is finally dependent on a fusion of contradictory qualities of personality. For although Maggie may be the slave of her sense of ideal possibilities ("You Americans are almost incredibly romantic," the Prince observes very early in the novel, and Maggie replies: "Of course we are.

That's just what makes everything so nice for us"), she must—and does—succeed in mastering the reality that she is forced to face.

And the reality, in this case, is full of the menace of particularly sordid possibilities. Indeed, there is no mistaking James's sense that for all its dazzling elegance and ostensible refinement of manners, the world of *The Golden Bowl* (especially as its dark dimensions are revealed through the daydreams and momentary fantasies of its characters) is in essence an "arena" into which the author has chosen to "get down . . . and do my best to live and breathe and rub shoulders and converse with the persons engaged in the struggle that provides for the others in the circling tiers the entertainment of the great game." Significantly, James describes the characters caught in this struggle as "the real, the deeply involved and immersed and more or less bleeding participants," and the force of this description is brought home again and again in the course of the novel as pressures mount and hover at the breaking-point until every conversation has the air of an encounter in which the characters are taking their lives into their hands, attacking, circling, backing off, seeking to conceal their intentions and defend themselves. Indeed, in this regard James might just as well have been defining the effect of his own novel when, in 1897, he observed of Ibsen's *John Gabriel Borkman:* "There is no small talk, there are scarcely any manners. . . . Well in the very front of the scene lunges with extraordinary length of arm the Ego against the Ego, and rocks in a rigor of passion the soul against the soul."

Thus, as Maggie sits one evening musing while a party of the main characters plays bridge nearby—a party from which she and Colonel Bob Assingham have temporarily removed themselves—her thoughts reveal that "erect above all for her was the sharp-edged fact of the relation of the whole group,

individually and collectively, to herself—herself so speciously
eliminated for the hour, but presumably more present to the
attention of each than the next card to be played"; at length,
as a consequence of her awareness of the awareness of these
"serious and silent" players at their game of cards in the
charged atmosphere of the smoking-room at Fawns, "the
amount of enjoyed or at least achieved security represented by
so complete a conquest of appearances . . . acted on her
nerves precisely with a kind of provocative force":

> She found herself for five minutes thrilling with the idea of the
> prodigious effect that, just as she sat there near them, she had
> at her command; with the sense that if she were but different—
> oh ever so different!—all this high decorum would hang by a
> hair. There reigned for her absolutely during these vertiginous
> moments that fascination of the monstrous, that temptation of
> the horribly possible, which we so often trace by its breaking
> out suddenly, lest it should go further, in unexplained retreats
> and reactions.

The emotion continues to rise and fill her mind, and "after
it had been thus vividly before her for a little that, springing up
under her wrong and making them all start, stare and turn
pale, she might sound out their doom in a single sentence, a
sentence easy to choose among several of the lurid—after she
had faced that blinding light and felt it turn to blackness," she
makes her way out to the terrace, seeking to "get away, in the
outer darkness, from that provocation of opportunity which
had assaulted her, within on her sofa, as a beast might have
leaped at her throat."

The full significance of the fusion of rage and terror represented by this image is disclosed in the final stages of the novel,
first in Maggie's perception of Charlotte as a "splendid shining
supple creature . . . out of the cage, . . . at large," then soon
afterward as she imagines herself as the beast's victim, "thrown

over on her back with her neck from the first half-broken and her helpless face staring up," and finally (for the intense economy of imagery and language in the novel is maintained until the end) as she becomes aware of her sense regarding her father's ultimate possession of Charlotte that "the likeness of their connexion wouldn't have been wrongly figured if he had been thought of as holding in one of his pocketed hands the end of a long silken halter looped round her beautiful neck. He didn't twitch it, yet it was there; he didn't drag her, but she came," and the "two or three mute facial intimations which his wife's presence didn't prevent his addressing his daughter . . . amounted perhaps only to a wordless, wordless smile, but the smile was the soft shake of the twisted silken rope. . . ." Perceptions of this kind serve as eloquent testimony to the force of Nietzsche's assertion that "almost everything we call 'higher culture' is based on the spiritualization of *cruelty*, on its becoming more profound. . . . That 'savage animal' has not really been 'mortified'; it lives and flourishes, it has merely become—divine."

In the course of *The Golden Bowl*, Maggie Verver succeeds in making something "splendid" out of the potentially vile human materials at hand; with enormous force of will she reduces the situation and everyone involved in it to means ultimately serving to strengthen her ideal self-conception. For the masterpiece that she is engaged in creating is, in the last analysis, herself, and it is only that masterpiece which "justifies" the sordid human situation, which redeems it by converting it to use as the price to be paid for the emergence of such glory. But this process requires that Maggie somehow extricate herself from the emotional situation in which she is so unavoidably and deeply involved, and that she bring herself to face it with the artist's eye, at one remove: hence, she must neither be possessed by her own rage nor paralyzed by her timidity and "vertiginous" fear, for in either case she would be merely the slave of the situation, powerless to transform it—to make the best of it. To be adequate to the situation Maggie must be free, and "the highest type of free men," as Nietzsche observes, "should be sought where the highest resistance is constantly overcome: five steps from tyranny, close to the threshold of the danger of servitude":

> For what is freedom? That one has the will to assume responsibility for oneself. That one maintains the distance which separates us. That one becomes more indifferent to difficulties, hardships, privation, even to life itself. That one is prepared to sacrifice human beings for one's cause, not excluding oneself.

Nietzsche goes on to explain that freedom "in individuals and peoples" is measured "according to the resistance which must be overcome, according to the exertion required, to remain on top"; moreover, he contends, throughout history, "the peoples who had some value, *attained* some value," and "it was great danger that made something of them that merits respect. Danger alone acquaints us with our own resources, our virtues, our armor and weapons, our *spirit*, and *forces* is to be strong. *First* principle: one must need to be strong—otherwise one will never become strong."

As for that highest type of free man posited by Nietzsche, the man who must "be sought where the highest resistance is constantly overcome" and whose character is thus conceived as a product of conflicting forces since at any moment he seems simultaneously to be approaching and resisting opposed poles of servitude and tyranny, Nietzsche goes on to observe of him that this description of his state is "true psychologically if by 'tyrants' are meant inexorable and fearful instincts that provoke the maximum of authority and discipline against themselves." Nietzsche concludes by selecting as the "most beautiful" exam-

ple of this type "Julius Caesar," but the full range of his meaning here does not seem completely clear until one consults a
note for *The Will to Power* in which he calls for "education in
those rulers' virtues that master even one's benevolence and
pity: the great cultivator's virtues ('forgiving one's enemies' is
child's play by comparison), the affect of the creator must be
elevated—no longer to work on marble!—The exceptional situation and powerful position of those beings (compared with any
prince hitherto): the Roman Caesar with Christ's soul." As
Karl Jaspers has observed, the idea of "the Roman Caesar with
Christ's soul" represents one of "the most amazing attempts
to bring together again into a higher unity what [Nietzsche]
has first separated and opposed to each other. . . . Nietzsche
imagines—without any power of vision and unrealizably—the
synthesis of the ultimate opposition!"

In the present context, it is perhaps enough to remark that
the moral paradox which remains at the center of the action of
The Golden Bowl, and which may be seen as accounting for the
puzzling doubleness of aspect of that action, is—to borrow
Nietzsche's cogent formulation—that "one cannot establish the
domination of virtue by means of virtue itself; with virtue itself
one renounces power, loses the will to power." Similar assertions
occur elsewhere in *The Will to Power*; for example: "The victory of a moral ideal is achieved by the same 'immoral' means
as every victory: force, lies, slander, injustice." And again: "Morality is just as 'immoral' as any other thing on earth; morality
is itself a form of immorality. The great liberation this insight
brings. Contradiction is removed from things, the homogeneity
of all events is saved—"

At this point it is important to recall our earlier discussion
of William James's view of the relationship between "the two
ideals" of "strong man" and "saint"; in his lectures on "The
Value of Saintliness" in *The Varieties of Religious Experience*

(1902), it will be remembered, James cites a passage from Nietzsche's *Genealogy of Morals* and goes on to argue that "the clash between the two ideals . . . revolves essentially upon two pivots: Shall the seen world or the unseen world be our chief sphere of adaptation? and must our means of adaptation in this seen world be aggressiveness or non-resistance?" Observing that this "debate is serious," for "in some sense and to some degree both worlds must be acknowledged and taken account of; and in the seen world both aggressiveness and non-resistance are needful," James eventually arrives at the conclusion that although the saint "would be entirely adapted" to a "millennial society" and "is therefore abstractly a higher type of man than the 'strong man,' because he is adapted to the highest society conceivable, whether that society ever be concretely possible or not," nevertheless "it must be confessed that as far as this world goes, anyone who makes an out-and-out saint of himself does so at his peril." Indeed, "Christ himself," as James points out, "was fierce upon occasion."

So far as the saint's possibilities for "success" in the world are concerned, James concedes that "the greatest saints, the spiritual heroes whom everyone acknowledges . . . are successes from the outset. They show themselves, and there is no question; every one perceives their strength and their stature. Their sense of mystery in things, their passion, their goodness, irradiate about them and enlarge their outlines while they soften them." Yet William James is finally inclined to take the position that there is no absolutely valid way of measuring the success of the saint: "How is success to be absolutely measured when there are so many environments and so many ways of looking at the adaptation?" he asks. "It cannot be measured absolutely; the verdict will vary according to the point of view adopted."

But the question does not seem to have struck Henry James

in the same way, as might be gathered from his refusal to regard
the success of his spiritual heroine in *The Golden Bowl* as subject to such limitations: in his view, Maggie Verver's efforts
must be judged in the light of her admission to Fanny Assingham that all that she "bears" she bears "for love"—not love of
her father or love of her husband, but love itself, the idea of
love.* Consequently, her success or failure must be regarded
as absolute. Moreover, James's conception of Maggie's apparently contradictory character does not simply involve a "realistic" combination of self-interested and altruistic motives
which allows her to do what is necessary to survive a nasty situation with her ideals and self-respect still more or less intact.
In Maggie's character as James conceives it two conflicting sets
of feelings, each at full intensity, related to the two opposing
ideal types discussed by William James—that of the "saint"
and that of the "strong man"—are held in perilous balance.
The impulse to acquisition, self-assertion, and aggressiveness
is thus reconciled in Maggie with the impulse to renunciation,
selflessness, and nonresistance. Were these antithetical feelings
not brought into this tense equilibrium, they might threaten to
tear the self apart; but as it is their immeasurably powerful

---

* As this discussion would suggest, especially when seen in relation to the
general theme of imaginative transformation at the novel's heart, we could
wish no better gloss for *The Golden Bowl*—the title of which refers to an
essentially flawed but exquisitely beautiful vessel—than a passage from
Yeats's "Crazy Jane Talks with the Bishop." Like James's novel, Yeats's
poem is very much concerned with the movement from love (lower case)
to Love (upper case):

> A woman can be proud and stiff
> When on love intent;
> But Love has pitched his mansion in
> The place of excrement;
> For nothing can be sole or whole
> That has not been rent.

union enables Maggie to achieve a success which is at the same time worldly and otherworldly, seen and unseen.

Dorothea Krook's evident misreading of the novel in this regard is important and instructive. In her view, when, in the scene between father and daughter at the end of the novel, Maggie says, " 'It's success, father' and he answers 'It's success,' the reader is meant to see that it might be one of two kinds of success—either the good and noble kind consistent with the redemptive theme, or a success fundamentally power-seeking and acquisitive, and not the more attractive for its admixture of self-righteousness." This reading, as sensitive as it is to the divergent strains of feeling woven into the fabric of the novel, is largely a product of Miss Krook's insistence on James's "ambiguity" as the underlying principle of coherence in the work. But Maggie's success is surely not "ambiguous" in the sense Miss Krook appears to have in mind, nor is it at all clear that the reader "is meant to see that it might be one of two kinds of success." For James, the significance of Maggie's triumph is not intended to be the kind of toss-up implied by Miss Krook's formulation: as he conceives it, that triumph is absolute, not simply, as William James's remarks might lead us to expect, a function of one "point of view" or another. Indeed, to the novelist's mind, precisely what is so extraordinary, so unequivocally "splendid" about Maggie's success is that it embraces two antithetical and ostensibly irreconcilable possibilities, for it represents a triumph in the actual world as well as a triumph of the spirit. Her shattering beauty is of the kind best grasped by Rilke when he observes that "beauty is nothing / but the beginning of terror we can just barely endure, / and we admire it so because it calmly disdains / to destroy us. Every angel is terrible."

Consequently, unlike most of James's central characters, Maggie is not finally caught between two mutually exclusive sets of values, two opposing worlds: she does not achieve success in this world only at the cost of her most exigent ideals, nor does her refusal to compromise her finest expectations make her failure in the world inevitable. For Maggie, there is only one world, and what she succeeds in proving in the course of the action of *The Golden Bowl* is that she possesses the single-minded power required to rule over it. (The reader inclined to suppose that Maggie's triumph in *The Golden Bowl* represents a form of self-deception, an illusion, should bear in mind that the effect of that illusion in the novel is such that in the end "it is the world," as R. W. B. Lewis has observed, ". . . which is struck down by aggressive innocence.") In the process, the demands of reality become continuous with Maggie's own ideal desires, an expression of her own impulse to perfection; what is demanded by the particular situation is no longer a question to be answered in two ways. Self-interest and selflessness have fused, and the currency of worldly success has become interchangeable with that of spiritual nobility.

Thus, just as the crack in the symbolic golden bowl is both there and not there, so too in the novel by that name antithetical possibilities, though they remain distinct, are wed (it is surely worth noting in this regard that James explicitly regretted not being able to title the book "The Marriages" because he had used the title once before); so joined, these possibilities represent the two sides of the coin of experience, for as James notes in the Prefaces, "No themes are so human as those that reflect for us, out of the confusion of life, the close connexion of bliss and bale, of the things that help with the things that hurt, so dangling before us for ever that bright hard medal, of so strange an alloy, one face of which is somebody's right and ease and the other somebody's pain and wrong." Maggie Verver's discovery, which is that of the artist, is that the coin of experience also serves as the coin of the imaginative realm: that realm which on

its near side embraces everyday reality, and at its furthest
reaches merges seamlessly with dream.

2.

In Chapter Twenty-five of A *Small Boy and Others*, James vividly recounts his experience as a young man in Paris, and in
particular recalls the sensation of happily crossing "that bridge
over to Style constituted by the wondrous Galerie d'Apollon,
drawn out for me as a long but assured initiation and seeming
to form with its supreme coved ceiling and inordinately shining
parquet a prodigious tube or tunnel through which I inhaled
little by little, that is again and again, a general sense of *glory*."
At first "simply overwhelmed" and "bewildered" by the array
of styles, the numberless possibilities for treatment which as-
sailed him "as if they had gathered there into a vast deafening
chorus," the young man, continuing to contemplate the spectacular gallery (which contains, as F. W. Dupee has significantly noted, "certain of the crown jewels of France, as well as
decorations by Delacroix and others"), gradually became aware
that "the glory means ever so many things at once, not only
beauty and art and supreme design, but history and fame and
power, the world in fine raised to the richest and noblest expression." Thus, for James, as Lionel Trilling has pointed out in
one of his most important and far-reaching essays, the "first
great revelation of art came as an analogy with the triumphs of
the world; art spoke to him of the imperious will, with the
music of an army with banners."

Indeed, the Louvre's spectacular gallery appeared to James to
incorporate all of "monumental Paris," the living city beyond
its walls but not beyond its irresistible artistic power, to form
part of its overall effect: the "magnificent parts of the great
gallery," James wrote, ". . . arched over us in the wonder of
their endless golden riot and relief, figured and flourished in per-

petual revolution, breaking into great high-hung circles and symmetries of squandered picture, opening into deep outward embrasures that threw off the rest of monumental Paris somehow as a told story, a sort of wrought effect or bold ambiguity for a vista, and yet held it there, at every point, as a vast bright gage, even at moments a felt adventure, of experience." This *trompe l'œil* effect described by James is achieved when actuality is made to lend its energies to art, and art, in return, heightens actuality and transforms it into a kind of *tableau vivant* in which elements still functioning in the real world are caught up and enclosed at the same time within another all-embracing pattern of meaning. Consequently, as they are subjected to the dynamic process of artistic conception, redefined in relation to an expressive whole, the details of actual experience seem to exist in two realms simultaneously, and the border between those realms no longer appears distinct: in this way, the quality of actual experience is altered in direct proportion to the enhancement of the artistic illusion.

Insofar as art thus serves to transform reality by redefining it, by establishing new relationships and categories in which experience may be comprehended, it follows that artistic triumphs must be reckoned triumphs in the world, and in James's view the power of the artist must therefore be seen as of a kind with that of conquerors and heads of state. Such are the intimations of "glory" revealed by the novelist's perception of the Galerie d'Apollon, that majestic corridor in which art and worldly power rush together like a wave to overwhelm the beholder with a sense of the vast range of possibilities for excellence and splendor.

It is of course significant that the scene so conceived by James and associated with this dizzying sense of potentialities should also serve as the setting of "the most appalling yet most admirable nightmare of [his] life":

The climax of this extraordinary experience—which stands alone for me as a dream-adventure founded in the deepest, quickest, clearest act of cogitation and comparison, act indeed of life-saving energy, as well as in an unutterable fear—was the sudden pursuit, through an open door, along a huge high saloon, of a just dimly-described figure that retreated in terror before my rush and dash (a glare of inspired reaction from irresistible but shameful dread,) out of the room I had a moment before been desperately, and all the more abjectly, defending by the push of my shoulder against hard pressure on lock and bar from the other side. The lucidity, not to say the sublimity, of the crisis had consisted of the great thought that I, in my appalled state, was probably still more appalling than the awful agent, creature or presence, whatever he was, whom I had guessed, in the suddenness wild start from sleep, the sleep within my sleep, to be making for my place of rest. The triumph of my impulse, perceived in a flash as I acted on it by myself at a bound, forcing the door outward, was the grand thing, but the great point of the whole was the wonder of my final recognition. Routed, dismayed, the tables turned upon him by my so surpassing him for straight aggression and dire intention, my visitor was already but a diminished spot in the long perspective, the tremendous, glorious hall, as I say, over the far-gleaming floor of which, cleared for the occasion of its great line of priceless vitrines down the middle, he sped for his life, while a great storm of thunder and lightning played through the deep embrasures of high windows at the right. The lightning that revealed the retreat revealed also the wondrous place and, by the same amazing play, my young imaginative life in it of long before, the sense of which, deep within me, had kept it whole, preserved it to this thrilling use; for what in the world were the deep embrasures and the so polished floor but those of the Galerie d'Apollon of my childhood? The "scene of something" I had vaguely then felt it? Well I might, since it was to be the scene of that immense hallucination.

Although it is not wholly unconvincing, Leon Edel's interpretation of this nightmare as an apparent reflection of "the fears and terrors of a 'mere junior' threatened by elders and

largely by his elder brother" represents what is perhaps the
least interesting way of understanding James's remarks. Moreover, as Trilling has pointed out (and most readers who do not
share Edel's enthusiasm for the practice of free-associating for
Henry James will certainly agree), "We do not have to presume very far to find meaning in the dream, for James gives us
all that we might want. . . ." Accordingly, after having recalled
the vision of power expressed by James immediately before his
recounting of the nightmare, Trilling goes on to identify the
psychological mechanism at work here ("aggression brings guilt
and then fear") and then to elucidate the significance of the
episode in the terms in which James himself depicted it: for as
Trilling notes, it is the novelist himself who "tells us that the
dream was important to him, that, having experienced art as
'history and fame and power,' his arrogation seemed a guilty
one and represented itself as great fear which he overcame by
an inspiration of straight aggression and dire intention and tri-
umphed in the very place where he had had his imperious
fantasy."

The nightmare itself thus embodies an extraordinary reversal
of antithetical possibilities, for within it intense anxiety manifests itself and is almost at once directly resolved ("An admirable nightmare indeed," Trilling concludes, for it may be that
"one needs to be a genius to counter-attack nightmare . . .");
but it seems equally significant from another point of view that
the scene of such a reversal should be the very "palace of art."
Acting on impulse with a rush of "life-saving energy" at a moment of "unutterable fear" and suddenly forcing his locked and
barred door outward against the pressure of that "awful agent
. . . making for my place of rest," what James sees before him
is "the tremendous, glorious hall" of artistic triumph, "in the
long perspective" of which "my visitant was already a diminished spot." Reflecting on this prospect, the novelist recalls that

the "far-gleaming" corridor in which the power of art had first
revealed itself to him had always impressed him as "a splendid
scene of things," though he had never before guessed just what
a "precious part" it was to play in his own life as the scene of
"that immense hallucination," the very spot in which terror
was to be converted into psychic victory; and it now seems to
him as if for all these years "the sense . . . deep within [him]"
of the "wondrous place and . . . [his] own young imaginative
life in it of long before . . . had kept it whole, preserved it to
this thrilling use. . . ."

3.

In a remarkable passage in *Beyond Good and Evil* Nietzsche
ponders the relation between waking reality and dreams and
indicates that that relation may be very different from the one
which is traditionally assumed to obtain:

> *Quidquid luce fuit, tenebris agit:* but the other way around,
> too. What we experience in dreams—assuming that we experi-
> ence it often—belongs in the end just as much to the over-all
> economy of our soul as anything experienced "actually": we are
> richer or poorer on account of it, have one need more or less,
> and finally are led a little by the habits of our dreams even in
> broad daylight and in the most cheerful moments of our wide-
> awake spirit. Suppose someone has flown often in his dreams
> and finally, as soon as he dreams, he is conscious of his power
> and art of flight as if it were his privilege, also his characteristic
> and enviable happiness. He believes himself capable of realiz-
> ing every kind of arc and angle simply with the lightest impulse;
> he knows the feeling of a certain divine frivolity, an "upward"
> without tension and constraint, a "downward" without con-
> descension and humiliation—without *gravity!* How could a hu-
> man being who had had such dream experiences and dream
> habits fail to find that the word "happiness" had a different
> color and definition in his waking life, too? How could he fail

to—desire happiness differently? "Rising" as described by poets must seem to him, compared with this "flying," too earth-bound, musclebound, forced, too "grave."

By representing unattainable forms of human perfection as realizable possibilities, the dream engenders expectations and awakens hungers which could never be satisfied by reality. As a consequence, the insatiable craving for the ideal manifested in Nietzsche's announced attempt to achieve "an absolute victory" over the actual circumstances of his life—"that is, the trans-formation of experience into gold and use of the highest order" —may ultimately lead to a dangerous devaluation of all experi-ence. At that point, as Freud has noted, reality comes to be regarded "as the sole enemy and as the source of all suffering, with which it is impossible to live, so that one must break off all relations with it if one is to be in any way happy." Thus, Freud continues, "the hermit turns his back on the world and will have no truck with it. But one can do more than that; one can try to re-create the world, to build up in its stead another world in which its most unbearable features are eliminated and replaced by others that are in conformity with one's own wishes." "But whoever, in desperate defiance, sets out upon this path to happiness," Freud warns, "will as a rule attain nothing. Reality is too strong for him. He becomes a mad-man. . . ."

But if this rage against the actual should be located within a cultural context which not only embraces it but virtually de-mands it as a sign of moral authority, then the consequences become considerably more ambiguous. "I have written a wicked book, and feel spotless as the lamb," Melville observes of that novel in which what appears at first a perfectly familiar com-mercial adventure is continually reconceived as an assault on the mute battlements of heaven. In the American situation, as we have seen, the overriding moral imperative is that one endlessly remake oneself and the world in accordance with one's most far-reaching expectations. "I learned this, at least, by my experiment," Thoreau tells us at the end of *Walden*: "that if one advances confidently in the direction of his dreams, and endeavors to live the life he has imagined, he will meet with a success unexpected in common hours. He will put some things behind, will pass an invisible boundary; new, universal, and more liberal laws will begin to establish themselves around and within him; or the old laws be expanded, and interpreted in his favor in a more liberal sense, and he will live with the license of a higher order of beings."

Conceived in these terms, the promise of America, like the promise of art, is the assurance of an available divinity. More precisely, it is the promise of power over all experience, and ultimately of sole authorship of one's very being. Every citizen of the republic is invited (indeed obliged, according to the terms of the national self-definition) to make something of himself, to become somebody, by exceeding the conditions of his history and overcoming the accident of his first, unwilled birth. Like Gatsby, he must change his given name; he must become the artist of his own life, and his success as an American will be judged in relation to his ability to attain and remain true to his ideal conception of himself. To the extent that he is able to align his actual experience with that elusive conception, he may find that seamless happiness which, in Hawthorne's words, weaves one's "mortal life of the selfsame texture with the celestial," and permits one "to look beyond the shadowy scope of time, and living once for all in eternity, to find the perfect future in the present."

The American thus able to grasp the ultimate character of his immediate situation may secure a sense of himself which persists through ceaseless change and contradiction, and which remains invulnerable to the wear and tear of circumstances and the encroachments of other wills:

Apart from the pulling and hauling stands what I am,
Stands amused, complacent, compassionating, idle, unitary,
Looks down, is erect, or bends an arm on an impalpable
    certain rest,
Looking with its sidecurved head curious what will come
    next,
Both in and out of the game, and watching and wondering
    at it.

And as the example of Whitman would also suggest, the transcendental American, participating in a national identity founded on the dream of triumph over every possibility of servitude, may move at times beyond the boundaries of his own artistic self-conception to take his refreshment in the stream of untransformed experience. At such moments, his sense of visionary power is sustained by a belief that the unrestricted freedom which may finally elude him even as an artist remains within his grasp as the defining condition of being an American. Thus, his needs as an artist may themselves come to be perceived playfully, as if from a great aesthetic height; and he may accordingly succeed in freeing himself from the potentially devastating logic of unconditional self-conquest which results—as it did in Nietzsche—when the artistic will to convert all experience to imaginative use labors under the weight of the ultimate Christian imperative to achieve, within the confines of one's mortal life, the unalterable state of perfection.

All through his life, the artist Henry James engaged in taking precise measurements of the strength of that reality which did not correspond to his own best expectations; in the process, he came to see that he would lose far more than he gained by breaking openly with it, and that he could never hope to triumph over it by acts of "desperate defiance." And once he had thus yielded to the fact that he was marooned in the real world, the world of "things we cannot possibly *not* know, sooner or later, in one way or another," it was his deepest joy to discover that he nevertheless could, simply by turning over the coin of experience, find himself at any moment contemplating that other realm of "things that, with all the facilities in the world, all the wealth and all the courage and all the wit and all the adventure, we never *can* directly know; the things that can reach us only through the beautiful circuit and subterfuge of our thought and our desire."

Abbreviations

Works by James and Nietzsche frequently cited in the text are referred to in the Notes according to the following abbreviations:

HENRY JAMES

AN   *The Art of the Novel* (Collected Prefaces to the New York Edition, 1907-1909), intro. by Richard P. Blackmur, New York, Charles Scribner's Sons, 1937.

LHJ   *The Letters of Henry James*, 2 vols., sel. and ed. by Percy Lubbock, London, Macmillan, 1920. (Until the completion of Leon Edel's new five-volume edition of the letters—published by Harvard University Press—this remains the most comprehensive source of letters dating from all periods of the author's life.)

SLC   *Selected Literary Criticism*, ed. Morris Shapira, introductory essay by F. R. Leavis, New York, McGraw-Hill, 1965 [1964].

Edel's five-volume biography of James is referred to in the notes as "Edel," followed by a Roman numeral indicating the volume cited.

FRIEDRICH NIETZSCHE

German texts:

WDB   *Werke in drei Bänden*, ed. Karl Schlecta, 3rd ed. (which includes a fourth volume containing a valuable *Nietzsche-Index* and bibliography), Munich, Carl Hansers Verlag, 1965.

Mus.   *Gesammelte Werke, Musarionausgabe*, 23 vols., Munich, Musarion Verlag, 1920-1929. (All references to the German text of *The Will to Power* are to this edition.)

English translations:

Except where otherwise indicated, the translations cited are those by Walter Kaufmann. Individual works by Nietzsche are referred to first by title and section number, then by the Kaufmann volume in which they appear. Thus, BGE 56, ML, p. 258, indicates *Beyond Good and Evil,* section 56, which may be found in Walter Kaufmann's Modern Library *Basic Writings of Nietzsche,* p. 258. Similarly, TI ix:1, PN, p. 513, indicates *Twilight of the Idols,* chapter 9, section 1, in Kaufmann's *The Portable Nietzsche,* p. 513. In every instance, the English citation is followed by a reference to the German text.

    A   *The Antichrist* (in PN; see below).
   BT   *The Birth of Tragedy* (in ML; see below).
  BGE   *Beyond Good and Evil* (in ML).
   CW   *The Case of Wagner* (in ML).
   EH   *Ecce Homo* (in ML).
   GM   *On the Genealogy of Morals* (in ML).
   GS   *The Gay Science.*
  LFN   *Selected Letters of Friedrich Nietzsche,* ed. and trans. Christopher Middleton, Chicago, Univ. of Chicago Press, 1969.
   SE   *Schopenhauer as Educator,* trans. James W. Hillesheim and Malcolm R. Simpson, Chicago, Henry Regnery Co., 1965.
   TI   *Twilight of the Idols* (in PN).
   UA   *The Use and Abuse of History,* in *Thoughts Out of Season,* vol. II, trans. Adrian Collins (*The Complete Works of Friedrich Nietzsche,* ed. Oscar Levy, vol. V), New York, Russell and Russell, 1964; 2nd ed. rev. available in The Library of Liberal Arts, Indianapolis, Ind., Bobbs-Merrill, 1957.
   WP   *The Will to Power* (see below).
    Z   *Thus Spoke Zarathustra* (in PN).

Kaufmann translations:

   GS   *The Gay Science,* New York, Random House, 1974.
   ML   *Basic Writings of Nietzsche,* New York, Random House, 1968.

PN *The Portable Nietzsche*, New York, Viking Press, 1968.
WP *The Will to Power*, trans. Kaufmann and R. J. Hollingdale, New York, Random House, 1967.

Works referred to in the translations which appear in the Levy edition of Nietzsche (*The Complete Works of Friedrich Nietzsche*, 18 vols., London, George Allen and Unwin Ltd., 1909-1913 [rpt. by Russell and Russell, New York, 1964]) are indicated in the notes by the translator's name, followed by "Levy" and the number of the individual volume in which the translation appears.

Kaufmann's valuable source book, *Nietzsche: Philosopher, Psychologist, Antichrist*, 4th ed., Princeton, N.J., Princeton Univ. Press, 1974, is referred to in the notes as "Kaufmann."

Notes

vii. "Two pictures . . .": *The Autobiography of William Butler Yeats*, New York, Collier-Macmillan, 1965, pp. 26-27.

ix. "desperate buffoonery": Karl Löwith, quoted in Werner Dannhauser, *Nietzsche's View of Socrates*, Ithaca, N.Y., Cornell Univ. Press, 1974, p. 40. "the furthest frenzies . . .": D. H. Lawrence, *Studies in Classic American Literature*, New York, The Viking Press, 1971 [1923], p. viii.

x. "the author who has been richest in ideas . . .": Nietzsche, quoted in Kaufmann's translation of the Musarion edition (XI:283), in the "Translator's Introduction" to *The Gay Science*, New York, Random House, 1974, p. 12. "Never have I felt . . .": *ibid.* "that most difficult . . .": "We Antipodes," in *Nietzsche contra Wagner*, trans. Anthony M. Ludovici (Levy, VIII), p. 67. For Kaufmann's translation, see PN, p. 670. [WDB, II: 1048.] An earlier version of this section of the work appears in *The Gay Science*: GS, Bk. 5, Sect. 370, p. 329. [WDB, II: 245.]

xi. "Theories which bring . . .": *Studies in the History of the Renaissance*, New York, Boni and Liveright, 1919 [1873], p. 2.

xvi. "it is, above all else . . .": Mazzino Montinari, "The New Critical Edition of Nietzsche's Complete Works," trans. David S. Thatcher, *The Malahat Review*, no. 24 [special Nietzsche issue], Oct. 1972, p. 128. "the key to a balanced understanding . . .": R. J. Hollingdale, *Nietzsche*, Routledge and Kegan Paul, 1973, p. xii.

3. "I have found . . .": Nietzsche, quoted in Kaufmann, p. 252. "under the extreme . . . collapse": MS diary of Sir Sydney Waterlow, entry for Nov. 9, 1907. (Berg Collection, New York Public Library.) Quoted by H. Montgomery Hyde, *Henry James at Home*, London, Methuen & Co., 1969, p. 119. Hyde uses this anecdote to demonstrate that James "hated cats"; his notes direct the reader seeking further information about the association between James and Waterlow to S. P. Waterlow, "Memories of Henry James," *New Statesman*, Feb. 26, 1926, and Leon Edel, "Henry James and Sir Sydney Waterlow," *The* [London] *Times Literary Supplement*, Aug. 8, 1968.

4. "radically powerful and unique . . .": Edmund Gosse, quoted in *The*

Legend of the Master, compiled by Simon Nowell-Smith, New York, Scribners, 1948, p. 5.

4-5. "the strange power . . . had": Elizabeth Jordan, quoted in *ibid.*, p. 6.

5. "My servants . . .": F. M. Hueffer (later Ford Madox Ford), quoted *ibid.*, p. 8. "I found him overwhelming . . .": Theodora Bosanquet, *Henry James at Work*, The Hogarth Essays, London, printed at the Hogarth Press by Leonard and Virginia Woolf, 1924[?], pp. 244-45. The portrait of James referred to is the one painted by Jacques-Émile Blanche in 1908, which Edith Wharton describes as "the only one that renders him *as he really was*." (Edith Wharton, *A Backward Glance*, New York, Scribners, 1964 [1934], p. 175. ". . . once I was seated . . .": Bosanquet, *op. cit.*, p. 245.

6. ". . . really the partial victory. . . .": Wharton, *op. cit.*, p. 178. ". . . magisterial, . . . upon the whole. . . .": Ford Madox Ford (F. M. Hueffer), quoted in H. Montgomery Hyde, *op. cit.*, p. 74. ". . . the spiral of depression . . .": Desmond McCarthy, quoted in Nowell-Smith, *op. cit.*, p. 127. "It all seems . . .": Bosanquet, *op. cit.*, p. 248.

7. "first by reason . . .": Ezra Pound, "Henry James," *Literary Essays of Ezra Pound*, London, Faber & Faber, 1960, p. 299.

8. "had a mind so fine . . .": T. S. Eliot, "On Henry James," in F. W. Dupee, ed., *The Question of Henry James*, New York, Henry Holt & Co., 1945, p. 110. "there never was a writer . . .": Philip Rahv, "Attitudes toward Henry James," *Image and Idea*, rev. and enlarged ed., Norfolk, Conn., New Directions, 1957, p. 85. "his Utopia was an anarchy . . .": Bosanquet, *op. cit.*, p. 276.

9-10. ". . . with the complete record . . . barbarous stupidity": Bosanquet, *op. cit.*, pp. 275-76.

9n. Joseph Warren Beach, "The Figure in the Carpet," in F. W. Dupee, *op. cit.*, p. 95.

11-12. "How you go . . .": *The Correspondence of Emerson and Carlyle*, ed. Joseph Slater, New York, Columbia Univ. Press, 1964, p. 567.

13. "that the necessity . . .": Alburey Castell, "The Humanism of William James," introduction to *Essays in Pragmatism* by William James, New York, Hafner Publishing Co., 1948, p. xi. "express the interests . . .": *ibid.*, p. viii. "the end of our youth": this estimate from Henry James's *Notes of a Son and Brother* is quoted in Gay Wilson Allen, *William James: A Biography*, New York, Viking Press, 1969, p. 169. "that pit of insecurity . . .": *ibid.*, p. 166.

13-14. "in accumulated acts of thought . . . ego to the world . . .": *ibid.*, p. 169. For a remarkably similar account of a period of mental crisis, see Henry James, Sr.: "One day, . . . having eaten a comfortable dinner, I remained sitting at the table after the family had dispersed, . . . when suddenly—in a lightning-flash as it were—'fear came upon me, and trembling, which made all my bones to shake.' To all appearance it was a perfectly insane and abject terror, without ostensible cause, and only to be accounted for, to my perplexed imagination, by some damnèd shape squatting invisible to me within the precincts of the room, and raying out from his fetid personality influences fatal to life. The thing had not lasted ten seconds before I felt myself a wreck, that is, reduced from a state of firm, vigorous, joyful manhood to one of almost helpless infancy. . . . by an immense effort I . . . determined not to budge from my chair till I had recovered my lost self-possession. This purpose I held to for a good long hour, as I reckoned time, beat upon meanwhile by an ever-growing tempest of doubt, anxiety, and despair. . . . Now, to make a long story short, this ghastly condition of mind continued with me, with gradually lengthening intervals of relief, for two years, and even longer. . . . At first, when I began to feel a half-hour's respite from acute mental anguish, the bottomless mystery of my disease completely fascinated me. The more, however, I worried myself with speculations about the cause of it, the more the mystery deepened, and the deeper also grew my instinct of resentment at what seemed so needless an interference with my personal liberty." (*Society the Redeemed Form of Man, and The Earnest of God's Omnipotence in Human Nature: Affirmed in Letters to a Friend*, Boston, Houghton, Osgood and Co., 1879, pp. 44-46.)

14. "My first act . . .": Allen, *op. cit.*, p. 168. "whether [William] finished . . .": *ibid.*, p. 164. The complex relation between Henry James, Jr.'s, imaginative work and his father's strange but compelling legacy of Swedenborgian ideas is the subject of a full-scale investigation in Quentin Anderson's *The American Henry James*, New Brunswick, N.J., Rutgers Univ. Press, 1957. "soon came to hate": Allen, *op. cit.*, p. 164.

15. "We fished in various waters . . .": reminiscences by Thomas Sergeant Perry quoted by Percy Lubbock in LHJ, I: 7-8. "after reading Plato . . .": Allen, *op. cit.*, p. 164. "pragmatism . . . a power philosophy": Bertrand Russell, *Power: A New Social Analysis*, London, George Allen & Unwin, 1962, p. 174. Russell's additional remarks along these lines, although somewhat loose and undeveloped, merit some attention: "For pragmatism, a belief is 'true' if its consequences are pleasant. Now human beings can make the consequences of a belief pleasant or unpleasant. Belief in the superior merit of a dictator has pleasanter consequences than disbelief, if you live under his government. Wherever there is effective persecution, the official creed is 'true' in the pragmatist sense. The pragmatist philosophy, therefore, gives to those in power a metaphysical omnipotence which a more pedestrian philosophy would deny to them. I do not suggest that most pragmatists admit these consequences of their philosophy; I say only that they are consequences, and that the pragmatist's attack on the common view of truth is an outcome of love of power, though perhaps more of power over inanimate nature than of power over other human beings." (*Ibid.*) For a reply made by William James to some of Russell's early criticisms of his pragmatic conception of truth, see the chapter entitled "Two English Critics" in *The Meaning of Truth* (1909), reprinted with a new introduction by Ralph Ross, Ann Arbor, Univ. of Michigan Press, 1970, esp. pp. 272-80.

16. "growth of one's 'taste' . . .": AN, p. 340.

16-17. "And you tell me, friends . . .": Z, Pt. I, PN, p. 229 [WDB, II: 373.]

17n. The bibliography may be found in Virginia Harlow's *Thomas Sergeant Perry: A Biography and Letters to Perry from William, Henry, and Garth Wilkinson James*, Durham, N.C., Duke Univ. Press, 1950, pp. 358-384.

18. "The charges . . . within themselves": Thomas Sergeant Perry, review of *Vom Nutzen und Nachtheil der Historie für das Leben*, *North American Review* 121, no. 248 (July 1865): 192.

19. "If anything is suggested . . .": *ibid.* Cf. Carlyle's "Characteristics" (1831): ". . . this is specially the Era when all manner of Inquiries into what was once the unfelt, involuntary sphere of man's existence, find their place, and, as it were, occupy the whole domain of thought. What, for example, is all this that we hear, for the last generation or two, about the Improvement of the Age . . . but an unhealthy state of self-sentience, self-survey; the precursor and prognostic of still worse health? . . . Never since the beginning of Time was there, that we hear or read of, so intensely self-conscious a Society." "the fatal futility of Fact": Preface to *The Spoils of Poynton*, AN, p. 122.

20. "try Émile Bourget's . . .": letter to T. S. Perry, March 6, 1884, included in the selection of letters from the Jameses which appears in Virginia Harlow, *op. cit.*, p. 316. "a great friend of mine": letter to T. S. Perry, Sept. 26, 1884, *ibid.*, p. 317. This chronology is confirmed by Edel (III: 113), who contends that James was introduced to Bourget in July by John Singer Sargent—the American painter who also counted a young woman author named Violet Paget ("Vernon Lee") among his friends. *Although this friendship* . . .: Bourget apparently reciprocated and kept all

of James's letters to him, and Edel notes (III: 114) that "this is one of the rare instances . . . in which both sides of the correspondence survive." But although Edel was given access to James's letters to Bourget by Bourget's executor, there is still no reason to suppose that I. D. McFarlane will be proved wrong in his assertion that "It is most unlikely that Bourget's notebooks, papers and letters will ever be published—before his death he left strict instructions that they should not be given to the public—and it seems, therefore, that we are now in possession of most of the material which can throw light on this friendship which lasted well over thirty years." (I. D. McFarlane, "A Literary Friendship—Henry James and Paul Bourget," *The Cambridge Journal* IV [1951]: 147.) "[Bourget] was the first . . .": Wharton, *op. cit.*, p. 179; see also letter to Charles Eliot Norton, July 4, 1892, LHJ, I: 199. "almost nothing to show us . . .": Henry James in "Pierre Loti," *Essays in London and Elsewhere*, London, 1893, quoted by René Wellek, *A History of Modern Criticism 1750-1950*, vol. IV, *The Later Nineteenth Century*, New Haven, Yale Univ. Press, 1965, p. 225. Cf. also Arnold L. Goldsmith, "Henry James's Reconciliation of Free Will and Fatalism," *Nineteenth-Century Fiction* 13 (Sept. 1958): 113-14.

21. "it was quite understandable . . . realm of psychology": I. D. McFarlane, *op. cit.*, p. 149. "from which, I hope [Bourget's] delicate . . .": letter to Hippolyte Taine, July 4, 1887, LFN, pp. 267-68. "the only psychologist. . .": TI ix: 45, PN, 549.* [WDB, II: 1021.] "mon ambition . . .": *Essais de psychologie contemporaine*, I, édition définitive, Paris, Librairie Plon, 1937 [1883]: xiii.

22. "his definition of decadence . . . under different names": René Wellek, *op. cit.*, p. 350. Similarly, Kaufmann, who specifies the particular passage from Bourget paraphrased by Nietzsche, in CW 7, ML, p. 626 [WDB, II: 916-17], observes that "Bourget's chapter . . . does not introduce an entirely new turn into Nietzsche's thought; it merely strengthens a previously present motif." (Kaufmann, p. 73n.) *The two men actually met.*

* In all citations from *Twilight of the Idols*, the lower-case Roman numerals correspond as follows to the individual parts as Nietzsche named them: (i) "Maxims and Arrows"; (ii) "The Problem of Socrates"; (iii) " 'Reason' in Philosophy"; (iv) "How the 'True World' Finally Became a Fable"; (v) "Morality as Anti-Nature"; (vi) "The Four Great Errors"; (vii) "The 'Improvers' of Mankind"; (viii) "What the Germans Lack"; (ix) "Skirmishes of an Untimely Man"; (x) "What I Owe to the Ancients"; (xi) "The Hammer Speaks." (All chapter titles refer to the Kaufmann translation.)

. . . It seems virtually certain, however, that Bourget did not know Nietzsche's work at first hand until 1892 or 1893. According to Michel Mansuy,
"le 21 mai 1893, Mme Bourget fait pour son mari un résumé assez som-
maire de sa doctrine, preuve que le romancier ne la connaissait guère
jusque là." (*Un Moderne, Paul Bourget de l'enfance au disciple*, Annales
Littéraires de l'Université de Besançon, 39, Paris, Les Belles Lettres, 1960:
492-93, n. 86.) "disappointed to find [Bourget]": a paraphrase of Nietzsche which appears in LFN, p. 304n; cf. *WDB*, III: 1319-20.

22-23. "a young Englishwoman . . . *Belcaro*": Edel, III: 115.

23. "I don't think I think . . .": letter to T. S. Perry, Sept. 26, 1884,
Harlow, *op. cit.*, p. 318. As her biographer points out, "Vernon Lee" was
reckoned a prodigious intellectual figure by many of her most exacting
contemporaries, and "her conversational powers were acknowledged as altogether extraordinary by friends and enemies alike; she shone even in an
age which knew both Whistler and Wilde." (Peter Gunn, *Vernon Lee:
Violet Paget, 1856-1935*, London, Oxford Univ. Press, 1964, pp. 2-3.)
"very radical and atheistic": letter to T. S. Perry, Sept. 26, 1884, Harlow,
op. cit., p. 318. "very bad, *strangely* inferior . . .": *ibid.*, p. 319. "dogmatic
and dictatorial . . . sympathy in what you do": quoted in Gunn, *op. cit.*,
p. 105. "interminable et plein de défauts": Michel Mansuy, *op. cit.*, p. 382,
n. 16. Bourget's essay appeared in *Débats* on May 6, 1885, and was later
included in his *Essais et Portraits* (*Oeuvres complètes: Critique*, vol. II).

24. *satirizing James in a story*: the story, *Lady Tal*, appeared in a collection by Vernon Lee entitled *Vanitas: Polite Stories*, published by William
Heinemann in 1892. This incident, and William James's angry response on
behalf of his brother, are recounted in Gunn, *op. cit.*, pp. 136-39, where
bibliographical references for further details may also be found. "draw it
mild . . . ": letter to William James, Jan. 20, 1893, quoted in Gunn,
op. cit., p. 139. "treachery to private relations . . . my fortune to know":
Edel, III: 333-34.

25. "the appearance of volition . . ." "Vernon Lee" [Violet Paget],
"Nietzsche and the 'Will to Power,'" *North American Review* 179 (Dec.
1904): 845. *personal as against philosophical* . . . : Cf. also William
James: "Not only Walt Whitman could write 'who touches this book
touches a man.' The books of all the great philosophers are like so many
men. Our sense of an essential personal flavor in each one of them, typical
but indescribable, is the finest fruit of our own accomplished philosophic
education. What the system pretends to be is a picture of the great universe of God. What it is,—and oh so flagrantly!—is the revelation of how
intensely odd the personal flavor of some fellow creature is." (*Pragmatism*,

A New Name for Some Old Ways of Thinking, together with Four Related Essays from *The Meaning of Truth*, ed. Ralph Barton Perry, New York, Longmans, Green, 1948 [1907, 1909], pp. 35-36.) "the proud and combative . . .": Vernon Lee, *op. cit.*, p. 846. "was never able to carry . . . sociological product": *ibid.*

27. "For, if the individual . . . moral manners?": *ibid.*, pp. 847-48. "To esteem is to create . . .": "On the Thousand and One Goals," Z, Pt. I, PN, p. 171. [*WDB*, II: 323.] "more than in any other . . . 'My Taste' ": Vernon Lee, *loc. cit.*, pp. 855-56.

28. *For Nietzsche* . . . : The passage explicitly concerned with the death of God occurs in *Die fröhliche Wissenschaft*, 125 ("Der tolle Mensch"). [*WDB*, II: 126-27.] GS, Bk. III, Sect. 125 ("The Madman"), pp. 181-82. "Give me, ye heavenly ones . . .": quoted by Vernon Lee, *loc. cit.*, p. 859. "in humility and confidence . . . self": *ibid.*

29. "the state or political community . . .": Aristotle, *Politics*, Bk. I (1252a), trans. by Benjamin Jowett, in Richard McKeon, ed., *Introduction to Aristotle*, New York, Random House, The Modern Library, 1947, p. 553.

30. "From this transfer of the world . . .": Emerson, "The Transcendentalist" (1842). "we have seen how . . .": Vernon Lee, *loc. cit.*, pp. 856-57.

31. "emotional condition . . . teaching": *ibid.*, p. 756. "vital lie . . . renunciation": *ibid.*, pp. 854 and 853.

32. "And what you have called world . . .": Nietzsche, "Upon the Blessed Isles," Z, Pt. II, PN, p. 198. [*WDB*, II: 344.]

33. "To redeem those who lived . . .": Nietzsche, "On Redemption," Z, Pt. II, PN, pp. 251-52. [*WDB*, II: 394.]

34. "I led you away . . .": *ibid.*, p. 253. [*WDB*, II: 395-96.]

35. "What, if some day or night . . .": GS, Bk. IV, Sect. 341, pp. 273-74. [*WDB*, II: 202-3.] "eternal recurrence is . . .": Karl Löwith, Appendix II, "Nietzsche's Revival of the Doctrine of Eternal Recurrence," *Meaning in History*, Chicago, Univ. of Chicago Press, 1949, p. 216. For an interesting discussion of the emotional logic which may be involved in producing the idea of the recurrence, see Pierre Klossowski, *Nietzsche et le cercle vicieux*, Paris, Mercure de France, 1969.

36. "the misapprehension that . . .": Kaufmann, p. 324, but see pp. 322-28 for the full development of his argument. "*Duration* coupled with . . .": Kaufmann, p. 327. WP 55, p. 35. [*Mus.*, xviii: 45.]

37. "the most scientific of all . . .": WP 55, p. 36. [*Mus.*, xviii: 46.]

38. "What he wanted was totality . . .": TI ix:49, PN, p. 554.

[WDB, II: 1024-25.] "the last disciple . . .": TI x: 5, PN, p. 563.
[WDB, II: 1032.] "*After the vision* . . .": quoted in Kaufmann, p. 327.

39. My formula . . .": EH II ("Why I Am So Clever"): 10, ML, p. 714. [WDB, II: 1098.] "By that big part . . .": quoted in Gay Wilson Allen, *op. cit.*, pp. 167-68.

40. "Tis the best use of Fate . . .": *ibid.*, p. 168. "the form that so lately moved . . . generations": William James, "An Address at the Emerson Centenary in Concord," May 25, 1903, in Bruce Wilshire, ed., *William James: The Essential Writings*, New York, Harper & Row, 1971, p. 287. "Beloved master . . .": *ibid.*, p. 293.

41. "Emerson. I have never . . . Milky glass": Nietzsche, quoted by Hermann Hummel in his own translation, in his essay entitled "Emerson and Nietzsche," *New England Quarterly* XIX, March 1940: 65-66. Readers interested in exploring the connections between Nietzsche and Emerson should begin by consulting Charles Andler, *Nietzsche, sa vie et sa pensée*, vol. I, *Les précurseurs de Nietzsche*, (2nd ed.), Paris, Éditions Bossard, 1920, Chap. II, "Emerson," *passim.*, esp. pp. 333-39. Similarly helpful is Charles R. West, Jr., "Nietzsche's Concept of *Amor Fati*," unpublished Ph.D. dissertation, Columbia University, 1957. Relying to some extent on Hummel (*op. cit.*), West argues convincingly that two early essays by Nietzsche were very heavily influenced by Emerson's essays "Fate" and "Power" from *The Conduct of Life*: the essays by Nietzsche are "Freedom of the Will and Fate, an Essay in Germania, Easter, 1862" and "Fate and History," both of which West translates from their originals in the *Jugendschriften*, ed. H. J. Nette, pp. 65-66, 67-69. West (*op. cit.*, p. 19) also summarizes the argument advanced by J. C. Lannoy (*Nietzsche, ou l'histoire d'un égocentrisme athée*, Paris, 1952, pp. 31-41) that "Nietzsche's essay 'Fate and History' was inspired by Emerson's *Conduct of Life* and that Emerson provided the key for Nietzsche's reconciliation of the ideas of freedom and necessity." Of additional value in determining the extent of the relationship is Eduard Baumgarten's *Der Pragmatismus*, Frankfurt, 1938, which is concerned with Emerson, William James, and John Dewey, and the same author's "Mitteilungen und Bemerkungen über den Einfluss Emersons auf Nietzsche" in the *Jahrbuch für Amerikastudien* I, ed. Walther Fischer, Heidelberg, 1956: 93-152; this last study provides an extensive account of Nietzsche's annotations of Emerson and the extracts which he copied out from his works. In recent years, the connection between Emerson and Nietzsche has been treated most fully in a dissertation written in German by an American at the University of Basel under the direction of the philosopher Karl Jaspers and Prof. Dr. Henry Lüdeke: see

Stanley Hubbard, *Nietzsche und Emerson*, Basel, Verlag für Recht und Gesellschaft, 1958, a study which focuses to a considerable extent on those passages in Emerson that Nietzsche marked in his German edition of the *Essays*. René Wellek's negative review of Hubbard's work surveys the general problem of the relation between the two thinkers and provides further bibliographical information (*Erasmus* 13, 1960: 134-35.) For a recent discussion of the relationship which calls attention to Emerson's application of the title "professor of the Joyous Science" to himself, see part 3 of Kaufmann's "Translator's Introduction" to *The Gay Science* (1974), pp. 7-13. "a little transformed . . . divine": Elisabeth Foerster-Nietzsche, *Das Leben Friedrich Nietzsches*, II, Leipzig, 1895-1904: 397 (cited in Hummel, *loc. cit.*, p. 63). ". . . I am having translated . . .": letter to Franz Overbeck, Dec. 22, 1884, translated in part in PN, pp. 440-41. It is worth noting that like many American critics Nietzsche felt that Emerson's later work represented a backing-off from his earlier radicalism. In this connection, Nietzsche remarked of the *Essays: Second Series* (1876): "The new Emerson has grown old . . . at last he is too much enamoured of life." (*Briefwechsel* II, no. 102, Sept. 24, 1876; cited in Hummel, *loc. cit.*, p. 65.)

42. "God is dead . . . skin": quoted in Cushing Strout, "William James and the Twice-Born Sick Soul," *Daedalus* (Summer 1968), Vol. 97, no. 3 of the Proceedings of the American Academy of Arts and Sciences, p. 1042. "transfigured victims": F. W. Dupee, *Henry James*, New York, William Sloane Associates, 1951, p. 64.

42-43. "the most inimical critic. . . . The sick . . . to be hatred": William James, Lectures 14 and 15 ("The Value of Saintliness"), *The Varieties of Religious Experience*, New York, Collier-Macmillan, 1961, pp. 294-95. For the passage in the *Genealogy*, see GM, III: 14, ML, pp. 557-59 [*WDB*, II: 863-64.]

44. "The carnivorous-minded 'strong-man' . . .": *ibid.*, p. 295. "According to the empirical . . ." . . . "strength and stature": *ibid.*, pp. 295-96.

45. "Their sense of mystery in things . . .": *ibid.*, p. 297. *Recent studies:* M. E. Humble observes that "in France [Nietzsche's] works were translated between 1898 and 1909 by Henri Albert and published by the *Mercure de France* with such success that an anonymous reviewer for the *Athenaeum* could state on March 7, 1903 that the series had already reached its tenth volume and that four volumes were in a fifth and three in a fourth edition. The first comprehensive French exposé in book form, by Henri Lichtenberger, appeared as early as 1898, and Nietzsche was dealt with at length in such periodicals as the *Mercure de France*, the *Revue Blanche*, the

Revue des Deux Mondes, and the *Revue de Paris."* ("Early British Interest
in Nietzsche," *German Life and Letters* 24 [Oct. 1970-July 1971]: 327-28.)
It seems worth noting, incidentally, that much of Albert's translation of
The Gay Science—a book which was, to judge from Nietzsche's *Nachlass,*
conceived under the pressure of Emersonian ideas—appeared during 1899
and 1900, before the writing of *The Golden Bowl,* and that Edmund
Gosse, one of James's closest friends, was counted as a subscriber to
Thomas Common's Nietzsche translation project—along with Edward
Garnett and George Bernard Shaw. (See Thatcher, *op. cit.* below, p. 36.)
For comprehensive accounts of the emergence of Nietzschean influence in
England during this period, see David S. Thatcher, *Nietzsche in England
1890-1914: The Growth of a Reputation,* Toronto, Univ. of Toronto Press,
1970, and Patrick Bridgwater, *Nietzsche in Anglosaxony: A Study of Nietz-
sche's Impact on English and American Literature,* Leicester, Leicester
Univ. Press, 1972.

   46. "Imagination, which . . .": William Wordsworth, *The Prelude*
(1850), Bk. 14, lines 189-90. "Beware when the great God . . .": most
of this passage is quoted by Nietzsche in the closing pages of SE, pp. 108-9.
[*WDB,* I: 364.]

   49. Friedrich Schiller, *On the Aesthetic Education of Man in a Series of
Letters.* All references to this work, hereafter cited as "Schiller," are to
the splendid edition and translation by Elizabeth M. Wilkinson and L. A.
Willoughby, Oxford, Clarendon Press, 1967. *Kant:* in his *Philosophy of
Fine Art,* Hegel pays tribute to Schiller and summarizes his relation to Kant
in the following manner: "It must in fact be admitted that the artistic sense
of a profound and, at the same time, philosophical spirit anticipated philosophy in the stricter sense by its demand for and expression of the principle of totality and reconciliation in its opposition to that abstract finite-
ness of thought, that duty for duty's sake, that understanding faculty devoid
of any substantive content, which one and all apprehend nature and reality,
sense and feeling, merely as a *limit,* something downright alien or hostile.
It is Schiller who must be credited with the important service of having
ventured the attempt to pass beyond the same by comprehending in
thought the principles of unity and reconciliation as the truth, and giving
artistic realization to that truth." (Georg Wilhelm Friedrich Hegel, *The
Philosophy of Fine Art,* 4 vols., translated by F. P. B. Osmaston, London,
G. Bell and Sons, Ltd., 1920, I: 83. "it is only . . . the aesthetic":
Schiller, Second Letter, p. 9. "the artist . . .": *ibid.,* Ninth Letter, p. 55.
"his theme . . . dark eddies below": *ibid.,* p. 57. "While the woman-
god . . .": *ibid.,* Fifteenth Letter, p. 109.

   50. "instrument not provided by the State . . . clear and pure": *ibid.,*

Ninth Letter, p. 55. "derived from a source . . .": *ibid.*, Tenth Letter, p. 69. "This pure rational concept . . .": *ibid.*, pp. 69-71.

51. "From now on . . .": *ibid.*, p. 71. *Schiller as precursor:* see notes to page 49 above. "the realm of . . . reality it contains": Hegel, *op. cit.*, I: 129.

52. "on the finite . . . is the Ideal": *ibid.*, p. 208. "the defects of immediate reality . . . lifted up . . . stare at us": *ibid.* "that region of more essential reality . . . may assume": *ibid.*, p. 136.

53n. "In protesting . . .": Richard Ellmann, "Introduction: The Critic as Artist as Wilde," *The Artist as Critic: Critical Writings of Oscar Wilde,* New York, Vintage Books, 1970, p. x. Hereafter this collection will be referred to simply as "Wilde."

53-54. "never expresses anything . . . its own progress": Wilde, "The Decay of Lying," p. 319.

54. "all beautiful things . . .": *ibid.*, p. 325. "nation of art critics," *ibid.*, "The Critic as Artist," Pt. I, p. 349. "the Critical Spirit . . .": *ibid.*, Pt. II, p. 407. "the realm of fine Art . . .": Hegel, *op. cit.*, I: 129. "The culture that . . . how to live": *ibid.*, pp. 384-85.

54n "addresses itself . . .": Wilde, p. 370. "Just as . . .": *ibid.*, p. 382.

55. "sit contented . . . and his only": *ibid.*, p. 407. "man only plays . . .": Schiller, Fifteenth Letter, p. 107.

56. "it was long ago alive . . .": *ibid.*, p. 109. "the highest of all bounties . . .": *ibid.*, Twenty-first Letter, p. 147. *paradoxically, then, full humanity* . . . : for later manifestations of this notion, see Sect. 6 ("The 'Human, Superhuman' Paradox") of Chapter III below, pp. 110-18. "from being a slave . . .": *ibid.*, Twenty-fifth Letter, p. 185. "contemplation . . . universe around him . . .": *ibid.*, p. 183. "as soon as . . . object": *ibid.*, p. 185. "Whatsoever is object . . . infinite form": *ibid.*

57. "gives form . . . his own self": *ibid.*, Eleventh Letter, p. 77.

57-58. "where . . . the formal drive . . . by our action": *ibid.*, Twelfth Letter, p. 83.

58. "man is under . . .": Hegel, *op. cit.*, I: 339. ". . . these two related . . .": *ibid.*

59. ". . . when we reach . . .": Wilde, pp. 406-7. "Is this dangerous?": *ibid.*, p. 407. "makes him Man . . . necessity": Schiller, Third Letter, p. 11.

59-60. "will not permit . . . decoration": Hegel, *op. cit.*, I: 42.

60. "a disposition . . . Personality": Schiller, Eleventh Letter, p. 77. "we must surely . . .": *ibid.*, pp. 75-77. "In conformity, then . . .": Hegel, *op. cit.*, I: 394.

61. "Rebels in the name . . . of utmost fascination": Thomas Mann,

"Wilde and Nietzsche," in Richard Ellmann, ed., *Oscar Wilde, A Collection of Critical Essays*, Englewood Cliffs, N.J., Prentice-Hall, 1969, p. 171.

62. "I believe America . . . ": D. H. Lawrence, letter of July 1917 to Waldo Frank, quoted in Richard Ruland, *America in Modern European Literature: From Image to Metaphor*, New York, New York Univ. Press, 1976, p. 37. "The Americans of all nations . . .": Walt Whitman, Preface to *Leaves of Grass* [1855 ed], ed. Malcolm Cowley, New York, Viking Press, 1959, pp. 5-9.

63. "entirely adapted . . . millennial society": see page 44 above. "Utopia was an anarchy . . . this commonwealth": Bosanquet, *op. cit.*, p. 276. "I was really too associated . . .": *ibid.*, p. 274.

64. "James was never really . . .": *ibid.* "was excusably reminded . . . doubtfully Anglo-Saxon": *ibid.*, pp. 244-45.

65. *Van Wyck Brooks* et al.: Van Wyck Brooks, *The Pilgrimage of Henry James*, New York, E. P. Dutton, 1925; V. L. Parrington's study is reprinted in F. W. Dupee, ed., *The Question of Henry James*, New York, Henry Holt & Co., 1945, pp. 128-130. The same collection includes the essays by Higginson (pp. 1-5) and Croly (pp. 28-39). Nuhn's book has been reprinted with a new foreword by the author and an introduction by Ellis Allen Johnson (Port Washington, N.Y., Kennikat Press, Inc., 1967). Edna Kenton's essay is also included in Dupee, *op. cit.*, pp. 131-37. "a Country of your Own . . .": quoted in Bosanquet, *op. cit.*, p. 274. "The truth is . . .": Edith Wharton, *op. cit.*, p. 175.

66. "the nonsense . . . at home there": *ibid.*, pp. 175-76. "If I were to live . . .": Simon Nowell-Smith, in whose collection this reminiscence is included, points out that Garland's visit "appears to have been about 1906 or 1907," and that James did return to the United States again (in 1910-1911). (Nowell-Smith, *op. cit.*, p. 104.)

67. "When he returned to Bolton Street . . .": Edmund Gosse, "Henry James," in *Aspects and Impressions*, London, Cassell and Co., 1922, p. 28. Higginson's remark actually appears in print in an 1879 essay ("Henry James, Jr.," originally published in *The Literary World* and included in Dupee, ed., *op. cit.*) It is possible, of course, that he liked the remark so well that he was given to repeating it years afterward in conversation, when an occasion to do so presented itself.

68. "His decision to settle . . .": LHJ, I: xii-xiii.

69. "could never . . . closed to him": *ibid.*, pp. xxiv-xxv. "items of high civilization . . . forty years ago": Henry James, *Hawthorne*, Ithaca, N.Y., Cornell Univ. Press, 1956 [1879], pp. 34-35.

72. "it is impossible . . . settled life": LHJ, I: xxv-xxvi. "the children's

extraordinarily haphazard . . .": *ibid.*, pp. 3-4. "wherever he might have lived . . .": Bosanquet, *op. cit.*, p. 275.

73. "Dearest Alice . . .": letter of April 1, 1913, LHJ, II: 317.

74. "I have not the least . . .": letter of Oct. 29, 1888, LHJ, I: 143. "He would do more . . .": Edel, II: 105. The Latin phrase is quoted by Arnold at the end of his essay on "Marcus Aurelius" (*Essays in Criticism: First Series*, 1865); it is, as Sister Thomas Marion Hoctor has pointed out, a line from Virgil's *Aeneid* (VI: 314), but Arnold has altered the syntax to fit his own sense. In his recent verse translation, Allen Mandelbaum renders the original line as "their hands reach out in longing for/ the farther shore." (*Matthew Arnold's Essays in Criticism: First Series*, ed. with an intro. and notes by Sister T. M. Hoctor, Chicago, Univ. of Chicago Press, 1964, p. 321; *The Aeneid of Virgil*, trans. Allen Mandelbaum, Berkeley, Calif., Univ. of California Press, 1971, p. 143.) "deep in the timorous recesses . . . any we have seen": letter to T. S. Perry, Sept. 20, 1867, in Harlow, *op. cit.*, pp. 284-85.

75. "the heir of all the ages": I am grateful to Steven Marcus for re-minding me that the source of this phrase, which James applies to Dr. Jackson Lemon in the story "Lady Barberina" (1884) and uses again more than twenty years later in his Preface to *The Wings of the Dove*, is Tennyson's "Locksley Hall" (line 178).

76. "Protean Man": Robert Jay Lifton, "Protean Man," published in the *Futuribles* series, Paris, Sedeis, 1967, and *Partisan Review*, Winter 1968, pp. 13-27; reprinted in Lifton's *History and Human Survival*, New York, Random House, 1970, from which all quotations are taken. "claim . . . that . . .": Lifton, *ibid.*, p. 312. "protean style . . . psychological quests": Lifton, *ibid.*, p. 319. "the classical superego . . . explorations": Lifton, *ibid.*, pp. 321-22.

76-77. "protean man's affinity . . . from all sources": Lifton, *op. cit.*, p. 331.

78. "technology (and technique . . .": Lifton, *op. cit.*, p. 328. "polymorphous versatility": Lifton, *op. cit.*, p. 319.

79. "I think that to be . . .": quoted in Harlow, *op. cit.*, p. 284.

80. "That's very crude . . .": *The Portrait of a Lady*, I: 287-88. A fine discussion of this passage appears in Frederick C. Crews, *The Tragedy of Manners: Moral Drama in the Later Novels of Henry James*, Hamden, Conn., Archon Books, 1971 [1957], pp. 13-17.

81. "The genius itself . . .": "Emerson" in SLC, p. 72. James's essay first appeared in *Macmillan's Magazine* in Dec. 1887; it was reprinted in his *Partial Portraits* the following year. "The doctrine of the supremacy . . .":

Henry James, *Hawthorne*, Ithaca, N.Y., Cornell Univ. Press, 1956 [1879], p. 67. *the prize* . . . "within": consider, in this context, Nietzsche's description of Emerson as "one who instinctively nourishes himself only on ambrosia, leaving behind what is indigestible in things. Compared with Carlyle, a man of taste. Carlyle, who loved him very much, nevertheless said of him: 'He does not give us enough to chew on'—which may be true, but is no reflection on Emerson." (TI: ix, 13, PN, p. 552.) [WDB, II: 998.]

82. "we must of course have something of our own . . .": letter to Perry in Harlow, *op. cit.*, p. 285.

83. "America is . . .": quoted by George E. Probst in his "Introduction" to Grund's *Aristocracy in America: From the Sketchbook of a German Nobleman*, New York, Harper & Bros., 1951 (based on the edition first published in London, 1839), p. xii. (See *The Americans, in Their Moral, Social, and Political Relations*, Boston, Marsh, Capen and Lyon, 1837, p. 149.)

84. "entirely adapted . . . possible or not": William James, *The Varieties of Religious Experience*, New York, Collier-Macmillan, 1961, p. 296. "The Americans love their country . . .": quoted by Probst, *loc. cit.*, p. xiii. (See Grund, *The Americans* . . . , p. 151.)

85. "the history of . . .": *Human, All-Too-Human*, II, translated by Paul V. Cohn (Levy, VII), p. 9. [WDB, I: 742.] "Trade and industry . . .": *Humans, All-Too-Human* 475, PN, pp. 61-62. [WDB, I: 685.] "We 'good Europeans' . . .": BGE 241, ML, p. 364. [WDB, II: 706.]

86. "those rarer and rarely contented . . .": BGE 254, ML, p. 385. [WDB, II: 722-23.] "I call you Kröger . . .": Thomas Mann, *Tonio Kröger*, in *The Thomas Mann Reader*, ed. Joseph Warner Angell, New York, Grosset & Dunlap, 1950, p. 12.

87. "free, *very* free spirits": ML. p. 194. [WDB, II: 566.] "You men of destiny . . .": *Human, All-Too-Human*, II (Levy, VII), p. 9. [WDB, I: 743.] "Call that in which . . .": BGE 242, ML, pp. 366-67. [WDB, II: 707-8.]

88-89. "We who are homeless . . . the sun has ever seen": GS, Bk. V, Sect. 377, pp. 38-39. [WDB, II: 251-52.] Nietzsche's reference to *chinoiserie* [*Chineserei*] in this passage reflects his animus against what he took to be the stagnation and rigidity of traditional Chinese society, which he regarded as having given up its capacity for change centuries before (see GS, Bk. I, 24, p. 99 [WDB, II: 58] for related remarks on "Chinese conditions and a Chinese 'happiness'").

91. "On the Thousand and One Goals": Z, Pt. I, PN, pp. 170-72. [WDB, II: 322-24.]

91n. The connection with Pater seems especially important here (though readers familiar with the "Hebraism and Hellenism" chapter of Arnold's *Culture and Anarchy* [1869] will also be aware of certain parallels). Michael Hamburger maintains that "though Pater never mentioned Nietzsche, it is generally agreed that his 'A Lecture on Dionysus,' given at the Midland Institute in 1876 and included in his *Greek Studies* (1895), shows an unacknowledged debt to Nietzsche's early writings." ("Nietzsche: A Craving for Hell," in *Contraries*, New York, E. P. Dutton, 1970, p. 203n.) This account is challenged in large part by Patrick Bridgwater in his book on *Nietzsche in Anglosaxony* (1972). "While it is . . . true," Bridgwater claims, "that the terms 'Dionysian' and 'Apollonian' belong fully as much to Pater's thought as to Nietzsche's, the crux of the matter is that these terms, which both writers arrived at independently within very few years of one another (Nietzsche first set forth the antithesis 'Apollonian: Dionysian' in a lecture on 'The Dionysian Principle' written in 1870), have in part quite different connotations in their respective works" (p. 26). The author goes on to argue that there is reason to suppose that Pater arrived at his own formulation of the contrast indicated by the names "Dionysus" and "Apollo" in 1864, years before Nietzsche's work was published.

Although it is interesting to speculate about what produced the evident parallel between the ideas of these two men (quite conceivably a reading of Hegel or Schiller), what is most significant for the purposes of our present discussion is the fact of that parallel. As Arthur Ransome observed in 1913, Pater "has never been compared to Nietzsche. Yet no student of Pater's ideas could avoid such a comparison, fantastic as it may seem. . . . Before *The Birth of Tragedy* was written, Pater had distinguished Apollo and Dionysus . . . as the particular deities of opposed artistic tendencies. At one with Nietzsche in his conception of the relative nature of truth, though he shrank from carrying it to battle *à l'outrance*, he says almost what Nietzsche says of the evil influence of 'the ideal,' 'the absolute,' on European thought. . . . Mildly, as if it did not matter, he murmurs what Nietzsche shouted." (Quoted in Bridgwater, *op. cit.*, p. 22.)

The apparent correspondence between certain notions of Nietzsche and Oscar Wilde may, therefore, be accounted for by the occurrence of related notions in the works of Pater—for example, *Plato and Platonism* (1893). The influence of Pater's aesthetic theories on Wilde is generally acknowledged, though it has not been explored in sufficient depth. (It is worth remembering that on the first day of his trial, April 3, 1895, in the course of his testimony Wilde referred to Pater as "the only critic of the century whose opinion I set high." [Wilde, *op. cit.*, p. 437.] In the "Four Years:

1887-1891" section of *The Trembling of the Veil*, Yeats recalls a similar—if somewhat more extravagant—estimate expressed by Wilde on the first evening the young poet spent in his company: "That first night," Yeats tells us, "he praised Walter Pater's *Studies in the History of the Renaissance*: 'It is my golden book; I never travel anywhere without it; but it is the very flower of decadence: the last trumpet should have sounded the moment it was written.'" [*The Autobiography of William Butler Yeats*, New York, Collier-Macmillan, 1965, p. 87.])

The chief conclusion to be drawn from these connections in the present context is that ideas of the kind we have been discussing were obviously circulating in the intellectual air which Henry James inevitably breathed in London during the closing decades of the nineteenth century, and that those ideas were of a kind that actually would have served, in complicated ways, to reinforce some of his own deepest convictions as a Transcendental American. (Consider, in this light, an allusion made to Emerson—and specifically to "Self-Reliance"—by one of the characters in Wilde's dialogue entitled "The Decay of Lying": "Who wants to be consistent? The dullard and the doctrinaire, the tedious people who carry out their principles to the bitter end of action, to the *reductio ad absurdum* of practice. Not I. Like Emerson, I write over the door of my library the word 'Whim.'" [Wilde, *op. cit.*, p. 292.]

92. "Nietzsche's reverence . . .": Leo Strauss, "Jerusalem and Athens," *Commentary* 43, no. 6 (June 1967): 45-46.

93. "the utmost honoring . . . supremacy": Strauss, *op. cit.*, p. 45.

94. "Highest Specimens": Nietzsche's term is *"höchsten Exemplare"* (". . . das *Ziel der Menschheit* kann nicht am Ende liegen, sondern nur *in ihren höchsten Exemplaren*." [WDB, I: 270.] Cf. UA, Chap. IX, p. 59. "not a German event . . .": TI ix:49, PN, p. 553. [WDB, II: 1024.] "In all the more profound . . .": BGE 256, quoted in Kaufmann, pp. 314-15. [WDB, II: 724.] "had been corrupted . . .": WP 1026, quoted in Kaufmann, p. 316. [*Mus.*, xix:350.] "synthesis of the inhuman . . .": quoted in Kaufmann, p. 315. [WDB, II: 797.] (See GM, I: 16, ML, p. 490.)

95. "When Napoleon . . .": *ibid. he becomes his own fiction . . .*: Some of the implications of this view are illuminted by Wilde in *Intentions* (1891) and, more obviously, *The Picture of Dorian Gray* (1891)—as well as by his behavior during his trials four years later—by Yeats in his account of the theory of masks (especially in *A Vision*, 1925), and by Sartre in *Les Mots* (1962), specifically in his remarks concerning the man who seeks to live his own autobiography. *Such a man is regarded as having freed himself . . .*": as we have seen, the general notion of

artistic self-creation as a means of liberation from the conditions of history owes a great deal to Schiller, but it is important to recognize, as Michael Podro points out in his excellent recent discussion of the *Aesthetic Education,* that Schiller's text there "is couched in terms which, as he notes himself, are derived from Fichte." (Michael Podro, *The Manifold in Perception: Theories of Art from Kant to Hildebrand,* Oxford, Clarendon Press, 1972, p. 48n.) And indeed, the most far-reaching formulation of the view is provided by Fichte—in *The Vocation of Man,* for instance: "What unity and completeness this view presents! What dignity it confers on human nature! Our thought is not founded on itself alone, independently of our impulses and affections. Man does not consist of two independent and separate elements; he is absolutely one. All our thought is founded on our impulses; as a man's affections are, so is his knowledge. These impulses compel us to a certain mode of thought only so long as we do not perceive the constraint; the constraint vanishes the moment it is perceived. . . . I shall open my eyes, shall learn thoroughly to know myself; I shall recognize that constraint—this is my vocation. This is what I shall do; and under that supposition I shall necessarily form my own mode of thought. Then shall I stand absolutely independent, thoroughly equipped and perfected through my own act and deed. The source of all my other thoughts and even of my life itself—that from which everything proceeds which can have an existence in me, for me, or through me, the innermost spirit of my spirit—is no longer a foreign power; it is, in the strictest possible sense, my own reasonable act. I am wholly my own creation. I might have followed blindly the leading of my spiritual nature, but I resolve to be a work not of Nature but of myself. . . . With freedom and consciousness I have returned to the point at which Nature had left me. I accept that which she announces, but I accept it not because I must—I believe it because I will." (Johann Gottlieb Fichte, *The Vocation of Man,* trans. by William Smith, rev. and ed. by Roderick M. Chisholm, Indianapolis, Ind., Liberal Arts Press, 1956, pp. 91-92.)

96. "great men . . . are explosives . . .": TI ix:44, PN, p. 547. [WDB, II: 1019.] "I am no man . . .": "Why I Am a Destiny," EH I, ML, p. 782. [WDB, II: 1152.] "What does the environment . . .": TI ix:44, PN, p. 547. [WDB, II: 1019.] "the case of Napoleon . . . the *only* master": *ibid.* "Great men are necessary . . .": *ibid.,* pp. 547-48.

97. "The revolution made possible . . .": WP 877, quoted in Kaufmann, p. 413. [*Mus.,* xix:273.] "The value of a man . . .": WP 878, p. 469. [*Mus.,* xix:273].

98. *Such figures exemplify* . . . : As Kaufmann has pointed out, Nietzsche's conception should be distinguished from Carlyle's view that (in Kauf-

mann's paraphrase) "Great men make history . . . society depends on
hero worship, and . . . without heroes there can be only anarchy. . . ."
(Kaufmann, p. 313.) For Nietzsche's almost consistently negative estimate
of Carlyle and "Carlylism," see, for example, Sect. 97 of *The Gay Science*
(GS, p. 150 [*WDB*, II: 102]), Sect. 252 of *Beyond Good and Evil* (BGE,
p. 380 [*WDB* II: 718-19]), Sect. 54 of *The Antichrist* (A, PN, p. 638
[*WDB*, II: 1221]), Sects. 12, 13, and 44 of *Twilight of the Idols* (TI: ix:
PN, pp. 521, 522, and 548 [*WDB*, II: 997, 998, 1020]), Sect. 1 of "Why
I Write Such Good Books," in *Ecce Homo* (ML, p. 717 [*WDB*, II:
1101]), and Sects. 27, 312, 343, 455, 747, and 968 of *The Will to Power*
(WP, pp. 19, 173, 188, 249, 395, 507 [*Mus.*, xviii: 24, 222, 243, 323;
xix: 176, 321]). In his essay on Nietzsche in *Contraries* (1970), Michael
Hamburger discusses the implications of Nietzsche's evident hostility toward
Carlyle in relation to the argument linking these two authors advanced by
Eric Bentley in *A Century of Hero-Worship: A Study of the Idea of Heroism in Carlyle and Nietzsche, with Notes on Wagner, Stefan George, and
D. H. Lawrence* (2nd ed., 1957). *Unzeitgemässe Betrachtungen*, II, *Vom
Nutzen und Nachteil der Historie für das Leben*, in WDB, I: 209-85. "be-
lieve that the meaning . . .": UA, Chap. I, p. 10.* [*WDB*, I: 217.]
" 'supra-historical' man . . . could not teach?": quoted in Kaufmann,
p. 147. Cf. UA, as in preceding note.

99. "of supreme importance . . . place and time": Kaufmann, pp. 147-
48. "Only strong personalities . . .": UA, Chap. V, p. 32. [*WDB*, I: 241.]
"elevated" . . . "intensified" . . . "symbols": quoted in Kaufmann, pp.
148-49.

100. "form a sort of bridge . . .": UA, Chap. IX, p. 59. [*WDB*, I: 270.]
"apparently scattered and . . .": quoted in Kaufmann, p. 313; cf. SE,
p. 59. [*WDB*, I: 327.] "The *goal of humanity* . . . specimens": quoted
in Kaufmann, p. 149. [*WDB*, I: 270.] Cf. UA, Chap. IX, p. 59. "supersubtle fry": Preface to *The Lesson of the Master*, AN, p. 221.

101. "If the life about us . . . to defend myself": *ibid.*, pp. 222-23.

103. "I was unlike . . .": *The Autobiography of W. B. Yeats*, New
York, Collier-Macmillan, 1965, p. 77. "a sort of bridge . . .": see first
note for p. 100 above.

104. "fatal futility of Fact": Preface to *The Spoils of Poynton*, AN,

* Here as elsewhere in the case of citations from UA, the quotation in the
text is from the Adrian Collins translation in the 1909 Levy edition (Vol.
V), but the page number given in the note refers to the somewhat revised
second edition published in 1957 in the Library of Liberal Arts and now
more generally available (see Note on Abbreviations).

p. 122. For a highly suggestive account of the sense of exhaustion, and of emotional and imaginative enslavement, which might be signified by—or at least continuous with—an unqualified commitment to literary realism, see Eugene Goodheart, "Flaubert and the Powerlessness of Art," *Centennial Review* XIX, no. 3, Summer 1975: 157-71. Goodheart's argument needs to be modified somewhat to take into account the complex religious intentions which manifest themselves in the late *Trois Contes* (1878), especially in *Un Coeur Simple* (the nature of these intentions is suggested by Lionel Trilling in his essay on *Bouvard et Pécuchet*—"Flaubert's Last Testament"—in *The Opposing Self*); on the whole, however, the claims he makes here are compelling, and the contrast which he proposes between Flaubert on the one hand and James and Proust on the other is especially to the point for our present purposes. "It is true of both James and Proust," Goodheart argues, "as it is not of Flaubert, that their imaginations have their sources in a life other than the immediate historical moment that they face. Flaubert remains the perfect exemplar of the self-loathing bourgeois imagination condemned to the reality which it loathes." In the course of his essay, Goodheart also suggests a contrast between the adventurousness of Nietzsche and the tendency toward immobility which seems most characteristic of Flaubert; this contrast has evoked an interesting response in the form of a brief essay by Michael Platt, entitled "Nietzsche on Flaubert and the Powerlessness of his Art" (*Centennial Review* XX, no. 3, Summer 1976: 309-13). Platt is primarily concerned with locating the implications of Nietzsche's negative estimate of Flaubert within the general scheme of the philosopher's thought, but the essay is also valuable for its convincing grasp of the intricate connections between Nietzsche's temperament and his intellectual and aesthetic judgments. "will always rise against . . .": UA, Chap. VIII, p. 54. [WDB, I: 265.] "How few living men . . . greater pride": *ibid*. "the spirit and the career . . . militant edge": see note to p. 101 above. "What does not destroy me . . .": TI i:8, PN, p. 467. [WDB, II: 943.]

105. "process of vision": AN, p. 308. "The unreality of the sharp distinction . . .": Preface to *The Princess Casamassima*, AN, p. 67.

106. *In the later James* . . . : as for the dialogue which is characteristic of those works, Ruth B. Yeazell (in *Language and Knowledge in the Late Novels of Henry James*, Chicago, Univ. of Chicago Press, 1977) has recently observed of the effects of such conversations that "when the characters in James's late fiction talk, the reader suffers from a kind of epistemological vertigo, for he is granted no secure position from which to judge the moral or even the factual truth of what is being said" (p. 71). Indeed,

"as readers witnessing" such exchanges "we are left to float in a world seemingly without solid fact—a world in which 'everything's possible,' and discourse does not so much reveal our truths as create them" (p. 73)—an exemplary Nietzschean predicament, it may be noted.

107. . . . *the paradoxical aspect of Maggie Verver's triumph* . . . : for negative estimates of the Ververs in general, see for example F. R. Leavis's essay on "The Later James" in *The Great Tradition*, New York, New York Univ. Press, 1964, and Sallie Sears, *The Negative Imagination*, Ithaca, Cornell Univ. Press, 1968, Charles Samuels, *The Ambiguity of Henry James*, Urbana, Univ. of Illinois Press, 1971, and Philip Weinstein, *Henry James and the Requirements of the Imagination*, Cambridge, Mass., Harvard Univ. Press, 1971. "the tangle, the drama . . .": Preface to *The Spoils of Poynton*, AN, p. 129.

108. "verily, even, I think . . .": Preface to *The Princess Casamassima*, AN, p. 67. "large lucid reflector": quoted in Morris Roberts, *Henry James's Criticism*, Cambridge, Mass., Harvard Univ. Press, 1929, p. 97. "a denser and duller . . . penetrating": Preface to *The Princess Casamassima*, AN, pp. 66-67. "the power to be finely aware . . . sense": *ibid.*, p. 62. "Their being finely aware . . .": *ibid.*

109. "The novelist of those . . .": quoted in Lionel Trilling, "Sherwood Anderson," *The Liberal Imagination*, London, Secker & Warburg, 1964 [1950], p. 32. Interestingly enough, James's account of the way people's lives are shrunken and distorted by their tendency to imagine themselves too narrowly is not very different from the one provided by Anderson in "The Book of the Grotesque" chapter which prefaces *Winesburg, Ohio* (1919). Referring to the "hundreds and hundreds" of "truths" of experience abroad in the world, the narrator tells us that it was the old writer's "notion that the moment one of the people took one of the truths to himself, called it his truth, and tried to live his life by it, he became a grotesque and the truth he embraced became a falsehood." It seems entirely possible to apply this notion to a Jamesian character like Kate Croy. As the early pages of *The Wings of the Dove* suggest, the truth she begins with is the truth of hunger; but as a consequence of her excessive preoccupation with that truth in relation to herself she becomes enslaved by it. In the end, her emotional life is distorted accordingly, and it comes to illustrate the "grotesque" (or "falsehood") version of the original truth: the truth of the predator. "I confess I never see . . .": Preface to *The Princess Casamassima*, AN, p. 67.

111. . . . *the influence of . . . evolutionary ideas:* pointing to Nietzsche's tendency "during the middle period, especially . . . to subsume both

moral and aesthetic arguments under the category of the physiological,"
J. P. Stern has maintained that in this "Nietzsche too, like so many thinkers
of his age, is a victim of a misunderstood Darwinism. He is therefore prone
to see this biological sphere above all as the sphere of victory and defeat,
achievement and failure. . . ." (J. P. Stern, "Nietzsche's Aesthetics?" *Journal of European Studies* V, no. 3, Sept. 1975: 215.) "If the teaching of
evolution . . . apt expression": Kaufmann, p. 150. "those true men . . .":
SE, Chap. V, p. 54. [WDB, I: 324.] "With their appearance . . .": *ibid.*

112. "truly *human* being": Kaufmann, pp. 152 and 312. "human, all-
too-human . . . superhuman": *ibid.*, p. 312.

112n. "In *The Origin* . . .": SE, n. 16, p. 114.

112n2. Letters of William James, ed. by his son, Henry James, Boston,
Atlantic Monthly Press, 1920, II: 141, 151, 157.

113. ". . . I shall suggest . . .": F. W. H. Myers, *Human Personality
and Its Survival of Bodily Death*, quoted from the abridged one-volume
version, London, Longmans, Green and Co., Ltd., 1935, pp. 45-46.

115. . . . *he can be only master or slave:* the importance of Hegel's
Phenomenology of Mind—especially the "lordship and bondage" section—
as a background for the present discussion should be noted. The most complete elaboration of the implications of this theme in Hegel (though one
which may in the end overestimate its importance in the economy of his
work as a whole) is Alexandre Kojève, *Introduction to the Reading of
Hegel*, ed. Allan Bloom, New York, Basic Books, 1969): this is an abridg-
ment of the original French version published by Gallimard in 1947. Also
valuable is George Armstrong Kelly, "Notes on Hegel's 'Lordship and
Bondage,'" *The Review of Metaphysics* XIX, no. 4, June 1966: 780-802;
for an illuminating treatment of these issues in their larger philosophical
context, see the same author's *Idealism, Politics, and History: Sources of
Hegelian Thought*, Cambridge, Cambridge Univ. Press, 1969. "in man
there is both . . .": Kaufmann, p. 310. BGE 225, ML, p. 344. [WDB,
II: 689.]

116. "esteems": See Zarathustra's speech "On the Thousand and One
Goals," Z, Pt. I, PN, p. 171. [WDB, II: 323.]

116n. "Art reminds us . . .": WP 802, p. 422. [*Mus.*, xix: 212.]

117. "lack of confidence . . .": letter to Franz Overbeck, Dec. 25, 1882,
LFN, p. 199 [WDB, III: 1198]. in its final and . . .": Kaufmann, p. 59.
"the winter of 1882/83 . . .": *ibid.*, p. 53. "This winter was . . .": LFN,
pp. 207-8. [WDB, III: 1201.] "a blessed comprehensive name . . .":
Preface to *The Golden Bowl*, AN, p. 340.

118. "the other side of the medal": F. W. Dupee, *Henry James*, New

York, William Sloane Associates, 1951, p. 25. "But let me . . .": Z, Pt. II,
PN, p. 198. [*WDB*, II: 344.]

119. "People who speak . . .": XI, 11, translated and with an introduction by R. S. Pine-Coffin, Baltimore, Md., Penguin Books, 1961, pp.
261-62.

120. *The Rhetoric of Fiction*, Chicago, Univ. of Chicago Press, 1961.

121. "more or less distant": *ibid.*, p. 156.

122. "the register . . .": Preface to *The Golden Bowl*, AN, p. 329. "fine
central intelligence": in his Introduction to AN, p. xviii. "instinctive disposition": Preface to *The Princess Casamassima*, AN, p. 70. "that the
novelist with a weakness . . . high lucidity": Preface to *The Spoils of
Poynton*, AN, p. 130. "a value intrinsic . . . finest order": Preface to *The
Princess Casamassima*, AN, p. 70.

123. "intense perceiver": *ibid.*, p. 71. "in placing advantageously . . .":
ibid., p. 70. "that magnificent end . . .": quoted in Morris Roberts, *op.
cit.*, p. 97. "*he* a mirror . . .": Preface to *The Princess Casamassima*, AN,
p. 70. "central light": Preface to *The Spoils of Poynton*, AN, p. 130. "To
lift our subject . . .": quoted in Roberts, *op. cit.*, p. 97. "my preference
for dealing with . . .": Preface to *The Golden Bowl*, AN, p. 327.

124. "the shorter things in especial . . .": *ibid.* "the lucid reflector . . .
each other . . .": Roberts, *op. cit.*, pp. 100-101. "mode of treatment":
Preface to *The Golden Bowl*, AN, p. 327.

124-25. "the possibility, which . . . *vice versa*": AN, p. xviii.

125. "the plea for the use . . .": *ibid.* "one on whom nothing . . .":
"The Art of Fiction," SLC, p. 57.

127. "penumbra" . . . "stupidity": Preface to *The Spoils of Poynton*,
AN, p. 130. "process of vision": Preface to *The Ambassadors*, AN, p. 308.
"conviction that 'seeing' . . . type": Ora Segal, *The Lucid Reflector: The
Observer in Henry James's Fiction*, New Haven, Yale Univ. Press, 1969,
p. xii.

128. "Tell me what the artist is . . .": Preface to *The Portrait of a
Lady*, AN, p. 46. "as the artist is only . . .": "In the Country of the
Blue," in F. W. Dupee, ed., *The Question of Henry James*, New York,
Henry Holt & Co., 1945, p. 191. "active sense of life": Preface to *The
Golden Bowl*, AN, p. 340.

128n. "I absolutely don't . . .": quoted in Edel, III: 322.

129. "adventures of perception . . .": LHJ, II: 2. "not long before
[James's] death . . . act of living": *ibid.*, p. xiv. "almost demonically both
sees . . .": Preface to *The Spoils of Poynton*, AN, p. 129. "Thus we get
perhaps . . .": *ibid.*, pp. 129-30. "the detestable tendency . . .": in

"Charles Nordhoff's Communistic Societies," *Literary Reviews and Essays by Henry James*, ed. Albert Mordell, New York, Vista House, 1957, p. 266.

130. "success": for a suggestive discussion of the changing idea of "success" in the nineteenth- and twentieth-century novel, see Lionel Trilling, "James Joyce in His Letters," *Commentary* 45, no. 2, Feb. 1968: 54-55. "the stupid, the coarse . . .": Preface to *The Princess Casamassima*, AN, p. 62.

131. "What is most striking about Minny . . .": *The American Henry James*, New Brunswick, N.J., Rutgers Univ. Press, 1957, pp. 132-33. "actually killed by the conditions . . .": in Dupee, ed., *op. cit.*, p. 193. "stretched out her wings . . .": *The Wings of the Dove*, II, New York, Scribners, 1937 (N.Y. Ed., vol. XX): 404.

132. "If I am talking . . .": in F. O. Matthiessen, *The James Family: A Group Biography*, New York, Alfred A. Knopf, 1947, p. 614. "the full ironic truth": Preface to *What Maisie Knew*, AN, p. 142.

133. "the perfect dependence of . . .": Preface to *The Portrait of a Lady*, AN, p. 45.

134. *the sales figures*: see the accounting of sales figures vs. publisher's advances in H. Montgomery Hyde, *Henry James at Home*, London, Methuen & Co., 1969, pp. 167-68. "authority": Preface to *The Spoils of Poynton*, AN, p. 123. "an immense increase . . .": "The Art of Fiction," SLC, p. 62. "throughout the Prefaces . . . the plea . . .": AN, p. xviii.

134-35. "consciousness . . . dim and meagre": AN, p. 67.

135. "full measure of truth": quoted in Wayne C. Booth, *op. cit.*, p. 44.

135n. "in the police court . . .": Joseph Conrad, *Lord Jim*, Boston, Houghton Mifflin Riverside Edition, 1958, pp. 22-23. For a useful recent account of the continuities of technique and philosophical concern between James and Conrad, see Elsa Nettels, *James and Conrad*, Athens, Ga., Univ. of Georgia Press, 1977.

136. "most polished of possible mirrors . . .": Preface to *The Princess Casamassima*, AN, p. 70. "picture" . . . "idea" . . . "interfused": "Guy de Maupassant," SLC, p. 101. "in the highest degree . . . dramatically and objectively": Preface to *The Princess Casamassima*, AN, p. 67.

137. "as an historian and . . .": quoted in René Wellek, *A History of Modern Criticism 1750-1950*, vol. IV, *The Later Nineteenth Century*, p. 222. "Might not an illusion . . . highest degree objective": UA, Chap. VI, pp. 37-38. [WDB, I: 246-47.]

138. *Stanley Cavell*: Cavell's remark, made in conversation, was reported to me by Roger Wertheimer, to whom I am also indebted for some clarification of the general formulation which follows. For a discussion of the ap-

propriation of Nietzsche by the Nazis, see Kaufmann's Prologue on "The
Nietzsche Legend" in Kaufmann, pp. 3-18, especially his remarks on Ernst
Bertram, pp. 12-14. It is presumably on the basis of accounts of this kind
that Conor Cruise O'Brien was moved to his rather free-swinging and unconvincing denunciation of Kaufmann for being too soft on Nietzsche, in
an essay which appeared to the incidental accompaniment of a David
Levine caricature of Nietzsche foaming at the mouth, evocative of World
War I allusions to "the werewolf of Turin" ("The Gentle Nietzscheans,"
The New York Review of Books, Nov. 5, 1970). Kaufmann's greatest po-
lemical weakness may well be his tendency to represent Nietzsche as essentially a late heir of the Enlightenment, a vigorous advocate of maximum
individual liberty and of the application of rational analysis to every area
of human affairs. The final irony here, however (provided that one has a
taste for the kind of irony that is central to works like Dostoevsky's *The
Possessed*), is that that is precisely what Nietzsche may be, and that this itself might be regarded as a rather telling judgment on the intellectual and
social consequences which may follow from Enlightenment values and expectations—just as the headlong, obsessive, unstoppable career of Ahab may
be seen, as D. H. Lawrence saw it, as the inevitable outcome of an absolute
commitment to ideals of rational control and personal freedom. But Kaufmann's unironic emphasis on these presumably positive aspects of Nietzsche's thought hardly makes him an apologist for anything that may be
sinister and unsettling in the philosopher's work. Moreover, his own efforts
over the past three decades have been extremely valuable in making Nietzsche more generally accessible to English readers who would otherwise be
likely to arrive at their sense of his significance on the basis of frequently
misleading paraphrases and translations, and who could not in any case be
expected to have more than a vague sense of the larger philosophical, historical, and moral contexts in which his work figures. It should be kept in
mind that Kaufmann's attempts to provide these contexts, which are essential to any responsible understanding of Nietzsche's necessarily controversial reputation, significantly predate the recent intensification of interest
in the German philosopher's thought among an influential group of literary
intellectuals in France and the United States. The reader seeking a precise,
detailed, and admirably balanced account of the limitations of Kaufmann's
assessment of Nietzsche should consult the introductory chapter of Werner
Dannhauser's book on *Nietzsche's Views of Socrates*, Ithaca, N.Y., Cornell
Univ. Press, 1974, pp. 26-41. "If such thinkers are dangerous . . .": SE,
Chap. VIII, p. 109. [WDB, I: 364.] "the presumption that the unity of
plan . . .": see second note for p. 137 above.

139. "must know man . . .": James, in "Our Mutual Friend," SLC, p. 9.

140. "the victim and the votary . . .": Ezra Pound, "Henry James," *Literary Essays of Ezra Pound*, London, Faber & Faber, 1960, pp. 298-99. "there are times when we might . . .": Booth, *op. cit.*, p. 46. "*c'est une rage . . . form*": letter of Feb. 6, 1891, LHJ, I: 183. "the sum of all intensities . . .": AN, p. 326. "the illusion . . . art of the novelist": "The Art of Fiction," SLC, p. 57. . . . *for Nietzsche, dramatic representation . . .* : cf. *The Birth of Tragedy* (esp. Sect. 8), ML, pp. 64-67. [WDB, I: 52.]

141. "real value" of history . . . "beauty exists in it": UA, Chap. VI, p. 39. [WDB, I: 249.] *an ideal aesthetic distance:* for an elaboration of some of the more far-reaching implications of the notion of artistic detachment alluded to here, see Edward Bullough's essay on " 'Psychical Distance' as a Factor in Art and an Esthetic Principle," *British Journal of Psychology* V, no. 2, 1913: 87-118.

142. "But this requires above all . . . called 'objectivity' ": UA, Chap. VI, pp. 39-40. [WDB, I: 249.] *not to* "believe in any history that . . .": *ibid.*, p. 40. [WDB, I: 250.] "no good novel . . .": "The Art of Fiction," SLC, p. 66. "There is one point at which . . .": *ibid.*; cf. also the preface to *The Portrait of a Lady*, AN, p. 45.

143. "as the picture is reality . . .": "The Art of Fiction," SLC, p. 51. "literature is an objective . . .": quoted in Wellek, *op. cit.*, p. 226. Consider the remarks, proceeding from similar assumptions, made by one of the characters in Oscar Wilde's dialogue entitled "The Decay of Lying," the first of the critical writings included in *Intentions* (1891): "My own experience is that the more we study Art, the less we care for Nature. What Art really reveals to us is Nature's lack of design, her curious crudities, her extraordinary monotony, her absolutely unfinished condition. Nature has good intentions, of course, but, as Aristotle once said, she cannot carry them out. When I look at a landscape I cannot help seeing all its defects. It is fortunate for us, however, that Nature is so imperfect, as otherwise we should have had no art at all. Art is our spirited protest, our gallant attempt to teach Nature her proper place. As for the infinite variety of Nature, that is a pure myth. It is not to be found in Nature herself. It resides in the imagination, or fancy, or cultivated blindness of the man who looks at her." Richard Ellmann, ed., *The Artist As Critic: Critical Writings of Oscar Wilde*, New York, Vintage Books, 1970, pp. 290-91. "most polished of possible . . .": quoted in Roberts, *op. cit.*, p. 97. "dramatically and objectively . . . case": Preface to *The Princess Casamassima*, AN, p. 67. "for

whom the world is finished . . .": UA, Chap. I, p. 10. [WDB, I: 217.]
". . . all is present": *Confessions* [see note to p. 119 above], p. 261. "It is
in this way, then . . .": *ibid.*, p. 259.

145. "elementary passions": "Our Mutual Friend," SLC, p. 10. "The
author must understand . . .": *ibid.* ". . . a large part of the very
source . . .": Preface to *The Spoils of Poynton*, AN, pp. 122-23. Despite
the qualifications delicately introduced at the conclusion, the Faustian dimensions of the novelistic enterprise as James conceives it are nowhere more
evident than in this passage. For a relevant account of some of the guises
in which such unbounded ambitions have appeared in art and philosophy
since the sixteenth century, as well as an immensely provocative analysis of
the kind of dilemma which they have invariably produced—a dilemma char-
acterized (in terms evocative of Ahab's fate in *Moby-Dick*|) as "the tragic
debate between the human mind's claim to autonomous sovereignty and
the universe's maneuvers to frustrate the mind's heroic experiments in absolute freedom"—see Erich Heller's highly important book, *The Artist's
Journey into the Interior and Other Essays*, New York, Random House,
1965. "the impersonal author's concrete . . .": Preface to *The Golden
Bowl*, AN, p. 327.

146. "the artist, the divine . . .": Preface to *The Tragic Muse*, AN,
p. 84. "the muffled majesty of authorship . . .": Preface to *The Golden
Bowl*, AN, p. 328. "by the light . . . all experience": "The Art of Fiction," SLC, p. 62. "power to guess the unseen . . .": *ibid.*, p. 57. "on
whom nothing is lost . . .": *ibid.* "experience is never limited . . . revelations": *ibid.*, p. 56. "in the gradual inward mastery . . .": in F. W. Dupee,
ed., *op. cit.*, p. 194. "a view of *all* the dimensions . . . atmospheric":
Preface to *What Maisie Knew*, AN, pp. 153-54.

147. "James 'was in love . . .'": quoted in F. O. Matthiessen, *The
James Family*, p. 592. "No privilege of the teller . . . at its best": AN,
p. 311. "constant and vast . . . nothing": in Matthiessen, *op. cit.*, p. 603.
"persons of a fine . . .": *ibid.*, p. 602. "conceivable that the possibility
. . . to it": *ibid.*, p. 603. "in proportion as we . . . relations": *ibid.*,
p. 612.

148. "through the individual fact . . .": "Address at the Emerson Centenary in Concord," May 25, 1903, in Bruce Wilshire, ed., *William James:
The Essential Writings*, New York, Harper and Row, 1971, pp. 289-93.
For a series of complementary assertions made by Henry James, see his
1887 essay on Emerson, reprinted in *Partial Portraits* (1888) [SLC, pp.
68-86].

149. "the danger of filling too full . . .": Preface to *The Princess*

Casamassima, AN, p. 63. "the illusion of life": "The Art of Fiction," SLC, p. 57. "intense perceivers . . . bewildered": Preface to *The Princess Casamassima,* AN, p. 63.

150. "a view of *all* the dimensions": Preface to *What Maisie Knew,* AN, p. 153. "the only reason for the existence of the novel": "The Art of Fiction," SLC, p. 50. "under the right persuasion . . .": Preface to *The Ambassadors,* AN, p. 326.

151. "little disquisition on the novel in general . . .": "Guy de Maupassant," SLC, p. 88. "there are simply as many different kinds . . .": *ibid.* "The house of fiction has . . .": AN, pp. 46-47.

153. "The real . . . represents . . .": Preface to *The American,* AN, p. 31. "I, for my part . . .": "Remarks on Spencer's Definition of Mind as Correspondence," in Bruce Wilshire, ed., *op. cit.,* pp. 23-24.

155. "that any form of the novel is simply . . .": "Guy de Maupassant," SLC, pp. 88-89. "the value of the artist . . . universal consciousness": *ibid.* "How childish, moreover . . .": *ibid.*

156. "one of the strong race . . .": EH II: 3 ("Why I Am So Clever"), ML, p. 700. [*WDB,* II: 1088.] "not that M. de Maupassant happens . . .": "Guy de Maupassant," SLC, p. 89. "of secondary importance . . . into that case": *ibid.* "a case is poor when . . .": *ibid.,* p. 90.

158. "the high price of the novel . . .": AN, pp. 45-46. "his life was one long conversation . . .": William James, in Bruce Wilshire, ed., *op. cit.* (see note to p. 148 above), p. 293. "the curiously generalized way . . .": "Emerson," SLC, p. 77.

159. "an experiment in the nurture . . .": *Henry James,* New York, William Sloane Associates, 1951, p. 25. "Within the last year . . .": entry for June 16, 1891, *The Diary of Alice James,* ed. Leon Edel, New York, Dodd, Mead & Co., 1964, p. 211.

160. "The sickness in this family . . . from loving them": *Daedalus,* Summer 1968, (Vol. 97, no. 3 of the Proceedings of the American Academy of Arts and Sciences): 1071. "The best thing I could say . . .": *The Joyful Wisdom* ("La Gaya Scienza"), trans. by Thomas Common (Levy, X): Sect. 98, p. 131. [*WDB,* II: 102-103.] For Kaufmann's translation see GS, Bk. II, Sect. 98, p. 150.

161. "love translated back into nature": CW 2, ML, pp. 614-17. [*WDB,* II: 907.] "Not the love of a 'higher virgin' . . .": *ibid.* Part of the classical background of this general line of thinking is discussed by Charles R. West, Jr., in his unpublished Columbia Ph.D. dissertation on "Nietzsche's Concept of *Amor Fati*" (1957). "Nietzsche's love," West points out, "is *not* the caritative love (based on sympathy and pity) propounded by the Chris-

tian tradition on the one hand and Schopenhauer on the other. Disinterested or selfless love is a contradiction in terms. A man's power to love is measured by the strength of his ego; and the noble man accepts the fact of his egoism without question. Love is the gift of the abundant spirit which seeks to pour itself out and is grateful to anyone who will receive it; it is Zarathustra's 'bestowing virtue.' Like the sexual impulse on which it is based, love also involves conflict, struggle, and competition. Nietzsche's love bears an affinity to the Platonic *eros* which flourished in competition for manly virtue and a high degree of personal perfection. Many of the ideas contained in the *Symposium* are incorporated into Nietzsche's own concept of the creative *eros*" (p. 3). "I know no case where . . .": CW 2, ML, p. 615. [*WDB*, *ibid*.]

162. "amiable ferocity . . .": quoted by Strout, *op. cit*., p. 1073. "the annihilation of ordinary bounds . . .": BT 7, ML, p. 59. [*WDB*, I: 48.] "the most immediate effect . . . of nature": *ibid*. [*WDB*, I: 47.]

163. "Greek tragedy in its earliest form . . .": BT 10, ML, p. 73. [*WDB*, I: 61.] There have, of course, been numerous investigations of the sources and historical development of Greek tragedy; one of the most interesting to have appeared in recent years is Gerald F. Else's *The Origin and Early Form of Greek Tragedy*, Martin Classical Lectures, vol. XX, Cambridge, Mass., Harvard Univ. Press, 1965. Acknowledging the greatness of Nietzsche's book, and confirming what is generally recognized, that "it has cast a spell on almost everybody who has dealt with the subject since 1871"–in this respect Nietzsche occupies a position not unlike that of D. H. Lawrence in relation to classic American literature—Else goes on to point unexpectedly to the "traditional and conventional basis" of Nietzsche's ostensibly revolutionary account: "*The Birth of Tragedy* does not present any new theory of the origin; it simply visualizes, *visionalizes*, an outline of events suggested in Aristotle's *Poetics*. The catalyst was Wagnerian opera, but the source was Aristotle." In the end, for Else, "the spiritual importance" of Nietzsche's work "vastly transcends its occasion and its evidence," and he concludes that "we nowadays can see it in broader perspective, as a milestone on the *via dolorosa* which led modern man into the twentieth century." (All quotations from Else, p. 10.) A consistently well-informed, carefully articulated, and highly compelling exposition of the whole course of development of Nietzsche's thought as that development reveals itself in his changing attitude toward classical philosophy is provided by Werner Dannhauser in his book *Nietzsche's View of Socrates*, Ithaca, N.Y., Cornell Univ. Press, 1974. For a valuable general discussion of Nietzsche's relation to classical scholarship (in his own time and ours), see Hugh Lloyd-Jones's essay on "Nietzsche and the study of the

ancient world," The [London] *Times Literary Supplement*, Feb. 21, 1975. A version of this essay appears in an important recent collection entitled *Studies in Nietzsche and the Classical Tradition*, edited by James C. O'Flaherty, Timothy F. Sellner, and Robert M. Helm (Chapel Hill, N.C., The University of North Carolina Press, 1976). Anyone who recognizes the centrality of this subject will wish to consult William Arrowsmith's complete translation—the first—of Nietzsche's *Wir Philologen*, as well as Arrowsmith's earlier work of selection, translation, and commentary, published in three parts under the title "Nietzsche on Classics and Classicists" (see Bibliography for full particulars). "that this dismemberment . . .": BT 10, ML, p. 73. [*WDB*, I: 61.]

163-64. "rebirth of Dionysus . . . augury of restored oneness": BT 10, ML, p. 74. [*WDB*, I: 62.] "form-giving." Kaufmann, p. 128. "the heroic effort of the individual . . .": BT 9, ML, p. 71. [*WDB*, I: 59.] "has to suffer for its individuation . . .": *ibid.*

165. "shattering of the individual": BT 8, ML, p. 65. [*WDB*, I: 47.] "fusion with primal being": *ibid.* "the metaphysical comfort . . .": BT 7, ML, p. 59. [*WDB*, I: 47.] "represents the world as vulnerable . . .": *Essays in Pragmatism*, ed. with an introduction by Alburey Castell, New York, Hafner Publishing Co., 1947, p. 59. "gives us a pluralistic, restless universe . . .": *ibid.*, p. 60.

166. "the indeterminism with its maggots . . .": *ibid.* "the effort of the artist . . .": Preface to *The American*, AN, pp. 37-38. "dramas within dramas . . .": "The Art of Fiction," SLC, p. 54. "had a mortal horror . . .": Preface to *The Tragic Muse*, AN, pp. 83-84. "loss of authority" . . . "The reason of this . . .": *ibid.*, p. 84.

167. "health and safety . . . dimensions": Preface to *What Maisie Knew*, AN, p. 153. "the aesthetic consciousness . . .": "Gabriele d'Annunzio," SLC, p. 288. "to live the life of others": quoted in Wellek, *op. cit.*, p. 223. "let anyone feel the urge . . .": BT 8, ML, p. 64. [*WDB*, I: 51-52.] "a continuum of cosmic consciousness": Matthiessen, *op. cit.*, p. 589.

168. "Ah! seest thou not, O brother . . .": included in Daniel Aaron and Alfred Kazin, eds., *Emerson: A Modern Anthology*, New York, Dell Publishing Co., 1958, p. 168. "Out of my experience, such as it is . . .": Matthiessen, *op. cit.*, pp. 588-89.

169. "left the question of immortality open . . .": Matthiessen, *op. cit.*, p. 590. "took the pluralistic view that God . . .": *ibid.* "most general effect . . . in this world": *ibid.*, p. 602. "Either one or the other of these opposed . . . speculative reckoning": *ibid.*

170. "it may very well be asked. . . .": *ibid.* "How *can* there be a per-

sonal . . .": *ibid.*, pp. 602-3. D. H. Lawrence, "Reflections on the Death
of a Porcupine" in the collection by that title, Bloomington, Indiana Univ.
Press, 1963, pp. 210-11.

171. *absorption into the* Ur-Ein: cf. Arthur C. Danto, *Nietzsche as Philosopher*, New York, Macmillan, 1965, p. 97.

172. "every center of force" WP 636, p. 339. [*Mus.*, xix: 105-6.] "in the
end . . . of modern physics": Kaufmann, p. 243. "Physicists believe . . .
process goes on—": WP 636, pp. 339-340. [*Mus.*, xix: 105-6.]

173. *Nietzsche as Philosopher*: Danto's discussion should be supple-
mented by John T. Wilcox's recent work entitled *Truth and Value in
Nietzsche: A Study of His Metaethics and Epistemology*, Ann Arbor, Univ.
of Michigan Press, 1974, as well Ruedigger Hermann Grimm, *Nietzsche's
Theory of Knowledge*, Berlin, Walter de Gruyter, 1977, and Jean Granier,
Le problème de la vérité dans la philosophie de Nietzsche, Paris, Éditions
du Seuil, 1966. "advanced a pragmatic criterion . . .": Danto, *op. cit.*,
p. 72. 'proclaims time and time . . . order to be true": *ibid.*, p. 75.

173n. "Any idea upon which . . .": "What Pragmatism Means" (see
note to page 174 below), p. 148.

174. "it converts the absolutely empty . . .": "What Pragmatism
Means," *Essays in Pragmatism*, New York, Hafner Publishing Co., 1948,
p. 152. "the state of private poetic intercourse . . .": "Gabriele D'Annunzio," SLC, p. 288. "tragic" . . . "that life is . . .": Danto, *op. cit.*,
p. 79. *the wisdom of Silenus in* The Birth of Tragedy: "There is an ancient
story that King Midas hunted in the forest a long time for the wise Silenus,
the companion of Dionysus, without capturing him. When Silenus fell at
last into his hands, the king asked what was the best and most desirable of
things for men. Fixed and immovable, the demigod said not a word, till at
last, urged by the king, he gave a shrill laugh and broke out into these
words: 'Oh, wretched ephemeral race, children of chance and misery, why
do you compel me to tell you what it would be most expedient for you not
to hear? What is best of all is utterly beyond your reach: not to be born,
not to *be*, to be *nothing*. But the second best for you is—to die soon.'" (BT
3, ML, p. 42. [*WDB*, I: 29-30.] The reference in this passage, as Kaufmann points out, is to Sophocles, *Oedipus at Colonus*, lines 1224ff. "the
would-be opponents . . . claim to truth": Danto, *op. cit.*, p. 76. "is but
one of an infinite number . . . of the world": *ibid.* "The question sometimes arises . . .": *ibid.*

175. "the world is in fact . . .": *ibid.*, pp. 77-78. "one cannot say . . .
where we are": *ibid.*, p. 78.

176. "the eye of Zarathustra . . . below": Preface to CW, ML, p. 611.

[*WDB*, II: 903.] "The doctrine that . . . of the herd": Danto, *op. cit.*, p. 77.

177. "the world is made up of points. . . . Will-to-Power": *ibid.*, p. 80. "every specific body . . . its extension": WP 636, pp. 339-40. [*Mus.*, xix: 106.] " 'First Law' of Nietzsche's theory . . . whole of space": Danto, *op. cit.*, p. 220. "a philosophical problem . . . overcome": *ibid.*, p. 70. "a will to impose . . . order": *ibid.*, p. 76.

178. *Accordingly . . . another man's conception of the world:* Cf. Blake's *Jerusalem* (1804-1820), Sect. II, line 24: "I must Create a System or be enslav'd by another Man's." ". . . what formerly happened . . . *causa prima*": BGE 9, ML, p. 206. [*WDB*, II: 573.] "Freedom from all kinds . . . of the concept": A 54, PN, pp. 638-39. [*WDB*, II: 1221-22.]

179 "Whatever I create . . . wills it": Z, Pt. II, PN, p. 227. [*WDB*, II: 371.] "Meanwhile I am still . . .": LFN, p. 214. [*WDB*, III: 1209.]

180. "had a more penetrating knowledge of himself . . .": Ernest Jones, *The Life and Work of Sigmund Freud*, II, New York, Basic Books, 1953: 344; cited by Kaufmann in his Introduction to EH, ML, p. 659. "addicted to seeing 'through' . . .": Preface to *What Maisie Knew*, AN, pp. 153-54. "One who is openly honest . . . hypocrisy": translated by Paul V. Cohn (Levy, VII), sect. 56, p. 38. [*WDB*, I: 763.]

181. *endless succession of perspectives:* for an interesting view of the history of modern science in roughly these terms, see Danto, *op. cit.*, p. 91. "Behold . . . I am . . . but all this is one . . .": Z, Pt. II, PN, p. 227. [*WDB*, II: 371.] "The phenomenon 'artist' . . . nature, etc.!": WP 797, p. 419. [*Mus.*, xix: 208.]

182. "I dreamed that I floated . . .": Emerson, *Journals*, V: 485, included in *Emerson: A Modern Anthology*, ed. Alfred Kazin and Daniel Aaron, New York, Dell Publishing Co., Inc., 1958, p. 21. "We need 'unities' . . . any actual unity": WP 635, p. 338. [*Mus.*, xix: 104.] "fiction," "the concept of activity . . . ," "the concept of motion . . .": *ibid.*, p. 339. [*Mus.*, xix: 104-5.] "lies are necessary . . . character of existence": WP 853, p. 451. [*Mus.*, xix: 251.] One of the most valuable discussions of the significance of necessary fictions and deliberate illusions in Nietzsche's work may be found in the last chapter of Hans Vaihinger's *The Philosophy of "As-If*," 2nd ed., London, Routledge and Kegan Paul, 1935. "We are fundamentally inclined . . .": BGE 4, ML, p. 202 [*WDB*, II: 569].

183. *"instrumental" value:* the fact that science relies extensively on such concepts as those of activity, identity, and motion does not, in Nietzsche's view, make those concepts any more "true": indeed, he generally appears to

regard the whole enterprise of science as no more or less than a form of art, a way of constructing the world which is still ultimately dependent on "our eye and our psychology," as he suggests in *The Will to Power*: hence the declaration in *Beyond Good and Evil that* "It is perhaps just dawning on five or six minds that physics, too, is only an interpretation and exegesis of the world (to suit us, if I may say so!) and not a world-explanation. . . ." For a useful discussion of this point, see Danto, *op. cit.*, pp. 71-72, 92-93. Two more recent studies which take up the issue of Nietzsche's relation to modern scientific theory are Wolfgang Yourgrau, "Nietzsche and Modern Physics," *The Denver Quarterly* VI, 1971, 20-32, and Alain Juranville, *Physique de Nietzsche*, Paris, Éditions Denoël, 1973. "that things possess a constitution . . .": WP 560, pp. 302-3. [*Mus.*, xix: 58-59.] "The world that we have not reduced . . .": quoted in Danto, *op. cit.*, p. 77.

184. "Verily, I have found you out . . .": Z, Pt. I, PN, pp. 186-87. [*WDB*, II: 336-37.] "disciplined himself" . . . "to wholeness": TI ix:49, PN, p. 554. [*WDB*, II: 1024.] "the 'life in God' " . . . "the subtlest and final offspring . . . at any price": BGE 59, ML, p. 261. [*WDB*, II: 620.] "it may be that . . . until now . . .": *ibid*.

185. "an illness, there is no doubt . . .": GM, II: 19, ML, p. 524. [*WDB*, II: 829.] "One should guard against . . .": GM, II: 18, ML, pp. 523-24. [*WDB*, II: 828.]

186. "a finer and more militant edge": Preface to *The Lesson of the Master*, AN, p. 223. "How much did this people have to suffer . . .": BT 25, ML, p. 144. [*WDB*, I: 134.] "want, if possible— . . . *to abolish suffering*": BGE 225, ML, p. 343. [*WDB*, II: 689.] "The discipline of suffering . . .": BGE 225, ML, p. 344. [*WDB*, II: 689-90.]

187. "This last bite of life . . .": Kaufmann, p. 59. [*WDB*, III: 1198.] (Cf. *LFN*, 198-99.) The phrase quoted by Nietzsche—"all experiences are useful, all days holy, and all human beings divine"—is a paraphrase of a sentence from Emerson's essay on "History" (*Essays: First Series*): "To the poet, to the philosopher, to the saint, all things are friendly and sacred, all events profitable, all days holy, all men divine." Nietzsche used a similar paraphrase as the motto at the beginning of the first edition of *Die fröhliche Wissenschaft*, published in 1882. (Cf. Elisabeth Foerster-Nietzsche, *Das Leben Friedrich Nietzsches*, II, Leipzig, 1895-1904: 397; cited in Hermann Hummel, "Emerson and Nietzsche," *New England Quarterly* XIX, March 1940: 63.)

188. "whatever lives, obeys" . . . "he who cannot . . .": Z, Pt. II, PN, p. 226. [*WDB*, II: 370.]

189. "It is practiced by those . . . the constraint of style": GS, Bk. IV,

Sect. 290, pp. 232-33. [WDB, II: 168-69.] "The noble type of man experiences *itself* . . . self-glorification": BGE 260, ML, p. 395. [WDB, II: 730.]

190. "the only right . . . the only wrong": compare these entries from Emerson's *Journal* for Sept. 1833: "A man contains all that is needful to his government within himself. He is made a law unto himself. . . . Good or evil that can [befall] him must be from himself. . . ." It is useful to keep such observations in mind in attempting to account for the ultimate admiration which the reader is invited to feel for a character like Kurtz in Conrad's *Heart of Darkness* (1899). Faced at last by "the chief of the Inner Station," a being to whose making "all Europe contributed," Marlow observes: "There was nothing either above or below him, and I knew it. He had kicked himself loose of the earth. Confound the man! he had kicked the very earth to pieces. He was alone, and I before him did not know whether I stood on the ground or floated in the air." (*Heart of Darkness* and *The Secret Sharer*, New York, New American Library, 1910, pp. 92, 122-23, 143.) "At the risk of displeasing . . .": BGE 265, ML, p. 405. [WDB, II: 739.]

190-91. "*knows itself to be at a height*": ibid. [WDB, II: 740.] "Ordinary human beings" . . . "poverty of their souls": BGE 61, ML, p. 263. [WDB, II: 622.]

191. "The essential characteristic . . .": BGE 258, ML, p. 392. [WDB, II: 728.]

192. "that of a woman whom I do not know" . . . "could have seen only at Mrs. Gardner's house": Louise Hall Tharp, *Mrs. Jack: A Biography of Isabella Stewart Gardner*, Boston, Little, Brown & Co., 1965, p. 170. "It is a portrait such as . . . masterpiece of this civilization": quoted *ibid.*, pp. 170-71.

193. *The Golden Bowl:* in a similarly revealing passage in that novel, an elevator also figures significantly; replying to a question by Fanny Assingham, the Prince explains what he regards as his lack of a moral sense in the following terms: "I've of course something that in our poor dear backward old Rome sufficiently passes for it. But it's no more like yours than the tortuous stone staircase—half-ruined into the bargain!—in some castle of our *quattrocento* is like the 'lightning elevator' in one of Mr. Verver's fifteen-storey buildings. Your moral sense works by steam—it sends you up like a rocket. Ours is slow and steep and unlighted, with so many of the steps missing that—well, that it's as short in almost any case to turn around and come down again." "Here we must beware . . . exploitation . . .": BGE 259, ML, p. 393. [WDB, II: 729.]

194. "the feeling of fullness . . .": BGE 260, ML, p. 395. [WDB, II: 730-31.] "the whole of nature is impelled . . .": SE, Chap. V, p. 54. [WDB, I: 324.] "And when the whole of nature . . .": *ibid.*, p. 52. [WDB, I: 322.] "those true men, *those no longer* . . . at her goal": *ibid.*, p. 54. [WDB, I: 324.]

195. "she fulfills her ends": *ibid.*, Chap. VII, p. 84. [WDB, I: 345.] "nature always wishes to be useful to all . . .": *ibid.*, pp. 83-84. "disgust at the valuelessness . . . clumsiness a little": *ibid.*, Chap. III, p. 26. [WDB, I: 304.] "at first, admittedly . . .": *ibid.* " 'blind instinct' is replaced by conscious will": *ibid.*, Chap. VI, p. 63 [WDB, I: 330.] "but eventually for everybody": *ibid.*, Chap. III, p. 26. [WDB, I: 304.] "every man is used to finding . . .": *ibid.*, p. 27. [WDB, I: 305.]

196. "the goal of all culture . . . redemption from itself": *ibid.*, Chap. V, pp. 56-57. [WDB, I: 326.] "it is only as an *aesthetic phenomenon* . . .": BT 5, ML, p. 52. [WDB, I: 40.] Cf. Sect. 24, ML, p. 141. [WDB, I: 131.]

197. "is the child of every individual's . . .": SE, Chap. VI, p. 61. [WDB, I: 328.] "Creation— . . . that is . . . if gods existed?": Z, Pt. II, PN, p. 199. [WDB, I: 328.] "himself to wholeness . . .": TI ix:49, PN, p. 544. [WDB, II: 1024.] "the deepest conviction that we meet nature . . . to become whole!": SE, Chap. VI, pp. 61-62. [WDB, I: 329.] "all is redeemed and affirmed in the whole": TI ix:49, PN, p. 554. [WDB, II: 1025.] Nietzsche outlines one of the more disquieting implications of this notion in *Beyond Good and Evil:* "If . . . a person should regard even the effects of hatred, envy, covetousness, and the lust to rule as conditions of life, as factors which, fundamentally and essentially, must be present in the general economy of life (and must, therefore, be further enhanced if life is to be further enhanced)—he will suffer from such a view of things as from seasickness. And yet even this hypothesis is far from being the strangest and most painful in this immense and almost new domain of dangerous insights; and there are in fact a hundred good reasons why everyone should keep away from it who—*can.*" (BGE 23, ML, p. 221.) [WDB, II: 587.] Compare Emerson in "Self-Reliance": "The doctrine of hatred must be preached, as the counteraction of the doctrine of love, when that pules and whines."

197-98. "I walk among men. . . . And this is all my creating . . . of accidents?": Z, Pt. II, PN, p. 251. [WDB, II: 394.]

198. "But my fervent will to create . . . gods to me now?": Z, Pt. II, PN, pp. 199-200. [WDB, II: 345-46.] "existence and the world . . .": BT 24, ML, p. 141. [WDB, I: 131.] "That which is in opposition . . .": Heracleitus of Ephesus, frag. 8, in Kathleen Freeman, *Ancilla to the Pre-*

Socratic Philosophers (a complete translation of Diels, *Fragmente der Vorsokratiker*, 5th ed., Walther Kranz, ed., Berlin, 1934-38), Cambridge, Mass., Harvard Univ. Press, 1957, p. 25. For an exceptionally lucid discussion of Heracleitus which is relevant to a fuller understanding of the background of much of Nietzsche's thought (in particular his notion of "perspectivism" and its relation to the will to power), the reader is directed to Freeman's *The Pre-Socratic Philosophers: A Companion to Diels, Fragmente der Vorsokratiker*, 5th ed.; 2nd ed., Cambridge Mass., Harvard Univ. Press, 1959, pp. 104-32, esp. pp. 109-17. Freeman's two volumes are referred to hereafter as *Ancilla* and *Companion* respectively.

    199. "convince us that even . . . artistically employed": BT 24, ML, p. 141. [WDB, I: 131.] "the tragic effect: For we now understand . . .": *ibid.*, pp. 141-42. [WDB, I: 131-32.] "All things are an exchange . . .": quoted in Freeman, *Companion*, p. 110 (cf. *Ancilla*, p. 31).

    200. "was ever and is and shall . . .": Heracleitus, frag. 30, *Ancilla*, p. 26. According to Freeman's reading of the fragments, Heracleitus maintained that "the material substrate was Fire. . . . real material Fire was the ultimate matter out of which all things come and into which all things return. It is able to undergo transformations, and so to produce the other substances Air, Water and Earth. . . . Particular things came out of Fire, and are destroyed back into it; their coming into being is 'in accordance with fate.'" (Freeman, *Companion*, p. 109.) ". . . just as the child . . . other worlds . . .": *Early Greek Philosophy and Other Essays*, trans. by M. A. Mügge (Levy, II), p. 108; cited in Richard P. Benton, "The Aesthetics of Friedrich Nietzsche: The Relation of Art to Life," unpublished Ph.D. dissertation, The Johns Hopkins University, 1955, p. 30. "existence and the world . . . aesthetic phenomenon": BT 5, ML, p. 52. [WDB, I: 40.]

    200n. "He was like a young god . . .": quoted in Alfred Kazin and Daniel Aaron, eds., *Emerson, A Modern Anthology*, New York, Dell Publishing Co., 1958, p. 379.

    201. "germ of a 'story' . . ." ". . . some sharp point. . . ." "virtue . . . operation": Preface to *The Spoils of Poynton*, AN, p. 119. "one's subject is in . . . happened to meet it": Preface to *The Spoils of Poynton*, AN, pp. 119-20.

    202. "clumsy life again . . .": *ibid.*, p. 121. "For the action taken . . .": *ibid.*, pp. 121-22. "amuses him again . . .": *ibid.*, p. 120.

    203. "has no direct sense . . . splendid waste": *ibid.* "waste is only life . . .": *ibid.*, p. 84. "the general and the only . . . illustrative": "The Art of Fiction," SLC, p. 58. "Hence the opportunity . . . of incomes": Preface to *The Spoils of Poynton*, AN, p. 120. An interesting perspective

on the financial metaphor in evidence here—and elsewhere in James's work—is provided by Donald L. Mull in his study entitled *Henry James's "Sublime Economy,"* Middletown, Conn., Wesleyan Univ. Press, 1973, particularly in the "Biographical" chapter, pp. 3-13. Also useful in this regard, though far more literal and less suggestive than Mull's discussion, is Jan W. Dietrichson, *The Image of Money,* Oslo, Universitetsverlaget, 1969. "a devastating lampoon . . .": H. Montgomery Hyde, *Henry James at Home,* London, Methuen & Co., 1969, p. 268. "I regard it as relevant . . .": July 10, 1915, LHJ, II: 508. For all the pertinent documents bearing on this important exchange, see Leon Edel and Gordon N. Ray, eds., *Henry James and H. G. Wells: A Record of Their Friendship, Their Debate on the Art of Fiction, and Their Quarrel,* Urbana, Ill., Univ. of Illinois Press, 1958. "a real and very fundamental difference . . .": July 8, 1915, excerpts quoted in LHJ, II: 505. "To you . . . it has a use": letter of July 13, 1915, *ibid.*

203-4. "There is no sense . . . of its process": letter of July 10, 1915, *ibid.,* pp. 507-8.

204. "When you say . . .": Wells, LHJ, II: 505. " 'Art' . . . has both a wide and narrow use . . .": Danto, *op. cit.,* p. 45. "it prolongs, it preserves. . . ." "in literature . . . the thing itself": quoted in Morris Roberts, *op. cit.,* pp. 85-86. "attempt to render the look . . ." "illusion of life" . . . "it is here in very truth . . .": "The Art of Fiction," SLC, p. 57.

205. "Art deals with what we see . . .": AN, p. 312. "Life being all inclusion . . . " "and art being all . . .": Preface to *The Spoils of Poynton,* p. 120. "while the dog desires . . .": *ibid.*

206. "melancholy outpouring" "how better to acknowledge . . .": letter of March 21, 1914, LHJ, II: 373. "I still find my consciousness . . ." "You see I still . . .": *ibid.,* p. 374.

207. "in many ways . . . and could be nothing else": F. R. Leavis, "James as Critic," introductory essay to SLC, p. xviii. "the imaginative representation of life": AN, p. xxxviii. "imposing on it the form . . .": *ibid.* "maintain his situation to have been . . . my best for it": AN, pp. 223-24. "observed reality" . . . "It was the fault . . .": *ibid.,* p. 224.

208. "The only real people . . .": Wilde, *op. cit.,* p. 297. "As the inevitable result . . .": *ibid.,* p. 303. "We have mistaken . . .": *ibid.,* p. 300.

209. "the *best* residuum of truth": Preface to *What Maisie Knew,* AN, p. 141.

209-10. "The only general attribute . . .": Preface to *The American,* AN, pp. 33-34.

210. *the truest realism is* "the real . . .": Roberts, *op. cit.*, p. 90. "It is
the real . . .": quoted in *ibid.* "physiological condition" ". . . aesthetic
doing and seeing": TI ix:8, PN, p. 518. [*WDB*, II: 995.] Cf. Plato,
Phaedrus, 245: "There is a third form of possession or madness, of which
the Muses are the source. . . . But if any man comes to the gates of poetry
without the madness of the Muses, persuaded that skill alone will make
him a good poet, then shall he and his works of sanity with him be brought
to naught by the poetry of madness, and behold, their place is nowhere to
be found." In his commentary on this passage, Hackforth points out that
"the idea of 'divine madness' . . . is no Platonic invention: it belongs in
origin to the religion of Dionysus, which was introduced into Greece many
centuries before Plato's day. . . ." *Plato's Phaedrus*, translated with an
intro. and commentary by R. Hackforth, New York, The Liberal Arts
Press, n.d., pp. 57-58. This classical background—always important in Nietzsche—seems especially pertinent to a consideration of a work in which he
celebrates what he regards as "the highest of all possible faiths: I have
baptized it with the name of *Dionysus*." (TI ix:49, PN, p. 554.) [*WDB*,
II: 1025.] "what is essential" . . . "Out of this feeling . . .": TI ix:8,
PN, p. 518. [*WDB*, II: 995.]

211. "You force all things . . .": Z, Pt. I, PN, p. 187. [*WDB*, II: 337.]
"he did not scruple . . . exist for us": LHJ, I: xv-xvi.

212. "art is not merely imitation . . .": BT 24, ML, p. 140. [*WDB*, I:
130.] "the delight in stinking": TI ix:1, PN, p. 513. [*WDB*, II: 991.]

212-13. "born psychologist" . . . "works 'from nature' . . . *whole*
artist": TI ix:7, PN, p. 517. [*WDB*, I: 994.] "one must know *who* one
is" . . . the factual": *ibid.* [*WDB*, II: 995.] "The belief that the world
as it ought to be . . . *as the impotence of the will to create.*" WP 585
(A), p. 317. [*Mus.*, xix: 78.]

214. "To deny the relevancy of subject-matter. . . ." "the crudity of
sentiment. . . ." "talk of morality . . . intellectual closet": "Charles
Baudelaire," SLC, pp. 30-31. "It is still expected. . . . This, of course,
any sensible . . .": SLC, p. 50.

214-15. "the fight against purpose in art . . . force of the prejudice":
TI ix:24, PN, p. 529. [*WDB*, II: 1004.]

215. "the purpose of moral preaching . . . *l'art pour l'art?*": *ibid.* "Art
is above all and first . . . mere accessary": *Human, All-Too-Human*, II,
trans. Paul V. Cohn (Levy, VII), sect. 174, pp. 91-92. [*WDB*, I: 944.]

216. "able to estimate . . . of my productions": AN, p. 309. "that
one's bag of adventures . . .": *ibid.*, p. 313. "depends so on what one
means . . . objective of the two": *ibid.*

216-17. "In outward manners . . . was never shaken": LHJ, I: xv.

217. "Henry James never took anything . . .": *ibid.*, pp. xii-xiv. "his life . . . undertaking to paint": *ibid.*, p. xiii.

218. "certain pencilled pages . . .": *ibid.*, p. xix. "which belong to . . .": *ibid.* "surrenders to the awe . . . of creation": *ibid.*, pp. xix-xx. "It was absolute for him . . . of the void": *ibid.*, p. xv. "it is as though . . . more closely": *ibid.*, p. xx. "I take this up again . . . kiss its hands": *ibid.*, pp. xx-xxi.

220. "although he had developed . . . in his language": Danto, *op. cit.*, p. 80. "Like many innovators . . . in his language": *ibid. the contradiction between two conceptions of truth:* for a full-scale exposition of the philosophical issues considered in the present chapter, see John T. Wilcox's *Truth and Value in Nietzsche* (Ann Arbor, Mich., 1974). Wilcox's work attempts in part to locate Nietzsche's concerns in this area in a larger philosophical context, and for this purpose his chapters on "Nietzsche as Noncognitivist," "Nietzsche as Cognitivist: General," and "Kant, the Thing-in-Itself, and Nietzsche's Skepticism" are especially valuable. "truth is the kind of error . . .": WP 493, p. 272. [*Mus.*, xix: 19.]

221. "by the feeling of enhanced power . . .": WP 455, pp. 249-250. [*Mus.*, xviii: 323.] "presuppositions concerning . . . involved at all—": *ibid.*, p. 250. [*Mus.*, xviii: 323-24.] "something might be true . . .": BGE 39, ML, p. 230. [*WDB*, II: 602.] "it might be a basic characteristic . . .": *ibid.* "there is only *one* world . . .": WP 853 (I), p. 451. [*Mus.*, xix: 250-51.]

222. "*We have need of lies* . . .": *ibid.* [*Mus.*, xix: 251.] A number of obvious parallels to Nietzsche's assertions in this context are set out, though in a characteristically (and deceptively) lighter tone, in Wilde's "The Decay of Lying," in which "Vivian," who has been arguing throughout the dialogue in favor of the benefits of lying, observes: "A short primer, 'When to Lie and How,' if brought out in an attractive and not too expensive a form, would no doubt command a large sale, and would prove of real practical service to many earnest and deep-thinking people. Lying for the sake of the improvement of the young, which is the basis of home education, still lingers amongst us, and its advantages are so admirably set forth in the early books of Plato's *Republic* that it is unnecessary to dwell upon them here. . . . The only form of lying that is absolutely beyond reproach is Lying for its own sake, and the highest development of this is, as we have already pointed out, Lying in Art. Just as those who do not love Plato more than truth [the allusion here is to a remark of Aristotle's in the *Nicomachean Ethics*] cannot pass beyond the threshold of the Academe, so those who do not love Beauty more than Truth never know the inmost

shrine of Art." (Wilde, *op. cit.*, p. 318.) Cf. also Patrick J. Keane, "On Truth and Lie in Nietzsche," *Salmagundi*, no. 29, Spring 1975, pp. 67-94. "metaphysics, morality, religion . . . faith in life"; WP 853 (I), p. 451. [*Mus.*, xix: 251.] "Life *ought* to inspire . . . an *artist*": *ibid.* "If we had not approved . . . of us . . .": *The Joyful Wisdom* ("La Gaya Scienza"), trans. Thomas Common (Levy, X), Bk. II, Sect. 107, pp. 145-46. For Kaufmann's translation see GS, Bk. II, Sect. 107, pp. 163-64. [*WDB*, II: 113-14.] "the great means of making life possible . . .": WP 853 (II), p. 452. [*Mus.*, xix: 252.]

223. "cannot endure reality . . .": WP 572, p. 308. [*Mus.*, xix: 65-66.] "to lie, to flight . . .": WP 853 (I), p. 452. [*Mus.*, xix: 251.] "Truth is ugly . . .": WP 822, p. 435. [*Mus.*, xix: 229.] "muffles the ache . . .": quoted in Roberts, *op. cit.*, p. 86. "he believes in life . . .": WP 853 (I), p. 452. [*Mus.*, xix: 251.] "man has once again . . .": *ibid.* [*Mus.*, xix: 251-52.] "expression is creation . . .": quoted in Roberts, *op. cit.*, p. 85. "whenever man rejoices . . .": WP 853 (I), p. 452. [*Mus.*, xix: 251.]

224. "*genius in lying*": *ibid.* " 'beauty' is for the artist . . .": WP 803, p. 422. [*Mus.*, xix: 213.]

225. "with much that is common ground . . .": LHJ, I: xxv. "Ah, how much there is . . . inner voices": letter of June 28, 1883, LFN, p. 213. "I am *solitude* become man": in a discarded draft for CW, ML, p. 799. The passage is taken by Kaufmann from Erich F. Podach, ed., *Friedrich Nietzsches Werke der Zusammenbruchs*, Heidelberg, Wolfgang Rothe, 1961, pp. 318ff.

226. "there is indeed a great *emptiness* . . .": letter of the end of July 1888. LFN, p. 302. [*WDB*, III: 1304-5.] "Has anyone ever had an inkling . . .": letter of Nov. 11, 1887, LFN, p. 276. "much as he always delighted . . .": LHJ, I: xv. "a cycle of vivid and incessant adventure . . . and most serenely": LHJ, I: xiv-xv. "About the profession of letters in general . . .": quoted in Simon Nowell-Smith's *The Legend of the Master*, p. 126.

227. "its host, soon to become . . .": quoted in Hyde, *op. cit.*, p. 108. "I had learned, as I may say . . .": F. O. Matthiessen, *The James Family: A Group Biography*, New York, Alfred A. Knopf, 1947, pp. 609-10.

228. "there was the wide, open Place . . .": Edel, I: 79. Although the account that follows relies heavily on Edel, some important information is derived from Hyde, *op. cit.*, esp. pp. 275-83. "What it somehow came to . . . that is represented": quoted by Edel, I: 79-80. In his biographer's view, this " 'general sense of glory' persisted" for James "far beyond the years of his childhood," and in an attempt to sketch out the general context of Napoleonic ambition with which it is associated he goes on to observe

that "Balzac, who later became [James's] supreme literary model, had placed as a sole ornament in his study in the Rue Cassini a plaster statuette of Napoleon and written under it: *'Ce qu'il n'a pas pu achever par l'épée, je l'accomplirai par la plume.'* James also in later life thought of himself as conquering worlds with his pen; the exhortations to himself which he wrote into his notebooks were summonses to literary conquest and power[,] 'splendid and supreme creation . . . *à l'oeuvre, mon bon, à l'oeuvre . . . roide!*'" (Edel, I: 72.)

229. "in later years [James] . . . during the 1890's": *ibid.*, p. 80. "the memoirs of Napoleon's . . . being searched": Edel, IV: 101. So far as James's own collection is concerned, Edel notes that "from the dates on the bindings and of publication, it is clear that James bought at this time a large number of volumes about the First Empire; some show signs of careful reading and contain marked passages. In his library the novelist had, in addition to the Marbot, the memoirs of Marshal Macdonald; Masson's book about Napoleon and women and his volume of anecdotes about the Emperor's private life; the reminiscences of General Bigarre, the aide to King Joseph . . .; Arthur Levy's *Napoléon Intime* of 1893; Barry O'Meara's earlier two-volume account of Napoleon on St. Helena. James also owned Lanfrey's five-volume life of Napoleon, as well as dozens of volumes of letters and biographies of figures in the Empire and after." (Edel, IV: 102-3.) "were dispatched in haste for . . .": *ibid.*, p. 55. "read in their French original . . .": *ibid.*, pp. 101-2. "was reported to have told . . .": quoted in Leon Edel, "Henry James's 'Last Dictation,'" *The* [London] *Times Literary Supplement*, May 2, 1968. Hereafter this article is referred to as "Edel, *TLS*." (A somewhat revised and more extensive account appears in Edel, V.) "he had had a stroke . . .": *ibid.*, p. 459. "on the next day . . .": *ibid.*

230. "a second stroke . . .": Hyde, *op. cit.*, p. 276. "Miss Bosanquet . . . feverish moments": Edel, *TLS*, p. 459. "his mind wandered . . .": *ibid.*, p. 460.

230-31. "I find the business of . . . amusement to them": *ibid. embolic pneumonia*: Hyde, *op. cit.*, p. 277. "Mind clouded . . . sick man": Edel, *TLS*, p. 459. "Wondrous enough certainly . . . hedge a king": *ibid.*

232. "Next statement is for all the world . . .": *ibid.* "The Bonapartes have a kind . . .": *ibid.*

232-33. "after luncheon [James] . . . peaceful sleep": *ibid.* "actually the first letter . . . sister-in-law Alice": *ibid.* "Dear and most esteemed . . .": *ibid.*

234. "Note that I do not . . .": Edel, IV: 102. "My dear brother and

sister . . . : Edel, *TLS*, pp. 459-60. "mostly by James's niece": *ibid.*, p. 460. "across the border . . .": *ibid.*

235. "several people who had seen . . .": Hyde, *op. cit.*, p. 285.

236. "almost without willing it so. . . . *depersonalization*": letter of Dec. 14, 1887, LFN, p. 280 [*WDB*, III: 1273.] "a new note appears . . .": "Nietzsche in his Letters," *Commentary* 38, no. 6 (Dec. 1969): 92. "I have just seen myself. . . .": letter of Oct. 30, 1888, LFN, p. 318. [*WDB*, III: 1326.]

237. ". . . since choosing Turin as my home. . . ." *ibid.* [*WDB*, III: 1326-27.] "I sometimes look at my hand . . .": *ibid.*, p. 319. [*WDB*, III: 1327.]

238. "All in all . . . grapes for me": letter of Dec. 21, 1888, LFN, p. 337. [*WDB*, III: 1344.]

238-39. "it is not only the right place. . . . become a destiny": Dannhauser, *op. cit.*, pp. 92-93.

239. "not the remotest conception of what . . . of my hand": letter of Dec. 1888, LFN, p. 339. "the task which is imposed . . .": *ibid.*, p. 340. "the riddle of self-conquest . . .": BGE 51, ML, p. 255. [*WDB*, II: 614.] "nature finally needs the saint . . .": SE, Chap. V, p. 57. [*WDB*, I: 326.] "we no longer understand the word 'I' ": *ibid.*

240. "And do you know what . . .": WP 1067, pp. 549-50. [*Mus.*, xix: 373-74.]

241. "we come to the paradoxical conclusion . . . 'nature of things' ": *Reflections on the Napoleonic Legend*, New York: Scribners, 1924, p. 260. "the obliteration of Self . . . doubts and fears": *ibid.*, p. 261. "eye of Zarathustra" . . . "for such a goal . . .": Preface to CW, ML, p. 611. [*WDB*, II: 903-4.]

242. "steadily more docile . . .": Dannhauser, *loc. cit.*, p. 89. "Actually I would much rather . . .": LFN, p. 346. [*WDB*, III: 135.]

243. "Fair and foul . . .": "Crazy Jane Talks with the Bishop" (1933), in *The Collected Poems of W. B. Yeats*, definitive ed., New York, The Macmillan Company, 1957, p. 254. "The way in which dreams . . .": Sigmund Freud, *The Interpretation of Dreams*, trans. and ed. James Strachey, New York, Basic Books, 1955, p. 318. "knowing only too well that precisely . . .": BGE 213, ML, p. 330. [*WDB*, II: 679.]

244. "success": *The Golden Bowl*, II: 366. "You Americans . . .": *ibid.*, I: 11.

245. "arena" . . . "get down . . . great game": Preface to *The Golden Bowl*, AN, p. 328. "the real, the deeply involved . . .": *ibid.* "There is no small talk . . .": quoted as the epigraph to R. W. B. Lewis, "The Vision

of Grace: James's *The Wings of the Dove*," *Modern Fiction Studies* III, no. 1, Spring 1957: 33. "erect above all for her . . .": *The Golden Bowl*, II: 232.

246. "She found herself . . .": *ibid.*, p. 233. "after it had been thus vividly . . . to blackness": *ibid.*, pp. 333-34. "get away, in the outer darkness . . .": *ibid.*, p. 235. "splendid shining supple creature . . .": *ibid.*, p. 239. "thrown over on her back . . .": *ibid.*, p. 242.

247. "the likeness of their connexion . . . silken rope . . .": *ibid.*, p. 287. "almost everything we call 'higher culture' . . .": BGE 229, ML, p. 348 [WDB, II: 693.]

248. "the highest type of free men . . . not excluding oneself": TI ix: 38, PN, p. 542. [WDB, II: 1015.] "in individuals . . . on top": *ibid.* "the peoples who had some value . . .": *ibid.*

248-49. "true psychologically . . ." . . . "Julius Caesar": *ibid.*

249. "education in those rulers' virtues . . . Christ's soul": WP 983, p. 513. [*Mus.*, xix: 329.] "the most amazing . . .": Jaspers, quoted in *ibid.*, p. 513n. "one cannot establish the domination . . .": WP 305, p. 171. [*Mus.*, xviii: 220.] "The victory of a moral ideal . . .": WP 306, p. 171. [*ibid.*] "Morality is just as 'immoral' . . .": WP 308, p. 172. [*Mus.*, xviii: 221.]

250. "the clash between the two ideals" . . . "was fierce upon occasion": *The Varieties of Religious Experience*, New York, Collier-Macmillan, 1961, p. 295. "the greatest saints . . . soften them": *ibid.*, p. 297. "How is success to be absolutely measured . . .": *ibid.*

251. "for love": *The Golden Bowl*, II: 116.

251n. Collected Poems of W. B. Yeats (see note for page 243 above), p. 255.

252. " 'It's success, father' . . . self-righteousness": Dorothea Krook, *The Ordeal of Consciousness in Henry James*, Cambridge, Cambridge Univ. Press, 1962, p. 316. "beauty is nothing . . .": Rainer Maria Rilke, "The First Elegy," *Duino Elegies*, translated by C. F. MacIntyre, Berkeley, Calif., Univ. of California Press, 1968, p. 3.

253. "it is the world . . .": *The American Adam*, Chicago, Univ. of Chicago Press, 1955, p. 154. "The Marriages": see *The Notebooks of Henry James*, ed. F. O. Matthiessen and Kenneth B. Murdock, New York, Oxford Univ. Press, 1961, p. 233. James had used the title for a story first published in August 1891, in the *Atlantic Monthly* and later reprinted in vol. 18 of the New York Edition. "No themes are so human . . .": Preface to *What Maisie Knew*, AN, p. 143.

254. "that bridge over to Style . . .": *A Small Boy and Others*, in

Henry James: Autobiography, ed. F. W. Dupee, New York, Criterion Books, 1956, p. 196. "as if they had gathered there . . .": *ibid.*, p. 195. "certain of the crown jewels . . .": see the note by Dupee on this passage, *ibid.*, p. 606. "the glory meant ever so many . . .": *ibid.*, p. 196. "first great revelation of art . . .": "The Princess Casamassima," *The Liberal Imagination*, London, Secker & Warburg, 1964 [1950], p. 82. "monumental Paris" "magnificent parts of the great gallery" ". . . arched over us . . .": *A Small Boy and Others*, in Dupee, ed., *op. cit.*, pp. 195-96.

255. "the most appalling yet . . .": *ibid.*, p. 196.

256. "The climax of this extraordinary experience . . .": *ibid.* "the fears and terrors of a 'mere junior' . . .": Edel, I: 75.

257. "We do not have to presume very far . . .": Trilling, *op. cit.*, p. 82. "aggression brings guilt and then fear": *ibid.* "tells us that the dream . . .": *ibid.*, pp. 82-83. "An admirable nightmare . . .": *ibid.*, p. 82.

258. "a spendid scene of things" . . . "precious part": *A Small Boy and Others*, in Dupee, ed., *op. cit.*, p. 196. "*Quidquid luce fuit, tenebris agit* . . .": BGE 193, ML, p. 296. [WDB, II: 651.] Kaufmann translates the Latin as "What occurred in the light goes on in the dark."

259. "an absolute victory" . . . "that is, the transformation . . .": letter to Franz Overbeck, Summer 1883, LFN, p. 214 [WDB, III: 1209.] "as the sole enemy . . ." "the hermit turns . . ." "But whoever . . ." "will as a rule . . .": *Civilization and Its Discontents*, translated and ed. by James Strachey, New York, W. W. Norton and Co., 1962, p. 28. "I have written . . .": letter of November 17, 1851, to Nathaniel Hawthorne, included in *Moby-Dick*, ed. Harrison Hayford and Herschel Parker, New York, W. W. Norton and Co., 1967, p. 566.

260. "mortal life of the selfsame texture . . .": "The Birthmark," in *The Complete Novels and Selected Tales of Nathaniel Hawthorne*, ed. with an intro. by Norman Holmes Pearson, New York, The Modern Library, 1937, p. 1033.

261. "Apart from the pulling . . .": "Song of Myself" (Sect. 4) in *Leaves of Grass* [1855 ed.], ed. Malcolm Cowley, New York, Viking Press, 1959, p. 28. *devastating logic of unconditional self-conquest:* see Z, pt. III: "The lust to rule: the terrible teacher of the great contempt, who preaches 'away with you' to the very faces of cities and empires, until it finally cries out of them themselves, 'Away with me!' " ("On the Three Evils," PN, p. 301. [WDB, II: 437.] Some of the implications of this passage which bear on the present discussion are suggested in my essay "Emerson, Christian Identity, and the Dissolution of the Social Order," in Quentin Anderson, Stephen Donadio, and Steven Marcus, eds., *Art, Politics, and Will:*

Essays in Honor of Lionel Trilling, New York, Basic Books, 1977, pp. 120-21. "things we cannot possibly *not* know . . .": Preface to *The American*, AN, p. 31.

   262. "things that, with all the facilities . . .": *ibid.*, pp. 31-32.

Bibliography

General

Abrams, M. H., *Natural Supernaturalism: Tradition and Revolution in Romantic Literature*, New York, W. W. Norton, 1971.

Adams, Henry, *The Education of Henry Adams*, New York, Random House, 1931.

Allen, Gay Wilson, *William James: A Biography*, New York, Viking Press, 1967.

Anderson, Quentin, *The Imperial Self: An Essay in American Literary and Cultural History*, New York, Alfred A. Knopf, 1971.

Anderson, Sherwood, *Winesburg, Ohio*, New York, Viking Press, 1960 [1919].

Arieli, Yehoshua, *Individualism and Nationalism in American Ideology*, Baltimore, Md., Penguin Books, 1966 [1964].

Aristotle, *Introduction to Aristotle*, ed. Richard McKeon, New York, Random House, 1947.

Arvin, Newton, *American Pantheon*, ed. Daniel Aaron and Sylvan Schendler, New York, Dell Publishing Co., 1966.

St. Augustine, *Confessions*, trans. R. S. Pine-Coffin, Baltimore, Md., Penguin Books, 1961.

Barrett, William, *Irrational Man*, Garden City, N.Y., Doubleday, 1962.

Barzun, Jacques, *Darwin, Marx, Wagner*, rev. 2nd ed., Garden City, N.Y., Doubleday, 1958.

Berenson, Bernard, *Selected Letters of Bernard Berenson*, ed. A. K. McComb, Boston, Houghton, Mifflin, 1964.

Beer, Thomas, *The Mauve Decade: American Life at the End of the Nineteenth Century*, New York, Vintage Books, 1961.

Blackmur, R. P., *The Lion and the Honeycomb*, New York, Harcourt, Brace and World, 1955.

312   BIBLIOGRAPHY

Blake, William, *Complete Writings*, ed. Geoffrey Keynes, London, Nonesuch Press, 1957.

Boas, George, "The Romantic Self: An Historical Sketch," *Studies in Romanticism* IV, no. 1 (Autumn 1964): 1-16.

Booth, Wayne C., *The Rhetoric of Fiction*, Chicago, Univ. of Chicago Press, 1961.

Bourget, Paul, *Essais de psychologie contemporaine*, vol. 1, édition definitive, Paris, Librairie Plon, 1937 [1883].

Bradley, F. W. H., *Ethical Studies*, 2nd ed., with an intro. by Richard Wollheim, London, Oxford Univ. Press, 1962 [1927].

Bullough, Edward, " 'Psychic Distance' as a Factor in Art and an Esthetic Principle," *British Journal of Psychology* V, no. 2, (1913): 87-118.

Butler, E. M., *The Tyranny of Greece over Germany: A study of the influence exercised by Greek art and poetry over the great German writers of the eighteenth, nineteenth, and twentieth centuries*, Boston, Beacon Press, 1958 [1935].

Carlyle, Thomas, *On Heroes and Hero-Worship* (printed with Emerson's *Representative Men*), Garden City, N.Y., Doubleday, n.d.

Commager, Henry Steele, *The American Mind: An Interpretation of American Thought and Character since the 1800's*, New Haven, Conn., Yale Univ. Press, 1950.

Conrad, Joseph, *Heart of Darkness* [1899] and *The Secret Sharer*, New York, New American Library, 1950.

——, *Lord Jim*, ed. Morton Dauwen Zabel, Boston, Houghton Mifflin, 1958 [1900].

Ellmann, Richard, ed., *Oscar Wilde: A Collection of Critical Essays*, Englewood Cliffs, N.J., Prentice-Hall, 1969.

——, and Feidelson, Charles, Jr., eds., *The Modern Tradition: Backgrounds of Modern Literature*, New York, Oxford Univ. Press, 1965.

Else, Gerald F., *The Origin and Early Form of Greek Tragedy*, Cambridge, Mass., Harvard Univ. Press, 1965.

Emerson, Ralph Waldo, *Emerson: A Modern Anthology*, ed. Alfred Kazin and Daniel Aaron, New York, Dell Publishing Co., 1958.

——, *The Correspondence of Emerson and Carlyle*, ed. Joseph Slater, New York, Columbia Univ. Press, 1964.

————, *Representative Men* (printed with Carlyle's *On Heroes and Hero-Worship*), Garden City, N.Y., Doubleday, n.d.

————, *The Selected Writings of Ralph Waldo Emerson*, ed. Brooks Atkinson, New York, Random House, 1950.

Fichte, Johann Gottlieb, *The Vocation of Man*, trans. William Smith, rev. and ed. Roderick M. Chisholm, Indianapolis, Ind., Liberal Arts Press, 1956.

Findlay, J. N., *Hegel: A Re-examination*, New York, Oxford Univ. Press, 1976 [1958].

Fitzgerald, F. Scott, *The Great Gatsby*, New York, Charles Scribner's Sons, 1953 [1925].

Frame, Donald M., "To 'Rise Above Humanity' and To 'Escape from the Man': Two Moments in Montaigne's Thought," *The Romanic Review* LXII, no. 1 (Feb. 1971): 28-35.

Freeman, Kathleen, *Ancilla to the Pre-Socratic Philosophers* (a complete translation of the fragments in Diels, *Fragmente der Vorsokratiker*, 5th ed., ed. Walther Kranz, Berlin, 1934-38), Cambridge, Mass., Harvard Univ. Press, 1959.

————, *The Pre-Socratic Philosophers: A Companion to Diels, Fragmente der Vorsokratiker* (5th ed.), 2nd ed., Cambridge, Mass., Harvard Univ. Press, 1959.

Freud, Sigmund, *Civilization and its Discontents*, trans. and ed. James Strachey, New York, W. W. Norton, 1962.

————, *The Interpretation of Dreams*, trans. and ed. James Strachey, New York, Basic Books, 1955.

————, "The Antithetical Sense of Primal Words," trans. Joan Rivière, in Benjamin Nelson, ed., *Freud on Creativity and the Unconscious*, New York, Harper and Bros., 1958.

Frothingham, Octavius Brooks, *Transcendentalism in New England: A History*, New York, Harper and Bros., 1959 [1876].

Garrett, Peter K., *Scene and Symbol from George Eliot to James Joyce: Studies in Changing Fictional Mode*, New Haven, Conn., Yale Univ. Press, 1969.

Geyl, Pieter, *Napoleon For and Against*, trans. Olive Renier, New Haven, Conn., Yale Univ. Press, 1949.

Goodheart, Eugene, "Flaubert and the Powerlessness of Art," *Centennial Review* 19, no. 3 (Summer 1975): 157-171. (See also response by Michael Platt listed below.)

Grattan, C. Hartley, *The Three Jameses: A Family of Minds*, New York, New York Univ. Press, 1962 [1932].

Grund, Francis J., *Aristocracy in America: From the Sketch-Book of a German Nobleman*, intro. by George E. Probst, New York, Harper and Bros., 1959 (1st American ed., based on the edition published in London by Richard Bentley in 1839).

———, *The Americans, in Their Moral, Social, and Political Relations*, Boston, Marsh, Capen and Lyons, 1837.

Guérard, Albert L., *Reflections on the Napoleonic Legend*, New York, Charles Scribner's Sons, 1924.

Gunn, Peter, *Vernon Lee: Violet Paget, 1856-1935*, London, Oxford Univ. Press, 1964.

Hale, Edward Everett, *The Man without a Country and Other Tales*, Boston, Roberts Bros., 1888 [1868].

Halsted, John B., ed., *Romanticism*, New York, Harper and Row, 1969.

Hardy, Barbara, *The Appropriate Form: An Essay on the Novel*, London, Athlone Press, 1964.

Harlow, Virginia, *Thomas Sergeant Perry: A Biography and Letters to Perry from William, Henry, and Garth Wilkinson James*, Durham, N.C., Duke Univ. Press, 1950.

Hawthorne, Nathaniel, *The Complete Novels and Selected Tales*, ed. Norman Holmes Pearson, New York, The Modern Library, 1937.

Hegel, Georg Wilhelm Friedrich, *On Art, Religion, Philosophy*, ed. J. Glenn Gray, New York, Harper and Row, 1970.

———, *The Phenomenology of Mind*, trans. with an intro. and notes by J. B. Baillie, New York, Harper and Row, 1967 [1931].

———, *The Philosophy of Fine Art*, 4 vols., trans. F. P. B. Osmaston, London, G. Bell and Sons, 1920.

———, *The Philosophy of Hegel*, ed. Carl J. Friedrich, New York, Random House, 1954.

———, *The Philosophy of History*, with prefaces by Charles Hegel and the translator, J. Sibree, and a new intro. by C. J. Friedrich, New York, Dover Publications, 1956.

Heine, Heinrich, *Selected Works*, trans. and ed. Helen M. Mustard, New York, Random House, 1973.

Heller, Erich, *The Artist's Journey into the Interior and Other Essays*, New York, Random House, 1965.

James, Alice, *The Diary of Alice James*, ed. Leon Edel, New York, Dodd, Mead, 1964.

James, Henry [Sr.], *Society the Redeemed Form of Man, and The Earnest of God's Omnipotence in Human Nature: Affirmed in Letters to a Friend,* Boston, Houghton, Osgood and Co., 1879.

James, William, *Essays in Pragmatism,* ed. with an intro. by Alburey Castell, New York, Hafner Publishing Co., 1948.

————, *Essays in Radical Empiricism and A Pluralistic Universe,* ed. Ralph Barton Perry, New York, E. P. Dutton, 1971.

————, *William James: The Essential Writings,* ed. Bruce Wilshire, New York, Harper and Row, 1971.

————, *Human Immortality: two supposed objections to the doctrine,* Boston, Houghton Mifflin, 1898.

————, *The Letters of William James,* 2 vols., ed. by his son Henry James, Boston, Atlantic Monthly Press, 1920.

————, *The Meaning of Truth: A Sequel to Pragmatism,* with a new intro. by Ralph Ross, Ann Arbor, Mich., Univ. of Michigan Press, 1970 [1909].

————, *Memories and Studies,* New York, Longmans, Green, 1911.

————, *Pragmatism: A New Name for Some Old Ways of Thinking,* together with Four Related Essays from *The Meaning of Truth,* ed. Ralph Barton Perry, New York, Longmans, Green, 1948 [1907, 1909].

————, *The Principles of Psychology,* 2 vols., New York, Henry Holt and Co., 1918 [1890].

————, *Selected Papers on Philosophy,* intro. by C. M. Bakewell, London, J. M. Dent, 1917.

————, *The Varieties of Religious Experience,* with a new intro. by Reinhold Niebuhr, New York, Collier-Macmillan, 1961.

————, *The Writings of William James: A Comprehensive Edition,* ed. John J. McDermott, New York, Random House, 1967.

Jones, Ernest, *The Life and Work of Sigmund Freud,* vol. II, New York, Basic Books, 1953.

Kaminsky, Jack, *Hegel on Art, An Interpretation of Hegel's Aesthetics,* New York, State Univ. of New York Press, 1962.

Kaufmann, Walter, *Hegel: Reinterpretation, Texts and Commentary,* London, Weidenfeld and Nicolson, 1966 [1965].

Kelly, George Armstrong, *Idealism, Politics and History: Sources of Hegelian Thought,* Cambridge, Cambridge Univ. Press, 1969.

————, "Notes on Hegel's 'Lordship and Bondage,'" *The Review of Metaphysics* XIX, no. 4 (June 1966): 780-802.

Kermode, Frank, *Romantic Image*, London, Routledge and Kegan Paul, 1957.

Kerrane, Kevin, "Nineteenth-Century Backgrounds of Modern Aesthetic Criticism," in O. B. Hardison, Jr., ed., *The Quest for Imagination*, Cleveland, Ohio, The Press of Case Western Reserve Univ., 1971.

Kojève, Alexandre, *Introduction to the Reading of Hegel*, ed. Allan Bloom, trans. James H. Nichols, Jr., New York, Basic Books, 1969.

Lawrence, D. H., *Reflections on the Death of a Porcupine and Other Essays*, Bloomington, Ind., Indiana Univ. Press, 1963.

————, *Studies in Classic American Literature*, New York, Viking Press, 1971 [1923].

Leavis, F. R., *The Common Pursuit*, Harmondsworth, Penguin Books, 1963.

————, *The Great Tradition*, New York, New York Univ. Press, 1964.

Lewis, R. W. B., *The American Adam: Innocence, Tragedy and Tradition in the Nineteenth Century*, Chicago, Univ. of Chicago Press, 1955.

————, "The Vision of Grace: James's *The Wings of the Dove*," *Modern Fiction Studies* III, no. 1 (Spring 1957): 33-40.

Lifton Robert Jay, *History and Human Survival*, New York, Random House, 1970.

MacIntyre, Alasdair, *Hegel: A Collection of Critical Essays*, Garden City, N.Y., Doubleday, 1972.

Mann, Thomas, "Tonio Kröger," in *The Thomas Mann Reader*, ed. Joseph Warner Angell, New York, Grosset and Dunlap, 1950.

Mansuy, Michel, *Un Moderne, Paul Bourget de l'enfance au disciple*, Annales Littéraires de l'Université de Besançon, vol. 39, Paris, Les Belles Lettres, 1960.

Meinecke, Friedrich, *Cosmopolitanism and the National State*, trans. Robert B. Kimber, Princeton, N.J., Princeton Univ. Press, 1970.

Melville, Herman, *Moby-Dick*, ed. Harrison Hayford and Herschel Parker, New York, W. W. Norton, 1967 [1851].

Mount, Charles Merrill, *John Singer Sargent: A Biography*, New York, W. W. Norton, 1955.

Mumford, Lewis, *The Brown Decades: A Study of the Arts in America 1865-1895*, 2nd ed. rev., New York, Dover Publications, 1955.

———, *The Golden Day: A Study in American Literature and Culture*, with a new intro. by the author, Boston, Mass., Beacon Press, 1957.

Myers, Frederic W. H., *Human Personality and Its Survival of Bodily Death*, ed. and abr. by S. B. and L. H. M., London, Longmans, Green, 1935.

Napoleon Bonaparte, *The Mind of Napoleon: A Selection from His Written and Spoken Words*, ed. and trans. J. Christopher Herold, New York, Columbia Univ. Press, 1955.

Napoleon III (Prince Napoléon-Louis Bonaparte), *Napoleonic Ideas*, ed. Brison D. Gooch, New York, Harper and Row, 1967.

Nuhn, Ferner, *The Wind Blew from the East: A Study in the Orientation of American Culture*, with a new foreword by the author, Port Washington, N.Y., Kennikat Press, 1967 [1942].

Otto, Walter F., *Dionysus: Myth and Cult*, Bloomington, Ind., Indiana Univ. Press, 1965.

Pater, Walter, *Studies in the History of the Renaissance*, New York, Boni and Liveright, 1919 [1873].

Perry, Ralph Barton, *The Thought and Character of William James* (briefer version), New York, Harper and Row, 1964 [1948].

Perry, Thomas Sergeant, Review of Nietzsche's *Von Nutzen und Nachtheil der Historie für das Leben* (Pt. II of the *Unzeitgemässe Betrachtungen*, 1874), *North American Review* 121, no. 248 (July 1875): 190-193.

Plato, *Phaedrus*, trans. with an intro. and commentary by R. Hackforth, New York, Liberal Arts Press, n.d. [1952].

Podro, Michael, *The Manifold in Perception: Theories of Art from Kant to Hildebrand*, Oxford, Clarendon Press, 1972.

Poirier, Richard, *A World Elsewhere: The Place of Style in American Literature*, New York, Oxford Univ. Press, 1966.

Rilke, Rainer Maria, "The First Elegy," *Duino Elegies*, trans. C. F. MacIntyre, Berkeley, Calif., Univ. of California Press, 1968.

318   BIBLIOGRAPHY

Roberts, Mark, *The Tradition of Romantic Morality*, New York, Barnes and Noble, 1973.

Ruland, Richard, *America in Modern European Literature: From Image to Metaphor*, New York, New York Univ. Press, 1976.

Russell, Bertrand, *A History of Western Philosophy*, New York, Simon and Schuster, 1945.

——, *Power: A New Social Analysis*, New York, Barnes and Noble, 1962.

Santayana, George, *Character and Opinion in the United States*, New York, W. W. Norton, 1967.

——, *The German Mind: A Philosophical Diagnosis*, New York, T. Y. Crowell, 1968 [1916, rev. 1940].

Savant, Jean, *Napoleon in His Time*, trans. Katherine John, New York, Thomas Nelson and Sons, 1958.

Schenk, M. G., *The Mind of the European Romantics*, with preface by Isaiah Berlin, Garden City, N.Y., Doubleday, 1969.

Schiller, F. C. S., Review of William James's *The Will To Believe and Other Essays in Popular Philosophy*, in *Mind* VI (London), N.S. (Oct. 1897): 547-554.

Schiller, Friedrich, *On the Aesthetic Education of Man, in a Series of Letters*, bilingual edition, ed. and trans. with an intro., commentary, and glossary of terms by Elizabeth M. Wilkinson and L. A. Willoughby, Oxford, Clarendon Press, 1967.

Shakespeare, William, *King Lear*, in *The Complete Works of Shakespeare*, ed. George Lyman Kittredge, Boston, Ginn and Co., 1936.

Shaw, Charles Gray, "Emerson the Nihilist," *International Journal of Ethics* XXV (Oct. 1914): 68-86.

Stace, W. T., *The Philosophy of Hegel: A Systematic Exposition*, New York, Dover Publications, 1955 [1924].

Stang, Richard, *The Theory of the Novel in England 1850-1870*, New York, Columbia Univ. Press, 1959.

Strauss, Leo, "Jerusalem and Athens," *Commentary* 43, no. 6 (June 1967): 45-57.

Strout, Cushing, "William James and the Twice-Born Sick Soul," *Daedalus* (Summer 1968), vol. 97, no. 3 of the Proceedings of the American Academy of Arts and Sciences, 1062-1082.

Tharp, Louise Hall, *Mrs. Jack: A Biography of Isabella Stewart Gardner*, Boston, Little, Brown, 1965.

Thoreau, Henry David, *Walden* and *Civil Disobedience*, ed. Owen
Thomas, New York, W. W. Norton, 1966.
Trilling, Lionel, "James Joyce in his Letters," *Commentary*, 45, no.
2 (Feb. 1968): 53-64.
————, *The Opposing Self*, New York, Viking Press, 1955.
————, *Sincerity and Authenticity*, Cambridge, Mass., Harvard
Univ. Press, 1972.
Wellek, René, *Confrontations: Studies in the Intellectual and Liter-
ary Relations between Germany, England, and the United
States during the Nineteenth Century*, Princeton, N.J.:
Princeton Univ. Press, 1965.
Whitman, Walt, *Leaves of Grass*, 1st ed. text (1855), ed. Malcolm
Cowley, New York, Viking Press, 1959.
Wilde, Oscar, *The Artist as Critic: Critical Writings of Oscar
Wilde*, ed. Richard Ellmann, New York, Vintage Books,
1970.
Wilshire, Bruce, *William James and Phenomenology: A Study of
"The Principles of Psychology,"* Bloomington, Ind., Indiana
Univ. Press, 1968.
Wilson, Edmund, ed., *The Shock of Recognition*, New York, Ran-
dom House, 1955.
Yeats, William Butler, *The Autobiography of William Butler Yeats*,
New York, Collier-Macmillan, 1965 [1916-1935].
Zetterbaum, Marvin, "Self and Political Order," *Interpretation* II
(Winter 1970): 233-246.

Henry James

Bibliography
Edel, Leon, and Laurence, Dan H., *A Bibliography of Henry James*,
2nd ed. rev., London, Rupert Hart-Davis, 1961.
Modern Fiction Studies XII, no. 1 (Spring 1966) [Special Henry
James number], "Criticism of Henry James: A Selected
Checklist," 117-177.
Ricks, Beatrice, *Henry James: A Bibliography of Secondary Works*,
Metuchen, N.J., Scarecrow Press, 1975.

Primary works
James, Henry, *The Art of the Novel* (collected Prefaces to the New

York Edition), intro. by Richard P. Blackmur, New York, Charles Scribner's Sons, 1937 [1907-1909].

———, *Autobiography* (containing *A Small Boy and Others, Notes of a Son and Brother*, and *The Middle Years*), ed. Frederick W. Dupee, New York, Criterion Books, 1956.

———, *The Future of the Novel*, ed. Leon Edel, New York, Vintage Books, 1956.

———, *The Golden Bowl*, 2 vols., New York, Charles Scribner's Sons, 1937 [1904; 1907-1909].

———, *Guy Domville*, ed. Leon Edel, with a biog. account of James as a dramatist (*Henry James: The Dramatic Years*), Philadelphia, Pa., J. B. Lippincott and Co., 1960.

———, *Hawthorne*, Ithaca, N.Y., Cornell Univ. Press, 1956 [1879].

———, *The Letters of Henry James*, 2 vols., sel. and ed. by Percy Lubbock, London, Macmillan, 1920.

———, *The Letters of Henry James*, ed. Leon Edel; vol. I: 1843-1875; vol. II: 1875-1883. Cambridge, Mass., Harvard Univ. Press, 1974, 1975.

———, *Literary Reviews and Essays by Henry James*, ed. Albert Mordell, New York, Vista House, 1957.

———, *The Notebooks of Henry James*, ed. F. O. Matthiessen and Kenneth B. Murdock, New York, Oxford Univ. Press, 1961 [1947].

———, *Parisian Sketches, Letters to the New York Tribune 1875-1876*, ed. Leon Edel and Ilse Dusoir Lind, London, Rupert Hart-Davis, 1958.

———, *Partial Portraits*, new intro. by Leon Edel, Ann Arbor, Mich., Univ. of Michigan Press, 1970 [1888].

———, *The Portrait of a Lady*, 2 vols., New York, Charles Scribner's Sons, 1936 [1881; 1907-1909].

———, *The Question of Our Speech; The Lesson of Balzac* (Two Lectures), Boston and New York, Houghton Mifflin, 1905.

———, *Representative Selections*, with intro., bibliog., and notes by Lyon N. Richardson, Urbana, Ill., Univ. of Illinois Press, 1966 [1941].

———, *Selected Literary Criticism*, ed. Morris Shapira, introductory essay by F. R. Leavis, New York, McGraw-Hill, 1965 [1964].

———, *Theory of Fiction: Henry James*, ed. James E. Miller, Jr., Lincoln, Neb., Univ. of Nebraska Press, 1972.

————, *William Wetmore Story and His Friends*, New York, Da Capo Press, 1969 [1903].

————, *The Wings of the Dove*, 2 vols., New York, Charles Scribner's Sons, 1937 [1903; 1907-1909].

Secondary works

Anderson, Quentin, *The American Henry James*, New Brunswick, N.J., Rutgers Univ. Press, 1957.

Banta, Martha, *Henry James and the Occult: The Great Extension*, Bloomington, Ind., Indiana Univ. Press, 1972.

Barzun, Jacques, *The Energies of Art*, New York, Vintage Books, 1962.

Bayley, John, *The Characters of Love: A Study in the Literature of Personality*, London, Constable, 1962.

Beach, Joseph Warren, *The Method of Henry James*, enlarged ed. with corrections, Philadelphia, Pa., Albert Saifer, 1954.

Benson, A. C., *Rambles and Reflections*, London, John Murray, 1926.

Bewley, Marius, *The Complex Fate*, with an intro. and two interpolations by F. R. Leavis, New York, Gordian Press, 1967.

————, *The Eccentric Design: Form in the Classic American Novel*, New York, Columbia Univ. Press, 1963.

Blackall, Jean Frantz, *Jamesian Ambiguity and The Sacred Fount*, Ithaca, N.Y., Cornell Univ. Press, 1965.

Bosanquet, Theodora, *Henry James at Work*, The Hogarth Essays, London, The Hogarth Press, 1924 [?], pp. 243-276.

Brooks, Peter, *The Melodramatic Imagination: Balzac, Henry James, Melodrama, and the Mode of Excess*, New Haven, Conn., Yale Univ. Press, 1976.

Brooks, Van Wyck, *The Pilgrimage of Henry James*, New York, E. P. Dutton, 1925.

Brownell, W. C., *American Prose Masters*, ed. Howard Mumford Jones, Cambridge, Mass., Harvard Univ. Press, 1963.

Buitenhuis, Peter, *The Grasping Imagination: The American Writings of Henry James*, Toronto, Univ. of Toronto Press, 1970.

Cargill, Oscar, "*The Portrait of a Lady*: A Critical Reappraisal," *Modern Fiction Studies* III, no. 1 (Spring 1957): 11-32.

Crews, Frederick C., *The Tragedy of Manners: Moral Drama in the Later Novels of Henry James*, Hamden, Conn., Archon Books, 1971 [1957].

Dietrichson, Jan W., *The Image of Money*, Oslo, Universitetsver-
taget, 1966.
Dupee, F. W., *Henry James*, New York, William Sloane Associates,
1951.
———, ed., *The Question of Henry James*, New York, Henry Holt
and Co., 1945.
Edel, Leon, *Henry James*, vol. I: *The Untried Years, 1843-1870*;
vol. II: *The Conquest of London, 1870-1881*; vol. III: *The
Middle Years, 1882-1895*; vol. IV: *The Treacherous Years,
1895-1901*; vol. V: *The Master, 1901-1916*. Philadelphia,
Pa., J. B. Lippincott, 1953-1972.
———, "Henry James's 'Last Dictation,' *The* [London] *Times
Literary Supplement*, May 2, 1968, pp. 459-460.
———, ed., *Henry James: A Collection of Critical Essays*, Englewood Cliffs, N.J.: Prentice-Hall, 1963.
———, and Ray, Gordon N., *Henry James and H. G. Wells: A
Record of Their Friendship, Their Debate on the Art of Fic-
tion, and Their Quarrel*, Urbana, Ill., Univ. of Illinois Press,
1958.
Egan, Michael, *Henry James: The Ibsen Years*, New York, Barnes
and Noble, 1972.
Emerson, Donald, "Henry James and the Limitations of Realism,"
College English XXII (Dec. 1960): 161-166.
Fergusson, Francis, "*The Golden Bowl* Revisited," *Sewanee Review*
63 (Winter 1955): 13-28.
Firebaugh, Joseph J., "A Schopenhauerian Novel: James's *The
Princess Casamassima*," *Nineteenth-Century Fiction* III
(Dec. 1958): 177-97.
———, "The Relativism of Henry James," *The Journal of Aes-
thetics and Art Criticism* XII (Dec. 1953): 237-242.
Furbank, P. N., "Henry James: The Novelist as Actor," *Essays in
Criticism* I, no. 4 (Oct. 1951): 404-420.
Gale, Robert L., *The Caught Image: Figurative Language in the
Fiction of Henry James*, Chapel Hill, N.C., Univ. of North
Carolina Press, 1964.
Goldberg, M. A., " 'Things' and Values in Henry James's Uni-
verse," *Western Humanities Review* XI (Autumn 1958):
377-385.
Goldsmith, Arnold L., "Henry James's Reconciliation of Free Will

and Fatalism," *Nineteenth-Century Fiction* XIII (Sept. 1958): 109-126.

Goode, John, ed., *The Art of Reality: New Essays on Henry James*, London, Methuen, 1972.

Gordon, Caroline, "Mr. Verver, Our National Hero," *Sewanee Review* 63 (Winter 1955): 29-47.

Gosse, Edmund, *Aspects and Impressions*, London, Cassell and Co., 1922.

Graham, Kenneth, *Henry James: The Drama of Fulfillment*, Oxford, Clarendon Press, 1975.

Greene, Graham, *The Lost Childhood and Other Essays*, New York, Viking Press, 1962 [1951].

Grover, Philip, *Henry James and the French Novel: A Study in Inspiration*, New York, Barnes and Noble, 1973.

Herrick, Robert, "A Visit to Henry James," *The Manly Anniversary Studies in Languages and Literature*, Chicago, Ill., Univ. of Chicago Press, 1923, pp. 229-242.

Hocks, Richard A., *Henry James and Pragmatistic Thought: A Study in the Relationship between the Philosophy of William James and the Literary Art of Henry James*, Chapel Hill, N.C., Univ. of North Carolina Press, 1974.

Holder-Barell, Alexander, *The Development of Imagery and Its Functional Significance in Henry James's Novels*, New York, Haskell House, 1966 [1959].

Holland, Laurence B., *The Expense of Vision: Essays on the Craft of Henry James*, Princeton, N.J., Princeton Univ. Press, 1964.

Hyde, H. Montgomery, *Henry James at Home*, London, Methuen, 1969.

Isle, Walter, *Experiments in Form: Henry James's Novels, 1896-1901*, Cambridge, Mass., Harvard Univ. Press, 1968.

Kimball, Jean, "Henry James's Last Portrait of a Lady: Charlotte Stant in *The Golden Bowl*," *American Literature* 28 (Jan. 1957): 449-468.

Krook, Dorothea, *The Ordeal of Consciousness in Henry James*, Cambridge, Cambridge Univ. Press, 1962.

"Vernon Lee" [Violet Paget], *The Handling of Words, and Other Studies in Literary Psychology*, Lincoln, Neb., Univ. of Nebraska Press, 1968 [1927].

Lubbock, Percy, *The Craft of Fiction*, New York, Viking Press, 1957.

Mackenzie, Manfred, *Communities of Honor and Love in Henry James*, Cambridge, Mass., Harvard Univ. Press, 1976.

Martin, Jay, *Harvests of Change: American Literature 1865-1914*, Englewood Cliffs, N.J., Prentice-Hall, 1967.

Matthiessen, F. O., *Henry James: The Major Phase*, New York, Oxford Univ. Press, 1963.

————, *The James Family: A Group Biography*, New York, Alfred A. Knopf, 1947.

McFarlane, I. D., "A Literary Friendship—Henry James and Paul Bourget," *The Cambridge Journal* IV (1951): 144-161.

Mull, Donald L., *Henry James's 'Sublime Economy,'* Middletown, Conn., Wesleyan Univ. Press, 1973.

Nettels, Elsa, *James and Conrad*, Athens, Ga., Univ. of Georgia Press, 1977.

Nowell-Smith, Simon, ed., *The Legend of the Master*, New York, Charles Scribner's Sons, 1948.

O'Neill, John P., *Workable Design: Action and Situation in the Fiction of Henry James*, Port Washington, N.Y., Kennikat Press, 1973.

Paget, Violet, *see* "Vernon Lee."

Poulet, Georges, *The Metamorphoses of the Circle*, trans. Carley Dawson and Elliott Coleman, Baltimore, Md., The Johns Hopkins Press, 1966.

Pound, Ezra, *Literary Essays of Ezra Pound*, ed. with an intro. by T. S. Eliot, London, Faber and Faber, 1960.

Powers, Lyall M., *Henry James and the Naturalist Movement*, East Lansing, Mich., Michigan State Univ. Press, 1971.

————, "*The Portrait of a Lady*: 'The Eternal Mystery of Things,' " *Nineteenth-Century Fiction* XIV (Sept. 1959): 143-155.

Rahv, Philip, *Image and Idea*, rev. and enlarged ed., New York, New Directions, 1957.

Roberts, Morris, *Henry James's Criticism*, Cambridge, Mass., Harvard Univ. Press, 1929.

Samuels, Charles T., *The Ambiguity of Henry James*, Urbana, Ill., Univ. of Illinois Press, 1971.

Sears, Sallie, *The Negative Imagination: Form and Perspective in* the Novels of Henry James, Ithaca, N.Y., Cornell Univ. Press, 1968.

Segal, Ora, The Lucid Reflector: The Observer in Henry James's Fiction, New Haven, Conn., Yale Univ. Press, 1969.

Spencer, James L., "Symbolism in James's The Golden Bowl," Modern Fiction Studies III, no. 1 (Spring 1957): 333-344.

Spender, Stephen, The Destructive Element, London, Jonathan Cape, 1938.

Stafford, William T., A Name, Title and Place Index to the Critical Writings of Henry James, Englewood, Col., Microcard Editions Books, 1975.

Stevenson, Elizabeth, The Crooked Corridor: A Study of Henry James, New York, Macmillan, 1961.

Stone, Donald David, Novelists in a Changing World: Meredith, James and the Transformation of English Fiction in the 1880's, Cambridge, Mass., Harvard Univ. Press, 1972.

Tanner, Tony, ed., Henry James: Modern Judgments, London, Macmillan, 1969.

Trilling, Lionel, The Liberal Imagination, London, Secker and Warburg, 1964 [1950].

Vaid, Krishna Baldev, Technique in the Tales of Henry James, Cambridge, Mass., Harvard Univ. Press, 1964.

Wallace, Ronald, Henry James and the Comic Form, Ann Arbor, Mich., Univ. of Michigan Press, 1975.

Wasserstrom, William, Heiress of All the Ages: Sex and Sentiment in the Genteel Tradition, Minneapolis, Minn., Univ. of Minnesota Press, 1959.

Weinstein, Philip M., Henry James and the Requirements of the Imagination, Cambridge, Mass., Harvard Univ. Press, 1971.

Wellek, René, A History of Modern Criticism: 1750-1950, 5 vols.; vol. IV: The Later Nineteenth Century, New Haven, Conn., Yale Univ. Press, 1965.

Wharton, Edith, A Backward Glance, New York, Charles Scribner's Sons, 1964 [1934].

Yeazell, Ruth Bernard, Language and Knowledge in the Late Novels of Henry James, Chicago, Ill., Univ. of Chicago Press, 1976.

Friedrich Nietzsche

Bibliography
Reichert, Herbert W., and Schlecta, Karl, *International Nietzsche Bibliography*, rev. and expanded, Chapel Hill, N.C., Univ. of North Carolina Press, 1968.
Reichert, Herbert W., "International Nietzsche Bibliography 1968 through 1971," *Nietzsche-Studien, Internationales Jahrbuch für die Nietzsche-Forschung*, II, Berlin, Walter de Gruyter, 1973: 320-339.
————, "International Nietzsche Bibliography 1972-1973," *Nietzsche-Studien*, IV (1975): 351-373.

Primary works
German texts
Gesammelte Werke, Musarionausgabe, 23 vols., Munich, Musarion Verlag, 1920-1929.
Werke in drei Bänden, ed. Karl Schlecta, 3rd ed. (which includes a *Nietzsche-Index* and bibliography), Munich, Carl Hansers Verlag, 1965.

English translations (see also note on Abbreviations)
Nietzsche, Friedrich, *Basic Writings of Nietzsche*, trans. and ed. with commentaries by Walter Kaufmann, New York, Random House, 1968.
————, *The Case of Wagner* (containing, in addition, *Nietzsche contra Wagner* and *Selected Aphorisms*, trans. Anthony M. Ludovici; and *We Philologists*, trans. J. M. Kennedy. (*The Complete Works of Friedrich Nietzsche*, ed. Oscar Levy, vol. 8.) London, George Allen & Unwin, 1911.
————, *The Gay Science*, trans. with commentary by Walter Kaufmann, New York, Random House, 1974.
————, *Human All-Too-Human*, 2 vols., vol. I: trans. Helen Zimmern; vol. II: trans. Paul V. Cohn. (*The Complete Works of Friedrich Nietzsche*, ed. Oscar Levy, vols. 6 and 7.) London, George Allen & Unwin, 1900, 1911.
————, *The Joyful Wisdom* ("La Gaya Scienza"), trans. Thomas Common. (*The Complete Works of Friedrich Nietzsche*,

ed. Oscar Levy, vol. 10.) New York, Russell & Russell, 1964 [1910].

———, "Nietzsche on Classics and Classicists," sel. and trans. by William Arrowsmith, in *Arion* II (1963); Part I (issue no. 1, Spring): 5-18; Part II (no. 2, Summer): 5-27; Part III (no. 4, Winter): 5-31.

———, "Notes for 'We Philologists,' " trans. William Arrowsmith, *Arion*, New Series 1/2 (Boston University), 1973/1974, pp. 279-380.

———, "On the Pathos of Truth" (one of "Five Prefaces to Five Unwritten Books" composed by Nietzsche and dedicated to Cosima Wagner at Christmas 1872), trans. David S. Thatcher, *The Malahat Review*, no. 24 (1972), pp. 134-138.

———, *Philosophy in the Tragic Age of the Greeks*, trans. with an intro. by Marianne Cowan, Chicago, Ill., Henry Regnery Co., 1962.

———, *The Philosophy of Nietzsche*, ed. with an intro. by Geoffrey Clive (selected from the 18-volume Oscar Levy translation; topical arrangement based on Karl Schlechta's new German ed. of Nietzsche's works). New York, New American Library, 1965.

———, *The Portable Nietzsche*, trans. and ed. with a critical intro. and notes by Walter Kaufmann, New York, The Viking Press, 1968.

———, *Schopenhauer as Educator*, trans. James W. Hillesheim and Malcolm R. Simpson, Chicago, Ill., Henry Regnery Co., 1965.

———, *Selected Letters of Friedrich Nietzsche*, ed. and trans. Christopher Middleton, Chicago, Ill., Univ. of Chicago Press, 1969.

———, *Thoughts Out of Season*, Part II: *The Use and Abuse of History*, trans. Adrian Collins (*The Complete Works of Friedrich Nietzsche*, ed. Oscar Levy, vol. 5). New York, Russell & Russell, 1964 [1909].

———, *The Use and Abuse of History*, 2nd. ed. rev., trans. Adrian Collins, Indianapolis, Ind., Bobbs-Merrill, 1957.

———, *The Will to Power*, trans. Walter Kaufmann and R. J. Hollingdale, ed. with commentary by Walter Kaufmann, New York, Random House, 1967.

*Secondary works**

Allison, David B., ed., *The New Nietzsche: Contemporary Styles of Interpretation*, New York, Dell Publishing Co., 1977.

Andler, Charles, *Nietzsche, sa vie et sa pensée*, 6 vols., 2nd ed.; vol. I: *Les précurseurs de Nietzsche*. Paris, Editions Bossard, 1920.

Barrack, Charles M., "Nietzsche's Dionysus and Apollo: Gods in Transition," *Nietzsche-Studien, Internationales Jahrbuch für die Nietzsche-Forschung*, vol. 3, Berlin, Walter de Gruyter, 1974, pp. 115-129.

Baumgarten, Eduard, *Der Pragmatismus: R. W. Emerson, W. James, J. Dewey*, Frankfurt, V. Klostermann, 1938.

————, "Mitteilungen und Bemerkungen über den Einfluss Emersons auf Nietzsche," *Jahrbuch für Amerikastudien*, vol. 1, ed. Walter Fischer, Heidelberg, 1956.

Bentley, Eric, *A Century of Hero-Worship: A Study of the Idea of Heroism in Carlyle and Nietzsche, with Notes on Wagner, Stefan George, and D. H. Lawrence*, 2nd ed., Boston, Mass., Beacon Press, 1957.

Benton, Richard P., "The Aesthetics of Friedrich Nietzsche: The

* This listing includes a number of studies which have appeared recently in France as a consequence of an intense and growing revival of interest there in Nietzsche's work. These publications contain many interesting arguments, but because they generally proceed from literary and philosophical assumptions unrelated to those of the present study, they are not addressed directly in the text. English readers may find a convenient sampling of such works in translation in *The New Nietzsche: Contemporary Styles of Interpretation*, ed. and intro. by David B. Allison (see full entry above). Readers of French and German may also be interested in consulting the proceedings of the conference on Nietzsche held at Cerisy-la-Salle in 1972 (subsequently published in two volumes as *Nietzsche aujourd'hui?* by the Union Générale d'Editions), as well as Maurice de Gandillac's report on that conference ("Le colloque de Cerisy-la-Salle," *Nietzsche-Studien, Internationales Jahrbuch für die Nietzsche-Forschung*, vol. 4, Berlin, Walter de Gruyter, 1975, pp. 324-333), and Rudolf E. Künzli's useful attempt to place these new developments in a larger critical perspective ("Nietzsche und die Semiologie: Neue Ansätze in der Französischen Nietzsche-Interpretation," *Nietzsche-Studien*, vol. 5 [1976]).

Relation of Art to Life," Ph.D. dissertation, The Johns Hopkins University, 1955.

Boudot, Pierre, *L'ontologie de Nietzsche*, Paris, Presses Universitaires de France, 1971.

Bridgwater, Patrick, *Nietzsche in Anglosaxony: A Study of Nietzsche's Impact on English and American Literature*, n.p., Leicester Univ. Press, 1972.

Brinton, Crane, *Nietzsche*, New York, Harper and Row, 1965.

Congdon, Lee, "Nietzsche, Heidegger, and History," *Journal of European Studies* III, no. 3 (Sept. 1973): 211-217.

Copleston, Frederick C., "Foreground and Background in Nietzsche," *Review of Metaphysics* XXI (March 1968): 506-523.

Dannhauser, Werner J., "Nietzsche in his Letters," *Commentary* 48, no. 6 (Dec. 1969): 86-93.

———, *Nietzsche's View of Socrates*, Ithaca, N.Y., Cornell Univ. Press, 1974.

Danto, Arthur C., *Nietzsche as Philosopher*, New York, Macmillan, 1965.

Deleuze, Gilles, *Nietzsche et la philosophie*, Paris, Presses Universitaires de France, 1973.

deMan, Paul, "Action and Identity in Nietzsche," *Yale French Studies*, no. 52 [1975] (*Graphesis: Perspectives in Literature and Philosophy*): 16-30.

———, "Genesis and Genealogy in Nietzsche's *The Birth of Tragedy*," *Diacritics* II, no. 4 (Winter 1972): 44-53.

———, "Nietzsche's Theory of Rhetoric," *Symposium* XXVIII, no. 1 (Spring 1974): 33-51 (includes discussion by respondents, among them Peter Heller and Walter Kaufmann).

Drimmer, Melvin, "Nietzsche in American Thought: 1895-1925," Ph.D. dissertation, The University of Rochester, 1965.

Eckstein, Walter, "Friedrich Nietzsche in the Judgment of Posterity," *Journal of the History of Ideas* VI, no. 3 (June 1945): 310-324.

Ellerman, Carl Paul, "Nietzsche's Madness: Tragic Wisdom," *American Imago* 27 (Winter 1970): 338-357.

Fischer, Kurt Rudolf, "Is Nietzsche a Philosopher?" *Bucknell Review* XVIII, no. 3 (Winter 1970): 117-130.

Flaccus, Louis William, *Artists and Thinkers*, Freeport, N.Y., Books for Libraries Press, 1967 [1916].

Foster, Grace R., "The Natural History of the Will," *American Scholar* XV (July 1946): 277-287.

Foucault, Michel, "Nietzsche, la généalogie, l'histoire," in *Hommage à Jean Hyppolyte*, Paris, Presses Universitaires de France, 1971.

Frenzel, Ivo, *Friedrich Nietzsche: An Illustrated Biography*, trans. Joachim Neugroschel, New York, Pegasus, 1967.

Furness, Raymond, "Nietzsche's Views on the English and His Concept of a European Community," *German Life and Letters* XXVII (1964): 319-325.

Gilman, Sander L., "*Incipit Parodia*: The Function of Parody in the Lyrical Poetry of Friedrich Nietzsche," *Nietzsche-Studien, Internationales Jahrbuch für die Nietzsche-Forschung*, vol. 4, Berlin, Walter de Gruyter, 1975, pp. 52-74.

Granier, Jean, *Le problème de la vérité dans la philosophie de Nietzsche*, Paris, Editions du Seuil, 1966.

Grimm, Ruediger Hermann, *Nietzsche's Theory of Knowledge*, Berlin, Walter de Gruyter, 1977.

Hamburger, Michael, *Contraries: Studies in German Literature*, New York, E. P. Dutton, 1970.

Heidegger, Martin, *What is Called Thinking?* trans. Fred D. Wieck and J. Glenn Gray, New York, Harper and Row, 1968.

──────, "Who is Nietzsche's Zarathustra?" trans. Bernd Magnus, *Review of Metaphysics* 20 (March 1967): 411-431.

Heller, Erich, *The Disinherited Mind*, New York, Meridian Books, 1959.

──────, "Zarathustra's Three Metamorphoses," *Salmagundi*, no. 21 (Winter 1973): 63-80.

Heller, Peter, *Dialectics and Nihilism: Essays on Lessing, Nietzsche, Mann and Kafka*, Amherst, Mass., Univ. of Massachusetts Press, 1966.

──────, "The Tragedy of Knowledge: Notes on Nietzsche's *Memorabilia*," *The Malahat Review*, no. 24 (1972): 150-163.

Hollingdale, R. J., *Nietzsche: The Man and His Philosophy*, Baton Rouge, La., Louisiana State Univ. Press, 1965.

──────, *Nietzsche*, Routledge Author Guides, London, Routledge and Kegan Paul, 1973.

Howey, Richard Lowell, *Heidegger and Jaspers on Nietzsche: A Critical Examination of Heidegger's and Jaspers' Interpretations of Nietzsche*, The Hague, Martinus Nijhoff, 1973.

———, "Some Reflections on Irony in Nietzsche," *Nietzsche-Studien, Internationales Jahrbuch für die Nietzsche-Forschung*, vol. 4, Berlin, Walter de Gruyter, 1975, pp. 36-51.

Hubbard, Stanley, *Nietzsche und Emerson*, Basel, Verlag für Recht und Gesellschaft, 1958.

Humble, M. E., "Early British Interest in Nietzsche," *German Life and Letters* 24 (Oct. 1970-July 1971): 327-335.

Hummel, Hermann, "Emerson and Nietzsche," *New England Quarterly* 19 (March 1940): 63-84.

Huszar, George de, "Nietzsche's Theory of Decadence and the Transvaluation of All Values," *Journal of the History of Ideas* VI, no. 3 (June 1954): 259-272.

Janz, Curt Paul, "Friedrich Nietzsches Akademische Lehrtätigkeit in Basel 1869 bis 1879," *Nietzsche-Studien, Internationales Jahrbuch für die Nietzsche-Forschung*, vol. 3, Berlin, Walter de Gruyter, 1974, pp. 192-203.

Jaspers, Karl, *Nietzsche: An Introduction to the Understanding of His Philosophical Activity*, trans. Charles F. Wallraff and Frederick J. Schmitz, Chicago, Henry Regnery Co., 1969.

———, *Reason and Existenz*, New York, Noonday Press, 1955.

Juranville, Alain, *Physique de Nietzsche*, Paris, Editions Denoël, 1973.

Kaufmann, Walter, *Nietzsche: Philosopher, Psychologist, Antichrist*, 4th ed., Princeton, N.J., Princeton Univ. Press, 1974.

———, "Nietzsche as Scapegoat: A Reply to Alasdair MacIntyre," *Encounter* XXXIII, no. 1 (July 1969): 47-50. (See also MacIntyre and Whitty.)

Keane, Patrick J., "On Truth and Lie in Nietzsche," *Salmagundi*, no. 29 (Spring 1975), pp. 67-94.

Klossowski, Pierre, *Nietzsche et le cercle vicieux*, Paris, Mercure de France, 1969.

Knight, A. M. J., *Some Aspects of the Life and Work of Nietzsche, and Particularly of His Connection with Greek Literature and Thought*, New York, Russell and Russell, 1967 [1933].

Kofman, Sarah, *Nietzsche et la métaphore*, Paris, Payot, 1972.

Krell, David Farrell, "Heidegger Nietzsche Hegel: An Essay in Descensional Reflection," *Nietzsche-Studien, Internationales Jahrbuch für die Nietzsche-Forschung*, vol. 5, Berlin, Walter de Gruyter, 1976, pp. 255-262.

Lacoue-Labarthe, Philippe, "Le détour (Nietzsche et la rhétorique)," *Poétique* 5 (Paris, 1971): 53-76.

Lea, F. A., *The Tragic Philosopher: A Study of Friedrich Nietzsche*, London, Methuen and Co., 1972 [1957].

"Vernon Lee" [Violet Paget], *Gospels of Anarchy and Other Contemporary Studies*, London, T. Fisher Unwin, 1908.

——, "Nietzsche and the 'Will to Power,' " *North American Review* 179 (Dec. 1904): 842-859.

Ledure, Yves, *Nietzsche et la religion de l'incroyance*, Paris, Desclée, 1973.

Lloyd-Jones, Hugh, "Nietzsche and the Study of the Ancient World," *The* [London] *Times Literary Supplement*, Feb. 21, 1975, pp. 199-201.

Love, Frederick R., "Prelude to a Desperate Friendship: Nietzsche and Peter Gast in Basel," *Nietzsche-Studien, Internationales Jahrbuch für die Nietzsche-Forschung*, vol. 1, Berlin, Walter de Gruyter, 1972, pp. 261-285.

Löwith, Karl, *From Hegel to Nietzsche: The Revolution in Nineteenth Century Thought*, trans. from the 3d German ed. by David E. Green, Garden City, N.Y., Doubleday, 1967.

——, *Meaning in History*, Chicago, Ill., Univ. of Chicago Press, 1949.

MacIntyre, Alasdair, "Philosophy and Sanity: Nietzsche's Titanism," *Encounter* XXXII, no. 4 (April 1969): 79-82. (See also replies by Kaufmann and C. W. M. Whitty.)

Marcuse, Ludwig, "Nietzsche in America," trans. James C. Fleming, *South Atlantic Quarterly* 50 (July 1951): 330-339.

McGinn, Robert E., "Culture as Prophylactic: Nietzsche's *Birth of Tragedy* as Culture Criticism," *Nietzsche-Studien, Internationales Jahrbuch für die Nietzsche-Forschung*, vol. 4, Berlin, Walter de Gruyter, 1975, pp. 75-138.

Morel, Georges, *Nietzsche: Introduction à une première lecture*, vol. 1: *Genèse d'une oeuvre*; vol. 2: *Analyse de la maladie*; vol. 3: *Création et métamorphoses*. Paris, Aubier-Montaigne, 1970-71.

Morgan, George Allen, *What Nietzsche Means*, New York, Harper and Row, 1965 [1941].

Neumann, Harry, "Superman or Last Man? Nietzsche's Interpretation of Athens and Jerusalem," *Nietzsche-Studien, Internationales Jahrbuch für die Nietzsche-Forschung*, vol. 5, Berlin, Walter de Gruyter, 1976, pp. 1-28.

Nietzsche, 7e Colloque philosophique international de Royaumont, 1964 [Cahiers de Royaumont, Philosophie, no. 6], Paris, Editions de Minuit, 1967.

Nietzsche aujourd'hui? vol. 1: *Intensités;* vol. 2: *Passion.* Publications du Centre Culturel de Cerisy-la-Salle, Paris, Union Générale d'Editions, 1973.

O'Brien, Conor Cruise, "The Gentle Nietzscheans," *The New York Review of Books* (Nov. 5, 1970): pp. 12-16.

O'Flaherty, James C., Sellner, Timothy F., and Helm, Robert M., eds., *Studies in Nietzsche and the Classical Tradition*, Chapel Hill, N.C., The Univ. of North Carolina Press, 1976.

Paget, Violet, *see* "Vernon Lee."

Pautrat, Bernard, *Versions du soleil: Figures et système de Nietzsche*, Paris, Editions du Seuil, 1971.

Platt, Michael, "Nietzsche on Flaubert and the Powerlessness of His Art," *Centennial Review* XX, no. 3 (Summer 1976): 309-313.

Reichert, Herbert W., "The Present Status of Nietzsche: Nietzsche Literature in the Post-War Era," *Monatshefte* 51 (Madison, Wisc.) (March 1959): 103-120.

Rey, Jean-Michel, *L'enjeu des signes*, Paris, Editions du Seuil, 1971.

Schacht, Richard, "Nietzsche and Nihilism," *Journal of the History of Philosophy* XI, no. 1 (Jan. 1973): 65-90.

Smith, John E., "Nietzsche: The Conquest of the Tragic through Art," in *The Tragic Vision and the Christian Faith*, ed. Nathan A. Scott, Jr., New York, Association Press, 1957.

Solomon, Robert C., ed., *Nietzsche: A Collection of Critical Essays*, Garden City, N.Y., Doubleday, 1973.

Stambaugh, Joan, "Thoughts on Pity and Revenge," *Nietzsche-Studien, Internationales Jahrbuch für die Nietzsche-Forschung*, vol. 1, Berlin, Walter de Gruyter, 1972, pp. 27-35.

———, "Nietzsche Today," *Symposium* XXVIII, no. 1 (Spring 1974): 86-93.

Stern, J. P., "Nietzsche's Aesthetics?" *Journal of European Studies* V, no. 3 (Sept. 1975): 213-222.

Thatcher, David S., *Nietzsche in England 1890-1914: The Growth of a Reputation*, Toronto, Univ. of Toronto Press, 1970.

————, ed., *Friedrich Nietzsche: A Symposium to Mark the Centenary of the Publication of The Birth of Tragedy, The Malahat Review*, no. 24 (special Nietzsche issue), Victoria, British Columbia, Univ. of Victoria, Oct., 1972.

Vaschide, N. and Binet-Valmer, G., "The Elite of Democracy," *Monist* XIV (April 1904): 427-451.

Wellek, René, Review of *Nietzsche und Emerson*, by Stanley Hubbard, *Erasmus* XIII, nos. 5-6 (1960): 134-135.

West, Charles R., Jr., "Nietzsche's Concept of *Amor Fati*," unpub. Ph.D. dissertation, Columbia University, 1957.

Whitty, C. W. M., Letter concerning Alasdair MacIntyre's observations with respect to Nietzsche and "General Paralysis of the Insane," *Encounter* XXXIV, no. 2 (Feb. 1970): 95-96.

Wilcox, John T., *Truth and Value in Nietzsche: A Study of His Metaethics and Epistemology*, Ann Arbor, Mich., Univ. of Michigan Press, 1974.

Willcox, Louise Collier, "Nietzsche: A Doctor for Sick Souls," *North American Review* 194 (Nov. 1911): 765-774.

Yourgrau, Wolfgang, "Nietzsche and Modern Physics," *The Denver Quarterly* VI (1971): 20-32.

Zuckert, Catherine, "Nature, History and the Self: Friedrich Nietzsche's Untimely Considerations," *Nietzsche-Studien, Internationales Jahrbuch für die Nietzsche-Forschung*, vol. 5, Berlin, Walter de Gruyter, 1976, pp. 55-82.

Index

This Index includes the names of fictional characters as well as actual persons. Individual works by James and Nietzsche are listed alphabetically by title under the author's name; in the case of Nietzsche, the titles are listed in English, and the German is given in parentheses. A lower case "n" following a page number indicates a footnote appearing in the text; a capital "N" refers to the note provided for that particular page in the Notes section at the end of the book.

Castell, Alburey, 13
Cat, killed by James, 3
Cavell, Stanley, 138, 138N
Christian piety, seen as will to "un-truth at any price," 184-85
"Civil Disobedience" (Thoreau), 30
Civilization: lack of requisite com-ponents of in America alleged by James, 69-70; commitment to values of, resulting in barbarism, 107
Civilization and Its Discontents (Freud), 259
Classicism and classical scholarship, Nietzsche's relation to, 142, 163N, 198N, 200N
Confessions of St. Augustine, The, 119, 143-44
Conrad, Joseph, 107, 135n, 135nN, 190N
Conscience, 107, 185
Consciousness: degree of, as basis for distinguishing God from man, 114; indivisibility of, in Emerson, 155
Constant, Benjamin, 162
"Conversion," James' family rule, 6-7, 74, 261-62
Correspondence Theory of Truth, 15, 173, 220
Cosmopolitan: inapplicability of the term to James asserted by his secretary, 64; and by Col. Higgin-son, 67; "der gute Europäer" as, 85
"Crazy Jane Talks with the Bishop" (Yeats), 243, 251n
Creator and creature, two aspects of human personality, 115, 133, 134, 187, 188, 239-40
Crèvecoeur, Hector St. John de, 79
Crews, Frederick C., 80N
Croce, Benedetto, 99
Croly, Herbert, 65
Croy, Kate, 109N, 131
Cruelle Énigme (Bourget), 20

Cruelty, spiritualization of as basis of "higher culture," 247
Culture: "historical," 27, 29, 79; "historical" contrasted with "in-ner," 18-19, 26, 93; production of genius as goal of, 195-96
Culture and Anarchy (Arnold), 91N

Dannhauser, Werner, 138N, 163N, 236, 238-39, 242
Danto, Arthur C., 173-77, 181N, 183N, 204, 220
Darwin, Charles, 12, 98, 111N, 112n, 138
Daudet, Alphonse, 210
"Death in Venice" (Mann), 87n
Decadence, Nietzsche's notion of compared with that of Bourget, 22
Dedalus, Stephen, as type of the artist, 86; linked with Tonio Kröger, 86
Delacroix, Eugène, 254
Democracy in America (Tocque-ville), 83
Densher, Merton, 131
Desaix [de Veygoux], Louis Charles Antoine, 228
Determinism, 12-13, 25, 36
Dickens, Charles, 70
Dickinson, Emily, 11
Dietrichson, Jan W., 203N
"Dilemma of Determinism, The" (William James), 165-66
Diogenes, 139
"Dionysian": tendency, as con-trasted with "Apollonian," 37n, 91N, 162-65; faith, exemplified by Goethe, 37-38, 95, 104, 186; as element of Greek tragedy, 162-65; man, described in Zara-thustra, 197
Dionysus, 162-65, 210N
Dog, artist likened to, by James, 205

340

"Hebraism and Hellenism," 91n,
91N
Hegel, Georg Wilhelm Friedrich,
48, 49N, 91N, 98, 111; *Philoso-
phy of Fine Art*, 51-60 *passim*;
Phenomenology of Mind, 115N
Heine, Heinrich, 94
Heller, Erich, 145N
Heller, Peter, 7n
Helm, Robert M., 163N
Hemingway, Ernest, 64, 120
Heracleitus, 36-37, 161, 198-200,
198N, 200nN
Higginson, Thomas Wentworth,
65, 67, 67N
Hillesheim, James W., and Mal-
colm R. Simpson, 112n
"Historical" culture, 18-19, 26, 29,
79, 93
Hoche, Louis Lazare, 228
Hoctor, Sister Thomas Marion,
74N
Hollingsdale, R. J., xvi
Howells, William Dean, 107
*Human Personality and Its Survival
of Bodily Death* (F. W. H.
Myers), 112-14
Humble, M. E., 45N
Huxley, Aldous, 64
Huxley, T. H., 13, 103
Hyde, H. Montgomery, 134N, 230,
235

Ibsen, Henrik, 13, 31, 245
"Illusion of reality," 208-9
Illusions, necessity of, 182N, 221-
24
Immortality: Henry James on pros-
pect of, 132; 227; William
James's view of, 148, 154, 167-69
Imperial Self, The (Quentin An-
derson), 11
Intentions, 95N, 143N, 208
Interpretation of Dreams, The
(Freud), 243
"Indeterminism," 165-66, 175
Individual, supremacy of the, 90, 93

Individuality, Emerson's conception
of, 135, 168; associated with full
humanity, 169-71
Individuation, seen as "primal cause
of evil," 162-65
Influence of Nietzsche in England
and America, 45N
"Inner" culture, 18-19, 26, 93
Instrumental view of truth, 173,
173n
Ishmael, 70, 90n
"Isolatoes," 70
"Is There a Life After Death?" 132

James, Alice (Mrs. William), 73,
233, 236
James, Alice (sister of William and
Henry), 159, 160, 233
James, Henry, Sr., 160, 162; mental
crisis of, 14N
James, Henry: failure of *Guy Domville*, 14, 139; on becoming a
British subject, 63; apparent
homelessness of, 64-73; education of described by Lubbock as
"promiscuous and haphazard,"
71-72; affirmation of his ambiguous literary identity, 74; ambitions as an author, 74-75; defense
of his "supersubtle fry," 100-102;
life at Lamb House, as viewed by
William James, 227; suffers first
stroke, 229; begins last dictations,
230; dictates two letters in character of Napoleon Bonaparte,
232-34; face after death likened
to that of Napoleon or Goethe,
236; most celebrated nightmare,
254-58; Writings: *A Small Boy
and Others*, 254-56; *Ambassadors, The*, 24, 123, 134; *Ambassadors, The*, Preface to, 137,
140, 147, 150-51, 205, 216;
American, The, 140; *American,
The*, Preface to, 153, 166, 209-
10; "Art of Fiction, The," 126,
134, 140, 142, 143, 146, 149,

LT   R83PC

            DONADIO

A3
lllw